REX HARRISON:
THE FIRST BIOGRAPHY

Following on his highly successful biographies of
Merle Oberon and Roger Moore, Roy Moseley
has now written a fascinating account of that
most celebrated and enduring star: Rex Harrison. This biography is a salute to the life of one of
Britain's greatest actors; it traces his diverse and
brilliantly successful international career in tan-
dem with a carefully researched account of a
most romantic private life which shares equally
the comedy and the tragedy which he performs
so well on stage and screen. From his brilliant
screen performances to his latest stage appearance, Rex Harrison has richly earned his accolade
as a great British actor.

About the Authors

Roy Moseley is one of the best-known show-business biographers on both sides of the Atlantic. He is the author of the first biographies of Merle Oberon, Roger Moore and Rex Harrison, and of a personal memoir of his friendship with Bette Davis, FASTEN YOUR SEATBELTS. He has also written his autobiography A LIFE WITH THE STARS.

Philip and Martin Masheter are brothers. After leaving university they joined Roy Moseley to write ROGER MOORE: A BIOGRAPHY and REX HARRISON: THE FIRST BIOGRAPHY.

**Also by the same author,
and available from NEL:**

Merle: A Biography of Merle Oberon
(with Charles Higham)
Roger Moore: A Biography
(with Philip and Martin Masheter)

Rex Harrison: The First Biography

Roy Moseley

with Philip and Martin Masheter

NEW ENGLISH LIBRARY
Hodder and Stoughton

Copyright © 1987 by Roy
Moseley with Philip and Martin
Masheter .

First published in Great Britain in
1987 by New English Library

First New English Library
Paperback Edition 1988

British Library C.I.P.

Moseley, Roy
  Rex Harrison: the first biography.
  1. Harrison, Rex
  2. Actors – Great Britain –
  Biography
  I. Title
  II. Masheter, Philip
  III. Masheter, Martin
  792.'028'0924   PN2598. H336

  ISBN 0-450-42138-4

Printed and bound in Great
Britain for Hodder and Stoughton
Paperbacks, a division of Hodder
and Stoughton Limited, Mill
Road, Dunton Green, Sevenoaks,
Kent (Editorial Office: 47 Bedford
Square, London WC1B 3DP) by
Richard Clay Limited, Bungay,
Suffolk. Photoset by Rowland
Phototypesetting Limited,
Bury St Edmunds, Suffolk.

Especially for my Mother, with gratitude and love for
making this book possible – and to my Father
Roy Moseley

To our parents, Heather and Harry, with love
Philip and Martin Masheter

ACKNOWLEDGEMENTS

In May 1985 the late Lilli Palmer came to England, and on the 7th she met me at a London hotel where we had a long conversation, followed by an in-depth interview. Miss Palmer's parting words to me concerning her life with Rex Harrison were:

'They were, after all, fifteen years of my life – some of them beautiful – and I will not have them denigrated and totally distorted. That's the only reason – against other people's better advice – that I wanted to see you.'

To Miss Palmer and her husband, Carlos Thompson, who initially brought about this eventual meeting, my sincere and profound gratitude.

To Mrs Kim Kendall Campbell, the sister of Kay Kendall, my grateful thanks for her generous help and concern.

Elizabeth Harrison risked life and limb to drive through the most appalling weather conditions to keep her promise to give us invaluable help.

Joan Carey and Sheila Taylor were kind and generous in their support, as was Simon Harrison.

They all have two things in common – they represent the family of Rex Harrison and they are all very proud to be a part of it.

Most grateful thanks for all their help to Dermot Carey, Lewis Packer, Jack Abel, Geoffrey Brocklebank, Commander R. H. Grist, The Revd M. D. A. Hepworth, N. R. Bomford, Henry E. Cotton, Sister Peggy, the late Vivien

Leigh, Damian Harris, Darren Ramirez, Terry Kendall, Cavan Kendall, the late Sir Terence Rattigan, Nora Swinburne, Esmond Knight, the late Sir Noël Coward, the late Dame Anna Neagle, Evelyn Laye CBE, Ann Todd, Jill Esmond, Larry Adler, Diana Churchill, the late Victor Saville, Valerie Hobson, the late George Cukor, Margaret Lockwood CBE, Elisabeth Welch, Leslie Phillips, Dame Wendy Hiller, Lady Richardson, Sir David Lean, Derek Farr, Constance Cummings CBE, Griffith Jones, the late Martin Stevens MP, Richard Lyon, Vanessa Brown, Barbara Lawrence, Alan Dobie, Kurt Kreuger, Mary Martin, Googie Withers, John McCallum CBE, Douglas Fairbanks Jnr KBE, Charlton Heston, Fannie Mae Bolden, Athene Seyler CBE, Dirk Bogarde, the late Alan Jay Lerner, Nancy Olson, Kitty Carlisle Hart, Mona Washbourne, Audrey Hepburn, The Hon. William Douglas-Home, Eloise Hardt, Tammy Grimes, Hermione Baddeley, Ross Hunter, Rosalind Knight, Hugh Latimer, Julie Harris, Mike Merrick, Alvin Rakoff, Peggy Cummins, Joyce Redman, Moira Lister, Ned Sherrin, Judy Tarlo, Lance Percival, Christopher Cazenove, Mark Lester, Peter Roberts, George Hulme, Sir Alec Guinness, Lord Miles of Blackfriars, Jean-Pierre Aumont, Wing Commander R. Stanford-Tuck, HRH Princess Lilian of Sweden, Colin Hankins, David Smith, Alan Levine, Sir John Mills, Marvin Paige, Maggie Unsworth, Peter Moore, Curtis Harrington, Derek Braeger, Rolla Campbell, John Marven, Jackie Frame, Bernard Barrington Sharpe, Keith Devon, Angus McBean, Janet de Cordova, Eric Harrison, Charles Higham, Edith Jackson, Richard Lamparski, Sir William van Straubenzee MP, Richard Sabat, Richard Green, Bruce Cohn Curtis, and Dr Robert Knutson and Ray Holland of the University of Southern California. Roberta Rubenstein, once again, was of invaluable help to us. To Toni Lopopolo, our editor in the United States, to Ion Trewin, who appeared, thankfully, at the crucial ninth inning, to Carola Edmond, and to Brian Durban who gave so much time and care, our very special thanks. The celebrated Milton Goldman was, as always, brilliantly diplomatic and wonderfully helpful. And finally, so much gratitude to our esteemed agent Mitchell Douglas, who is not only our business partner but our friend.

ROY MOSELEY

1

Rex Harrison was born on Thursday, March 5th 1908 in Huyton, Merseyside to William and Edith Harrison, and christened Reginald Carey Harrison. The birth was at their home, Derry House, in Tarbock Road, where his arrival had been eagerly awaited by his two sisters, Marjorie, aged eight and Sylvia, aged four.

Compared with some of their neighbours' homes, Derry House was small, but the Harrisons were fortunate to live in Huyton which, eighty years ago, was an attractive village of pleasant country houses with large gardens. Located only seven miles east of the bustling centre of the northern city and port of Liverpool, it still retained enough of its rural character to be a popular residential suburb among the more affluent merchants, professional men and industrialists. Well served by the South Lancashire system of electric tramways, as well as a regular train service from the two local railway stations, the residents were assured of quick and easy access to their work in Liverpool or the nearby industrial towns of Prescot and St Helens. The only signs of industry in the village were the local brewery and the Huyton Quarry coal mine on its western boundary. Otherwise, with its attractive village green and open fields stretching beyond its eastern boundary it was the epitome of the typical English village. Huyton Cricket Club, which also had facilities for tennis and bowls, was the popular centre of village life.

In common with their neighbours, the Harrisons were a solid middle-class family. Mrs Harrison, née Edith

Mary Carey, came from a family where Baptist mission-aries, parish clerks and schoolmasters predominated, and was said to be distantly related to the great nineteenth-century actor, Edmund Kean. Her grand-father, Eustace Carey, had been born in Northampton-shire in 1791 and, following the example of an uncle and four cousins, had gone to India as a missionary in 1814. He and his wife, Mary, stayed for eleven years, during which time she gave birth to six children, although only two lived past the age of five. In 1829, four years after their return to England, Mary died. Eustace remarried five years later. His second wife, Esther, had two chil-dren, Eustace and Annie. Eustace was born in 1836 in Camberwell, South London. By 1855, the year his father died, it was clear that he did not feel the call towards missionary work, preferring instead to train as an analyti-cal chemist, eventually becoming secretary of the United Alkali Co. in 1890. In 1863 he had married Mary Jane Picard, and together they raised a family of four children, in which Edith was the second child and only daughter.

By the time she met William Harrison, Edith was a tall, slim woman with dark hair, her face dominated by a strong, determined mouth and distinctively hooded eyes – a feature which her son would inherit. Immaculately well-dressed in the long, high-collared dresses so fashionable at the turn of the century, she stood in contrast to her husband who favoured Norfolk jackets and loose-fitting collars, disliking more formal attire with starched collar and tie. A well-built man with deep-set eyes, brown hair and a thick moustache set on a rounded face, he had an air of wistful detachment about him which did not invite close contact. William Reginald Harrison, known to everyone as Bill, was the third-born son of a large family of seven boys and one girl. His father was the possessor of a considerable fortune, although its source remains obscure. Family legend has spoken openly of slave-trading – a not uncommon livelihood in nineteenth-century Liverpool – but, whatever its origins, his wealth enabled him to purchase a family yacht, a shoot on the Scottish moors and a large country house called Belle Vale, equipped with its own stables, tennis court and even a cricket ground.

Brought up with all the advantages that money could offer, Bill Harrison developed a keen interest in sport from an early age, playing tennis and cricket at home with his brothers. Like his father, he was educated at Harrow. Intelligent, extremely well-read and an excellent sportsman, Bill Harrison would earn a certain fleeting fame by running a hundred yards in 10.5 seconds, as well as being picked to represent England in international hockey. After leaving Harrow he went to Germany to study engineering but, returning home and setting about pursuing a career as a mechanical engineer in the industrial north of England, he lost some of his previous zest for life. When he met and fell in love with Edith Carey the family fortune was still intact, but it was not long before his father lost everything and was declared bankrupt, leaving his son no option but to earn a living from his profession.

The final indignity came when Belle Vale, the house in which he had spent such a happy childhood, was sold and converted into a jam factory. The factory has since been demolished, and in its place today is the appropriately named Belle Vale Housing Estate. The family motto, 'Courage Sans Peur' (Courage Without Fear), engraved on a gold signet ring which Rex himself has worn on the little finger of his left hand since the death of his father, would remain as a lasting reminder of the former wealth and prestige of the Harrison family.

With the birth in 1900 of their first daughter, Marjorie, followed by Sylvia in 1904 and a son, Reginald, four years later, Bill had a family of three to support but lacked any real ambition and was despairing of ever finding a job to which he felt he was ideally suited. His wife had constantly to goad him to greater responsibility towards her and the children. Despite her efforts he remained a dreamer who quickly settled into their modest middle-class existence, content to drift through life as easily, and with as little trouble, as possible. Their son would recall that his parents argued frequently when he was a child, usually over his father's stubborn refusal to upset himself about anything. Bill Harrison turned his back on mechanical engineering in later years, and instead could be found walking the floor of the Liverpool Stock Exchange, where he worked as a produce broker. Lacking his own father's gift for making money, his efforts to make his fortune there were, by all accounts, unsuccessful. He was happiest sitting reading a book by himself, playing chess with his son or joining his children in the games he had enjoyed as a boy. Rex would later say that he never got to know his father well. 'My father had innately a lot of charm and gaiety, but I saw him being slightly squashed by my normally doting mother.' Rex would, however, recall his childhood as a happy time, praising his father as being 'marvellous with us as children' and a 'great companion on holidays' who was 'endlessly patient' when trying to teach them new games.

Work held no interest for Bill Harrison – it was a necessity to which he was resigned. Unable to find fulfilment in any form of gainful employment, he had a reputation for being distant and remote, and it was rumoured that he sought consolation elsewhere. Joan Carey, a daughter of Edith's brother Edward, and one of Rex's several cousins, recalls Bill Harrison as being 'rather too fond of the ladies. He was known as a woman-iser by all the relatives, and disliked because of it.'

As a child, Rex Harrison was thin and pale, and it was not uncommon for the young boy, with his mop of brown hair and clear blue eyes, to be confined to bed under the care of his devoted mother. One of his earliest memories is of kettles of hot water on the boil in his room. Thrown into an unusually close relationship with his mother, as she slavishly attended to every wish of her sickly-looking son, he was to become totally reliant upon her. In retrospect, Rex would refer to himself as a 'seedy child': 'As a boy I was very dependent on my mother. I was a delicate child, and constantly going back to Mum. Rather a "mother's boy" I suppose.' His cousin, Joan Carey, confirms that, 'he was much closer to his mother than his father.' As a result of his mother's preoccupation with his health, he grew into a remarkably self-obsessed child and, as he developed into manhood, he would become neurotically concerned about his health. Edith's over-indulgent treatment of her son did not go unnoticed by his cousin: 'Rex I considered rather a spoilt wee boy. When he was very young he used to call himself Baa, and I can remember him saying, "Baa wants it!" – and I imagine he got it!' She recalls that his sisters were totally different: 'Marjorie was very much the elder sister and was older than all of us. Sylvia was a dear little girl and shy.' Joan does add, however, that 'they spoilt him too.'

It must have been a disappointment for Bill Harrison that his son had not inherited his own robust constitution, as it limited his role as father when Rex was more in need of his mother's nursing than anything else. Rex enjoyed playing with his numerous cousins who lived nearby. Edith's brothers, Edward and Arthur, both had large families – totalling eleven children altogether, most of whom were girls. Rex was among the youngest and as a result was smothered by the attentions of his female cousins. With Joan's two young brothers, Dermot and Brian, he used to play in the garden at Derry House climbing trees, although she says that they were 'often unable to climb down again!' She also recalls the first hint of the actor in young Rex, as at parties he loved 'charades' and was always acting them.

In 1912, aged four, Rex had started school, attending the kindergarten at Huyton College. Founded twenty years before as a school for girls, Huyton College accepted boys in the kindergarten between the ages of four and seven, and most of the children in the village attended. Lewis Packer, a contemporary of Rex's at the school, recalls that 'Miss Baster was the tireless and indefatigable mistress in charge,' and that the school had 'extensive shrubberies which provided a marvellous location for games of cowboys and Indians in term time and holidays.' Of the young Rex Harrison he remembers only that, 'Reggie was very much under the protection of his sisters,' and also says that 'the Harrisons, father and mother, did not involve themselves much in local affairs.'

Summer holidays in the Harrison household required a good deal of careful organisation as, more often than not, they were accompanied by Edward and Arthur Carey with their large families. The holidays were spent either on the coast at Penmaenmawr in North Wales, or visiting grandfather Eustace Carey at his home, Ferney Green, at Bowness-on-Windermere in the Lake District. Cousin Dermot Carey vividly remembers the start of one of their journeys from Liverpool to North Wales, led by Bill Harrison in his straw boater: 'We set off on a wagonette to Lime Street Station where we had a coach on the train reserved for us – which impressed me very much.'

Rex enjoyed the holidays in Wales, although he later recalled that, after swimming in the bitterly cold Irish Sea, his parents would have to feed him sugary buns to help him warm up. He loved playing ball games on the beach with his father, and looked forward to the long walks with his parents and two sisters through the countryside. His sense of childish fun was no different from other boys'. He would run ahead and hide, and just before they walked past him, would suddenly spring out onto the path, screaming and making faces, in an attempt to frighten them. It was on one of these holidays that he was observed standing on top of a sandcastle he had built, looking around at everybody on the beach with his hands on his hips, defying anyone to dispute him as he bellowed, 'I'm the King of the castle!'

During their Welsh holiday in August 1914 war broke out. Rex later remembered an argument between his parents in which he heard his mother urging his father to take some sort of action. Annoyed that his holiday had been disturbed, and unwilling even to think about committing himself to anything which might entail their moving from Huyton, Bill Harrison stubbornly refused to discuss the subject. Despite his customary reluctance to trouble himself, he eventually relented under his wife's constant pressure, and offered his services to an armour-plating factory in Sheffield. Nor was the move across the Pennines to Rex's liking. Now five, he was forced to leave his first girl friend, Sheila Brunner, who lived in a large house opposite the Harrisons. Worse still, there were no fields to run in, or trees to climb. In Sheffield he caught measles. It was evidently a severe attack as his cousin Sheila remembers hearing that 'Rex had fainted in bed!' When the rash finally disappeared, Rex found that he had lost most of the sight of his left eye. It was a traumatic experience for a boy of only seven, and a disability which would hinder his progress at school, and remain with him for the rest of his life.

Rex was lonely in Sheffield, feeling that he had nothing in common with his two sisters, who were now growing up fast. He hardly saw them during this period other than when they all stood around the piano with their mother and sang Gilbert and Sullivan songs, or when they were all huddled under the stairs, hiding from the Zeppelins which occasionally flew over Sheffield on bombing raids.

At eight, he became a pupil at Birkdale Preparatory School, where he was only faintly remembered as being academically undistinguished, although extraordinarily neat for a schoolboy. With poor eyesight making it difficult for him to see the blackboard, he found himself unable to concentrate on his lessons and was usually at the bottom of the class. He would refer to himself as 'the backward boy' and recalls, 'I had no real education, largely because I wasn't capable of taking one in.'

A welcome interruption to the routine of daily life was

the arrival of Bill Harrison's brother, Vivian, on leave from his Canadian regiment. Colourful and adventurous, he had left England in a hurry some years before – for reasons Rex was never able to discover – and emigrated to Canada. When war broke out he joined up and was sent to France. On his first leave from the front he decided to visit his brother in Sheffield. He arrived at the doorstep blind drunk and covered in lice, so before presenting him to the family properly Bill Harrison took him to the local Turkish bath to clean him up. Vivian quickly became Rex's hero; he would follow him everywhere, never more content than when his uncle sat him on his knee and regaled him with stories of his adventures in Canada, as well as gruesome accounts of the war. All too soon his visit came to an end and life reverted to normal. But not for long. A new world opened up for Rex when his parents took him to the theatre for the first time. The show, a pantomime, made such a deep impression on him that when they returned home, Rex immediately placed two chairs for his parents in front of the bay window in the sitting room. With curtains on either side, it looked enough like a stage to him, and he began practising taking bows – apparently feeling it unnecessary to give any kind of performance.

Unlike his father, Rex was not sent to Harrow. It was not just the financial burden and the school's proximity to London during wartime. With Rex's uncertain health, his parents felt it unwise for him to be educated away from home. Rex was, he recalls, 'too delicate . . . I was always nervous and never felt well.' He discovered many years later that, as a child, he had the beginnings of tuberculosis. Fortunately, by the time he was ten, it had cleared up.

When the war ended the Harrisons returned to Liverpool but instead of going back to live in Huyton they moved into a small house at 5, Lancaster Avenue in the Sefton Park district of the city. Rex decided to dispense with the name of Reginald, which he felt was necessary because: 'Reginald became Reggie and I didn't like Reggie, so Reggie became Rex.' In his autobiography he says that he cannot recall why he chose the name Rex, although he assumes that he must have been attracted to the sound of it after hearing someone calling after a dog. The derivation of the name Rex, from the Latin word for 'king', would surely not have gone unnoticed by him, especially at an age when he would have begun studying Latin at school. He must have felt it was an appropriate replacement for the more commonplace Reginald, for which he felt such an aversion. His parents gave their reluctant approval, while Rex ignored the mutterings of his two sisters who felt the name entirely inappropriate.

The newly-named Rex Harrison entered Liverpool College at the age of eleven and began to cultivate his interest in the stage, although academically he continued to be backward and often enlisted his father's help with his homework. He joined the school's Junior Dramatic Society, ably run by Fred Wilkinson, whom Rex would remember as 'a kind and gentle man'. His first dramatic appearance was in the annual school play, a much-praised production of Shakespeare's *A Midsummer Night's Dream*, which had two performances at Liverpool's Crane Hall in May 1922. The hall was filled to capacity on both nights and the applause was loud. R. C. Harrison, as he was listed in the programme, played the double part of Flute and Thisbe, wearing for the latter part a corn-coloured wig and a long dress, made especially for him by his mother. The Liverpool College Magazine, reporting on the production, said: 'It will be a long memory with many of us: and we shall be well satisfied if we never see a performance of *A Midsummer Night's Dream* less worthy than this one . . . for we all, like Nick Bottom, the weaver, had "had a most rare vision".'

Rex also appeared as the Cat in the school production of Maurice Maeterlinck's children's fantasy *The Blue Bird*, again wearing a costume made by his mother. His parents nurtured his interest in acting by taking him regularly to the theatre in Liverpool, giving him the opportunity to see such performers as Gerald du Maurier, Seymour Hicks, Ralph Lynn and Charles Hawtrey, whose stylish performances in the popular drawing-room comedies of the period would greatly influence him.

Jack Abel, who was in the same class as Rex at Liverpool College and also appeared in the school plays, remembers an incident shortly afterwards, at the beginning of the next school year. 'We had started in a new form and the form master asked us to go up to his desk and tell him what we had in mind when we left school. Most of us did not know, but Rex did. "I want to go on the stage in musical comedy," he said. The master did not reply.'

Whether or not, at such an early age, Rex told his parents of his intentions is unknown, although he once said: 'I don't suppose I ever thought of anything else but going on the stage.' However, his father's hopes were fulfilled when Rex began to take an active part in school sports, and he was very proud when Rex earned a place in the 1st XI Cricket team during his last year at school. His classmate Jack Abel recalls: 'Rex was a bowler and I can see him now, a long run intending to put the fear of God into the batsman, but not always achieving its object.'

Rex certainly looked dapper and self-assured in his blazer and cricket flannels, with his hair carefully parted in the centre, but his elegance of dress and the flamboyant 'fright-tactics' which he employed for his left-handed bowling style failed to uplift his cricketing skill sufficiently to justify his position in the 1st XI. His father's face must have dropped when he read the analysis of his son's cricketing abilities in the College Magazine:

R. C. Harrison: The disappointment of the season. His bowling has possibilities but owing to his temperament he has only 'come off' once. His batting is weak and his fielding, though good at times, is often very poor.

Along with other members of the team, Rex enjoyed practising in the cricket nets during the long summer evenings, but the coach found it difficult to convince them that the lively few minutes' hitting in the nets was not guaranteed to improve their batting strokes or remove bad habits. But Rex did, at least, inherit his father's enthusiasm for the game and has remained a devoted follower all his life.

Nor could Bill Harrison gain consolation from his son's performance at rugby, as a member of the 2nd XV. Not heavy enough for the scrum – he weighed just under ten stone – he was placed at wing where he was reported to be: 'Rather slow for a wing, but is very keen. Has still a lot to learn; a useful kick.'

It had long been clear that Rex was not an academic and as his formal education approached its end, his family discussed what career he should follow. His sister Sylvia's fiancé, a young Scottish barrister, David Maxwell-Fyfe, whose career in British politics over the next forty years would take him to two of the highest offices in the land – those of Home Secretary and Lord Chancellor – suggested that the young man should become a solicitor, while Bill Harrison thought he should apply for a position as a clerk in his office. Both suggestions filled Rex with horror and, determined to stand his ground, he announced his intention to pursue an acting career. To his surprise, 'There was no opposition at all. My family was wonderful and helpful.'

Bill Harrison knew one of the board of governors of the Liverpool Repertory Theatre, and through him was able to arrange for Rex to have an interview with William Armstrong, the then director of the Liverpool Playhouse.

2

THE LIVERPOOL Playhouse, in Williamson Square, could seat one thousand people. Before being bought by the Liverpool Repertory Company it had been called the Star Theatre, and was well-known for its productions of cheap melodramas such as *Driving a Girl to Destruction* (its final production). From the outset the repertory company had established it as a citizen's theatre with a large number of shareholders, designed to give Liverpudlians the opportunity to see plays performed in the city other than pantomimes, 'girl' shows and touring musical comedies.

Thanks to his parents, Rex was familiar with the high standard of the productions presented there. In the fourteen years since it had opened – on November 11th 1911 – its reputation had grown considerably. In due course J. B. Priestley would refer to it as 'the best repertory company in the kingdom'.

Many famous theatrical names had already been associated with the Playhouse early on in their careers, including Ronald Squire, Estelle Winwood and James Whale, who eventually went to Hollywood and made his name as a film director with *Frankenstein*. Others who had appeared there included C. Aubrey Smith, the sisters Hermione and Angela Baddeley, as well as Noël Coward and Gertrude Lawrence, as children, in a production of Gerhart Hauptmann's *Hannele*.

In addition to employing a resident company of sixteen or seventeen, the Rep also took on about ten students every season to watch rehearsals, understudy and act small parts until such time as they showed sufficient promise to join the official company themselves. It was in the hope of his son being accepted as a student that Bill Harrison arranged for him to see William Armstrong.

This tall, energetic Scotsman from Edinburgh, with thinning red hair, had been the producer and director of the Playhouse since 1923. He had previously been an actor with the Liverpool Rep between 1914 and 1916, but had left to pursue his career elsewhere. When he received the Rep's offer to return he was touring with Mrs Patrick Campbell in *Hedda Gabler*. He accepted the opportunity immediately – to the utter disgust of Mrs Campbell, although he was later able to persuade her to appear at the Playhouse.

As director of the Rep, Armstrong was responsible for selecting all new entrants and so it was that the precocious Rex Harrison found himself being interviewed by the imposing Scotsman. It was a task that Armstrong did not relish and this communicated itself by his impatience and apparent boredom, which he found difficult to hide. Rex, who later described himself at this time as 'tall for my age, lanky, uninterestingly pale, and happy-go-lucky', was unnerved by the older man's apparently uninterested attitude as he explained the routine of life with the company. Armstrong told him of the hard work involved, which demanded total dedication to the profession. The working day began at 10.30 a.m. and finished twelve hours later, after a performance on-stage in the evening. Fully-fledged members of the company would perform one play at night, while rehearsing their roles in the next production during the day. The theatre was open from the beginning of September until the third week in June – a season of about forty-two weeks – and was closed for ten weeks during the summer when preparations would be made for the start of the new season in September. Fifteen or sixteen full-length plays were produced each season, as well as a number of one-act plays, performed as curtain-raisers to the evening's entertainment.

Rex was informed that he would be contacted when a student vacancy occurred. Armstrong must have been sufficiently impressed, for not long after Rex received a card requesting his presence at the Playhouse, where he was officially engaged as a student at a weekly wage of ten shillings and sixpence.

Fortunate enough to live at home with his parents in Liverpool, Rex was able to manage on this small salary, happy in the knowledge that membership of the repertory company would give him security and stability, as well as the prospect of opportunities to play a wide range of parts. Unlike many of his celebrated contemporaries, Rex did not attend drama school (his parents could not afford the fees). John Gielgud studied at RADA, while Laurence Olivier, who was less than a year older than Rex, had won a scholarship at the age of seventeen to London's Central School of Dramatic Art. Between 1926 and 1928 Olivier was a member of Sir Barry Jackson's Birmingham Repertory Theatre where he scored great success as a contract player, earning up to £20 a week when performing leading parts. Rex, however, was not destined to duplicate this achievement at the country's other leading repertory theatre of the period. He began his theatrical career doing odd jobs backstage and watching rehearsals, before making his first professional appearance on November 17th 1925 in a half-hour curtain-raiser written by Beatrice Mayor, entitled *Thirty Minutes in a Street*. He was cast as an anguished father, and in an interview over thirty years later he still vividly recalled that important night: 'For my first entrance in my first play, I had to rush on, call distractedly, "It's a baby. Fetch a doctor." Terrified, I slipped full length and gasped: "It's a doctor. Fetch a baby."'

Three months would elapse before Rex was given the chance to appear again, when he was given the part of a footman in John Galsworthy's *Old English*, which opened on February 15th, 1926. It was to be his last role of the season, as business was badly affected by the General Strike in May and this, together with the financial loss from taking a much praised but otherwise unsuccessful production to London over Christmas, forced William Armstrong to call an emergency meeting. In poor health and due to have a serious operation, he warned of the possibility of a cut in salaries but, reluctant to take such drastic action, he urged them all to economise wherever possible. Having gained their unanimous support he closed the meeting, only to be told as he was leaving that the light in one of the dressing rooms had been left on the entire weekend. It was the final straw. Armstrong collapsed and was rushed to hospital. Rex spent the remainder of the season trying to learn whatever he could from his fellow players in the company, particularly the two juvenile leads, Cecil Parker and Hugh Williams, both of whom left at the end of the season and went on to achieve great success in London. Rex's attention also wandered in the direction of an attractive young actress, Primrose Morgan, who was completing her second and last season with the company. She was generally cast in *ingénue* parts – and Rex dated her briefly.

He also became friendly with two fellow students, Basil Moss and Jack Minster, and, together with Arthur Barbosa, who was attending the Liverpool Art School, they would go to the local dance-halls. They were particularly fond of the Bear Garden at the Adelphi Hotel, which was a popular place for music and dancing. Caught up in the heady atmosphere of flappers and jazz in the roaring twenties, Rex was gradually transformed into a dapper young man, and soon took to wearing a monocle, which he justified because of the poor sight in his left eye. A friend from those days recalls: 'He was addicted to plus-fours and that infernal monocle. We used to go to local dances on Saturday nights. Rex was expert at the Charleston and the Black Bottom and would teach the young maidens how to dance.' Even during his school days – according to Jack Abel – he had been known as 'Sexy Rexy' – a nickname he would later grow to despise. Jazz became a life-long passion for Rex and, being in Liverpool, he had the opportunity to see many of the great jazz men of the period, including Paul Whiteman and the Rhythm Boys.

With the departure in the previous June of a number of actors, Rex became a member of the resident company for the 1926–1927 season, and was much more active than before, although still only entrusted with relatively minor roles. However, in accordance with his elevated position, his salary rose to one guinea per week – still far less than the majority of the company who received a minimum of £3 a week, while leading players received up to £20.

He started the season with a brief appearance in Jules Romains' *Doctor Knock*, which opened on October 11th, and followed this with the more substantial part of a native, Jimmy Kanaka, in Eugene O'Neill's *Gold*. It was the first production of the play in England, and the first night, on November 9th, was attended by a number of London critics.

For the part of the native, Rex was obliged to cover himself in black make-up as he only wore a loin-cloth on-stage. In the scene in which he appeared he had to climb a palm tree in the centre of the stage and pretend to sight a ship. Unfortunately, nobody had thought to warn him that the palm tree had been fire-proofed just before the performance, but the flame-resistant chemical had had insufficient time to dry. Consequently, while climbing up and down the tree some of his make-up rubbed off, revealing white patches of skin which he tried vainly to hide during the remainder of the scene.

Rex was next in the company's Christmas offering, J. M. Barrie's *A Kiss For Cinderella*, and early in 1927 was cast in the Arnold Bennett and Edward Knoblock play *Milestones*, which attracted his first critical notice in the *Liverpool Echo*: 'Mr Rex Harrison was nicely in the picture in a minor part.'

Next came his most important role so far, in the last production of the season, John Drinkwater's *Abraham Lincoln*, which was revived specifically to allow Herbert Lomas, who had been the company's leading character actor since 1922, to take leave of his Liverpool audience in one of his most popular roles. The theatre filled to capacity at every performance, a tribute to the much-loved Lomas. Rex had a small but telling part and, despite the emotional focus on Lomas, was noticed once again by the *Liverpool Echo*: 'Two of the younger members of the company, Mr Basil Moss and Mr Rex Harrison, again showed themselves to be the possessors of definite talents. Mr Harrison's dumb show as the messenger from Fort Sumter was finely effective.'

Like Lomas, Rex had also decided that this was to be his final appearance with the Liverpool Rep, and on June 18th he was officially off the payroll. Now aged nineteen, he was impatient to try his luck in London, feeling that he had learnt a great deal since his first appearance at the Playhouse nearly two years before. However, William Armstrong, whom Rex would remember as 'one of the wittiest men I have ever known', felt that he should give the young man some fatherly advice. Harrison claims that he strongly advised him to give up any thought of a career on the stage, and says that he begged him: 'Please do not go on with this.'

Although this sudden plea from the man who had been responsible for giving him his start in the theatre must have come as quite a shock, Rex was determined to carry on – and in London. His Aunt Evelyn had gone to live in Bayswater after the death of her husband Arthur in 1923, and it was arranged that Rex would stay with her and his cousins while he looked for work. His mother accompanied him on the journey and returned to Liverpool after a short stay, leaving Rex to begin making the rounds of the theatrical agents in London.

Despite Armstrong's discouraging advice, his luck was in when he landed the plum part of Jack Chesney in a twelve-week tour of *Charley's Aunt*. Mrs Brandon Thomas, whose company had been performing her husband's tremendously popular farce all over the country for years, desperately needed a young actor at very short notice to play the part, and Rex was sent to be interviewed by her son, Jevan Brandon Thomas, who passed him as acceptable. Jevan, who often played Jack Chesney himself, could not embark on the tour as he was busy finalising arrangements for the company's visit to Canada, scheduled to begin early in December.

The tour opened at the Grand Theatre, Hull, on July 25th. The *Hull Daily Mail* critic remarked: 'Mrs Brandon Thomas's company gave an adequate if not wholly brilliant presentation of the ever-popular farce,' and continued: 'Richard Cooper in the title role gave a delightful study which thoroughly deserved and received the appreciation of the audience, and he was ably supported by Rex Harrison and Michael Shepley-Smith as Jack Chesney and Charles Wykeham, his fellow undergraduates. The former was not always easily audible but he appeared to be suffering from a cold.' Apart from the discomfort of having a cold, Rex also had to cope with the eccentric behaviour of James E. Page, an actor who had made a career of playing Stephen Spettigue in the play. Twenty years later, Rex would recall:

'Almost immediately, I was nearly sacked. An old boy in the cast who had played in the play for thirty years made me hysterical with laughter. The only kick left in his life for him was to try to "dry up" the other actors – make them go up in their lines. He'd turn his back to the audience, take out his false teeth and put them into his hat and it was difficult not to laugh.' After their engagement in Hull, they performed in Leicester for a week, followed by three days at the Spa Theatre in Whitby, where their efforts on the first night were rewarded with several curtain calls. In Whitby, by way of relaxation over the August Bank Holiday, Rex partnered a local barmaid in a dancing competition, which earned him the title of 'The Best Fox-Trotter on the East Coast'.

Rex battled on in the show, trying to ignore the antics of James E. Page, but he was not always successful. As the tour continued with a three-day engagement at Bridlington, followed by a week in Bristol, reports of Rex's on-stage laughing fits reached Jevan Brandon Thomas in London, and he decided to visit the company in Salisbury where they had been booked to appear next. Fortunately Rex got through the performance without incident, although Jevan Brandon Thomas had warned him: 'If you don't stop laughing, young Rex, and behave yourself, you'll have to go.'

After a week in Gloucester, they next travelled to Reading, where Rex's life, not just his career, very nearly came to a dramatic end:

> 'One afternoon, I hired a canoe and went sailing on the Thames alone. Out at Caversham Reach I was horrified to see a woman driving crazily upstream in a motor launch. My boat was caught in the wash and capsized in mid-stream. I tried to swim ashore, but the strong current caught me. After a desperate struggle, I succeeded in arriving at a point about six feet from the bank.
>
> 'I imagined I could easily wade ashore. But, as soon as I lowered my feet, I became hopelessly entangled in riverside vegetation. I actually went down three times!
>
> 'Yelling for help, I suddenly glanced upwards and was astonished to see a hay-rake being waved above my head. I managed to clutch the implement, and was pulled to safety by an elderly man who had been clearing weeds from the water's edge.
>
> 'The fellow undoubtedly snatched me from my doom. But you can imagine my reaction when, walking to the theatre that evening, my eye caught a

newspaper contents bill on which these words were boldly printed: *Actor Saved by Rake!'*

After appearing in Morecambe, Warrington and Dundee the tour ended on October 17th, after a week at the Borough, Stratford.

Rex was well on the way to becoming a seasoned touring actor, and over the next three years he would play the provinces exclusively, appearing in a different town every week. 'Those were the days when people said only fish and actors travel on Sundays.' He quickly became used to the realities of life as a wandering actor, living out of a suitcase and staying in actor's 'digs', often run by severe landladies who kept a tight rein on their guests. Breakfast would be served in a small communal dining-room and an evening meal would usually be available before or after the show. The landladies were wary of actors who did not return at a proper time at night and there was no 'bringing home'.

In those days an actor's life on tour was anything but glamorous, although Rex would recall his struggling days in the provinces with affection in later years: 'I enjoyed life. I never thought I'd be any good as an actor. I didn't care. I lived for the day . . . My only ambition was to have a good time. Something would turn up. This may have started my reputation as a playboy. But who isn't at that age?' However, he did add: 'I have always taken my work dead seriously. I have never played at that. What probably saved me from becoming a wastrel was the development over the years of a strong dedication to my job. I enjoyed playing around, of course. But any contemplated fun came second to my work as an actor.'

Of his generation, Rex Harrison is probably the only top actor who was subjected so intensely to the most rigorous form of the British theatrical repertory company tradition, serving his apprenticeship in often third-rate plays and productions, among a cast of players of whom only a very few would make any real progress in their chosen profession.

With the departure of Mrs Brandon Thomas's company for Canada early in December, with Jevan Brandon Thomas once again in the part of Jack Chesney, Rex began looking for work. He was accepted for a supporting part in *Potiphar's Wife* by Edgar C. Middleton. The play, a society melodrama which relied on the prospect of an evening's titillation to bring in its audience, dealt with the story of a young countess, bored with her much older husband, who unsuccessfully attempts to seduce her chauffeur. The play ended with a lengthy courtroom scene, the result of the countess having accused the chauffeur of assault.

The touring rights to the play, which had been presented in London at the Globe and Savoy theatres, were secured by Lionel Bute who, in marketing his product, publicised it as 'the most discussed play of recent times' and 'the play that shocked London'. He sent out two separate touring companies simultaneously, identified as the red and the blue tours. Red opened in Swansea in January 1928, the Blue, of which Rex was a member, a month later at Devonshire Park in Eastbourne.

Elizabeth Vaughan had a principal role as the Countess, with Rex cast as the Hon. Maurice Worthington, a member of the Countess's worthless social circle. Once again, he played theatres from one end of the country to the other, from Brighton to Edinburgh. Also in the cast, playing Rosita Barlow, another of the Countess's friends, was a seventeen-year-old from Cardiff, Christine Barry, whose real name was Grace Underwood. She and Rex fell in love and when the tour ended at the King's Theatre in Glasgow, after sixteen weeks on the road, Rex took her home to Liverpool to meet his parents. His cousin, Joan Carey, remembers Miss Barry as 'very attractive' and says, 'I always thought she was such a contrast in looks with Rex.'

In July, Lionel Bute again sent out two companies with

Potiphar's Wife, and Rex and Christine Barry were engaged to repeat the roles they had played earlier in the
year. Their first booking was on July 23rd at the Royal
Artillery Theatre in Woolwich, with the two principal
roles in the play now taken over by Bertha Cross and
Roland Gillet.

The tour lasted twenty-one weeks, finishing at the
Empire, Preston on December 16th. It was long enough.
When appearing in *Potiphar's Wife* Rex was gripped by an
irrational fear that he would be sick on-stage and make a
public spectacle of himself. He was most affected during
the lengthy courtroom scene in the last act when he had
to sit in the witness box and say nothing.

In the new year Rex and Christine were both given
supporting roles in the Lionel Bute and B. A. Meyer
touring version of *Alibi*, a play adapted from Agatha
Christie's novel, *The Murder of Roger Ackroyd*. They were
in the Blue tour which starred the portly British actor
Francis L. Sullivan as the Belgian detective, Hercule
Poirot – a role which had been played with great success
by Charles Laughton during the London run at the Prince
of Wales. Rex and Christine, who were now engaged to
be married, were cast respectively as Ralph Paton and
Ursula Bourne. Their first booking was at the Hippodrome, Darlington, on January 7th 1929, and the tour
came to a conclusion in Bolton eighteen weeks later on
May 11th.

Rex was next cast as Richard Marquess, an English
planter, in *The Chinese Bungalow*, which had been a great
success for Matheson Lang in London. Set in the tropics,
the plot centred around a Chinaman who kills his English
wife and her lover when he discovers that she has been
unfaithful, and then abducts his sister-in-law to take her
place. She is held against her will, and her fiancé then
comes to the rescue. Being cast in the tour meant a
lengthy separation for Rex and Christine, as it opened in
Harrogate on June 17th and did not close until December
21st, concluding with a final four weeks in music-halls in

the London suburbs of Woolwich, Brixton, Stratford and Walthamstow. Rex would recall that the audiences in these suburban London music-halls were particularly rowdy, and often took a violent dislike to the actor playing the Chinaman.

The drudgery of touring continued the following year when Rex played Charlie Tutt in Ben Travers' Aldwych farce *A Cup of Kindness*. Under the management of Barry O'Brien, two separate companies were sent on tour. Rex's company made their first appearance at the Hippodrome, Gloucester on January 13th 1930, Rex scoring a personal triumph, his interpretation of Charlie Tutt being warmly applauded. In the short time since he had left the Liverpool Repertory Company he had already shown clear signs of a gift for playing comedy and farce.

After seven weeks Rex and Phil Ray, the actor playing Charlie Tutt in Barry O'Brien's other tour, switched companies, which gave Rex the opportunity to make his first appearance on a Liverpool stage since he had left the Playhouse nearly three years before. The Liverpool correspondent for *The Stage* wrote, 'Rex Harrison does very well indeed.' The tour closed after a week's engagement at the Empire, Kingston on May 3rd. Rex had made such an impression that Barry O'Brien sent him out with the play again in the summer, beginning at the Opera House, Blackpool on July 7th and finishing at the Empire, Wood Green on August 30th.

Rex used his spare time between tours to mix with fellow actors in London at popular haunts, and in 1930 he even appeared in two films, although in a very minor capacity. His film debut was in a severely abridged screen version of Sheridan's *The School for Scandal*. Madeleine Carroll played Lady Teazle while Rex was at the bottom of the cast in a bit-part. When *Theatre World* reviewed the film they dismissed it as 'stilted and tedious' and a waste of the talents involved. Rex's other brief film appearance was as George in a 'quota-quickie', *The Great Game*, a story about a football team's hard battle to win the Cup.

Having completed the second tour of *A Cup of Kindness*, Rex went once more in search of work. He was forced to take a very minor part in Baliol Holloway's production of *Richard III* at the New Theatre in St Martin's Lane, which had opened on September 1st for a five-week season. With Holloway in the title role, supported by Nancy Price and Alan Napier, the cast also included Bernard Miles making his West End debut, who recalls:

'I was the second Messenger and a fellow actor whose name I now forget was first Messenger. First Messenger fell ill and as part of the stage management I was involved in choosing a replacement. My notion was that if I could find the right man to replace myself I could step up into the role of first Messenger. I revealed my plot to my agent, George Altree, asking if he could find a substitute for me, thus automatically elevating me into first Messenger. George said he had a very promising young actor on his books – inexperienced but of high potential and at that time 'resting'. This was Rex. I was commanded by leading man Baliol Holloway to take Rex through his lines and he gave a resounding performance of his single line, "His regiment, my liege, lies half a mile south from the mighty power of the king." This Rex delivered with true Shakespearean authority and as far as I can remember I was instrumental in getting his weekly salary raised from £3 a week to £4.'

Having finally graduated to playing leading roles on tour it must have been a hard decision for Rex to accept so minor a part, but it was a notable production and it would be some time before he could afford to turn down any work that was offered to him.

Following *Richard III* he gained a more substantial role in a comedy called *Getting George Married* by Florence Kilpatrick, presented at the Everyman Theatre in Hampstead. The comedy revolved around the plight of a shy young man, the Hon. George Tremayne, who inherits a dukedom he does not want and as a result has to contend with the interference of the domineering Lady Thripple-ton, who is determined to see her now very eligible relative suitably married, ignoring the fact that he is in love with his secretary. Louise Hampton was cast as the formidable Lady Thrippleton, with Rex playing her son, the Hon. Frederick Thrippleton. The play opened on November 26th, but closed shortly before Christmas.

Rex always took a great deal of care over his appearance, and dressed in a fashionable camelhair coat, still with a rather forbidding monocle over his right eye and a cigarette holder clenched between his teeth, he presented an image of confident upper-class affluence.

A fellow actor, who appeared in *Getting George Married*, described Rex at this time: 'He looked, dressed and behaved as if he had pots of money and a whole forest of rich connections. Usually, he hadn't a shilling, but there was a charming thing about him – he was as interested in your part as his own. If he could see a way of improving your part, he'd suggest it – very tactfully of course. So tactfully, you'd generally think you thought of it.'

He would eventually discard the monocle, being naturally sensitive to the derisive reaction it occasionally provoked, especially outside London and particularly in local pubs. Indignant at the lack of understanding of its use he would later say: 'It was purely functional. I can see perfectly well out of my left eye and I'm almost blind in the right. If you've got just one bad eye, it's much easier to wear an eyeglass than heavy spectacles. The connotation of an eyeglass, of course, is affectation, and I suppose that's why I stopped wearing one.'

It also had its impractical side, as was demonstrated on one occasion when Rex and his cousin Brian were driving in his car and decided to call in for a cup of coffee at his cousin Dermot Carey's house in Knutsford. When it was time to leave Dermot remembers that as it had to be started manually, 'Rex had difficulty starting the car while wearing a monocle – much to the amusement of my brother, Brian, and my wife, Audrey.'

For Rex, as a touring actor, the realities of his life continued to be a succession of cheap theatrical boarding houses, living on fish and chips, baked beans, digestive biscuits, double-Gloucester cheese and beer. Although he had managed to break into the inner world of the West End theatre in a very minor way, he would remain a touring actor for some time to come. Despite his outward assurance he was privately full of self-doubt, questioning the wisdom of embarking on a theatrical career, and he once admitted: 'I used to be a terrible worrier, health, every damned thing, always thinking inwards. I just couldn't stop.' He already had experience of a large number of tours, enjoying the cameraderie of their close-knit existence, but he knew that few touring actors would progress beyond the continual drudgery of travelling around provincial England in small repertory groups. Look at the programmes of the productions in which he appeared: few names are remembered today.

Harrison has said, 'My worry used to be that I would end up as a waiter in the Green Room Club for actors. That was when I was twenty, and my mother used to send me a ten-shilling note every week to help me out.'

What appeared to be his first real opportunity to make an impression on West End audiences came when he was chosen to play Rankin, a detective in a new play written by Frederick Jackson called *The Ninth Man*, which was to be presented at the Prince of Wales Theatre. Set in New York and dealing with the destruction of a Chinese opium gang, the stars of the play were the renowned West End actress Nora Swinburne and the then-popular British film actor, John Longden. They opened at the Theatre Royal, Brighton on January 19th 1931, where the play was enthusiastically received, although this was primarily due to it being its premiere engagement. The company then embarked on a short tour before the London opening, appearing in Southsea, Eastbourne,

Newcastle and Croydon. Edward Ashley, who was to marry Nora Swinburne soon after, was also in the cast. Nora Swinburne recalls: 'On the tour before coming to town we three became good friends. We stayed in the same digs and used to go for long walks together, and have a lot of giggles. Rex was tall, slim, very amusing and frightfully good in the play. We enjoyed his company tremendously – he was great fun.'

When *The Ninth Man* opened at the Prince of Wales on February 11th it was hammered by the London press. The *Daily Telegraph* critic called it 'a thriller without a thrill' and thought it 'thoroughly clumsy and badly constructed', while James Agate, in the *Sunday Times*, found the play totally implausible and began his review: 'This thriller will not do, for the reason that it has not been put together with enough care.' He went on: 'Mr Frank Royde gave a good performance as the Chinese thug, and a competent cast, headed by Mr John Longden and Miss Norah Robinson, did all that was possible with the material. The second detective, whose name escapes me, did rather more by introducing us to a new face, a new personality, and at the moment [a] new method of entertaining us.'

Under the critical barrage it received, *The Ninth Man* was not destined to run for very long. On March 9th they transferred to the Duke of York's Theatre, but closed after less than two weeks. The only consolation for Rex was that he had scored a personal success as Rankin and been singled out for praise (albeit anonymously) by the most prominent theatre critic in London.

With the failure of *The Ninth Man*, Rex left London to join Robert Redford's Repertory Company, who were playing a two-month season at the New Theatre in Cardiff. There he was professionally reunited with Christine Barry, who had been with the company since they had opened there on February 21st.

Rex recalled that 'I lived in digs. Had a sitting room and bedroom for 36 shillings a week, all-in. I saved up to £4 a week on my salary of £10.' As a member of Robert Redford's company, he acted in a number of plays, starting on April 6th as 'Larry' in *Square Crooks*, and followed over the next two months by appearances in at least four others, *The Berg, The Joan Danvers, Meet The Wife* and *Other Men's Wives*. It was a successful stay. Cardiff's correspondent for *The Stage*, reporting on one of the group's productions at the beginning of May, wrote: 'Frank Stayton's play, *The Joan Danvers* is given a very capable interpretation by the Repertory Players here. Christine Barry and Rex Harrison are prominent; both of them sustaining parts that are exacting in the curtain-raiser, *The Rest Cure*, as well as the main play,' and he concluded, 'Rex Harrison reveals a pleasing resource in the two productions.'

Whereas Christine Barry now went to London and made her first West End appearance in June at the Garrick Theatre, in *What Woman Wants*, Rex was forced to continue touring. The separation was more than professional. The following year Christine appeared in Walter Hackett's comedy *Road House* at the Whitehall Theatre, starring Gordon Harker, a popular cockney comedian of the time. Although Harker was twenty-six years her senior, the couple were married soon after.

Rex, meanwhile, was on the road playing Ralph in John Van Druten's play *After All*, a role which had been created in London by Laurence Olivier. The cast was distinguished by the presence of Violet Vanbrugh and her daughter, Prudence Vanbrugh, who played mother and daughter in the play too.

The tour began at the Knightstone Pavilion in Weston-super-Mare in August, and for the first six weeks they played the coastal resorts of southern England. In Brighton the critic from the influential *Evening Argus* wrote: 'Rex Harrison is a huge success as the son.'

A future actor friend of Rex's who saw his performance in the play at one of its other engagements, was also impressed, and says: 'It was a very long part in this play and he was absolutely wonderful. I remember I sat there and thought, "My God, this fellow's got the most marvellous timing."'

During the second week in September, when they were at the Palace Theatre in Westcliffe-on-Sea, Rex was introduced to Anna Neagle for the first time. In the evenings she was appearing at the London Hippodrome with Jack Buchanan, but she was in Westcliffe visiting an aunt for the day and had been invited to their cast picnic on the beach at Thorpe Bay. Anna Neagle recalled: 'Rex was just a boy really – but fine looking.'

The *After All* company left the coast soon after and headed north, playing Manchester, Glasgow and Edinburgh before closing at the Theatre Royal, Newcastle on November 28th.

The following year Rex undertook another major role in H. F. Maltby's 'farce with tunes', *For The Love of Mike* which had been a phenomenal success for Bobby Howes and Arthur Riscoe at the Saville Theatre in London the year before. Taking over Riscoe's part for the tour, Rex played Conway Paton, a private detective, with Leslie Hatton replacing Bobby Howes as Bob Seymour. Opening at the Royal Artillery Theatre in Woolwich in January, the production was received enthusiastically wherever it went, and Rex's performance was highly praised. It gave him his first opportunity to sing on-stage, in a duet with Leslie Hatton entitled 'The Prisoner's Blues', but at the Lyceum in Sheffield early in February, the correspondent for *The Stage* wrote: 'The piece is well-received and the songs are enjoyed, although singing is not the company's strongest point.' *Film Weekly*'s Freda Bruce Lockhart, who saw Rex in the show, recalled his performance in an article she wrote about him five years later: 'He had a great deal of the vigorous freshness he has now, though his work was much less polished.'

Throughout March Rex continued with the tour, including a week in Liverpool just after his twenty-fourth birthday, but after appearing at the Opera House, Leicester at the beginning of April, Barry O'Brien replaced him with Fred Kitchen, Jr. Rex recalled the reason: 'The whole company kicked up against playing twice nightly and three shows on Saturday. I led the revolt. We agreed we would rather have a week out. The management read the riot act. Not one member of the company backed me up. So much for the sticking together of actors. So I sacked myself. I was out of work five months. Had no money. Not a bean.'

At some time during this period Rex decided to rent a flat in Hertford Court, Shepherd Market in Mayfair with an actor friend, Tom Macaulay. Previously, whenever he had been in London between tours, he had stayed at a dilapidated hotel in St Martin's Lane, but now felt that he needed a more permanent base. Macaulay remembered:

'Rex was always very smart. Beautifully groomed in lounge suits, very suave, an elegant walker. He had tremendous ambition and sacrificed everything to his acting. Except girls. To be a successful actor, you had to be smart, know how to wear a dinner jacket, how to pour a cocktail. Shows were directed to the stall public, the educated public, and the actor had to have at least the veneer of education, the smell of aristocracy. Rex managed that quite nicely. To be a successful actor was a difficult thing. You had to have luck. It's no good knocking them dead in Ashby-de-la-Zouch for a night or two. You must be a hit in a hit. And that's all Rex ever thought about.

'He was a great one for living secondhand. If he didn't have a car, he knew girls who did. He was always considered dangerously attractive. I suppose men like that always are . . . When he was through with one of his bus-stop affairs he would shrug and say, "I've always got the job." And it was true, he was rarely without work.'

At the beginning of 1933 Rex replaced Louis Hayward as Peter Hallam in Rose Franken's *Another Language*, which was coming to the end of its brief run at the Lyric Theatre, Shaftesbury Avenue. Herbert Marshall and Edna Best, who were married at the time, had originally headed the cast but Miss Best left the play on January 9th; it closed early in February.

Rex then went on tour in *Road House*, the comedy in which Christine Barry had appeared with Gordon Harker at the Whitehall Theatre the year before. Cast as Dick D'Arcy, a member of a 'smash and grab' gang, he opened at the Pavilion in Torquay on July 31st, and played engagements at other South Coast resorts until leaving the company on September 9th after their appearance at the Theatre Royal, Brighton. Rex was transferred immediately to the more prestigious post-London tour of *Mother of Pearl*. This musical comedy with the dazzling Alice Delysia, the French star whom England had adopted as their own, had just completed a successful run at the Gaiety Theatre.

Delysia had the central role of Pavani, a middle-aged operatic star with a whole legion of male lovers, while Rex played Lord Amber, a nobleman who is a columnist for a Sunday newspaper. Also in support was another young actor, Robert Coote, who would become one of Rex's life-long friends. Both men had a gift for light comedy, specialising in playing urbane men-about-town. In the past they had often auditioned for the same roles, and Coote had even taken over as Conway Paton in the summer tour of *For The Love of Mike* after Rex's departure. It has been said that often on their way to the theatrical manager's offices in the West End to audition for a part, they would meet and, quickly passing the time of day, would blankly assure the other that there was no work around. Then, ducking around a corner in the hope of giving the other the slip, they would confront each other fifteen minutes later in the same manager's office, casually explaining their presence there by claiming to have heard about the job just after they had parted in the street.

Mother of Pearl marked the first time that the two men found themselves performing together in the same production. Beginning at the Hippodrome, Golders Green on September 11th, (Rex had closed only two days previously in *Road House*) the tour took them to all the major provincial theatres in England and Scotland. Madame Delysia was fêted wherever they played, while Robert Coote, as a cricketer, stole the notices for the supporting cast. He was reported to have kept the house in continuous laughter during the last act. Rex became acutely aware that his friend could be relied upon to steal his thunder, and although his own contribution was praised, he could not overcome Coote's adept ability to grab the audience's attention whenever he appeared. The tour ended in Scotland at Christmas.

The year had begun with Rex a debonair bachelor. Then, at twenty-five, he met and fell in love with an attractive honey-blonde who had worked occasionally as a fashion model. The daughter of a retired army major and his wife who lived in a small village near Bude in Cornwall, she had been christened Noel Marjorie Collette Thomas, but preferred to be called Collette. Rex and Collette met at a party in London in 1933 and were soon seeing a lot of each other. Her parents saw no future for their daughter as the wife of a penniless actor who had yet to make his name in the West End. On Rex's side, Joan Carey recalls, 'The family would not have been happy for Rex to marry Collette.' In spite of the objections of both the Thomases and the Harrisons, the couple began 1934 by getting married.

The newly-weds moved into a small flat in Bruton Mews, which Collette found, but very soon they were faced with the harsh economic realities of living in London without a regular source of income. Early on there were unmistakable signs of strain between the two of them as they began to argue more frequently, occasionally reaching the stage of throwing crockery at one another. Rex appeared to be destined for a series of poorly-paid engagements, waiting for his luck to turn. He recalled their life together: 'No security, small-part jobs for me in reps and touring companies, living in a tiny mews flat we could not afford. Bills, debts, the lot.' On one occasion Rex said that they were even sued for payment of an outstanding grocery bill.

1934 was a difficult year for them both as work was hard to find and when it did come it was spasmodic and of short duration. Rex appeared in minor roles in two film comedies: *Get Your Man* and *Leave It To Blanche*, but otherwise worked solely in the theatre. In May, he returned to the West End stage in *No Way Back* at the Whitehall Theatre, a play written by a retired Bengal Cavalry officer, Graham Hope, which *Theatre World* described as 'one of those stupidly trivial plays that irritate rather than entertain.' The play opened on May 17th and closed within a week.

Rex's most regular employment was at the Shilling Theatre in Fulham. The actor Robert Newton had found the theatre derelict in 1931 and borrowed £20 in the hope of running it on the shilling-a-seat arrangement. The London County Council had then informed him that he would have to spend £3,000 on repairs and renovation work and, with this in mind, he formed a company, called simply the Shilling Theatre Ltd, and let the theatre to repertory groups while fulfilling engagements elsewhere as an actor. When the theatre was reopened in January 1933, Newton himself appeared in the programme of four one-act plays, with scenery designed by Augustus John. Newton's performance with Rex in the film version of *Major Barbara* in 1940 would establish him as a fine actor, while his Shilling Theatre provided a useful platform to help actors such as Rex to get a foothold in London, as well as enticing an audience of young artists, including Alec Guinness, hungry to see good theatre.

Rex's introduction to the Shilling Theatre came when he was asked to appear, at very short notice, in a murder mystery, *Death at Court Lady* by Sydney Horler. The play opened on September 24th, with a cast including Nigel Patrick, a young actor also struggling for recognition. Rex desperately needed employment, as Collette was expecting their first child early in the new year. Fortunately he scored a success in the play and was offered the chance to return in *Division*, a 'drama of the tropics', which was to play a week from October 14th. Rex was cast as Basil Markham, an Assistant District Officer for a community on the Malay peninsula, while the Assistant Commissioner of Police was played by Donald Wolfit who, at this period of his career, accepted any work going so as to establish a touring company to take Shakespeare to the provinces. *Division* was produced by Jack Minster, one of Rex's old friends from the Liverpool Playhouse, who asked him to return again in *Anthony and Anna* by St John Ervine for a week from November 12th. Rex had the title role of Anthony Fair, a young man who despises work and prefers to earn his living as a hired guest at dinner and weekend parties. The supporting cast included Herbert Lomas, who had been such a dominating personality at the Liverpool Playhouse when Rex was there. The play was a success and *The Stage* noted: 'The figure of Anthony, with his glib impudence and his self-confidence is obviously one that would have been quite at home in a Shavian extravaganza. Moreover, if Mr Ervine's wit rather lags behind that of Bernard Shaw, his energy is always to the fore, with the result that the character, which was capitally handled by Rex Harrison, caused plenty of amusement.'

Before appearing in *Anthony and Anna*, Rex had a supporting role in *Our Mutual Father*, a new comedy by John Beanes presented by the Repertory Players at the Piccadilly Theatre for one Sunday only. Although Rex and his fellow cast members, who included Eric Portman and Basil Radford, did the best that they could with the material, the play was not well received.

Sunday theatre groups were popular at this time and, in the case of the Repertory Players, had been founded by a number of actors in 1921 with the specific aim 'to afford those connected with the theatre an opportunity for furthering themselves in their profession.' They attempted to sell a play, complete with most of the cast, to a commercial management, usually choosing plays which had already been rejected by West End managers, in the hope of changing their minds. The plays, performed only once and with a different cast for each play, gave a useful opportunity to new playwrights who would otherwise have little hope of attracting the notice of producers in London and to actors looking for long-term employment. Rehearsals were haphazard, as it was often impossible to gather the cast together at the same time because of other commitments elsewhere during the week. Margaret Rutherford, on the brink of making a name for herself in the theatre, was also a member and particularly admired Rex's 'authority and accurate timing.'

On January 29th 1935 Rex became a father when Collette gave birth to a son, whom they christened Noel. A week later Rex was in Glasgow for the first performance of *Man of Yesterday*, adapted by Dion Titheradge from Jean Bommart's play *Le Revenant*. The cast was headed by Leslie Banks in the principal role of a banker who suffers from amnesia after an accident and reverts back to his carefree, youthful self when he is hospitalised with a head wound after the battle of the Somme. Although Banks stole all the notices, Rex's appearance in the first act as Paul Galloway, a medical student in the hospital, attracted some attention and *The Stage* said that he was 'most effective' in the part. Other members of the cast included Ann Todd as a nurse with whom Banks falls in love, and Gillian Lind as his suffering wife. After engagements in Glasgow and Edinburgh, they opened at the St Martin's Theatre in London on February 19th and played for three months before closing on May 25th.

In 1935 Rex made only one film, a low-budget comedy directed by Anthony Kimmins entitled *All At Sea*, in which he played Aubrey Bellingham, the hero's main rival for the affections of Googie Withers, then only seventeen and already starring in her second film. Although Miss Withers enjoyed working with Rex she says: 'I didn't see that he was going to be a star. He was a clever actor with a throw-away style, but it didn't really show until I saw him in *French Without Tears*.'

In fact, the British trade paper, *Kinematograph Weekly*, was less than impressed with his performance and wrote in their review: 'Rex Harrison overacts as Aubrey.' Googie Withers says, 'Rex was a very sophisticated man with a worldly air about him,' and she recalls her reaction when he drove her back from the studio on one occasion: 'I was told he had a reputation and I was quite frightened when he suggested I go up to his flat for a drink. Collette was out but he behaved impeccably, perhaps because he wasn't attracted to me or maybe because I somehow gave him the "stop" sign and he saw that I wasn't going to enter into "another woman" situation. I wasn't that kind of girl.' She also adds, 'I am happy that I was one of the ones who were never involved romantically with him.'

Miss Withers' attitude towards Rex was certainly not unusual among the many actresses with whom he worked. Although all acknowledged him to be an attractive man, most seemed to avoid any romantic attachment. However, Miss Withers thinks, 'The attraction grew stronger in his middle years – as with all men.'

In August Rex played the lead in a new light comedy by Graham Ward Bain called *The Wicked Flee*, which included his friend Tom Macaulay in the supporting cast as a journalist. They opened at the Alhambra, Glasgow on August 12th for a week, and then went to Edinburgh and Nottingham. The *Nottingham Evening News* thought that Rex played his part with 'infectious drollery' and commented: 'The author's dialogue was bright and breezy, and sometimes rather sophisticated, and the company saw to it that all the excitements he planned were realised for a house which obviously enjoyed the evening.'

Despite the generally warm reception given to the play, Rex knew that it would not reach the West End and he grasped the opportunity to extricate himself from the production when he was asked to read for the part of Mark Kurt, a young American film producer, in a new comedy, *Short Story* by Robert Morley.

On Monday, August 26th he began rehearsing at His Majesty's Theatre in London before catching a train to Nottingham in time for the evening performance of *The Wicked Flee*, a heavy routine which was to continue for the next five days, until the play finally closed. The cast of *Short Story*, headed by Marie Tempest and Sybil Thorndike, also included A. E. Matthews and Ursula Jeans, with a supporting cast which included Margaret Rutherford. Was this the breakthrough Rex had been awaiting?

Following a brief tour (Edinburgh, Glasgow, Manchester, Birmingham and Leeds) *Short Story* opened in London at the Queen's Theatre, Shaftesbury Avenue on November 2nd. Distinguished by its cast, the modest play was lucky enough to receive moderate reviews, with most critics singling out as the highlight an encounter between Rex and Margaret Rutherford. James Agate wrote: 'The scene in which the tigerish mouse wrestles with another caller (of all people, Rex Harrison) for the telephone, and finally secures it with a kick on the ankle, is the best thing in the play.'

The only positive aspect of the engagement was the opportunity it gave Rex to share the stage with Tempest and Thorndike, and appear with his long-time light comedy idol, A. E. Matthews. Rex did not stay for the whole of the comparatively short run of the play, as a more promising offer presented itself when, shortly after the opening in Edinburgh, the play's director Tyrone Guthrie asked him if he would be interested in appearing in the New York production of *Sweet Aloes* which he was to direct. Written by Joyce Carey, the daughter of another theatrical Dame – Lilian Braithwaite – under the pen name of Jay Mallory, the play, with its story of child substitution within the English upper classes, had been a success in the West End, and Rex readily agreed. He asked Hugh Beaumont, then a budding theatrical impresario, if he would arrange his release from the Robert Morley play, and was soon able to prepare for his first assault on Broadway.

Between the time when Rex left *Short Story* and his embarkation for New York, he agreed to appear, for one night only, in *Charity Begins—*, a comedy presented by the Repertory Players at the Aldwych Theatre on Sunday, January 12th 1936. In February Collette took Noel down to Cornwall to stay with her parents, before she and Rex sailed for New York. They arrived with very little money, but were helped out by the generosity of the play's leading lady, Evelyn Laye and its author, Joyce Carey, who was also appearing in the production. But Rex and Collette remained so hard up in America that they had to live on a diet of cookies and baked potatoes.

Sweet Aloes opened in Washington on February 24th to promising reviews, although when they reached the Booth Theatre in New York on March 4th, the critics were less enthusiastic and, once again, Rex found himself in an insubstantial play which stood very little chance with New York audiences. Brooks Atkinson wrote in the *New York Times*: 'Everything about the performance is captivating except the play,' but he was very complimentary about Evelyn Laye and gave Rex a glowing notice: 'As Tubbs Barrow, the friend and wit, Rex Harrison has the most attractive part in the play, or, at any rate, gives that impression, for he plays it with ingratiating animation.'

While they were in New York, 'Boo' Laye stayed in a luxurious duplex apartment on Fifth Avenue. She was already a darling of New York audiences, having played in Noël Coward's *Bitter Sweet* six years before. She frequently invited Rex and Collette up to dine after the show:

> 'I liked Collette. She was an enchanting young thing: gentle and shy, and sweet and very pretty. I found Rex a very fascinating young man. I knew he was very highly-strung and nervy and I tried to teach him to relax and be quiet, and made him practise yoga on the floor, but he couldn't. He was, and always has been, insecure. It was all bubbling up inside him. He was quite nice, but self-possessed – a difficult man to know and to get inside.'

Rex, for his part, acknowledged Miss Laye's kindness towards him and said later: 'She practically saved my reason. I was very run down, nervous and generally wretched. Coming to New York for the first time is exhausting.' He would also say, '"Boo" was the first person to teach me how to relax.'

While in New York Rex was invited to the Warner Brothers' Manhattan office, as they intended to film *Sweet Aloes* and had even put money into the New York production. They wanted to test Rex to see if they should engage him to repeat his role as Tubbs Barrow for the film. A contract was drawn up for a possible option on his services for two films, one of which would be *Sweet Aloes*, both to be made between May and September, earning Rex a salary of one thousand dollars a week, but whether or not they signed him depended on the outcome of the screen test made at their Brooklyn studio on March 9th.

By the time the test was made Rex's marriage was in tatters and the play already in difficulties. Collette returned to England soon after the New York opening, and the play closed shortly afterwards, notching up only twenty-four performances. The Warner executives had not been sufficiently impressed with Harrison's screen presence to take up the option on his services and, with the closure of the play, Rex left New York and sailed back to England on the *Aquitania*. Despite its failure on Broadway, Warner Brothers still went ahead and filmed the play, changing the title to *Give Me Your Heart*, with Roland Young playing Tubbs Barrow.

Back in England, Rex saw very little of Collette who had not even been there to greet him when he disembarked from the *Aquitania*. She had taken a job in a fashionable London hat-shop and spent most of her evenings out, while Rex passed the time with their infant son, waiting for his career to receive a much-needed boost. His marriage to Collette was to limp on for a number of years with neither party inclined to end it, if only for the sake of their child. Over the following years they would have short-lived reconciliations, but for the majority of the time of their legal marriage they led separate lives. As Rex's career prospered, he had even less time for Collette and inevitably they drifted further apart.

Rex was not long out of work after his return, accepting the role of Tom Gregory in *Heroes Don't Care*, a comedy by Margot Neville. After a preliminary week at the New Theatre in Oxford, they opened at the St Martin's Theatre on June 10th to enthusiastic reviews. Set during a night and early morning at the Grand Hotel, Bergvaag – the most northerly hotel in Norway – the play dealt with the complications which arise when Tom Gregory, a member of Sir Edward Pakenham's latest expedition to the North Pole, gets cold feet and wants to back out. Rather than admit it, he sets about sabotaging the trip by seducing a not-unwilling Lady Pakenham while Sir Edward has even more trouble with the arrival of Connie Crawford, a celebrated aviatrix recently returned from a record flight to Tibet, who is determined to be the first woman to accompany an expedition to the North Pole. *Theatre World* wrote: 'What ensues is purest – and occasionally impurest – farce, studded with witty lines, packed with hilarious situations and played at lightning speed.' Of Rex's performance they remarked prophetically: 'Rex

Harrison proves himself one of the best light comedians on the English stage with his study of a timorous yet resourceful youth, warring with circumstances beyond his control or seeking. I am very much afraid that the film magnates will be after Mr Harrison in a clamorous body.'

The play was the boost Harrison had been looking for. In the cast he was reunited with Carol Goodner as Lady Pakenham, with whom he had co-starred in *Anthony and Anna*. The play also included Felix Aylmer as Sir Edward, and Coral Browne as Connie Crawford. It ran for several months before finally closing on October 17th, vastly raising Rex's stock in the eyes of both theatre and film producers alike.

No less a figure than Alexander Korda, then the most successful producer of British films, saw the potential in Harrison and signed him to an exclusive contract with an annual salary of £2,500. The contract allowed Korda to use Rex in his own films or lend him out, with any earnings which he made either in the theatre or with other studios being set against the basic contract payments. For the first time in his working life, Rex was financially secure, and he took the opportunity presented by the turn in his fortunes to move into a Chelsea flat in Cadogan House, off Sloane Square.

Korda's Denham studios were busy with Laurence Olivier and Vivien Leigh in *Fire Over England*, their first film together, and Marlene Dietrich, who had come over from Hollywood to appear in *Knight Without Armour* with Robert Donat. Another production, which began shooting in September, was *Men Are Not Gods*, a comedy in which Korda put Rex to work in a supporting role as Tommy Stapleton, a newspaper reporter who writes the obituary columns. The film was notable for the presence of Hollywood star Miriam Hopkins heading the cast, along with Gertrude Lawrence in one of her rare screen appearances, and also boasted cameos by Noël Coward, Marlene Dietrich and Charles Laughton in a hotel-lobby scene.

Men Are Not Gods was directed by the German-born Walter Reisch, whose mastery of the English language was somewhat limited, making him a less than ideal choice to take charge of a comic subject. Rex was unable to relax completely in front of the cameras and the producer/director Victor Saville, who would be a helpful influence on Rex's early cinematic career, felt that he was hindered by Reisch's heavy-handed approach: 'A foreign director whose command of English is not complete is more than likely to have his actors speak deliberately and not at a colloquial pace. Unfortunately, Walter Reisch's direction fell into this category and Rex Harrison, who was very inexperienced in films, gave a very loud and studied performance.'

Rex worked on the film during the day, while continuing to appear in *Heroes Don't Care* in the evenings, beginning the pattern of an extremely heavy work schedule which was to dominate his life for over two years.

3

UNKNOWN TO Rex, his stage career was on the brink of a major breakthrough which would cement his position as one of the foremost exponents of light comedy in England. Bronson Albery was faced with the imminent closure of *The Lady of La Paz* starring Lilian Braithwaite, which had been playing at the Criterion since July. Business had unexpectedly fallen off and Albery needed to find a replacement play quickly. John Gielgud recommended to him *Gone Away*, a light comedy by Terence Rattigan, then relatively unknown. Set in a French-language cramming school on the west coast of France, run by the forbidding Monsieur Maingot, it was a frothy and lively play about the havoc wrought on the all-male students by the arrival of Diana Lake, the attractive sister of one of them. Intent on mischief, she makes advances towards them all and, playing one off against the other, makes them look complete fools. Only the Hon. Alan Howard, a star prospect for the diplomatic service, sees through her schemes and watches cynically from the sidelines.

With himself as senior partner, Albery financed the production with Rattigan's literary agent, A. D. Peters, and a theatrical producer, Alban Limpus – each putting up a sum of £500. For this delicate and very light comedy the players had to be perfect to ensure that the humour was brought out and, with Harold French engaged to direct, a hand-picked cast was quickly assembled, including Kay Hammond, Roland Culver, Trevor Howard, Robert Flemyng, Percy Walsh, Alec Archdale and Jessica Tandy. Miss Tandy signed only for an initial six-week run, having a prior commitment to play Katharine to Laurence Olivier's Henry V at the Old Vic.

Albery, aware of the success that Rex had scored in *Heroes Don't Care*, suggested that Harold French should go and see the play as he knew that Harrison would soon be available and thought that he might be suitable for the leading role of Alan Howard. The director, accompanied by Kay Hammond, who had been engaged to play Diana Lake, went to see the play and, by the time the curtain fell, they knew that Rex was ideal.

The first read-through of the play took place in Bronson Albery's office at the New Theatre, on the evening of October 15th, with Harold French, Terence Rattigan and the whole cast attending. The reading went satisfactorily and when Rattigan returned home late that night only the play's title worried him. This he changed, in a moment of inspiration, to *French Without Tears*.

Rex had accepted the role, although not without hesitation, as he admitted later: 'I am always indecisive at the beginning of anything and I spend a lot of time making up my mind . . . I was always like that – even when I was a young and unknown actor and I was offered the lead in *French Without Tears* on stage. I kept them hanging about then while I tried to make up my mind whether I should do it or not.'

Heroes Don't Care concluded its run at the St Martin's and for the next two weeks Rex was involved in a frantic period of rehearsals to get *French Without Tears* into shape for the opening at the Criterion on October 31st. The cast worked well, with the exception of Alec Archdale as Brian Curtis, who was clearly wrong in the part. Curtis was one of the play's most amusing characters, a rakish Englishman complete with a dapper moustache and sports car and an eye for the girls. A replacement was needed quickly and the only actor who came to mind was Guy Middleton, who had made a great impression in the play *Young England*. Albery again sent Harold French to investigate and he returned convinced that the part could only be played by Middleton. But as Albery told French, Middleton was having an affair with Collette.

But he was so right for the part that the management risked Harrison's wrath and cast Middleton. With little more than a shrug of the shoulders, Rex agreed. Although working with Middleton every night could not have been pleasant for him, he knew that his marriage to Collette was a marriage in name only, even though they did sometimes appear in public together during the run of the play to keep up appearances. One member of the cast recalls: 'Guy and he weren't exactly close – but the matter wasn't discussed.'

Except for a few minor problems, the first dress rehearsal on November 4th went well, although Rex was considerably annoyed to discover that the sleeves of the German sports jacket he was to wear were too short. The final dress rehearsal was called for six o'clock the following evening, the night before they were due to open. Apart from Terence Rattigan and his mother, and the play's financial backers, the audience that night included Ralph Lynn, the great farceur, and Irving Asher, the head of Warner Brothers in England. What followed was a complete disaster, as Harold French recalled:

'At six-fifteen the curtain rose. Trevor Howard "dried" on his second line, Rex Harrison played as though he were constipated and didn't care who knew it, Roland Culver put in more "ers" than he had done at the reading, Jessica Tandy was so slow she might have been on a modern strike, Percy Walsh forgot he was playing a Frenchman and every now and then lapsed into an Oxford accent; only Guy Middleton and Kay Hammond knew what it was all about. At a few minutes after eight the final curtain descended. Not so much as a titter had I heard from my manager sitting

behind me, nor a sound from the dress circle where
Terry and his mother were sitting . . .'

The first reaction on the part of the play's backers was
complete panic. A furious Bronson Albery began racking
his brains for another play to put on in its place, while
Alban Limpus wasted no time and rushed to the nearest
telephone and sold his share in the production to the
theatrical producers, O'Bryen, Linnit and Dunfee. Even
Rattigan's agent, A. D. Peters, made an unsuccessful
attempt to sell his share for £200 to anyone who would
take it, and Ralph Lynn advised: 'Don't open it. It's a
complete waste of time.'

While this frantic activity was going on, Harold French
stormed backstage, berated the cast for giving such a
disgusting performance, and told them to prepare for
another dress rehearsal in fifteen minutes.

When he returned to his seat out front, the theatre was
deserted except for the stage hands and a crestfallen
Terence Rattigan. The curtain rose once again but this
time the cast pulled themselves together and performed
perfectly. Some time after ten o'clock that night they left
the theatre with a sense of relief, although they were
understandably nervous about what would happen the
following evening.

The night of the opening could not have been more
miserable. With rain pouring down outside the theatre it
was the perfect setting for a disaster but in a packed
house, led by Cicely Courtneidge, *French Without Tears*
established itself as a success with the audience almost
from the start. *The Stage* called it, 'a delightfully bright,
almost effervescent light comedy of modern sophisticated youth', and the only critic who was not carried
along by the general enthusiasm was James Agate, who
thought that it was trivial and contributed nothing to the
development of better standards in the theatre. But nothing could dampen its runaway success which, above
all, was the joint triumph of Rex Harrison and Terence

Rattigan. In one enormous leap, it sent them soaring to the top of their respective professions, and marked the beginning of a lifelong friendship.

Rex's performance was admired by both colleagues and public alike. *Theatre World* noted that, 'Rex Harrison's sense of comedy and timing are invaluable in the role of Alan Howard.' Robert Flemyng recalls that 'Rex was wonderful in it – nobody has ever touched him in the part.' The producer Charles B. Cochran rated his performance as one of the greatest that he had witnessed in his long career: 'I have never considered that perfection of playing the lightest of comedies need be unworthy to rank as art. I would place on very high pedestals the performance of Rex Harrison in *French Without Tears* and the electric brilliance of Gertrude Lawrence and Noël Coward in *Private Lives*.'

Business at the theatre was phenomenal, which had an added advantage for Rex and Kay Hammond, since they both had a 5 per cent share of the house takings over and above a certain weekly level. However, Rex did not sit back on his laurels, unlike Rattigan who, flushed with his overnight critical and financial success, stopped writing for a year and went on a wild spree of gambling and spending, cultivating the playboy image that he loved so much. Harrison, who appeared 'by permission of London Films' still had to fulfil his obligations towards Alexander Korda.

Just prior to the opening of *French Without Tears*, Victor Saville had cast Rex as the leading man, opposite Vivien Leigh, in his production of *Storm in a Teacup*, based on Bruno Frank's successful play. After he had announced his intention to use Harrison, United Artists – the distributors for Korda's films in America – contacted Saville and let him know what they thought of Rex Harrison, after having seen his contribution in *Men Are Not Gods*. Saville recalled: 'I received a cable from their Managing Director in New York telling me that if I cast Harrison in the film they would not distribute it. The inexperienced executive side of showbusiness is not too bright at assessing who to blame and who to praise; hence the strict instructions to give Rex the heave-ho, which of course I ignored.'

Rex was fortunate to have the support of a man of such influence in the British film industry as Victor Saville, and with his help he gave a finely-etched and spirited performance in the film. The fast-moving comedy, adapted for the screen by James Bridie, transferred the setting of the original play from Germany to Scotland, with Rex playing Frank Burden, a crusading reporter who thwarts the political ambitions of the local provost, played by Cecil Parker, who orders a dog to be destroyed when its owner is unable to pay the licence fee. Making an issue out of the case, he eventually succeeds in saving the dog while simultaneously romancing the provost's daughter, played by Vivien Leigh. Rex and Vivien Leigh made an effective screen partnership and the film marked the beginning of a lifelong friendship between the two of them. They would often drive home together from the studios and Rex, like most men, fell madly in love with her.

Korda appeared at a loss as to how to employ his new contract artist, having great difficulty in finding leading roles which were suited to Rex's unique personality. In June 1937 his forthcoming production schedule included two films with Rex: a Technicolor musical to be produced by Victor Saville called *Bicycle Made For Two*, in which he would be cast alongside Binnie Barnes and Sydney Howard from a script by R. C. Sherriff, and the second, *The Playboy*, another musical which was to star Jack Hulbert, with Rex in the supporting cast. Nothing came of either project.

Korda had also considered Rex for the sequel to his popular success, *The Scarlet Pimpernel*, which had starred Leslie Howard and Merle Oberon, but after testing Rex in costume he thought better of the idea and the principal role in *The Return of the Scarlet Pimpernel* was given to newcomer Barry K. Barnes. In an interview given towards the end of 1937, Rex was surprisingly open about what some people felt was his unsuitability to play romantic leads in films: 'I wish I knew whether the trouble is something I can't help, like my physical appearance, or something I can alter, like my mental attitude. I imagine that was what killed the idea of my doing *The Scarlet Pimpernel*. I thought the test wasn't bad, but I'm terribly glad I didn't do it. I've never done a stitch of costume work, and it would have been too big a risk.'

Instead, Korda lent him out to producer Richard Wainwright for *School for Husbands*, a comedy adapted from a play by Frederick Jackson, the author of *The Ninth Man*. Rex was cast as Leonard Drummond, a successful novelist who prides himself on his knowledge of women, and helps two husbands, played by Romney Brent and Henry Kendall, get their revenge on their wives, played by Diana Churchill and June Clyde, after they have both been making advances towards him.

The film was directed by the Hungarian-born Andrew Marton, at Shepperton studios. Rex was not required for work until the film was well into production and when he was finally called, Diana Churchill recalls that there was a completely different atmosphere on the set:

'I started the film before Rex and I was with these lovely chaps, Romney Brent and Henry Kendall, who sparked off each other like mad. They were both funny, wicked and very witty but it changed at once when Rex came. Things didn't bounce off him. He walked on and I thought, "We've got to behave at once." One wasn't encouraged to be jolly about life at all. He wanted to get on with the job. I found him extremely easy to get on with but he has got that remote quality and tends to lock himself away a bit and I don't think he wanted to do anything but work.'

Filming at Shepperton, Rex had to be up early in the morning. He would then travel back to the West End in time for the evening performance of *French Without Tears*, which continued to play to packed houses with no signs of business slacking off. Occasionally Collette would drive her husband to the studio, and once or twice Miss Churchill accompanied them. She remembers Collette as 'a charming girl – very chic and very attractive.'

Korda next cast Rex in his Technicolor production *Over The Moon*, a starring vehicle for his future wife, Merle Oberon. The taxing routine of working on a film sound-stage during the day and in the theatre in the evening began to take its toll on Rex. After he finished shooting at the studios at five-thirty he only had time to rush back to the flat in Sloane Square for a quick meal before rushing out again to the Criterion Theatre for the evening per-formance of *French Without Tears*. While making *Over The Moon*, he talked about his punishing work schedule: 'Trying to do both at once is simply desperate. All day in the studio I am trying to learn from Merle, who can express everything just with her eyes in a way one never learns on stage, and from Bill Howard, who has helped me tremendously with my timing. Then at night I have to unlearn it all.'

Mid-way through shooting, the film ran into diffi-culties and the American director William K. Howard was fired from the picture following a disagreement with Korda. Thornton Freeland was given the unenviable task of completing the film. He recalled: 'I was under contract to Korda and was between pictures, so Alex assigned me to do re-takes, shoot the balance of the script – which was a poor one from a poor story – and put the bits and pieces together so that the picture could be released. It was a great help that Merle Oberon and Rex Harrison were great friends and worked very well together.'

Despite Rex's good working relationship with Miss Oberon, nothing could salvage the film which was little more than an excuse to promote Miss Oberon in a variety of dazzling costumes, photographed against a background of fashionable European locations. The film was completed in February of 1938, after seventeen weeks of shooting (extraordinarily lengthy for the period), but was not released until two years later by which time war-torn England was desperate for any kind of entertainment.

As soon as Rex had completed *Over The Moon*, Charles Laughton negotiated for him to appear in *St Martin's Lane* which was to star himself and Vivien Leigh, under the direction of Tim Whelan. Laughton, with his partner Erich Pommer, was also producing the film under his own independent banner, Mayflower Productions, at Associated British studios at Elstree. Rex made such an impression on Laughton and Pommer over dinner that they changed the young male lead from an American newspaperman to a successful English songwriter, and Clemence Dane rewrote the part with Rex in mind. During the shooting, Laughton lived in a tree house and Rex said later: 'It was during his most eccentric period. He used to come on the set every day with flowers he'd picked on the way down. I'm only sorry I never had the nerve to ask why he wanted to live up a tree.'

The story was a contemporary one, dealing with a group of buskers who entertain the people queueing for tickets at the West End theatres. Vivien Leigh played Libby, who joins Laughton's buskers, bringing them great success until she is tempted away by Harley, a well-known songwriter who falls in love with her and helps her realise her ambition to become a star on the legitimate stage. The film was finished at the end of April and was highly praised by the critics when it was released, but it was Laughton's marvellous character study which dominated the film, closely followed by a lively performance from Miss Leigh. Although third-billed, Rex's part was once again a supporting role, which gave him little scope to appear as anything but a very sophisticated and elegant man-about-town. The film was not released in the United States until 1940, where it was retitled *Sidewalks of London*, by which time Miss Leigh had shot to international stardom playing Scarlett O'Hara in *Gone with the Wind*. One of the members of Laughton's buskers was played by Tyrone Guthrie in a rare screen appearance. Guthrie had directed Rex in *Sweet Aloes* on Broadway and was to become, as Sir Tyrone, one of the greatest and most innovative directors in the British theatre.

Rex was next reunited with Victor Saville, who was producing the film version of A. J. Cronin's best-selling novel *The Citadel* for Metro-Goldwyn-Mayer in England. Saville had co-written the screenplay with John Van Druten; King Vidor came over from Hollywood to direct. Robert Donat was the star, with Rosalind Russell, who had also made the journey from Hollywood, as his leading lady. Rex was given the part of Freddie Lawford, a prosperous Harley Street doctor who preferred to live off his wealthy patients, while Donat played the hero who, despite temptations and setbacks, remains true to the 'citadel' of his ideals, formed during his early struggles in a grim mining community in Wales, to help those who really need him.

The film was an enormous popular and critical success when it opened in London, breaking all house records at the Empire, Leicester Square, and after it was shown in America it was given the New York Film Critics Award as the Best Film of 1938. *Kinematograph Weekly* described Rex's performance as a 'flawless cameo', and on the strength of it, he was offered a seven-year contract by M-G-M if he would move to Hollywood. But with the crisis in Europe gathering momentum, Harrison decided that it was not the time to think about leaving his country. The film was also responsible for providing Ralph Richardson with his final stepping-stone to screen stardom.

Having played in *French Without Tears* for nearly two years, as well as appearing in five films over the same period, Rex was totally exhausted and felt that he needed a rest. Like the other members of the cast he had signed a contract for the run of the play, but he asked for, and was granted, his release. Roland Culver said: 'He had wanted to leave for some time. Rex is a character who has, through life, usually managed to get his own way.'

Kay Hammond had already left some time before, in early January 1938, when she had become pregnant. The play later transferred to the Piccadilly Theatre and when it finally closed, on May 6th 1939 after 1,039 performances, the only remaining members of the original cast were Guy Middleton, Roland Culver, Trevor Howard and Percy Walsh.

In the summer of 1938, Rex and Collette decided that they would like to take a well-earned holiday together and, along with Harold French and his wife, they motored down to St Tropez in the South of France. They had planned to stay for four weeks but the Munich crisis interrupted their holiday, and they were informed that Europe was on the brink of war and that they should return to England. As if this were not enough, on the journey back, Rex suffered facial burns when the radiator of his sports car spouted out a jet of boiling water while he was investigating the cause of some steam pouring from the engine. Fortunately, he escaped permanent damage to his face, but had to suffer the inconvenience of spending ten days in a Paris hospital with his face shrouded in bandages before he could finally return home to England.

Early in November it was announced that Rex would appear in a forthcoming production of Noël Coward's play *Design for Living* with Diana Wynyard and Anton Walbrook, to be directed by Harold French. Diana Wynyard who, like Rex, had started her career at the Liverpool Playhouse, had appeared in several films in Hollywood during the early thirties, including *Rasputin and the Empress* with the three Barrymores, while Anton Walbrook had escaped from the Nazis to forge an exceedingly successful career on the British stage and screen.

Rex got along very well with Miss Wynyard, and he said that she was 'Wonderful to be with in the theatre . . . She was invariably unruffled and calm.' *Design for Living*, a comedy about the relationship between two men and a woman who live together, had been written by Coward as a parody of himself, Alfred Lunt and Lynn Fontanne, which they had all three subsequently performed in New York at the Barrymore Theatre in 1933. The play is one of Coward's lesser efforts which, although controversial for its time because of its underlying suggestion of homosexuality, was not successful. A disastrous film version was made in the same year, with Gary Cooper, Frederic March and Miriam Hopkins, but all of Coward's intent was replaced by an even more ludicrous and tedious screenplay, and it was not until six years later that the play finally reached London for the first time with Diana Wynyard playing Gilda, Anton Walbrook as Otto, and Rex Harrison as Leo, the part that Coward had played on Broadway.

Rehearsals began in the middle of December, with a week out of town at the Theatre Royal, Brighton before opening in London at the Theatre Royal, Haymarket. When, on the packed first night in Brighton the company received thunderous applause, the audience called for Coward, but Miss Wynyard had to inform them that he was in America.

The play was a hit with the London audience, glad to have something trivial and light-hearted to take their minds off the worsening situation in Europe. *The Stage* said: 'Rex Harrison knows exactly how to get quick-fire charm into the character of the lady's man so popular at the moment.'

By early 1939, Rex was such a major personality in London that he only just missed being voted 'Britain's Best-Dressed Man', losing to Anthony Eden, as it was stated that Rex had only lately been 'noticed' by tailors for the smartness of his clothes while 'Mr Eden, on the other hand, has long been strictly "correct" in his clothes and has probably influenced the style of formal wear to some extent.'

Rex enjoyed his new-found prosperity and was often seen roaring around town in his powerful car, cutting a dashing figure in the West End. Many friends of long acquaintance had become aware of a gradual change in Rex's personality with the advent of success. Baron, the theatrical photographer, who had met him years before when he was still touring in plays around the provinces, was less than complimentary. 'Rex Harrison has become, in my opinion, one of the world's most accomplished and technically perfect actors – but the fun has gone from him, as it has from so many people who have become stars. What a pity they change.'

Baron felt that too many actors fell victim to their own star complex: 'Rex Harrison succumbed to it hardest,' he said. 'Bit by bit the mask of artifice stole over their faces, and the spontaneity died from their laughter. Their eyes became dull and anxious, quick to suspicion at the fear that they might not be recognised or appreciated. Even if you don't know the face you can always spot a movie star by the enormity of his *amour propre*.'

Another friend thought that the man he had known as a struggling actor had gradually disappeared, to be engulfed inside the manufactured image of Rex Harrison the actor, and he remarked: 'In a way, Rex is a fraud. There's still a lot of Reginald in him somewhere.' Harrison has said on many occasions that his early touring days were hard – 'I have had my whack of being knocked about by the world' – and there can certainly be no actor who worked harder at his craft, putting up with living in 'digs' for so long and then, having once achieved success in the West End, working almost sixteen hours a day for two years, on stage and in films. When the good life came he was determined to keep it, whatever the cost. One of the casualties was his marriage which, after numerous partings and reconciliations, finally came to an end – although the formalities of divorce were left until 1942.

Rex, recalling his first marriage, once said: 'We had some happy times. But after many separations and startings-again, we decided to call it a day.'

Collette said in retrospect, 'I remember the first time I saw Rex on stage. I thought then, as I do now, that he was a contributor, a contributor to all our enjoyment. He may have put on or acted up as a man, but never as an actor. I don't think he grew in himself, but his acting did.'

Rex continued to make films during the day while appearing in *Design For Living* and in February 1939 began work on *Peace in our Time* at Denham under the direction of Herbert Mason. It was a Paramount film adapted from the novel *The Chinese Fish* by the prize-winning French author Jean Bommart, with much of the action taking place on the Simplon-Orient Express, and brought up to date with current political events to include a crisis in the Balkans threatening the peace of Europe; mid-way through shooting the film's title was changed to *The Silent Battle*. Rex played Sauvin, a mysterious secret-service agent known as the 'Chinese Fish', co-starring with John Loder as a newspaper reporter investigating the prospective Balkan revolution, and Valerie Hobson as an attractive young woman who unwittingly becomes involved.

Valerie Hobson had returned to England in 1936 after appearing in a number of Hollywood films, including *The Bride of Frankenstein* with Boris Karloff. Within the next two years Korda starred her in his production of *The Drum*, after which she co-starred with Conrad Veidt in *The Spy in Black* and *Contraband*, and with Laurence Olivier and Ralph Richardson in *Q Planes*.

'In 1939 I was asked to appear in *The Silent Battle*, which my husband, Anthony Havelock-Allan, was producing. I can remember being amazed when I was told that I was to have two leading men: one the extremely hand-some John Loder who was already well known, the other an up-and-coming young actor, Rex Harrison, who was already attracting considerable notice for his charm and elegance. He was not handsome – but attractive. Even then he had personality and charm.

'He came on the set with a reputation for "not suffering fools gladly", and there was some apprehension that he wouldn't relish the sequence in which he had to spend most of a day hanging upside down out of a railway carriage while a wind machine blew smoke into his face full-force. Surprisingly, he survived with unruffled calm and his good temper complete.'

Rex finished *The Silent Battle* in March, and was then cast in Columbia's *Ten Days in Paris*, again being directed by Tim Whelan, in which he was co-starred with new-comer, Karen Verne. Rex played a young Englishman who wakes up in a Paris nursing home with a bullet wound in his head, suffering a complete loss of memory regarding his movements over the past ten days. In tracing the events which led to his injury he finds that, mistakenly identified as a foreign spy, he had become involved in trying to prevent a munitions train, carrying a time bomb, from penetrating the Maginot line. On its release *Kinematograph Weekly* said: 'Rex Harrison has an easy, nonchalant way with him, and his talent and attractive personality do much to keep the fantastic yet intriguing story in some perspective. He also injects considerable feminine appeal into the role of Robert.'

In May, with the final closure of *French Without Tears*, Anthony Asquith began work on the film version for Paramount. Only Roland Culver and Guy Middleton repeated the roles they had played on-stage, as Paramount sent over Ray Milland and Ellen Drew from Hollywood to interpret the parts played so perfectly by Rex and Kay Hammond, feeling that the film needed the drawing power of two established box-office stars for the American market. They were poor substitutes for the originals and the film was not a success.

4

ALONG WITH every man, woman and child in Britain, Rex Harrison's world was thrown into confusion on Sunday, September 3rd 1939, when a state of war was declared between Great Britain and Germany.

At the time, Rex was still appearing in *Design For Living*, now at the Savoy Theatre where it had transferred on June 13th. It was known that all places of entertainment in central London would automatically close on the outbreak of war, so initial plans for such an eventuality had already been made. A meeting was hastily convened in the H. M. Tennent Organisation offices above the Globe Theatre in Shaftesbury Avenue. The *Design For Living* cast were prominent among those present.

Rex had also been attempting to enlist. On the morning of September 4th, he received a telephone call at his Sloane Street flat from his agent, Vere Barker, a major in the reserve, who informed his client that he was trying to secure a place for him in the Inns of Court Cavalry Regiment. Rex hastened to the Inns of Court to see the regimental colonel but found they were not taking any more recruits and that he would receive his call-up papers when he was required. As Rex recalled in his autobiography: 'I thanked him and left, feeling rather as if I had auditioned for a part that I was not quite sure I wanted.'

Collette had already left to join the Red Cross and would be trained somewhere outside London, effectively consolidating their separation. Their son Noel had been sent down to Collette's parents in Cornwall, leaving Rex alone in Sloane Street, with not even *Design For Living* to bolster his spirits. With his life in limbo while the future of *Design For Living* and his possible future in the army were both being decided, Rex felt too oppressed to remain in London and went to stay with his cousin, Bat Tonge, and her husband Buster, at their home, Rudlow Manor, near Bath. While there, Rex was further exasperated to discover that his call-up papers had gone astray and all the places in the Inns of Court Cavalry Regiment were filled before it could be sorted out. It was an annoying set-back. The almost total blindness in his left eye would certainly bar him from active service at the front and he was anxious to make himself available for service elsewhere as soon as possible.

Rex was finally rescued from this uneasy idleness by a telephone call from Hugh 'Binkie' Beaumont, who had solved the problem of the future of *Design For Living*. The play had been presented to capacity houses and permanent closure would undoubtedly have been premature. There remained only one solution beyond closure. It was clearly out of the question to remain in London. The Home Office had imposed a six o'clock curfew and had restricted public transport, with the result that evening performances were impossible. To remain in the West End meant surviving on six matinees a week, (Sundays were forbidden) which effectively wrecked the financial chances of a production. One of the few productions which did continue at its old home was the already phenomenally successful Noël Gay musical *Me and My Girl* at the Victoria Palace, starring Lupino Lane.

Design For Living was just one of a number of notable attractions forced to close – John Gielgud's production of Oscar Wilde's *The Importance of Being Earnest* at the Globe Theatre, with Gielgud, Edith Evans, Peggy Ashcroft and Margaret Rutherford, and Emlyn Williams's *The Corn Is Green* at the Duchess Theatre, which starred Williams himself and Sybil Thorndike, both closed. A further casualty was Ivor Novello's *The Dancing Years*, and it was

Novello who summed up the feeling at the time in an interview he gave to the October issue of *Theatre World*. The solution was obvious. Theatres throughout the provinces were still open and eager for new attractions, as Novello proclaimed,

> Keep the footlights burning! . . . if we cannot play in the West End for a while, then the theatre will carry on its work throughout the country. One thing is certain, we must all make sacrifices. There can be no big star salaries; instead there must be a flat, uniform figure, with a sliding percentage. The whole point is to get back to work again, as soon as possible, and you can realise how much that means to the thousands of people suddenly deprived of a living overnight and faced with an indefinite period of unemployment.

The first production to reappear was *The Importance of Being Earnest*, which reopened at the Golders Green Hippodrome in north-west London just two weeks after war had been declared. Golders Green proved to be the embarkation point for several important tours including *The Corn Is Green*. But *Design For Living* after opening there on September 25th, went further afield immediately, to Southport on October 9th, followed by, among other centres, Leicester, Oxford, Cardiff, Birmingham and Manchester.

So it was that Rex Harrison found himself appearing in *Design For Living* at the Theatre Royal, Birmingham in November 1939. At another of the city theatres, the Alexandra, Leslie Banks and Margaret Rawlings were making a pre-West End tour in a play called *You of All People*, which had opened a few days before. The cast of Mr Banks's offering could not help but be aware of the presence of the rival attraction, not only because it was making a notable dent in their potential audience, but because the *Design For Living* company was also staying in the same hotel, it being one of the few still open.

One evening early in his stay, Rex entered the hotel's restaurant and glancing towards the table occupied by Leslie Banks and his company, was immediately aware of a strikingly attractive young woman. Through his monocle, Rex surveyed her approvingly; she was a slim, well-rounded girl with blonde hair and large green eyes which dominated her small, elegant face. Her name, as Rex quickly discovered, was Lilli Palmer, a twenty-five-year-old German actress who was steadily making a name for herself in Britain.

Rex made no approach that evening but determined to collar Leslie Banks, with whom he had appeared in the play *Man of Yesterday* four years earlier, to bring about an introduction. Over the next few days Miss Palmer became very much aware of the interest which one of Britain's most dashing young leading men was showing towards her and which he made no attempt to hide. It therefore came as no surprise when she looked up one evening from where she was sitting in the dining room to see Leslie Banks approaching her table followed by the elegant Mr Harrison. No sooner had the introductions been made than Rex discovered her plans for the next day and invited himself along, displaying a confidence which defied her to refuse.

The following day, Rex and Lilli visited the private zoo of Lord Dudley just outside Birmingham. As an animal-lover the young actress had become a Fellow of London Zoological Gardens which gave her special privileges whereby she was able to visit zoos outside normal opening hours and could even enter some of the cages.

Rex's unflappable composure and ubiquitous monocle became a challenge to her and as the couple wandered around the zoo, Lilli felt a growing and irrepressible desire to see if she could break down this remarkably confident young man. She saw her chance when they reached the snake house. Lilli calmly stepped into a cage and picked up a long snake which she gently patted before draping it around Rex's neck. Lilli failed in her purpose utterly however: the monocle stayed firmly in place and so did Rex's composure. His only reaction was to express surprise at how warm the creature was when he had fully expected it to be cold. Rex further endeared himself to Lilli by demonstrating a genuine love of animals and a refreshing willingness to allow his clothes to get dirty in order to get closer to them.

Having spent the entire day together, the couple arranged to meet after their separate shows, when they walked about the darkened streets of Birmingham, talking mainly about the theatre. Over the next couple of days Rex and Lilli each saw the other play their matinees. Lilli's visit demonstrated to her that Rex was undoubtedly one of the most talented leading men in England while Rex, in his turn, offered concrete criticisms concerning Lilli's part revealing a thorough knowledge and passionate devotion to the theatre.

Their interest in each other quickly developed and Rex learnt that this young lady had already crammed a great deal into her life. Lilli Palmer was born Maria Lilli Peiser on May 24th 1914 in Posen, Germany but had lived most of her life in Berlin where her father, Dr Alfred Peiser, was head of surgery at a major hospital following four years in the army when he ran a field hospital at Verdun, earning an Iron Cross for his services. Lilli was the middle sister of three; the older one was named Irene and the younger Hilde. Before her marriage their mother had been an actress under her maiden name of Rosa Lissmann, but she gave that up to devote herself to her husband and children.

Theirs was a close family and Rosa and Alfred's marriage a loving one. Both were German and Jewish and their three daughters were all brought up in that faith, living a comfortably middle-class existence. Lilli's ambition to go on the stage was set from the age of ten despite her father's hopes that she would choose the medical profession and follow his example. From the age of sixteen, while still at school, she attended a drama school, taking on this double work-load for the remaining two years before she graduated in April, 1932. The end of her drama course was marked by a collective stage performance, and by the end of the evening Lilli had gained a twelve-month contract with the Darmstadt State Theater, one of the best repertory companies in Germany.

Unfortunately for Lilli the growth of Nazism intervened. As it became obvious that Germany was unsafe for a young Jewish girl, her parents decided she should go to Paris where her older sister Irene had already been for the past month. She was followed there by her boyfriend, Rolf Gérard, a painter and medical student who was six years her senior, and together they shared an apartment.

At this time Lilli was a rather chubby, moon-faced girl trying to get work on the stage in a foreign country. She changed her name to Lilli Palmer as it was easier for the French to pronounce and when, after much persistence, she got work in nightclubs it was as part of a double-act with her sister under the name of 'Les Sœurs Viennoises', a name which helped to soften any connection with Nazi Germany by implying Austrian origin.

Tragedy struck on January 31st 1934 when Lilli's father died suddenly of a heart attack. The two sisters returned briefly to Berlin but were soon back in Paris with a new plan – to go to England. Alexander Korda, Britain's most powerful film producer, had shown some interest in Lilli and on the strength of this Lilli crossed the English Channel. There were, however, the inevitable problems over work permits, and Lilli's first job was not with Alexander Korda but in a 'quota quickie' called *Crime Unlimited* with Esmond Knight, made for Warner Brothers at their Teddington studios. As a result of her appearance in this she was offered a contract by Gaumont-British, but the necessary labour permit was refused and Lilli had briefly to leave the country. On her

return both her contract and a permit which had to be
renewed every three months, came through. On this
precarious basis, Lilli's mother and two sisters set up
house with Lilli in north-west London in Parsifal Road,
Hampstead.

Lilli hired a drama teacher to improve her technique,
but was not short of work, her early films including *Good
Morning Boys* with Will Hay, and Alfred Hitchcock's
Secret Agent with John Gielgud, Madeleine Carroll and
another refugee, Peter Lorre. Her stage work included
The Road To Gandahar at the Garrick Theatre and *The Tree of
Eden*. She returned to the cinema to appear with Margaret
Lockwood, who was then well on the way to becoming
the British cinema's premier actress, in the Carol Reed
film of *A Girl Must Live*.

The outbreak of war brought a major blow for Lilli
when her contract with Gaumont-British was cancelled.
At least the Home Office now granted Lilli a permanent
labour permit, although with London's theatres tempor-
arily closed, work was in short supply. Then her relationship with Rolf Gérard ended. Altogether, life for Lilli
was very depressing until she gained a part in Leslie
Banks's touring production of *You of All People*, opening
in Birmingham in November.

The timing of her meeting with Rex could hardly have
been better; she was unattached for the first time in years
and Rex's stormy marriage to Collette had settled into
what looked like a permanent separation. Rex and Lilli
soon shied away from the haunts of their colleagues, sure
that they would meet knowing glances at every encounter. Rex explained his precarious married state and Lilli
was no less open about herself. They spent all the time
they could together and, since both companies were
moving on to Liverpool the following week, Rex offered
to drive Lilli there in his second-hand Bentley, along with
his friend Arthur Barbosa who had come up to Birmingham to see Rex before travelling on to Liverpool to see his
family.

This further week together in Liverpool cemented their relationship and when their separate tours branched off they arranged to meet again in London. Rex journeyed on to Newcastle where one evening the film director Carol Reed offered him the leading male role opposite Margaret Lockwood in a new film to be called *Gestapo*. The film was scheduled for the following spring. Rex finally returned to London in late December when *Design For Living* capped its tour with a run at the Savoy Theatre, opening on 23rd December, just one day after *You of All People* had opened at the Apollo. Rex quickly renewed his relationship with Lilli whose honesty and integrity he found attractive in the aftermath of the failure of his marriage. The war had cast a different light over his marriage to Collette, and with its frequent separations and reconciliations neither had valued faithfulness very highly. Collette was a naturally vivacious creature whereas Lilli, in contrast, was a much more withdrawn, serious woman. With the country thrown into turmoil, a steadfast and reliable woman like Lilli held a great attraction; so little else was certain in this unstable time.

Rex's days were now filled with the shooting of *Gestapo* at the Gaumont-British studios in Shepherd's Bush, for Twentieth Century Productions, the British arm of Twentieth Century-Fox. The script, originally titled *Report on a Fugitive*, and based on a story by Gordon Wellesley, had a screenplay written by Sidney Gilliat and Frank Launder, and finally emerged as *Night Train to Munich*. A spy thriller, it was very much along the lines of Alfred Hitchcock's *The Lady Vanishes*, made two years earlier with Margaret Lockwood and Michael Redgrave, also with a screenplay by Launder and Gilliat.

The film industry, like the theatre, had gone through a hard period at the outbreak of the war when all cinemas were closed for a short time. So bad was the situation that Twentieth Century-Fox, who had founded a base in Islington, were preparing to abandon their holdings in Britain due to the cessation of all British film production.

That production did begin again was mainly due to the efforts of producers Edward Black and Michael Balcon who managed to persuade the Board of Trade of the value the film industry held for a country at war. The studios which had been turned into warehouses (the Denham and Pinewood studios were being used to store sugar and flour respectively) or had been closed as a precaution in case of bombing raids, as in Islington's case, were reopened.

Black's first film following the reopening was *Night Train to Munich* which emerged as an entertaining piece of propaganda. Hurried into production at the earliest opportunity, the film had to be made at Shepherd's Bush because Fox's Islington studios were still closed. Set just prior to the outbreak of war, *Night Train to Munich* concerned the rescuing of a valued Czechoslovakian scientist and his daughter Anna, played by Margaret Lockwood, from Nazi Germany. It is left to Rex as Gus Bennett, a government agent and part-time song plugger, to don the disguise of a Nazi officer and rescue father and daughter before they reach Berlin via the Munich train under the watchful eye of Gestapo officer Karl Morse, played by Paul von Hernreid, who soon after changed his name to Paul Henreid and went to Hollywood, appearing most notably in *Now Voyager* and *Casablanca* for Warner Brothers. Rex is helped along the way by the cricket- and golf-loving Charters and Caldicott – Basil Radford and Naunton Wayne reviving their roles from *The Lady Vanishes*. Rex finally succeeds in his mission after some amusing confrontations and deceptions, with the film reaching its climax in a car chase to the border and a final escape by cable car.

It is interesting that our first introduction to Rex's character gives us an early taste of his singing voice. He is seen wearing a straw boater and bow tie at a pier sheet-music stall in a fictitious coastal town called Bright-bourne, singing a ballad entitled 'Only Love Can Lead the Way'. Although Rex's singing is played for comedy, he reveals a pleasant, light voice of limited range, worth noting because of what lay in the future.

Unfortunately, the merits of the film have all too often been overlooked because of its similarity to *The Lady Vanishes*. Margaret Lockwood herself says, 'I don't think *Night Train to Munich* was a patch on *The Lady Vanishes* and I was very disappointed after the excitement that *The Lady Vanishes* caused.' But it remains a very well constructed adventure film and in some ways has actually stood the test of time better than the Hitchcock film. With three members of the cast from the previous film present and with an important section of its action taking place on a trans-European train journey, the parallels are easy to draw but there is still enough originality to merit a higher reputation than it enjoys at present.

Miss Lockwood, however, does not recall Rex Harrison with much enthusiasm, 'He was just another leading man, although I liked him as a person. But I do remember that he wouldn't suffer fools gladly. I didn't have many scenes to play with him as his principal work constituted one part of the film and mine the other. It was not the usual playing opposite of hero and heroine.' Her abiding memory of the film is of an accident on the set which could easily have killed or severely injured both herself and Rex. During the filming of a sequence in a hotel where Rex, disguised as a German officer, is supposed to be reawakening an old passion in Margaret's heart in order to get to her father through her, Miss Lockwood, recalls:

'sitting up in bed in the luxurious hotel bedroom set while they were getting ready to shoot a scene with me leaning against the pillows on the bed. My stand-in, Katie, was standing at the foot of the bed, as I had now replaced her in the bed ready to shoot the scene with Rex. Amusing myself doing a crossword, I was stuck for a word and leant forward to seek Katie's advice. There was a large mirror that covered the whole wall at the back of the bed and Rex and I had to play the scene immediately in front of it. As I leaned forward, the whole wall mirror fell and shattered barely missing me. If I had not leaned forward when I did, I would most certainly have been killed . . .'

If Harrison had taken his place beside Miss Lockwood at that moment, that might have been the end for him, too. Viewing the film, one can see that the mirror has been replaced by a very large room-divider which does not match the decor of the rest of the room.

The film proved a great popular success, in no small degree due to Rex's polished performance, displaying immense charm and a deftness in handling the comedy. It must also rank as one of Rex's most physical roles in which we have the rare sight of him blasting away with a gun and even jumping in mid-air from one cable car to another during the exciting climax of the film – two images hardly in keeping with the accepted vision of Rex as a hero of the drawing-room school.

The success of the film was not just confined to Britain. Under the title *Night Train*, the film ran for fifteen weeks in New York at a time when British films found it difficult to infiltrate the lucrative American market, and it was this film which first made Hollywood take notice of Rex Harrison, leading ultimately to his being offered a contract with Twentieth Century-Fox.

Rex got along well with Carol Reed during the making of the film, respecting his diligence and perfectionism, qualities Rex has valued throughout his career. He has always been willing to go to any lengths to bring the best that he can to a part and is quick to recognise and appreciate the same qualities in others. The friendship which developed between the two men also led to Rex's first active involvement in the war effort. Like Rex, Carol Reed lived in Chelsea and when the filming of *Night Train to Munich* ended in June 1940, both men joined the Chelsea Home Guard. Following the evacuation at

Dunkirk, Home Guard units were set up all over England in response to the very real threat of invasion. Rex had not given up his attempts to enlist but his partial blindness proved an insurmountable obstacle. The Home Guard, however, did not require a medical test.

The Chelsea Home Guard was commanded by General Sir Hubert Gough who had begun a distinguished career when he joined the 16th Lancers in 1889 serving in India, and had risen to the position of first commander of the Fifth Army in France in the Great War. Under his direction Rex's unit went through a makeshift training programme, drilling every day despite a lack of arms and uniforms. As a well-known figure, Rex not unnaturally was made CO of a platoon which included several veterans. Rex's only military experience was the Officers' Training Corps at Liverpool College and, as a result, he did not take easily to his new role. Surprisingly, for an actor, he found it difficult to arrive at a suitably authoritative tone. Confronted by his platoon, he hesitantly tried to enforce some kind of order without being at all clear about what exactly he should be doing. Seeing his difficulty, one of the old soldiers asked him if he could be of any assistance, to which a grateful Rex replied, 'I'd love you to.' 'Don't love me to – tell me to!' was the instant and unexpected rebuff and Rex felt more at sea than ever. Rex's taste of command was short-lived and he was quickly demoted in favour of someone who possessed the necessary aggressive qualities.

Although Rex still lived in Sloane Street and Lilli in Parsifal Road in Hampstead with her family, they managed to see a great deal of each other, in spite of the fact that as an enemy alien Lilli was prohibited from leaving her home after dark.

Rex was not out of work for long before he was offered the major part of Adolphus Cusins in a proposed screen version of George Bernard Shaw's *Major Barbara*, which would follow the hugely successful film version of *Pygmalion*, with Leslie Howard and Wendy Hiller, which had been produced by Gabriel Pascal two years previously.

Before he started the film Rex moved from Chelsea to a small cottage near Denham Studios where the film was to be made. With bombing raids increasingly frequent in London, the dangers in remaining in central London were becoming too great, so Lilli moved into the cottage with Rex for the duration of the filming. Rex had not been the first choice to play the part of Cusins. Leslie Howard, who had been so successful as Professor Higgins in *Pygmalion*, had declined, reportedly because he would only consider the part if he was also able to co-direct, as he had done in the previous film in partnership with Anthony Asquith. However, Gabriel Pascal was determined to direct *Major Barbara* himself. With Leslie Howard's refusal, Pascal searched through the pages of *Spotlight*, the casting directory, and picked a young actor called Andrew Osborn, a choice which was approved by George Bernard Shaw himself.

Gabriel Pascal was a flamboyant and temperamental Hungarian who, as a penniless emigré, had managed to persuade Bernard Shaw to allow him the film rights to produce *Pygmalion*. With barely any experience of the film industry, Pascal's success in persuading Shaw, in the wake of failure by Alexander Korda, Universal Pictures and the American actress Marion Davies, was mainly due to his exhibiting a proper veneration for every word that Shaw had written, an attitude which the great man felt would protect his play from being mutilated on the screen. Such was the success of *Pygmalion* that Shaw encouraged the Hungarian to film another of his plays and, in July 1939, the two men agreed on *Major Barbara*. Shaw's parable shows how the might and power of industry can lead to a social reorganisation whereby poverty and injustice are eliminated far more effectively than through religious salvation alone.

Following some location shooting in Devon, filming began at Denham Studios on June 17th 1940. From the beginning, Pascal and Osborn clashed. Osborn was far too young and inexperienced an actor to take on such a part and Pascal, lacking any directorial experience or aptitude, was not the man to put the actor at his ease and help him through what was inevitably a daunting task. Within a few days of their return to Denham, Osborn was replaced. It has often been suggested that Shaw's young actor friend, Alec Guinness, was a possible contender for either the part of Cusins or that of Charles Lomax, but Guinness firmly refutes this:

'It is not true that I turned down a part in *Major Barbara* and suggested Rex Harrison. I would have been mad in 1939, at the age of 25, to have turned down anything. And Rex was an experienced star actor by that time. Shaw wrote a postcard to Pascal in Hollywood (where Pascal was seeking financial backing) suggesting me for a part but it was never taken up in any way. They in Hollywood weren't mad either! I wonder how these garbled stories get started and I am glad to have scotched this one.'

Accounts differ as to how far Rex was actually Gabriel Pascal's choice. Whatever the truth, Rex accepted the part in July, to join an impressive company.

Apart from Wendy Hiller, whose desire to play the title role and whose availability to do so had been the impetus for the entire project, the assembled cast included Robert Newton, Robert Morley, Sybil Thorndike, Emlyn Williams, Marie Lohr, Donald Calthrop, Penelope Dudley Ward, Stanley Holloway and a young discovery of Pascal's, Deborah Kerr, making her screen debut. Those involved behind the scenes were no less distinguished: David Lean and Harold French as assistant directors; Cecil Beaton designed the costumes, William Walton composed the music, the cinematographer was Ronald Neame, and Vincent Korda and John Bryan designed the sets.

Unfortunately, the disrupted first few days in the production were but a foretaste of the chaos which was to reign throughout the filming. Originally scheduled to be completed in ten weeks, it actually took six months and cost more than double its original budget. The major cause of the prolonged production was the war – on July 10th the Germans began bombing London and the Battle of Britain had begun. Shooting was continually interrupted by air-raids: there were spotters on the studio roof who would raise the alarm upon sighting enemy aircraft, at which the whole cast and crew would evacuate the sound stage to shelter in the storage areas underneath the concrete studio floor. There they would remain until the all-clear when they would return to the studio floor and try to get back into the momentum of the scene they were filming. An estimated one hundred and twenty-five bombs fell in the vicinity of the studio during filming, which was further disrupted by aircraft noise which made sound recording impossible. On one particular day such was the profusion of enemy aircraft in the skies that the company only managed to film one shot out of the seventeen that had been scheduled.

Location shooting also had its added hazards and delays. On one occasion, the unit returned to a street in London where they had been filming, to discover that the street had disappeared overnight, a victim of the previous night's bombing raid.

With such delays it is not surprising that the shooting of the film dragged on for so long. The tension that the threat of danger and the necessarily disjointed method of filming put on all those involved did not make working on the film a very happy experience. Even today, Wendy Hiller can only recall the film with dismay, 'I waited two years for *Major Barbara* and I was so disgusted by the whole thing that I have never seen it all. I saw a quarter of it and went to the Ladies and wept – because it wasn't *Major Barbara* and all I could think was that I wasted all that time of my life while there was a war on. Which, of course, meant nothing to Gaby Pascal. I hated every minute of it and hated every bit I saw.'

Pascal should never have directed the film. He was pushing himself beyond his capabilities, swept up by the success of *Pygmalion*, and convincing himself that he could match or even surpass that film if he took on the role of director himself. But, as Wendy Hiller recalls, it was to the film's detriment.

It was not long before David Lean and Harold French were forced to take on more active roles themselves because Pascal proved himself incapable of handling actors properly or of being able to conceive and execute a scene in cinematic terms while keeping within the bounds of what was actually technically possible. There was a vain attempt to play down the increased role of these two men at the expense of Pascal, but it was clear to everyone, including Rex, that David Lean's frequent whisperings into the Hungarian's ear were to give advice and this attempt at subtlety deceived no one. Lean himself recalls this situation on the film:

'Gaby Pascal didn't really know the right end of the viewfinder and so he employed me and Harold French as what is known as "Assistants In Direction" – not "Assistant Directors". Harold was there for the dialogue because he was a stage director and I was there for the camera set-ups and did a fair amount of the direction. I was a sort of *film* director; I was the camera end of it – but I've never had any credit for it.'

While no bombs actually fell on Denham Studios during the production of the film, the cast suffered one casualty. Robert Newton and Donald Calthrop were notorious drinkers and the two men were watched continually to ensure that no alcohol reached their lips. But both men had hiding places for their whisky and often, instead of sheltering during an air-raid, would take the opportunity to drink together. But they never let alcohol spoil their performances, indeed in Newton's case it would produce a marked improvement. Unfortunately, and more as the result of his alcohol intake than the war, Calthrop died on July 15th before he had finished his final scene. Lean recalls this incident: 'We had the most macabre scene where we were waiting for Donald Calthrop and we then found that he had died the night before. We had only two or three shots left with him and so we dressed up his stand-in in his clothes and put him back to camera and we had a voice mimic for a couple of lines – very macabre. I liked Donald Calthrop. He was very good and very nice – he used to drink too much, of course.'

George Bernard Shaw was kept in touch regarding the progress of filming, largely through visits and correspondence from Pascal, but he did make at least two appearances on the set when Rex was present. At the first, on July 26th, his eighty-fourth birthday, the company were shooting a spectacular Salvation Army meeting at the Albert Hall and Shaw enthusiastically joined in the filming, suggesting various bits of comic business that the members of the band could do with their instruments, and even joining in with the extras who were singing and waving their arms.

His second visit was on September 12th at Denham where he came to film a prologue which was to be added to the American copies of the film. The set had been cleared of everyone except the technicians and Rex Harrison and Wendy Hiller who, as the stars of the film, were to be photographed with Shaw for publicity purposes. Lean recalls: 'Gaby always used to call him "Master" and he used to have a great big armchair waiting for Shaw when he was expected to arrive. I remember when Shaw arrived, Gaby sat him down and kissed the top of his head. I thought, "Don't do it! That won't go down." But it did. He loved it.'

Rex was suitably impressed by Shaw's erect, self-possessed appearance and watched intently as the great man sat down at a desk to give his speech. When Shaw had finished, Pascal asked him to read through the last scene between Major Barbara and Cusins and to give the two actors some guidance. Rex and Wendy Hiller sat on either side of him while the author silently read the scene. Shaw paused after finishing it and his only comment was to express his extreme dissatisfaction with his own work, leaving his two actors no more enlightened as to the significance of the scene than they had been before.

Lean recalls an incident which occurred between Shaw and Rex on one of the author's rare appearances: 'Rex had a scene where he had to say the line and then bang on the drum to give it emphasis. Rex was being very polite about it – saying his lines and "boomph" – not banging hard. And Shaw said, "No, no, no, no! Let me take it!" He took the drumstick and he stood opposite Rex, who had the drum around his neck, and he delivered the line and "crash!" He was damn good – but I think Rex still rendered it in a polite version.'

Similarly, Shaw attempted to advise Rex with regard to the scene where Cusins quotes some verses from Euripides' *The Bacchae* at Andrew Undershaft. Always inclined towards the natural style of acting, Rex recited the verse in character, feeling that Cusins would say it, as Shaw himself noted, in a manner that was 'as colloquial as possible, so as to make it sound like cup-and-saucer small talk.' Shaw, in rehearsal notes to Pascal, informed the director how he had advised Rex to alter his interpretation so as not to 'throw' the verse away. 'When I write verse, it must be deliberately declaimed as such – I mentioned this to Rex.'

Apart from this comment Rex seems to have passed the author's approval and was even regarded by George Bernard Shaw as an ideal for a Shavian actor; an opinion which, however, did not prompt Rex to an immediate return to Shaw. Indeed, his only other Shavian involvements have been on stage in the past decade, with *Caesar and Cleopatra* and *Heartbreak House*, although of course, much of Shaw undoubtedly remains in *My Fair Lady*.

It was with Wendy Hiller's performance that Shaw was least happy, as he again wrote to Pascal following his visit to Denham: 'I doubt whether Wendy understands Barbara. As Eliza [in *Pygmalion*], whom she did understand, her face changed marvellously with every wave of feeling. In *Barbara* her face never changes at all.' Only Robert Newton, out of the entire cast, was actually singled out by Shaw for praise.

The film was finally completed in December 1940 and opened on April 17th 1941 to a predictably mixed critical reaction. The general consensus was that it was a distinctly inferior film to *Pygmalion* and did not make clear its issues and themes. Rex and Robert Newton came out of the film most successfully, both being almost universally acclaimed for their separate contributions, while Wendy Hiller suffered against comparisons with her Eliza Doolittle in *Pygmalion*. The film was only moderately successful, just about managing to earn back its cost, which had been exceptionally high for a British film at that time.

Over forty years after its release it is hard to understand why *Major Barbara* received so much negative criticism. It has possibly the finest cast of actors ever assembled for a British film, each and every contribution from them serving the distinguished playwright immaculately. The production values of the film are all you would expect from those involved in the making of it, and with hindsight, the film bears the obvious hallmark of David Lean. It must be considered one of Britain's finest film achievements and one of the best examples in that toughest of all genres – translating a play to the screen. As for Rex, it is one of his most important screen appearances and he is faultless as Adolphus Cusins.

During the long period when Rex was involved in the making of *Major Barbara*, his own personal life had not been without its upheavals. As soon as Rex and Lilli started living together, the pressure increased for the couple to marry. The arrangement had initially been that Lilli would join Rex in Denham while *Major Barbara* was being filmed, but since production went on for such a long period their domestic arrangements took on a more permanent appearance. Rex did not find it easy to obtain a divorce from Collette who was quite happy to continue their married existence in the manner in which it had been run for several years. But Rex was adamant, and he finally managed to persuade Collette to sue him for divorce, naming Lilli as co-respondent. Rex and Lilli planned to marry as soon as his divorce came through, but that would not be for some time.

The tragedy of war came closer to Rex than hitherto in those first months at Denham. Harold French, who had been a friend of Rex's since *French Without Tears*, had moved out of London, but his wife, Phyl, had remained because she had a war job in the capital. One morning French telephoned home as was his usual practice each day; unable to get through he rushed off to London and discovered that his house had received a direct hit and that his wife was dead. A distraught French returned to Denham and within a few days he left his own lodgings and moved in with Rex and Lilli who did their best to console him. The two men became close as a result of this shared experience and Harold French remains one of Rex's few long-standing friends.

Indeed, it was French who directed Rex in his next theatrical appearance. As soon as *Major Barbara* was completed Rex was offered a part in the London production of S. N. Behrman's *No Time for Comedy* which was being presented by Hugh Beaumont for H. M. Tennent. It was planned that the production would first go on tour and then open at the Haymarket, marking the reopening of the theatre following its closure at the outbreak of war.

Again, Diana Wynyard would be Rex's leading lady with a supporting cast which included Elisabeth Welch, Walter Fitzgerald and Arthur Macrae. Rex played a world-weary young playwright, Gaylord Easterbrook, who is torn between his aptitude for writing light plays and his ambition to write serious ones. The play had already opened on Broadway, at the Ethel Barrymore Theatre, on April 17th 1939 with Laurence Olivier as Easterbrook, starring opposite Katharine Cornell, in her first modern comedy, as his actress wife, Linda Paige. Among others, they were supported by Robert Flemyng who had appeared in *French Without Tears* with Rex. The play was a huge success in New York, rivalling the production of Philip Barry's new comedy *The Philadelphia Story*, starring Katharine Hepburn.

For the London production Rex suggested to Beaumont that Lilli should play the part of Amanda Smith, the attractive girl with whom Easterbrook philanders. That Lilli was given the role indicates the strength of the position Rex had achieved for himself by this time, although Lilli did have a reputation as a reliable actress and so neither Beaumont nor Diana Wynyard felt the need to raise any objections to her joining the company. There is no doubt that at this stage in her career her involvement with Rex brought her on to a higher theatrical plane, which meant that important producers and directors were made more aware of her talent.

It is interesting to conjecture whether during this wartime period she would so easily have made the step up without Rex's support. This is not in any way to denigrate her undeniable talent, but merely to point out that she was in a very difficult position following the outbreak of war between Britain and Germany. To most people the difference between a German and a German Jew was academic and, as Elisabeth Welch, who played the Easterbrooks' maid Clementine, recalls, this manifested itself quickly during the run of the play:

'There was that anti-German smell around because we were in the war and she was German. And, of course, she got into trouble. We opened in Blackpool at the Grand Theatre during the week before Christmas. As an alien you had to report your presence if you changed cities; when you got into town you had to go to the police station and they stamped your passport to show that you were okay.

'We were there for about a week before we opened because we rehearsed there. So, about two days before we opened we were in the middle of the rehearsal and two detectives made an appearance. They asked for "Peiser/Palmer" and, of course, we had to stop the rehearsal and she went away.

'Binkie was livid because they would not let her open and René Gad, who was understudying both Diana and Lilli, had to open the show. Binkie was very annoyed; we were all annoyed. Rex was livid but he didn't show it to us – how could he? And it threw us into a terrible tizz. We were already nervous about opening and the Blackpudlians didn't know anything about *No Time for Comedy* anyway and the audience was very scarce!'

Lilli herself recalled the incident and how it was ultimately resolved,

'Binkie Beaumont had neglected to inform the police – so it took a few days. But it was Binkie who met me on a draughty platform three days after the play had opened – and everything was all right. It was very distressing for me and also distressing for Rex; he was very upset about that.'

Rex, as the leading man of the production, was not a pillar of strength to look up to for moral support on opening night at Blackpool, or on any other night, as Elisabeth Welch continues: 'The only nerves he showed were before he went on. Pacing every night; he was terrible. In Blackpool I went out to the wings and there was Rex pacing with a glass of bicarbonate of soda to calm his nerves – walking like a caged lion.'

Rex's behaviour before going on seemed at odds with his previous confidence. He is a quick learner and knew all his lines without a book by the second week of the four-week rehearsal period, which had begun at the Globe Theatre in London and finished in Blackpool. But, as often happens with quick learners, they are the first to start losing their lines. By the time the company had reached the Haymarket in April Rex was stumbling over lines – although not enough to detract from his performance. This is a characteristic of Rex's acting which has continued to the present day. Lilli, by comparison, seemed almost nerveless, displaying a strength before going on which hid any nervousness she might have felt and which helped to calm Rex to a certain extent.

The tour lasted from December 1940 until March 1941, and as they travelled the country, staying in the most important hotel at each destination, it became the practice that Diana Wynyard and Rex would take a suite on alternate weeks to provide a meeting place for the company after the play. Rex and Diana were very friendly towards each other, having already appeared together in *Design For Living*, but they were never involved romantically. In Elisabeth Welch's opinion, 'Rex wasn't her type at all,' and in any case at this time she was having a big affair with Carol Reed whom she would call every night from wherever they were staying and whom she married in 1943.

Lilli was always present at these gatherings but made little effort to be sociable, as Miss Welch recalls, 'She was always there in the corner, huddled up and very, very distant. We called her "the pussycat"; she had no joy, no life.' Lilli would cling on to Rex who provided her with a sense of security. Her behaviour was probably partly due to the way that her alien status was stressed, which would obviously have made her feel unhappy and a little isolated. Because of what was perhaps unjustly regarded as her aloof manner she was not popular among the cast and Miss Welch admits that at the time she was inclined to 'avoid her'.

But if Lilli clung to Rex, then Rex was equally possessive of Lilli, to the point where on one occasion during the tour he threw the company into disrepute. The incident occurred at the Black Boy Hotel in Nottingham, when *No Time for Comedy* was playing at the Theatre Royal. One night early in the week's run, they returned to the hotel after the performance with Rex in a terrible mood because two army officers had sent a note backstage asking Diana Wynyard and Lilli Palmer to dine with them at the Black Boy after the show. It was difficult for Diana and Lilli to refuse because as officers these two men not only had to be treated with a certain amount of respect, but also would in all likelihood soon be going overseas to fight for their country. The two women conferred and decided that the only gracious response would be to accept the invitation, and Rex had no option but to agree that Lilli should go.

Rex's mood was not improved by the fact that as he, Elisabeth Welch and the rest of the company entered the dining room to eat together as they usually did, he was greeted by the sight of Lilli and Diana already installed at a table on the other side of the room with the two officers. Rex sat morosely looking at the foursome through his glasses as the first course of smoked salmon was placed in front of him. Elisabeth Welch expressed enthusiasm for her portion and prepared to eat it.

'I was sitting next to Rex and I cut the piece and was just about to put it in my mouth when Rex smacked my hand and said, "Don't eat it, Liz!" And I said, "Why?" He said, "Have you smelt it?" Rex was a smeller; one of our most embarrassing things on the tour was Rex's habit of smelling things – he always smelt things before he ate them. So I said, "No, I haven't smelt it." So I did and I couldn't smell anything. He, of course, said, "Send for the waiter!" The waiter was brought over

and the awful thing was that they were all Italians –
whom we were fighting. The waiter was terribly rude;
he said, "It's not my fault – it's the chef's fault!" So then
Rex said, "Bring in the chef!"

'He was in a terrible mood but it was really because
of Lilli and the officer. The waiter said, "Certainly not!"
Anyway, they were rude instead of apologising, which
they should have done. The waiter cuffed Rex, who
was sitting there with his glasses on, and back went
Rex's chair – but not that far because it was so crowded.
The chair was pushed up again and I pulled Rex's tails
and said, "Don't Rex! Don't Rex!" And of course, the
whole dining room stood still.

'We calmed Rex down and we left. We went upstairs
with no dinner because we couldn't stay after that. It
was so embarrassing; poor Rex's glasses had gone
flying – it was terrible.'

Rex tried to speak to the manager but was told that he
was away until the next morning, so he had to be content
with leaving a message demanding to see the manager at
ten o'clock that morning. The members of the company
all went dejectedly to their beds and had to make do with
eating the fruit in their rooms to stave off hunger, while
Rex was left alone to wait impatiently for Lilli to come
upstairs.

The next morning at half-past ten Diana Wynyard
came upstairs to tell those of the company who were still
in their rooms that the manager had decided to take his
waiter's side and that not only Rex but the rest of the
company would have to leave the hotel.

Rex telephoned a small hotel a few hundred yards up
the hill from the Black Boy Hotel and was able to secure
only four rooms for the whole company, which meant
that doubling-up was necessary. There was no possibility
of getting any more rooms because Nottingham was
surrounded by big army camps and visiting wives and
sweethearts managed to take up almost every bed in the

city. So up the hill, carrying all their luggage and in disgrace, trudged the entire *No Time for Comedy* company to their less salubrious accommodation, which they occupied for the rest of their week's stay in Nottingham.

Fortunately, apart from this incident, the tour went smoothly and the company settled into an easy routine. The only problem which occasionally faced them was trying to avoid an excessive alcohol intake each night. This arose because, as in London, the blackout applied in larger places like Manchester and so there were no evening performances in the theatres. Instead there were two morning shows per week, with the curtain rising at about ten-thirty in the morning, and six matinees at two o'clock, so that the performance ended well before the blackout. As a result, after about half-past five in the evening the actors had the whole night free to do as they wished. The hotel bar was usually the most notable social venue, but once there it was difficult to avoid getting drunk as they frequently found themselves obliged to join the officers in the hotel who were only too keen to mix with well-known theatrical faces as a change from their normal routine.

The tour finally closed at the end of March and the play came to London, marking the reopening of the Haymarket Theatre, an event which prompted the well known critic Ivor Brown to comment, '. . . how nice it is to have the Haymarket open again, to see a new play instead of a revival – and that mounted with a glitter of pre-war style!'

By this time the bombing of London had become even more severe and the Haymarket itself came close to being hit one night, when a hotel next to the theatre was completely destroyed leaving just a pile of rubble to indicate where it had stood. Amazingly, the Haymarket was not damaged at all. This incident brought home to everyone in the company the frightening impermanence of life and property in London. However, the continual air-raids had become such a regular part of life in the capital that a silent warning system now operated in the

Haymarket so that it did not interrupt the play. An illuminated box sign installed immediately in front of the footlights would be operated, giving patrons the opportunity to leave if they wished to, even though the play would continue as long as was practicable.

When they had been touring in the provinces no such system operated so if an air-raid warning sounded, Rex would stop the play and step up to the footlights to explain the location of the nearest shelter to those in the audience who wanted to leave. One of Rex's first tasks whenever they arrived at a new location was to find out where the air-raid shelters were situated. This unnatural break in the play would continue for several minutes while people left the auditorium, although usually most of the audience remained. However, their concentration was more often than not directed towards the noise of the aircraft flying overhead, as was also the case with the actors, who continued with only half their attention on their lines. But at the Haymarket, Rex was able to continue as Gaylord Easterbrook with the minimum of interruption, allowing the play to run smoothly while the silent air-raid warning operated discreetly at the front of the stage.

The return to London was a triumph, with Rex and Diana Wynyard in particular receiving a rapturous reception on opening night. It was to continue there for almost a year, playing to packed houses, and could have continued for much longer if Rex had not joined the Royal Air Force. Lilli even received co-star billing under Diana Wynyard and Rex Harrison; no small achievement when among such prestigious company. But Miss Palmer modestly put down her achievement: 'I wasn't a star – I was a leading lady. Rex was a star. *No Time for Comedy* was not a success for me. I played a role that I don't know anything about: an American intellectual. I had never been in America, I didn't know that particular woman. So the success of the play was that Rex and Diana played enchantingly.'

One reviewer described Rex as 'long-limbed, moody
. . . and magnetically attractive,' while Ivor Brown
wrote:

> The part of the tetchy Gaylord is played by Mr Rex
> Harrison with great ability and no less charm; he . . .
> puts a gleam of humour and of charm on the dull
> surface of a boor's behaviour . . . enthralled by a
> well-graced actor, we sit chuckling sympathetically at
> the kind of fellow whom, in actual life, we would itch
> to kick downstairs.
>
> Accordingly one may regard such texts as Mr Behr-
> man's and such performances as Mr Harrison's, which
> make the bear with a sore head seem excellent com-
> pany, as a dreadful incitement to bad manners.

Among those who saw Rex in the play was his future
co-star in the film of *Blithe Spirit*, Constance Cummings,

> 'I remember one marvellous bit of business that Rex
> did which I have never forgotten. There is a moment
> where he is left alone in the drawing room and he
> wanders around the room and looks at the *objets d'art* –
> filling in time. Then suddenly he sees the grand piano
> and he goes over and he sits down at it and he does all
> these limbering exercises with his hands, gets the seat
> very well adjusted – and then he starts to play "Chop-
> sticks". It was one of the funniest things I have ever
> seen in my life; you really thought he was going to play
> Rachmaninov or Chopin. The house just fell about. It's
> the concentration; it wasn't done like a gag, it was done
> with great seriousness.'

Arthur Macrae was the first member of the cast to be
called up, and his exit from the play only increased Rex's
own impatience to get into uniform himself. He felt
terrible pangs of guilt as he walked about London in his
civilian clothes, surrounded wherever he went by uni-

formed men and women who filled the auditorium of the
Haymarket every day. Apart from his acting Rex's only
contributions to the war effort were the two occasions a
week when he was on firewatch duty at the Haymarket.
He had to patrol the building looking for incendiary
bombs and would sleep on a bed in his dressing room.
The theatre became a second home to him and it served to
consolidate his affection for the Haymarket. Even today it
remains Rex's favourite theatre.

Eventually, Rex could bear his deprivation no longer
and went before an RAF Board, determined to over-ride
any talk of his being exempt from service due to his high
ranking in the theatrical world. The government had
stated that certain 'key actors' should be exempt from
service but had not actually named the actors whom they
felt were in that category, although Rex would undoubtedly have been one of them.

Rex's stubborn persistence paid off. His bad eyesight
did prohibit him from active service so he was sent to the
RAF depot at Uxbridge for the six-week Officers' Training Course. Rex's departure from *No Time for Comedy* left
a gap that could not be filled and the play closed on
January 24th, 1942 with his final performance.

Lilli had tried to contribute to the war effort early on by
offering to drive ambulances but her status as an enemy
alien automatically excluded her from any active service.
While Rex was at Uxbridge, Lilli remained nearby at the
Fulmer Woods cottage in Denham. She found herself
much in demand for films, beginning with *Thunder Rock*
with Michael Redgrave and James Mason.

Rex, for his part, entered a world which was totally
foreign to him. Having spent almost his entire adulthood
living the nomadic existence of a touring actor, he was
used to sleeping in endless hotels and boarding houses
with very little contact outside the theatre. He now found
himself sleeping in the same room as forty other men
from assorted backgrounds with whom he had very little
in common. Rex was horrified by the noises that came

from these men during the night as he tried to settle into an uneasy sleep, and he was further displeased when his hair was cut close to the head in accordance with service regulations, ruining his traditionally well-groomed appearance.

Rex's initial training took place mainly outside in the bitter cold and provided him with more physical exertion than he had ever experienced. The endless rifle drill, square-bashing, spit-and-polish and assault courses were a considerable shock to his system. Lilli recalled with some amusement Rex's induction into service life,

'When he came out of this ordeal of being in the ranks, like everybody else, he was in splendid physical health, after having been out square-bashing at five o'clock in the morning. He was rather proud of himself. There were some star actors who never went into the forces. Rex could have been spared because he was exempted, but he chose to join although he had a bum eye. He overcame all the difficulties because there was something in him that said, "At this moment everything else goes sour – I must go into the forces."'

Rex and Lilli found it difficult to meet; Lilli was not allowed more than thirty miles from her local police station without special permission and had to be home before midnight. Rex was able to get out twice to see her at Denham during the time he was at Uxbridge but later they had to stay in contact by letter and telephone.

After his six weeks at Uxbridge, Rex was transferred as a Flying Control Officer to the Photographic Reconnaissance Unit at RAF Benson, where his commanding officer was an acquaintance from the past, the actor Hugh Wakefield. Benson was just outside Oxford and the distance made it impossible for Rex and Lilli to meet.

Meanwhile Rex's divorce from Collette finally came through in the late summer of 1942 and he formally proposed to Lilli over the telephone. Rex managed to get

leave and he and Lilli were married at Caxton Hall
Registry Office in London on January 25th 1943, accompanied by Arthur Barbosa who, now an officer in the Pay
Corps, was Rex's best man, although Lilli herself disliked
him intensely.

The wedding reception was attended by several RAF
friends, among them fighter aces Rhys Thomas and his
wife Lilian, and Robert Stanford-Tuck, who attended 'a
rollicking party' at a pub near Marble Arch. Afterwards
Rex and Lilli returned to the Denham cottage which was
to remain their home while Rex was in the RAF.

Lilli remembered an incident immediately following
their marriage which reflected their disparate reactions
towards their families.

'I don't think Rex is a great family person. Lots of
English people have this kind of typical English remote
feeling for their families. I remember when we got
married I asked Rex, "What do I call your mother?"
And he was amazed and said, "Well, you call her Mrs
Harrison." I said, "Well, I can't do that. I mean it
would be really impossible to call someone . . ." So he
said in amazement, "What else do you want to call
her?" I said, "I'll call her mother," and sat down and
wrote a letter to her saying "dearest mother" and
"dearest father", and got a sweet letter back saying
"dearest daughter" – and we immediately established
a great relationship.

'Now with my mother, this was a bit more difficult.
While my mother and Rex were perfectly civil to each
other, the language problem was greatly in the way.
With one of my sisters he got on very well; the other
one was mainly away. But then, you see, it was never a
question during the war of bringing people into the
house. We lived most of the war in our little house in
Uxbridge and there was no getting together of families.
Also, I should say that they were really miles apart in
mentality. It didn't really worry me very much.'

Upon his return to RAF Benson, Rex was sent to be trained as a Flying Control Liaison Officer. His training actually took place in a familiar location: Rudlow Manor near Bath, the home of Bat and Buster Tonge who had taken Rex in during the first uncertain days of the war, and which was now 10-Group Operational Command.

As a Flying Control Liaison Officer Rex helped to guide returning bombers into the nearest aerodrome on the English coast or to send air-sea rescue units to rescue survivors. It was a difficult and demanding course, but Rex passed the examination and after several months was transferred to 11-Group Headquarters at Uxbridge. This move meant that Rex and Lilli were able to settle down into something approaching a normal married life; Lilli has recalled this time with particular affection, convinced that Rex was never happier than during his time in the RAF, 'It gave a form to his life, he knew where to be, at what time, and knew what to wear when he appeared. Life had order . . .' Many years later Lilli elaborated:

> 'He had something important to do that had nothing to do with *him* and he was transported by that, I felt. With his watches and his work, I think it is right when I say it was his happiest time. He came home fulfilled. We had seven years of true happiness together. We were very much in love. Our love during the war was a very strong love. I remember us lying in each other's arms when the bombs were falling and I used to think, "Nothing could ever replace that."'

Rex's working hours were spent hundreds of feet underground in the operations room which was only accessible via huge iron lifts and a maze of passages. This was the operations group for the whole of southern and eastern England and consisted of a large oval room dominated by a huge table on which lay a large-scale map of the area from the Wash in Norfolk to Southampton on the south coast, as well as the French and Belgian coasts up to the Dutch islands. On one side of the room, behind glass and overlooking the table, were the operations controllers, while on the other side were boards which listed the various squadrons and their states of readiness. Twenty or so earphoned WAAFs sat around the map table and plotted the positions of allied and enemy aircraft.

Rex was installed in one of the glass cages overlooking the table and his task was to watch out for and deal with any SOS aircraft, represented on the table by an indicative counter. Seated in front of a desk on which were placed five telephones, Rex often had to deal with up to twenty SOS aircraft at any one time and it was his responsibility to contact each one and guide them to aerodromes where they could land. If an aircraft was unable to reach land he had to arrange for the naval authorities to put up beacons on the headlands at Portland Bill and Beachy Head, and notify Air-Sea Rescue.

The busiest time for Rex was around dawn at which time the British bombers were returning from their missions. It was frequently exhausting work and Rex was aided by a WAAF who logged down every action he made so that he could answer any subsequent queries. The job carried a heavy responsibility, saving hundreds of lives which would otherwise have been lost. As Rex recalled with justifiable pride, '. . . if you got all the SOS aircraft of the night down safely you really did feel you had done something to help.'

As well as his tours of duty in the operations room, Rex, along with other Flying Control Liaison Officers, would visit aerodromes to see at first-hand how successful their efforts were in practice. On one occasion, at RAF Manston in south-east England, Rex actively participated in guiding in a damaged aircraft and in getting the crew out in dangerous conditions. While Rex was serving with 11-Group Lilli attempted to bolster his meagre pay by doing what film work she could get. Neither Rex nor Lilli had any savings and Rex not only had to support himself and Lilli, but also pay maintenance for Collette and Noel. The money coming in did not even begin to cover all these responsibilities and Lilli's film work provided a much needed boost to their finances. But even this extra income was cut off when Lilli became pregnant, although she worked as long as she could before her condition became too obvious to hide from the cameras.

On one occasion during her pregnancy Lilli was fortunate that she did not lose the baby. It was a cloudy afternoon and Rex and she were entertaining Harold French and Deborah Kerr who were then director and star of the film *The Day Will Dawn*. The peace of the afternoon was broken by the familiar sound of an air-raid warning which caused the foursome to pause momentarily. Rather than take shelter, they decided to stay in the house and continue their talk and after a short time the all-clear sounded. Rex, who was standing by the window, looked out casually and glanced at the overcast sky. At that moment, to his horror, he caught sight of a German aircraft breaking through the clouds and as he watched it approach he saw a bomb silently leave the bomb bay and begin its whining descent towards them. Rex shouted a hasty, 'Get down!' and everyone scrambled to the floor. Immediately there was a massive explosion which threw the four of them to the farthest wall of the lounge and engulfed the room in smoke and debris.

Gradually the air cleared and the extent of the damage became plain. Fortunately no one received more than superficial injuries: Rex escaped with a cut across the forehead and the resilient Lilli with only a cut to her wrist, while Deborah Kerr and Harold French were unhurt, but covered, as they all were, in plaster dust. They struggled to their feet and became aware of the noise of people outside shouting to see if they were all right. They called out in unison and an air-raid warden broke the door down and helped them to safety. Luckily, the bomb had landed in the vegetable garden. The earth being particularly soft due to recent heavy rainfall, it had burrowed into the ground before exploding, thereby cushioning its destructive power and saving the four of them from otherwise certain death.

Lilli's pregnancy continued uneventfully, although the baby was to be born during one of London's worst air-raids. On the evening of February 19th 1944, Rex returned home from his duties at 11-Group and was almost immediately faced with Lilli experiencing violent cramps. He hastily called for an ambulance in which Lilli was rushed to the London Clinic while Rex followed in his own car. Shortly after her arrival there Lilli gave birth to a baby boy while outside the sound of bombs falling on London could be plainly heard. Lilli was handed the baby wrapped in a towel and Rex moved to the edge of the bed to sit next to his wife and child. Both were a little disconcerted by the ugliness of the newborn baby, and Rex declared to Lilli, 'Darling, he's ours and we'll love him. But don't let's show him to anybody, please!'

Rather than expose his wife and son to further danger from German bombs, Rex collected them from the Clinic the next morning and took them back to the comparative safety of Denham. The baby was christened Rex Carey Alfred, Carey being in honour of Rex's mother and Alfred for Lilli's father, and was henceforth known as Carey Harrison.

Soon after Carey's birth Rex's tour of duty with 11-Group came to an end and the Air Ministry decided that he should be released from the RAF and return to his entertainment duties. Sufficient Flying Control Liaison Officers having now been trained, it seemed far more practical and useful to exploit Rex's acting talent. Rex had been away from acting for two and a half years during which time he made no public appearances either on film or stage. Rex claims to have been with Edward G. Robinson, Richard Attenborough and Ronald Squire in the 1944 film *Journey Together* made by the RAF Film Unit, but on viewing the film today his contribution appears to have been cut.

Rex was honourably discharged from the Royal Air Force in the spring of 1944 and immediately joined the cast of the film version of Noël Coward's comedy *Blithe Spirit* which was to be made by J. Arthur Rank at Denham Studios. Rex was cast by Coward himself and by David Lean who had already directed, as his first film, Coward's *This Happy Breed*, having been responsible for the action sequences on Coward's film tribute to the British Navy, *In Which We Serve*, and as we have seen, having been closely involved in the direction of *Major Barbara* with Rex. *Blithe Spirit*, like *This Happy Breed*, was to be made in Technicolor, a process which at the time was used only on the most prestigious British productions, due to its high cost.

Blithe Spirit had been a tremendous success on the stage. Indeed, the play did not close until March 9th 1946, ending its run at the Duchess Theatre, to which it had been transferred, after an incredible one thousand nine hundred and ninety-seven performances.

The cast of the original stage production, which had opened at London's Piccadilly Theatre in July 1941 and was still running, included Cecil Parker and Fay Compton as Charles and Ruth Condomine, Kay Hammond as Elvira and Margaret Rutherford as Madame Arcati, the eccentric spiritualist. Coward himself had actually toured the provinces in the play, in the role of Charles, in September 1942.

Kay Hammond and Margaret Rutherford recreated their stage roles in the film version, but Cecil Parker and Fay Compton were replaced by Rex Harrison and Constance Cummings, who joined a new cast which also included Joyce Carey and Hugh Wakefield, Rex's former commanding officer in the RAF. It was felt that Rex and Constance Cummings would have greater drawing power at the box office since they were more established as film actors and had proved their popularity.

Furthermore, Cecil Parker and Fay Compton were both comfortably into middle age and clearly a younger, more romantic couple would improve the chances of selling the film outside Britain, particularly to the United States where Rex and Miss Cummings were familiar to American audiences. In fact, *Blithe Spirit* would be the first Rank film to be shown at the huge Winter Garden Theatre in New York.

Noël Coward, however, was not involved. He went off to the Far East on one of his tours for the war effort, simply leaving instructions that the script was not to be tampered with and that they should just photograph the play – not the most encouraging remark to make, particularly to a perfectionist like David Lean. But Coward's absence from the set of *Blithe Spirit* was not unexpected, as David Lean explains, 'After *In Which We Serve*, Noël got terribly bored with the making of films. He used to say to Gladys Calthrop [his theatrical designer and close friend], "Gladys! Four-pack bezique", and they always used to go off and play cards. Noël was very highly keyed in those days and he just couldn't bear waiting about for the lighting – which, I must say, took a long time. It was nothing to wait for an hour for a medium shot to be lit.'

No-one was to recall the making of the film with much affection. Rex was understandably a little insecure after several years away from a stage or film-set. He was also uncertain whether David Lean was the right director for a comedy and felt that Lean had similar doubts. Forty years on, Lean himself corroborates this:

'I was terribly out of my depth. I knew nothing about high comedy. Most things that you do, do have some sort of yardstick to compare it with real life, but high comedy has nothing to do with real life even though when you watch it you think it is vaguely connected. Rex and I had quite a few strong passages because Rex knew a lot about high comedy. He knew I was out of my depth. I wouldn't call him a help to me as a director but we got on fine despite our difficulties.'

Because of wartime shortages of materials and David Lean's own meticulous methods of film-making, progress was agonisingly slow, severely damaging, in the opinion of Constance Cummings, the essential light and frothy mood of the piece. Coward himself was disappointed with the final result, as Lean recalls:

'When Noël arrived back in England I had a final cut of the film and I said to him, "Do come and see it." And he saw it at Denham. After the film the lights went on; there was a ghastly silence and I said, "Well, what do you think?" He said, "My dear, you've just fucked up the best thing I ever wrote!" And that was that. Later I saw a television show of *Blithe Spirit* that Noël produced in New York [in 1956] and I was able to return the compliment.'

The film did not do as well at the box-office as had been hoped, supporting Coward's view of the film. As Lean asserts, '*Blithe Spirit* wasn't a great success in Britain. It's got a better name now than it had then. I think the place where it was absolutely a mad success was India. The Indians still talk about it. Ghosts, mediums and that sort of thing went down well.' However, Coward's disappointment did not shake his faith in David Lean whom he chose the following year to direct *Brief Encounter*, which remains one of the classic films of British cinema and was a triumph for both author and director.

Constance Cummings enjoyed working with Rex on *Blithe Spirit* despite the various problems which beset the production, and some of the lighter moments during the filming were the result of Rex's behaviour. 'We used to tease him a bit because he was very concerned about himself. He was very concentrated on his performance because he is a perfectionist. It does mean that sometimes he is not quite aware of other people and other people's problems. He was very worried about his clothes and how he looked and whether the scene was going well. His attitude to life in general really depended on how the film was going.'

Rex's attitude towards his baby son Carey was subject to wild variation, depending on the progress of the film, as Constance Cummings continues:

'On one occasion there was some worry that they might have to reshoot a scene because they weren't quite happy with something about Rex: the clothes he was wearing or how he looked. There had been a little buzz that maybe they would have to retake this and Rex was beside himself with worry because he thought that anything less than perfect was no good as far as he was concerned. And I remember asking him, "How's the baby?" And he said, "Oh, poor little thing. He's going to be like me. He's a long, long baby. He's going to be a tall, thin chap. He's going to look exactly like me and be like me. Poor little thing – isn't it terrible?" The baby was a disaster to Rex.

'Then two or three days later word came through that the scene was fine. Rex was so relieved, and the next time somebody asked him, "How's the baby looking now?" he said, "Oh, he's a splendid little chap. He's absolutely adorable; he's going to be wonderful."'

Only when the day's filming was over was Rex really able to relax and enjoy himself. He was particularly flattered to be invited to a big party held by Alexander Korda at his home. To be invited showed that Rex had achieved an eminence in the industry that had not been lost during his absence in the RAF. Unfortunately, the party did not live up to Rex's hopes due to an incident with Anthony Havelock-Allan, the producer of *Blithe Spirit*, as Constance Cummings remembers:

'He hadn't been back long and he thought it would be fun to go to a big party with all these film people. He hadn't got a suit to wear so he borrowed one of his suits from his *Blithe Spirit* wardrobe. But when we saw him the next day he was rather crestfallen; we said, "How did you enjoy it? How did it go?" And he said, "Well it was a bit shaming really . . ." And he told us how he had arrived there and had been handed a cocktail and was introduced to one or two people and was moving around, feeling very pleased with himself and very happy. And suddenly Tony Havelock-Allan came up to him; Rex thought that was very nice and he said, "Hello Tony!" and Tony said, "Rex! Isn't that suit that you're wearing from the film?" And Rex said, "Er, well, yes, as a matter of fact it is." And Tony said, "Well, be careful. Don't spill anything on it!" And then he turned round and walked away. Rex said that he felt so dashed, he felt like a little boy who had been scolded by his nanny.'

Rex told the story, with himself as the butt of the humour able in retrospect to recall the incident as being very amusing, and revealing a refreshing, and perhaps not totally expected, sense of humour about himself.

The unexpectedly long shooting schedule finally drew to a close and, although he does not regard the film highly, Lean still counts it as an experience that taught him a great deal.

'Of all the films I have done, *Blithe Spirit* is the most static, stagey film. It is just dialogue – and rightly so. I don't think anybody should pick it out as an example of the art of film-making. It is really Noël's play.

'I had wonderful people who helped me. I learnt a lot from Rex on the delivery of lines. As a cast you couldn't ask for better. I just love working with real professional actors and that whole film was very professional.'

Lean views the minor friction between Rex and himself as a difference in interpretation.

> 'Where we had disputes was that I wanted Rex to play the part harder. Rex is a great charmer and I think that in a lot of the stuff we had in that film he was just a touch too charming and, in my opinion, he should have been rather more irritable – because I think it spoilt a little bit of the comedy. I know I got a bee in my bonnet that that part should have been played harder; he should have snapped more at the ghost wife. He may have been right. I'm not sure.'

If there was a certain amount of artistic tension between Rex and his director, it was not enough to prevent them from seeing each other off-set. With their social life limited through the obvious restrictions that the war imposed, Rex and Lilli mostly relaxed at the homes of their colleagues, David Lean among them, who all lived within the same area. Lean fondly remembers those days. 'We all lived out there in that neighbourhood – Gerrards Cross, Denham and Fulmer – and we all knew each other. They were good days; we were all very young and we did have a lot of fun. I liked Rex. He's tremendous company: very good company and a good raconteur – and Lilli's an attractive woman. They were a marvellous couple.' As well as Lean's wife, the actress Kay Walsh, the circle of friends included Mary and John Mills, Anthony Havelock-Allan and Valerie Hobson, the cinematographer and future director Ronald Neame and Vivien Leigh and Laurence Olivier, who would all get together on Saturday evenings to play poker.

Rex and Lilli also became involved in entertaining the troops in a touring show to which Constance Cummings was heavily committed. Lilli had previously appeared in some of these shows – called *You Asked For It!* – and once Rex was out of the RAF he willingly took part too. They were normally performed on Sundays, playing one or two houses depending on how long it took the company to get to their destination. The limit of the area that they covered was governed by whether they were able to get to and from the military base in a day. Constance Cummings recalls, 'We were straight actors and we used to sing and dance and do sketches. Lilli sang and danced as well as appearing in sketches. Rex did a sketch of Herbert Farjeon's called "Father and Son", in which a father is trying to tell his young son the facts of life and is terribly shy and never gets anything out at all. Rex was the son and Michael Shepley-Smith played the father.'

On completion of *Blithe Spirit*, Rex was eager to secure more work in order to restore his bank balance after the long period on service pay. He was offered one of the leading roles in Herbert Wilcox's latest vehicle for his wife Anna Neagle, *I Live In Grosvenor Square*, a romantic triangle in which Miss Neagle has to choose between her English lover and an American soldier stationed in England.

Although Rex received star billing, his part was really little more than a supporting role as the suitor who ultimately loses Anna Neagle's affections to Dean Jagger. With distinctly propagandist undertones, the film shows us entertainingly how the American and British way of life can comfortably merge when the two different cultures are thrown together in time of war. Anna Neagle plays an upper-class girl doing her bit for the war effort, while Rex is her very eligible suitor, being both an officer in the RAF and a parliamentary candidate. If the film has a fault within its own unambitious pretensions it is that Rex plays his part with such dash that it is very difficult to comprehend how she could choose Dean Jagger who, while playing with sincerity, is clearly miscast as a romantic lead, being of a staid and serious character which only serves to accentuate Rex's appeal in the film. Essentially a character actor, whose most notable role had been the title part in *Brigham Young* in 1940 for Twentieth Century-Fox, Dean Jagger was among the few

Hollywood actors to cross the Atlantic to film over here during the war and his pedigree and the novelty of a Hollywood figure appearing in a British film made him appear more interesting at the time of the film's release than he does when the film is viewed today. It remains, however, an enjoyable curiosity which provides an interesting reflection of Britain at war.

The film was made in the late summer and autumn of 1944 at studios in Welwyn Garden City and on location in Totnes in Devon, where the company filmed in and around Dartington Hall for a month. Lilli accompanied Rex, bringing eight-month-old Carey and his nanny with her. Anna Neagle remembered their stay there, 'It was a very colourful time in Totnes because it was where troops had been training for D-Day and so it had been full of Americans and there were still a lot left when we started filming.' Of Rex, she had reservations. 'I do say categorically that he is the most brilliant actor that I have ever worked with. I've liked others very much more, but it is not unusual for a very great and talented person to be self-centred – and Rex is very self-centred.'

Upon completion of the film, so impressed was Herbert Wilcox with the screen partnership of his wife and Rex that he made plans to star the two of them together again. *I Live In Grosvenor Square* was a huge popular success when it opened so Wilcox contacted Rex to discuss a possible next film, as Anna Neagle recalled:

'Rex and Lilli were staying at the Savoy and Rex invited us to come up and have dinner one night and *Piccadilly Incident* was discussed. Herbert was sure that he had got him but Twentieth Century-Fox, who distributed *I Live In Grosvenor Square* in the United States (under the title *A Yank In London*), signed him up. But it was not unexpected.'

Piccadilly Incident was eventually made with Michael Wilding substituting for Rex Harrison: it proved an enormous success and marked the beginning of the Neagle–Wilding partnership. In retrospect, Rex's career probably benefited.

With money now coming in, Rex and Lilli were able to buy a small house just off the sixth green of Denham golf course, above the village, and it was here that the Harrison family were based while Rex made *I Live In Grosvenor Square* and his next film, *The Rake's Progress*, in which he and Lilli appeared on the screen together for the first time. Their new home, modern, airy and attractive, was called The Little House. Lilli recalled it with affection, 'That was our first home. We were very proud of it. I sewed the curtains – very badly – and we had a lovely garden. The baby was already born and there we were very happy; in fact, these were very sunny days.'

Rex was very enthusiastic about his new film which had been crafted for him by Frank Launder and Sidney Gilliat. *The Rake's Progress*, directed by Gilliat, was the story of a young man from a well-to-do family who successively ruins the lives of various women through callousness in the pursuit of pleasure. It is told in flashback from the time where the rake, Vivian Kenway, facing imminent death while fighting for his country, recalls a life, from his university days until the present, which until the war has been entirely destructive. He rather incongruously vindicates his past and ends his life as a war hero, which prompted critic James Agee to write of Rex's character in the film as, 'one of those irresistibly forgivable and seductive top-drawer skunks, worthless in all of an interminable series of relationships and dangerous in some, who turns out to be just what our side needs once he gets into a war.' The uneasy ending to the film was probably mainly due to the censorship trouble that the production ran into, especially in America where the film was initially rejected. When it was accepted it was released under the title *Notorious Gentle-*

man. As well as Lilli Palmer, the cast included Godfrey Tearle, Guy Middleton, whose romance with Collette was long since over, Jean Kent and Griffith Jones.

The film does not succeed as well as it should have. Its picaresque construction places the entire weight of the film on Rex and while he acquits himself well personally, he is handicapped by the script which never focuses itself sufficiently to involve the audience as it rambles along. If the film was popular at the time it was because of its title and the character which Rex plays in it, which was a consolidation of his public image, whether he wanted it or not, as 'Sexy Rexy', the appellation which Rex detested. Beyond providing him with some effective publicity, the film did not tax his talents, giving him perhaps the most unattractive character of his career.

Lilli and Rex did not share much screen time together as her appearance, late on, is brief: the cameo role of a young Jewish girl whom Kenway marries in order to help her get out of an Austria threatened by the Nazis. His motives are strictly financial, since she pays off his accrued heavy debts which have made Kenway a prisoner in his Vienna hotel.

The film was made at the Gainsborough Studios in Shepherd's Bush, and while they were filming, Rex and Lilli lived in Lexham Gardens in Kensington. Griffith Jones recalls Lilli's 'wonderful parties. Everybody liked her. But, of course, one wasn't certain about Rex; one never quite knew him. But Lilli was warm and friendly.'

As usual Rex was demanding of himself during the shooting of the film. He would stop a scene if he felt in the least bit uncomfortable with his own performance, insisting on as many takes as he felt he needed until he achieved what he wanted. Griffith Jones recalls a scene they played together;

'Sidney Gilliat was well aware that he had a very restive racehorse who had to be humoured. Rex has got an excessive nervous energy but, let me tell you, in the end it was marvellous. It was light, it was impeccable, it was beautifully timed – and I was bloody awful because I was in such a dithery state. It wasn't deliberate. It was that he was determined to get it right, determined to get it as good as he could get it – for himself. The expenses and everything else – none of that mattered.'

Jones had a fight scene with Rex, set in an elevator in a department store. After running through the sequence for the first time Rex took Jones aside to say:

'"You're being a bit rough, old boy." I said, "I'm just out of the army. I'm bound to be a bit rough." I was so tough and strong and he had to fight back, but he felt that it ought to be faked – and of course, he was right. But I had such physical energy then that I was overdoing it and I hit him once accidentally. Sidney Gilliat had to come and stop us as I was well into the fight. Rex nursed his jaw and said, "Now look, there's a way of hitting where you don't hurt people, isn't there Sidney?" And he said "Yes." Rex said, "Griff, you stand there. All you've got to do is put your head to one side to miss it when I hit you." I said, "Certainly I'll do it Rex." So I did and he hit me very hard – he got his own back.'

During the filming of *The Rake's Progress*, the war in Europe ended. Basil Dean, then the head of ENSA (the Entertainments National Service Association), asked Rex if he would entertain the troops who were still stationed in Europe. It was decided that a production of *French Without Tears* would be taken through Holland and Belgium for six weeks and end in Paris.

The tour was organised by Roland Culver's wife, Daphne Rye, who was a producer for H. M. Tennent. The choice of *French Without Tears* came at the suggestion of Hugh Beaumont himself since he knew that neither

Rex nor Culver had other immediate engagements. Anna Neagle took Kay Hammond's old part and Percy Walsh, another member of the original London cast, also joined them. Daphne Rye directed and managed the company during the tour, which was ENSA in name only. With Beaumont involved, it had the invariable star values of a Tennent production.

Initial preparations and rehearsals took place in London. Anna Neagle recalled that the company:

'had to go and have injections for tetanus and cholera and then went on to rehearsals in a hall in London. Rex was the first one to go green and he was off from the rehearsal for about two days. All the rest of us stood up to it – not one of us had missed rehearsals.

'Then we had to go for a briefing to Drury Lane which, with all the seats moved out, was the headquarters of ENSA. We arrived there about two days before we were due to be flown out and we were all in our khaki uniforms. A forbidding lady came onto the stage and said, "Now, you have your uniforms—", she was talking to us as though we were a lot of children. "You understand that anything you have to report, you report to whoever is in charge of the hostel where you are – I mean, should you damage your uniform in any way. These are the property of ENSA, so you must report it immediately." And she continued, "Now, the labels for your luggage – Neagle: number so-and-so; Harrison: number so-and-so . . ."

'Rex put up his hand and said, "Well, what's that?" She said, "Oh, don't you know? You've been a number to me for weeks!" We were just numbers to her.'

With the presence of three members of the original production, rehearsals went smoothly. The company flew from Croydon to Brussels, the European headquarters of ENSA. Their first destination was Eindhoven in Holland, where the company was installed in a hostel which had reputedly been a brothel for the Luftwaffe. They were faced with a town that had reached the brink, as Anna Neagle recalled, 'They were literally starving. I don't think there was a black market or anything there. There just wasn't any food. I went out on the first morning with the girls in the company to look at the shops and there was nothing there.'

Despite the famine and privation that surrounded them, Rex could not disguise his displeasure at his own rations; Anna Neagle continued, 'I realised very quickly when we were in this hostel at Eindhoven that the food didn't appeal to him at all – but you couldn't get anything else in Holland, which had been through such a terrible time.'

If Rex had realised the extent of the distress around him he might have been more grateful to be getting any food at all, as Anna Neagle explained. 'Eindhoven was a dispersal centre for people from concentration camps. An army man who had seen a performance of the play spoke about the disease there and I went alone with him to see this. The Dutch people at Eindhoven, particularly the children, were black under the eyes because they were starving. For three solid weeks there had been no food at all.' Rex Harrison and Roland Culver preferred not to experience the horrors of war at first hand. 'I suppose they managed to play golf,' Anna Neagle commented.

As before, when Rex had appeared with her in *I Live In Grosvenor Square*, Anna Neagle found him a pleasure to work with, but even when they were thrown together in the intimate atmosphere of a small theatrical troupe, she still felt that she did not get to know him any more than she had before.

'I don't think anybody formed a friendship with Rex unless he was wanting them to get close. I so loved working with him that I would have liked to have got closer to him, but I can't even remember really having a conversation with him. We used to go out as little groups when, for instance, we were in Brussels. Here there were places to go to have something to eat and dance a bit after the show. He did that, but he is so self-centred that you don't ever get any mileage. Mind you, he's managed to collect a number of wives, so he must have been more out-going with them than he was with me.'

The tour included Ostend, Bruges, Brussels and finally Paris. Anna Neagle remembered their stay in Paris.

'The exciting one was when we got to Paris. That was our last date and we were put up by the Opéra Comique in a hostel that had been a small family hotel. And the other people who were there were the Old Vic company with Laurence Olivier, Ralph Richardson, Sybil Thorndike and Margaret Leighton. We each had a long trestle-table: two separate tables for two companies. Rex enjoyed himself in Paris. We were playing in the Marigny Theatre in the Champs-Elysées, where the troops came to see us.'

With the tour almost over there was some talk of it continuing. Anna Neagle was enthusiastic. 'I wanted to go into Germany – most of us did, although I don't think Rex did particularly. Basil Dean was out there whipping around all the places where his ENSA companies were and he came in to us and I said, "Why can't we go into Germany? We're really needed there." It was a small company with only one set and a cast of ten; we could easily have been taken into Germany.'

So keen was Anna Neagle to take *French Without Tears* into Germany that she had even secured the services of several officers from an RAF station who agreed to fly the company out and even guaranteed to bring them back. But it was to no avail.

Rex, she said, preferred to return to England. 'If you

say you'll do another six weeks, I'll murder you!' he remarked.

The death-knell for the tour came when Roland Culver was offered a role in *To Each His Own* with Olivia de Havilland. Culver was required to depart for Hollywood within two days of their arrival in Paris leaving Rex to play opposite Culver's understudy for the remaining ten days of the tour. Rex was shocked that Culver was adamant about going, as Culver recalled in his auto-biography. 'Said Rex, "If I may say so, dear boy, your attitude is that of the shit which you undoubtedly are . . . What do you want to go to Hollywood for? It's finished, old man; last legs, dear boy. You are making a big mistake. Take it from me, Hollywood's had it . . ."'

Any plans to continue the tour faded away and the company left Paris, returning by sea to England. Upon his arrival, Rex immediately joined Lilli in London and found urgent messages from Taft Schreiber, representative of the MCA agency in Hollywood, who had been trying to get in touch with him while he was in Europe. Schreiber urgently wanted to meet Rex to discuss the offer of a lucrative contract from Twentieth Century-Fox in Hollywood: seven years with options, at four thousand dollars a week for forty weeks a year. The proposed first film was *Anna and the King of Siam*, based on the book by Margaret Landon which chronicled the relationship between King Mongkut and an English governess who travelled to Bangkok in 1862 to teach his sixty-seven children. Rex would play the King opposite Irene Dunne as Anna.

Always careful in career matters, Rex first asked to read the script by Talbot Jennings and Sally Benson. Finding it to his liking he took the plunge. Such a radical career move had not been expected by Rex or Lilli and its suddenness and the necessity of an almost immediate departure for California required a hasty sorting-out of their affairs. Clearly, with a seven-year contract with a Hollywood studio in Rex's hand, it was impractical to consider holding on to their home in Denham. In any case, despite their fondness for it, the couple had already been making the first tentative steps towards moving into something larger. Having got to know Herbert Wilcox and Anna Neagle quite well, the Harrisons had considered buying the home that Wilcox had lived in with his former wife. The former Mrs Wilcox, now re-married, was moving to Ross-on-Wye so their house, Cokes Farm, in Chalfont St Giles, not far from Denham, was on the market. But the plan fell through as Anna Neagle recalled. 'Rex and Lilli loved the house and he was buying it for her. Then, of course, he went to Hollywood and dropped the whole idea. It was the sort of business thing that Herbert wouldn't discuss with me. I knew there was a little upset but it didn't undermine the appreciation or the admiration I had for Rex at all.' Wilcox felt let down by Rex twice over. He had also been confident that he was close to clinching a deal for Harri-son's services on other film projects, and the actor's departure for Hollywood dashed his hopes on that score too.

Having disposed of their own house to Mary and John Mills, Rex and Lilli departed for Hollywood on November 21st 1945 when, each carrying a single suitcase, they boarded the boat-train in London. Their destination was Southampton where the Cunarder *Queen Elizabeth* would transport them across the Atlantic to New York.

By this time Lilli was involved in talks with Hollywood producer Milton Sperling so her prospects in America were also optimistic. Carey and his nanny, Pat Jennings, were to stay with Lilli's mother and follow later as the *Queen Elizabeth* was still a troopship. Rex and Lilli were only able to sail on the *Queen Elizabeth* by special permit, secured by Twentieth Century-Fox who needed Rex immediately. The couple were the only civilians among thousands of returning American soldiers.

Seen off at Victoria Station by Rex's sister, Sylvia, and her husband, David Maxwell-Fyfe, and by Lilli's mother and two sisters, they left on their new adventure with hope mingled with trepidation about what Hollywood would hold for them. It seemed certain that California would be their home for the next seven years. It was not to be. Less than three years later they would depart in the aftermath of one of Hollywood's biggest scandals. The star roles would be played by Rex Harrison and Lilli Palmer.

5

WHEN REX HARRISON arrived in Hollywood in 1945, he was already a familiar figure to American audiences. As early as 1941 he had been hailed in New York as a new star – without ever having made a film in America – when his name appeared in lights three times on Broadway within five months, first in *Night Train* (the American title of *Night Train to Munich*), then in *Ten Days In Paris* (under the title *Missing Ten Days*) and finally in *Major Barbara*. Since then he had also been seen in *Blithe Spirit* and *A Yank In London*, and his latest film, *The Rake's Progress*, was soon to be released in America under the title *Notorious Gentleman*.

Rex never was in the conventional mould of the Hollywood hero. His is a distinctive personality which in many ways did not lend itself to conventional Hollywood fare. The screen image of Cary Grant, who had come out to California more than a decade earlier and who had established himself as one of Hollywood's foremost stars, is the closest that Hollywood ever got to the Rex Harrison style. But even when comparing the two, Grant is a much more physical man, with conventional good looks, whereas Rex is unprepossessing in terms of physical bulk and is far from the accepted view of male handsomeness, although he was always a most attractive man. Intriguingly, neither Cary Grant nor Rex Harrison studied at drama school, thus being the only two celebrated English actors ever to start their careers in this manner. By 1945 Rex Harrison had a reputation as a very able leading man and a true original and as such he arrived in a Hollywood which could not easily categorise him. Rex had come to California as an acknowledged star but curiously, unlike most Hollywood imports from overseas, his parts would not be a consolidation or extension of his previous roles. In *Anna and the King of Siam* he had a character role and this was the first opportunity of his career to prove that he could play a part beyond the restrictions of a conventional leading man.

The Hollywood into which Rex and Lilli settled was a Hollywood on the brink of change. During the war the great ladies of the screen had held the cinema audience tight while many of its leading men, including Clark Gable, James Stewart, Tyrone Power, Henry Fonda and Robert Taylor, were away at war. Although their return had been eagerly awaited, it was soon apparent that their experiences had aged them considerably and few of them now fitted the description of 'heart-throb'.

Within this changing professional world it was also apparent that the studio system was moving into a new phase. Rex Harrison himself was in the vanguard of the last group of foreign artists to be offered the once-standard seven-year studio contract. Highly skilled and well-proven moguls such as Louis B. Mayer, Jack L. Warner and Darryl F. Zanuck, still headed their respective studios, but behind them a new generation of producers, directors, writers and actors were impatient to take over. Just as the war had changed many people's lives irrevocably, so it altered Hollywood's direction. It had proven beyond doubt the potential power of the cinema as a propaganda machine, able to articulate the feelings of the common man at a time of crisis, and capable of bolstering flagging morale far more effectively than any other form of public entertainment. The war had made film-makers less superficial. Men like the head of Twentieth Century-Fox, Darryl F. Zanuck, returned to Hollywood with a different viewpoint which they were to bring to their future films. Life now seemed a very serious thing and old film-makers and newcomers alike came to Hollywood with the desire to articulate the thoughts of a generation that had lived through a world war of massive proportions.

The latter half of the forties was dominated by much more serious films. Gone were the screwball comedies and light-weight adventures that had dominated the thirties. A cynicism settled into Hollywood films and the great stars would reflect that change in their new roles. Rex Harrison had really arrived in Hollywood just too late for his potential to be fully exploited, for his was a talent ill-fitted to the climate of the time, as the stops and starts in his ensuing Hollywood career were to prove.

Darryl F. Zanuck had admired Rex Harrison's work since 1940 and indeed it was his studio that had already released two Harrison films in the United States. It was therefore not unexpected that Zanuck would acquire Rex's services for Fox, and that Rex would have felt that his film career was safe in the hands of one of the top moguls. However, whether it was the right choice for the actor to go to Zanuck is debatable. While Twentieth Century-Fox had a reputation as one of the most successful studios, it cannot be viewed, in retrospect, as having itself created many great stars, particularly leading men. The only top-ranking male stars ever to emerge from the studio had been Tyrone Power and Henry Fonda and before them, only Don Ameche had made any real impact. The great Fox stars were female: Alice Faye, Betty Grable, Shirley Temple, each of whom thrived in musicals. It was a studio curiously lacking in the requirements for building up a male movie star and Rex Harrison's talents needed a more careful exploitation than most actors'. Henry Fonda openly voiced his dislike of the way that Zanuck handled his career and finally bought out his contract.

Rex was not without qualms about going to Hollywood and this was reflected by his self-justification to the press for his presence there. Rex had often voiced his disapproval of the film capital and his wish not to work there but when interviewed now he seemed to have convinced himself that his going there was for the good of King and country. Rex's explanation, in an English film magazine, for being in Hollywood was so practical and sensible that it bears recall:

'One of the difficulties facing British films in the American market is that our stars in competition with the Hollywood names are often not sufficiently well-known to attract people into the cinemas. A British star who has been seen in American films has a great advantage.

'I went to Hollywood in the first place for what I still think are good reasons. It was a logical step in my film career. It was a good thing that I should, if possible, become known to the American public, not merely for my own professional sake but also for the sake of future British films I might play in.'

Rex and Lilli stayed first at the Beverly Hills Hotel but soon afterwards rented a house from actor Clifton Webb who was also at Fox. The house was situated high up in the hills of Bel Air, one of the largest and most exclusive residential areas in Los Angeles, and it was to this home that Carey, accompanied by his nanny, finally came three months later. The previous three months had been unexpectedly fraught for both Rex and Lilli.

The first signs of crisis had emerged while the couple were still ensconced in their suite at the Beverly Hills Hotel. Rex was understandably keyed-up about his role in *Anna and the King of Siam* and keen for support and advice for his playing of a part which was so completely removed from anything he had ever tackled before. The director was to be John Cromwell, an experienced craftsman responsible for such films as *Of Human Bondage* with Leslie Howard and Bette Davis, *The Prisoner of Zenda* with

Ronald Colman and more recently the Selznick production of *Since You Went Away*, the epic wartime drama with Claudette Colbert and Jennifer Jones. On his first day in Hollywood Rex went to meet him, anxious to hear the director's views on his role.

Cromwell was a one-time actor and a veteran stage director who had come to Hollywood, with the advent of sound films, to direct, and had achieved considerable success. By his own confession a self-made man, proud of the achievements he had made without the help of others, he was not always easy on his actors. He once recalled, 'I was forty-two when I went to Hollywood to direct pictures, had made my own way on the stage without any help, and I'm afraid had pretty stuffy ideas about obligations and what was generally expected from actors.'

Unfortunately for Rex, who desperately needed reassurance, it is obvious that Cromwell disliked him on sight and surprisingly, being a former actor himself, gave Rex short shrift when the actor wanted to discuss and analyse with him how the king should be played. His only words to Rex were curt and dismissive and a crushed Rex returned to Lilli in their hotel room, resigned to the fact that he was not going to get any help from his director. His initial reaction was to want to leave Hollywood rather than remain there playing an unfamiliar role in which, without proper guidance, he could easily damage his reputation, particularly at such a crucial time, when his debut appearance in an American film would be shown throughout the world. The despondent couple viewed their Hollywood future as an almost certain disaster. As the shock wore off, Rex realised that only bold action would save him and he resolved to take what was in those days a courageous and unprecedented step. He appealed straight to the head of the studio and was rewarded with Zanuck's total support – the only recorded time that Zanuck ever supported an actor against his chosen producer or director.

With three weeks to go before filming started, Rex set about creating the character of King Mongkut, entering into the task with his customary diligence and with very little help from anybody else. On the first day of filming, Rex walked onto the set and sat himself on his throne, prepared to give his first speech, with John Cromwell beside the camera. Rex was dressed in the elaborate silk robes of King Mongkut and, with slight rubber attachments fixed near his eyes to give them an Oriental slant, he looked every inch a Siamese king.

The camera started to turn and Rex began speaking in the peculiar twittering, bird-like way which he had developed to reproduce an Oriental speech pattern. The actor had only uttered a few words when a horrified John Cromwell stopped him and asked him what he was doing. When Rex replied that he was speaking in the manner in which King Mongkut would have spoken, Cromwell dismissed the accent entirely. Rex, however, proved as adamant as Cromwell and the first day ended with antagonism on both sides and Zanuck having to mediate. From this point on, director and actor went their separate ways. Neither did anything to help the other. Similarly, Irene Dunne went her own way, although she certainly had a much better relationship with Cromwell. She was a long-time Hollywood film actress, happily married for over twenty years and known for her professionalism and aloof cordiality. Rex did not find her an over-sympathetic leading lady, despite the fact that she was profoundly pro-British.

The only good news in the first, slow weeks of filming came from Lilli who had secured her first part in a Hollywood film, the thriller *Cloak and Dagger*, to be directed by another emigré from Germany, Fritz Lang, and starring Gary Cooper.

But for Rex, the ordeal of making his first Hollywood film proved gratifyingly worthwhile. When *Anna and the King of Siam* opened it was a personal triumph for the actor, who was universally praised for his remarkable performance. Critic Alton Cook wrote, 'During the filming, one of the unpredictable visitations of greatness blessed the work . . . the remarkable performance of Rex Harrison as the King. This characterisation is so vividly and imaginatively detailed, the whole emphasis has been altered, and it is the King, not Anna, who becomes the central figure.' Howard Barnes of the *Herald Tribune* described Rex's portrayal as 'nothing short of perfect' and 'unquestionably the finest' role of his career.

At the Hollywood premiere, which took place at Grauman's Chinese Theatre on July 8th 1946, Rex received the honour of being asked to put his hand- and foot-prints in concrete outside the theatre, a further indication of the great success of his Hollywood debut.

Unfortunately, Lilli's first Hollywood film did not fare so well and quickly disappeared. But the newly arrived Harrisons both enjoyed the social side of the Hollywood scene which seemed all the more impressive and decadent when compared with the war-scarred Britain that they had just left. The couple's initial friendships were naturally formed within Hollywood's English colony, notably Ronald Colman and his wife Benita Hume, and Bunny and Nigel Bruce. As well as these more established Hollywood Englishmen there were also Roland Culver, who had only preceded Rex to the film capital shortly before, and Robert Coote, a friend from his touring days. A routine quickly established itself whereby Rex and Lilli, along with other members of the English colony, would meet every Sunday afternoon at one another's homes. Despite being American, Douglas Fairbanks Jr. and Tyrone Power were very much a part of this circle.

With the success of *Anna and the King of Siam*, Rex began to feel more comfortable in his new life, although with the Hollywood press he was never at ease. Considering himself a serious actor, he was alarmed by the way in which the Hollywood publicity machine set about selling him to the American public. The drooling prose of fan magazine writers understandably made Rex uneasy; after interviewing the Hollywood newcomer one female writer wrote, 'He looked at me – or should I say *into* me? – intensely, probingly. After a while, my blood began to circulate again,' while another, in the best tradition of romantic fiction, gushed, 'Under his drilling gaze I was having a difficult time keeping my wits about me. *Ye gads*, I thought, *is my soul showing?*'

The label 'Sexy Rexy' was minted anew, becoming progressively more grating to his sensibilities as time wore on. Rex's own explanation for the description was tinged with humour, 'The formation of my eyes may be sexy but what I really think fools people are the bags I have under them.'

When treated in this manner by the press, it is not surprising that Rex began to avoid interviews whenever possible. The two most important columnists in Hollywood were Louella Parsons and Hedda Hopper who between them covered the whole American continent in their syndicated gossip columns which retailed rumour, innuendo and fact concerning the private lives of Hollywood figures. These two women had the reputation of being able to make or break an actor, and even the studios acknowledged their power by ensuring that their contract artists toed the line and danced attendance when summoned. But even in their case, Rex behaved otherwise. He was an actor and he was there to do his job as well as he could, and all other concerns did not bear consideration. Rex viewed the Hollywood press system as a rather silly game and decided that he was not going to play, unaware that such an attitude would be considered a calculated snub.

As a result Rex became fair game for snide personal attacks, which initially manifested themselves as reports of his aloof and rude behaviour towards his co-workers at Twentieth Century-Fox. The columnists had nothing else they could pin on Rex, but reckoned that if they waited patiently the actor would one day stumble and make a mistake on which they could pounce.

With all the publicity Rex received, particularly that which lauded his sexual magnetism, the female population in Hollywood could hardly be unaware of the dashing English newcomer, and Rex became their target at parties. As Lilli recalled, such a situation was difficult, 'Firstly, Hollywood is already a great strain on any marriage, particularly for two people who came out of the blackout of England as we did. And suddenly all the ladies in Hollywood threw themselves into Rex's arms as the gentleman with class – genuine class.' Rex did not always find it easy to resist the temptation of the many attractive women who pointedly made themselves available to him, but while discretion prevailed the Harrison marriage continued on an essentially untroubled course, although Lilli herself kept a tight hold on the marital reins, as she recalled, 'As far as I was concerned, I would have stayed with one man all of my life.'

Lilli naturally found other men attractive, particularly Gary Cooper who had been the idol of her youth. As she continued,

'Gary Cooper was like hanging a lollipop in front of a baby. But from there to wrecking my marriage . . . I was, I hope, a little too wise to throw it all away for the sake of a fling. If you went through what I did in my early teens – years of being a refugee – I think you appreciate all the more when good, enduring luck comes your way. And I suppose that was the difference, because Rex really took it all for granted that luck came his way. I didn't. So he was all the more ready to chance something. But at no point did he want to break up our marriage.'

At the time that Rex's autobiography came out, Lilli was quoted as saying, 'One woman wasn't enough for Rex – he just couldn't be faithful . . . He'd see some

woman and believe he'd fallen head over heels in love
with her. It was just his personality, I suppose.' Lilli was
able to accept Rex's occasional infidelities because she
knew that they were purely physical conquests which
never altered the way that Rex felt towards her.

With Rex and Lilli both settling gradually, if a little
uneasily, into the Hollywood way of life, Rex had to
consider his next film. He had made an auspicious Hollywood debut but it was certainly not a role that provided
any obvious indications of how Fox should nurture their
new star. Rex himself may not have been completely sure
what to do next, but he certainly knew what to avoid. In a
seven-month period after the completion of his first Fox
film Rex turned down every script submitted to him. He
was keen to follow on with a comedy, which would not
only be a marvellous change of pace after the heavy
dramatics of King Mongkut, but would also provide him
with the opportunity to display the gifts which had made
him a star in his own country. However, such was the
impression he had made in his first character part that
Fox found it difficult to imagine him in comedy, particularly when the accepted view of an English light-comedy
actor was Cary Grant.

Surprisingly the studio did not suspend him. Zanuck
would have been completely within his rights to force
Rex to appear in whatever film he chose for him, but
instead he allowed Harrison an exceptional freedom
while continuing to pay him his large weekly salary.

With nothing else to do Rex sank deeper into the
indulgent Hollywood style of life, leading an aimless
existence of continual socialising. Lilli, on the other
hand, had started another film soon after the completion
of *Cloak and Dagger*, this time appearing in the classic
boxing drama *Body and Soul*, in which John Garfield gave
one of his finest performances. Rex admits that he
allowed himself to be seduced by Hollywood, despite his

best intentions, and despite having seen the destructive effect it had had on others. He recalled in his autobiography,

'. . . the whole thing went to my head. The lavish living, the size of the steaks, the flowers, the alcoholic content of the whisky, the beauty of the women: it was all too much for me. There was nothing to do but to go to parties, play golf and go to the beach. This was ruinous for me . . . and I think those months of not working go to explain in part why, while I was out there, my behaviour was not all that could be desired.'

Even Zanuck was able to see the slow disintegration of his contract actor, as Rex and Lilli quickly became part of the producer's inner circle, and were regularly invited to his Palm Springs home, 'Ric-Su-Dar' – an amalgam of the names of Richard, Susan and Darryl Zanuck. The other guests at the polo and croquet weekends included, among others, Douglas Fairbanks, Jr and his wife Mary Lee, Clifton Webb, Howard Hughes, Olivia De Havilland and Moss Hart, who a decade later would be responsible in no small part for the greatest success of Rex's career. Rex always declined the invitation to indulge in either of Zanuck's two sporting passions, preferring a drink while watching the others play in the hot sun.

In Hollywood most parties were held on Saturday night and Rex developed a habit of never quitting a party while both the host and hostess were still circulating among their guests. Once one or other went to bed, then Rex felt that he could leave – which was usually not until dawn on Sunday morning. Lilli, being a non-drinker, might have one gin and tonic to be polite but inevitably she would slip away after a few hours to find somewhere quiet to sleep, while Rex continued eating, drinking, and enjoying himself.

Lilli's role at these functions became more and more that of a chauffeur who waited to drive Rex home. Lilli had doubts about married life with Rex at this time, while Rex was either unaware or unconcerned that his wife did not enjoy the parties they frequented with quite the same enthusiasm. A common misconception was that Lilli was the stronger of the two and that Rex had had to make concessions to satisfy her – but his behaviour belied this. Rex was once asked about whether he had to adjust his lifestyle to suit his wife and replied, looking 'politely astonished', 'I should say it was the other way round. If anything, she's had to adjust herself to my life . . . When I make a trip . . . she goes with me. She even adjusts in regard to food – I don't like German food, you know, while she does. So I'm afraid we eat English food . . . Once she accepts you, she's a wonderful person.'

Lilli's disenchantment with their Hollywood life began after she and Rex had been in California for barely six months. Until this point, Lilli had been as enthusiastic socially as Rex, but they were both involved in a tragic incident which cast a heavy cloud over their activities. It had become the common practice for Rex and Lilli to join the other younger members of the English colony every Sunday evening. The usual meeting place was the home of Tyrone Power and his wife Annabella and there was a regular crowd who would come not only to chat and drink but to play 'The Game' together. The big craze in Hollywood at the time, 'The Game' was a sophisticated form of charades, and this regular group, which included Cesar Romero and David Niven, could be found leaping about and giggling like children as they indulged their addiction each weekend. One of these gatherings was a special occasion because it was to be the first Hollywood party for David Niven's wife, Primmie, who had just arrived from England with their two young children. Primmie Niven was still dazzled by the luxurious climate and prosperity of Hollywood and this was to be her introduction into the circle. The evening started with an early barbecue around the pool after which they all went indoors into the Powers' spacious mansion to play 'The

Game'. As they settled themselves in the living room, Cesar Romero suggested a different game before starting the main event. He outlined 'Sardines', in which the lights are turned out and one person hides. The others then try to find that person and, if they do, secretly join him or her in the hiding place until only one person is left searching. Agreeing to try it, the guests eyed the various corners and exits from the room for a suitable hiding place. The lights were off and the game was in progress when the sound of someone falling was suddenly heard, followed by a cry. Cesar Romero immediately rushed to the light switch and, having turned it on, raced towards a door at one end of the living room where the sound had come from. Knowing the house well, he realised what had happened. Only Primmie Niven was unfamiliar with the lay-out and in rushing to hide in the coat closet had picked the door next to it, which led down a flight of stairs to the cellar. Romero reached the open door and saw Primmie lying unconscious at the bottom of the stairs on the stone floor where she had fallen head first.

Primmie was brought up to the living room and Lilli laid the unconscious girl's head on her lap while Annabella put cold compresses on her forehead. There was no sign of any significant injury and she started to regain her senses. David Niven had already called a doctor, who arrived within twenty minutes and took Primmie to the hospital, accompanied by her husband. At Power's suggestion the rest of them continued playing, but unenthusiastically, as they waited for news. David returned a couple of hours later with assurances that his wife would be fine and they all departed. Rex and Lilli checked with Niven on Primmie's condition the next evening and were told that she was still stable. However, soon afterwards a blood clot formed on her brain and she died in surgery. She was only twenty-five.

Rex and Lilli did what they could to bolster Niven's spirits. They bought him a Boxer puppy to keep him company and on Sundays and whenever Niven was not working, went to the house which Niven had been furnishing for his wife and children, along with David's other friends, to ensure that he was never alone.

If this incident made Rex and Lilli stop in their tracks, it was only for a short time. Rex was still unoccupied, and the round of parties soon began again. Lilli may have been inclined to hold back now but Rex, who was pleased to get out and mix with people, was in his element, particularly since there was nothing else with which to fill his days. While Rex's occasional extra-marital adventures caused little if any comment, a curious example of Hollywood's double standards occurred when Rex and Lilli entertained a guest from England – Collette Harrison. Much to Hollywood's surprise, she was not Rex's mother or sister but his first wife, who was greeted by Rex and the present Mrs Harrison in a manner which was considered unnecessarily broad-minded, particularly on Lilli's part. What really shocked the Hollywood gossips was the fact that the former Mrs Harrison ended up staying in Rex and Lilli's Bel Air home with them.

Lilli had not initially been very enthusiastic about the visit. Collette had written to them shortly before her arrival stating that she would be visiting Los Angeles with Noel who was now thirteen and, in his mother's opinion, should see his father again. They arrived in the summer of 1946 and booked into the Beverly Hills Hotel, but after two weeks they were forced to leave as that was the maximum stay permitted during the peak summer months. Rather than leave Hollywood so soon, Collette made some hints regarding the spare room in Rex and Lilli's home and it was agreed that she and Noel could stay there for a further week.

On the very day that their guests moved in, Rex and Lilli were invited to a party at the Santa Monica beach house of Norma Shearer, the great Metro-Goldwyn-Mayer star who had retired in 1942. Not wanting to leave Collette out of it, Lilli obtained an invitation from a nevertheless surprised Norma Shearer for the other Mrs Harrison as well.

That evening Rex arrived with a wife on each arm, an act of bravado that was not viewed very favourably by the other guests who were used to discretion regarding marriage. In a town where the temptations for infidelity abounded, the residents tried to keep as low a profile as possible in order to protect themselves from gossip, and the action of the Harrisons seemed to them a deliberate flaunting of the values that Hollywood liked at least to appear to uphold.

A further incident occurred later in the week when Collette and Lilli were alone in the house while Rex was appearing in a radio play. Lilli decided to take Collette out to dinner and, her curiosity having got the better of her, she decided to try to match Collette drink for drink. They began by having three cocktails before they left for Romanoff's, one of Hollywood's most famous restaurants, where they polished off a couple of bottles of wine and finished the meal with coffee and brandy.

Rex arrived home at half-past twelve that night and was greeted by the sight of their car wrapped around the centre pillar of the garage. He went into the house and found Lilli sprawled out unconscious across their double bed. Understandably anxious, Rex rushed into the guest room and woke up Collette, who explained that Lilli was drunk. Rex flew into a temper, blaming Collette for Lilli's condition, and sent her off to nurse his ailing wife who was starting to feel the full effects of too much alcohol. Collette undressed Lilli and put her to bed and spent half the night helping her over the wretched sickness she felt. Exhausted, Collette finally passed out on the double bed next to Lilli. When the maid entered the master bedroom carrying breakfast the next morning, she was somewhat surprised to find the two Mrs Harrisons fast asleep on the double bed together while Mr Harrison was asleep in the guest room, where he had retired in disgust and annoyance.

Lilli never again touched alcohol – nor was Rex keen to offer it to her. It had been an unfortunate incident, partly the result of Lilli's growing dissatisfaction with life in Hollywood and her annoyance over the double standards that she had unwittingly exposed at the Shearer party. Collette and Noel departed at the end of the week after their brief but eventful holiday in California. For Rex and Lilli the continual socialising went on, still holding its charms for Rex but becoming more and more vacuous for Lilli.

Fortunately, Rex's idleness finally came to an end and he started a new film in late November 1946 having found a script that appealed to him: *The Ghost and Mrs Muir*, adapted by Philip Dunne from a novel by R. A. Dick. His leading lady was Gene Tierney with whom Rex enjoyed a happy professional association. The film also featured George Sanders, the eight-year-old Natalie Wood and Rex's old friend Robert Coote. As director he had Joseph L. Mankiewicz and it was the first of four films the two men would make together. A respected writer and director, Mankiewicz's response to Rex varies. As a writer he is full of praise for Rex's technique and considers him to be his 'Stradivarius': the actor above any in the world whom he would choose to play his high comedy. However, as a director he has described the actor as egotistical, elaborating on this by explaining that Rex is, 'a very difficult man to work with. He gives everybody problems and he knows it. Everybody knows it.'

The Ghost and Mrs Muir did solid business without being a great success and remains a charming, effective film, stunningly photographed by Charles Lang – who received an Academy Award nomination for his work – and the bonus of one of Bernard Herrmann's most beautiful film scores. Rex gave a memorable performance showing that despite his months of easy living he was still the same painstaking professional when it came to work.

The Ghost and Mrs Muir was completed by the middle of

February 1947 and Rex immediately started work on another film, *The Foxes of Harrow*, based on a bestselling novel by Frank Yerby, which Rex was enthusiastic about since he was keen to play the part of an Irish Mississippi gambler in the New Orleans of 1820. Having worn a beard in *The Ghost and Mrs Muir*, Rex was now required to sport a dapper moustache and had no less than eight different instructors and technical advisers assigned to him on the film: one each for card-sharp tricks, fencing, jumping horses, dancing, singing, French and Irish dialects, and ju-jitsu.

However, despite Rex's initial enthusiasm, he was clearly miscast. Nor was filming an enjoyable experience, mainly because his relationship with his leading lady, Maureen O'Hara, was completely the opposite of the one he had enjoyed with Gene Tierney. As Vanessa Brown, who played Miss O'Hara's sister in the film, recalls,

'She was so mean to Rex – really mean. She would spread it around the set that Rex was a difficult man. She was just a horror on that set, absolutely awful, but I never saw Rex retaliate. I guess he wanted to do the picture. His only retaliation was when the publicity lady, Sonja Wolfsen, tried to get them to have lunch together so that it would appear to everyone, particularly the press, that they had made it up. But Rex refused to have lunch with her.'

Maureen O'Hara's attacks were not just confined to Rex. 'Sometimes she would leave her dressing room door open and talk very loudly to her make-up man – so that you could hear her outside. It was awful, the anti-semitism that was coming out of her mouth. There was no cause for it. I don't know what brought it on. It was just part of her venomous self at that point.' The shock of Maureen O'Hara's anti-semitism must have been particularly difficult for Rex who not only had a Jewish wife and a Jewish son, but beyond that he had just come out of his admirable war service.

Rex himself recalled Maureen O'Hara in less than flattering terms when interviewed a decade later. 'An unfortunate experience with Miss O'Hara. I am only able to waltz in one direction. I can't make a left turn. Only the right. We were dancing together in a take of a scene. I was doing my usual right turns. Miss O'Hara saw fit to stop the action and accuse me, loudly, of always getting my face in the camera, and the back of her head. Nothing could have been further from my mind.'

While Rex was making *The Foxes of Harrow*, Lilli was filming *My Girl Tisa*, a period romance set in New York's immigrant quarter at the turn of the century.

With their fortunes continuing at a satisfactory, if not overwhelming, pace Rex and Lilli decided to quit Bel Air for nearby Mandeville Canyon, convenient for the Twentieth Century-Fox studios which were only about fifteen minutes away by car. The house they moved to was smaller but it had bigger grounds and a five-stall stable.

At this time Rex received another battering from the press, reminding him that they were still waiting for him to falter. The actor was scheduled to make a guest appearance on Eve Arden's network radio show and in a sketch that he was to appear in he was supposed to answer a comment about five thousand people attending a garden party at Buckingham Palace with: 'Oh, yes, King George is the English Atwater Kent.' Atwater Kent was a millionaire whose only claim to fame was the fact that he chose to spend his fortune on gaudy, tasteless parties as a means of entering the Hollywood social scene. Rex objected to his King being compared with such a man and angrily walked out, explaining that the line, 'wounded my sensibilities' and that the trite script was 'not worth the time of any actor'. Rex had to be replaced immediately and the gossip columnists began attacking him again, accusing him of snobbery and rudeness.

But if the atmosphere was strained at the studio and with the press during this period, Rex found consolation with a beautiful blonde actress whom he encountered when on a weekend break in Palm Springs. Rex first met Carole Landis in the bar of the Racquet Club in the desert resort. He was sitting with Lucille Ball and Charles Farrell, who had by now retired from the screen and was the owner of the exclusive club, when Carole entered with a group of friends. They were immediately attracted to each other. Rex could not help but be struck by her physical beauty and soon found himself drawn into a lively conversation, admiring her easy and confident way with men and ability to tell funny stories with zest.

Carole Landis had been very popular with the public during the war years when, as a Twentieth Century-Fox contract artist, she had supported Betty Grable, Sonja Henie and Rita Hayworth. But with the war over and her professional break-up with Darryl F. Zanuck and Twentieth Century-Fox, she found it difficult to get work with the major studios. Ostracised by Hollywood society, who regarded her disdainfully as an uncomfortably liberated woman, she was only twenty-eight but found life had lost most of its charm. Rex, having more than his fair share of grievances against the Hollywood gossip writers, found that he had much in common with Carole and sympathised with her rebellious stand against the hypocritical scandal-mongers who infested Hollywood.

Carole had been born Frances Ridste on January 1st 1919, in Fairchild, Wisconsin of Polish/Norwegian parents. In 1922 Mr and Mrs Ridste and their son and two daughters moved west to California and by the time Frances was seven she was already taking part in amateur nights and beauty contests. At the age of fifteen, while still a schoolgirl, she married a writer, a short-lived affair which effectively ended after only twenty-five days, at which time Frances returned to school from where she graduated in 1936. By the time she was legally divorced from her husband, the already worldly Frances was working as a singer and hula dancer at the Royal Hawaiian nightclub.

In 1937 she decided to try her luck in Hollywood. After walk-ons in several films, she was spotted by Busby Berkeley. She changed her name to Carole Landis and made her mark in 1940 in the Hal Roach production of *One Million BC* in which she appeared with the up-and-coming Victor Mature. In the same year Carole was married for the second time, to a yacht broker, but again the relationship came to a swift and stormy conclusion with the couple separating after two months and divorcing after five. But Carole was consoled by the fact that her appearance in *One Million BC* brought her to the attention of Darryl F. Zanuck who signed her, together with Victor Mature, to a contract with Twentieth Century-Fox.

Zanuck had a reputation for being partial to sampling the new starlets on the lot and Carole proved no exception. Milton Sperling, before becoming an independent screenwriter and producer, was Zanuck's secretary from 1936 until 1941 and has recalled the 'four o'clock routine' at Fox, where a girl from the lot, usually a starlet, would visit Zanuck in his office. 'The doors would be locked after she went in, no calls were taken, and for the next half hour nothing happened. Headquarters shut down. Around the office, work came to a halt for the sex fiesta. It was an understood thing. While the girl was with Zanuck, everything stopped.' Afterwards the girl would leave by a side door, Zanuck's office would be unlocked, and business would return to normal. It was rare for the same girl to visit Zanuck's office more than once, but with Carole he made an exception and she was known to be called in regularly as one of his 'four o'clock specials'; Sperling even referred to her as 'the studio hooker'.

At Twentieth Century-Fox Carole appeared in lavish musicals such as *Moon Over Miami* with Betty Grable and Don Ameche and *My Gal Sal* with Rita Hayworth and Victor Mature, quickly gaining an ardent following. With

America's entry into the war, she was active in War Bond sales and in late 1942 embarked on a USO tour of North Africa with fellow actresses Martha Raye, Kay Francis and Mitzi Mayfair. While in London, en route to Africa, Carole married a Captain in the US Air Force, but although they were not divorced until 1945, they spent most of their marriage living apart.

After her tour of North Africa, Carole returned to California in 1943 and wrote about their experiences in a book which she called *Four Jills In A Jeep* which was filmed in the following year by Twentieth Century-Fox. On the completion of this film Carole undertook a tour of the Pacific, entertaining the troops on that front. However, Carole's admirable contribution to the war effort was unfortunately blighted somewhat in 1945 when she received some lurid publicity following her accusations of criminal assault against a man whom she claimed became 'unduly familiar' when he burst into her dressing room at the studio and tried to unzip her scanty, shoulderless costume.

With her third divorce through, Carole married her fourth husband in the same year – a Broadway stage producer named W. Horace Schmidlapp. However, by the time Carole met Rex at Palm Springs, she and Mr Schmidlapp were, predictably, living apart, his wedding ring comfortably on display on the third finger of her left hand, next to the rings of her previous three husbands, like the trophies of a huntress.

Rex quickly succumbed to the undeniable charms of Miss Landis, embarking on another little extra-marital adventure. However, if Rex's original intention was to have a quick fling and return to an understanding wife, the relationship soon became more intense – to the point where the affair began to be noticed by others. Rex and Lilli's marriage continued, but Lilli was aware that it was in trouble, though unable to pinpoint the source of their difficulties.

While Rex's affair continued, he finished *The Foxes of*

Harrow, giving a sigh of relief as he completed the final scene of what had proved to be an unpleasant film to work on. He already had his next project in view. He had always had an affection for the original film version of John Galsworthy's play *Escape*, made in 1930 with Gerald Du Maurier. Rex liked the idea of following in his idol's footsteps, playing the hunted gentleman-convict who escapes from Dartmoor Prison. Rex persuaded Zanuck to buy the rights to the property and plans were made to film it around the actual locations in England, thus providing an authentic background to the story, and, more importantly, taking advantage of a special tax-settlement agreement between Britain and the United States designed to revitalise the British film industry. *Escape* was not only the first post-war American production under this scheme, but it would also mark Rex's first visit to his home country for two years. Joseph L. Mankiewicz would direct.

Rex was accompanied on his journey by Lilli and three-year-old Carey and also by Mary and John Mills, who had been the Harrisons' house guests for the two weeks prior to their departure for England. Rex and Lilli ensured that their guests saw all the sights in and around Los Angeles and introduced them to such luminaries as Spencer Tracy and Tyrone Power. John Mills recalls their return journey on the *Super Chief* from the West Coast to New York and on the *Queen Elizabeth* to England with some amusement, 'On the way Mary and I and Rex and Lilli stayed with Frank Sinatra in the desert. It was a frantic and eventful journey for all of us from the start – when Rex nearly forgot the tickets – until we finally arrived back in England.'

Rex's trip did not, however, mean that he and Carole Landis would be separated for that period. They had fallen into a routine where they would meet to swim, play tennis or laze about on a beach together, preferring to avoid the more public socialising of Hollywood parties where Carole was not always a welcome guest and at which Rex would be expected to attend with his wife. Rex already knew that Carole had been signed up to make a film in England and so she would be following him across the Atlantic.

Rex's leading lady was Peggy Cummins who, like Rex, had recently been lured to Hollywood from Britain after being brought to Zanuck's attention by her appearance just after the war on the London stage in a production of the American hit comedy *Junior Miss*. She was also making her first appearance in her home country since her departure the year before.

The contrast between British and American film-making proved to be greater than expected, particularly for Mankiewicz who had to deal with troublesome unions which did their best to disrupt filming. The industry was no longer the one that Rex had left behind. The war being over, the unions were flexing their muscles. Mankiewicz has described the situation at the time, 'The British unions were the world's toughest, most erratic, unpredictable, and irritating to work with. On *Escape* they had just come into power and they were enjoying it. All the unions were doing this in England at that time. They were paying back for a hundred years' humiliation of their fathers and grandfathers.'

Filming began in September 1947, much of it on Dartmoor. This location shooting was already uncomfortable enough, having to contend with fog and heavy rain (and consequent mud), but the film crew made it even worse by always being on the verge of striking, which created totally unnecessary tension for the director and his actors. Mankiewicz again recalled,

'The electricians on high received lime juice every afternoon at four-thirty and if the mixture was not exactly right, they would strike. We'd have these sudden rainstorms in Devonshire, and electrical equipment was expensive and scarce just after the war. In one squall I grabbed a lamp to get it under cover and the crew struck because I was not a member of the electrical union. When we were using fog machines for some interior, they struck again. They wanted "fog money", an extra one-sixth for working in artificial fog.'

Rex consoled himself over these tensions in the company of Carole Landis who was by now also in England, making a film in London. The happy coincidence that Rex and Carole were in England at the same time did have its darker implications. Unlike Rex, who had chosen to travel to Britain to work, Carole was working in England because she was unable to find work in Hollywood. She was one of the first Hollywood personalities to follow this route to employment, but it was a movement which would gradually gather momentum as the decade drew to a close, with many Hollywood stars whose careers had lost much of the lustre they possessed in the pre-war years, attempting, more often than not in vain, to bolster their flagging positions by accepting leading roles in British productions. Unfortunately, most of these productions were shoddy, cut-price efforts which cashed in on a familiar Hollywood name to bolster the profits on what would otherwise be just another British supporting feature.

Carole had signed to make two films in England: *The Brass Monkey* and *Noose*, neither of which was a notable production, although the latter, based on a play of the same name which had had a successful run at the Saville Theatre, afforded her a slightly better opportunity. Her leading man in *Noose*, Derek Farr, remembered her with affection. 'I enjoyed working with her enormously. Everyone adored her in the unit – she was a real Hollywood pro.'

While the affair between Rex and Carole was generally known, she maintained absolute discretion about it, as Derek Farr testifies. 'I never saw Carole socially after work and she never talked about Rex at all to me. He never came to the studios but, of course, we all knew what was going on. I was told by someone who knew her that she adored him. It was all very sad.' With Rex on Dartmoor and Carole filming in London, the couple usually contrived to meet at weekends in Plymouth, a convenient meeting point between their two bases and far more discreet than London where Lilli remained with Carey. Carole was seen occasionally at public functions during this time but never in the company of Rex. She was in the line-up of invited film personalities at the second Royal Film Performance in November 1947 at the Odeon, Leicester Square when King George VI and Queen Elizabeth attended the chosen film, *The Bishop's Wife*, starring Cary Grant. Two of the film's other stars, Loretta Young and David Niven, came over especially. Carole arrived looking ravishing and was besieged by admirers anxious to catch a glimpse of the beautiful Hollywood actress. A keen amateur photographer herself, Carole took advantage of being in London at the time of the wedding of Princess Elizabeth (the future Queen Elizabeth II) to Philip, Duke of Edinburgh.

Rex finally completed *Escape* on December 18th 1947 and he and Lilli, along with Carey, returned to Hollywood where he was to start another film. Carole was still working on her film commitments in England and would not be returning to Hollywood for a few more weeks. While Carole remained there, she and Rex kept in close contact by telephone and Rex wrote to her regularly.

Initial announcements had stated that Rex would be returning to Hollywood to appear in Ernst Lubitsch's proposed production of *That Lady In Ermine* opposite Betty Grable, but circumstances and the film's leading man, Douglas Fairbanks, Jr, refute this possibility completely. Fairbanks says, 'I would be surprised that Rex would turn it down. Everybody was all over each other to work with Lubitsch. Lubitsch called me himself when he only had an outline for the script, so I came in a good six or eight months before the picture went into production.'

Shooting of the film began months before Rex's scheduled return to Hollywood, so it seems likely that Rex's name only appeared for publicity purposes to emphasise that Fox's English contract star would be returning to California after making *Escape* in his home country.

But if Rex missed the opportunity to work with Hollywood's most prestigious exponent of sophisticated comedy, it proved grimly fortuitous. Only eight days into production, Lubitsch suffered the sixth of a series of heart attacks and was replaced by the less suitable Otto Preminger while he recuperated. He seemed to rally, but then had a seventh and fatal heart attack and died on November 30th 1947. What might have been a frothy, witty entertainment in his hands proved to be a cheerless and lifeless production. If Rex had been available it would have involved him in an unmitigated disaster, something he could ill afford since *Escape* already showed all the signs of being no money-spinner.

However, the film that Rex did make held the promise of being the good picture he was well aware he needed. Having turned down several other projects Rex was finally offered the part of Sir Alfred de Carter in *Unfaithfully Yours*, a new Preston Sturges comedy. Rex admired Sturges who already had behind him such classic films of the forties as *Sullivan's Travels*, *The Lady Eve*, *The Miracle of Morgan's Creek* and *Hail the Conquering Hero*. *Unfaithfully Yours* was to be his first production in two years and Rex felt fortunate to work with an acknowledged master, in whose hands he could feel secure while making his first American comedy, which would enable him to display to its best advantage his supreme talent in that field. Rex's leading lady was Linda Darnell and the cast also included Rudy Vallee, Edgar Kennedy, Lionel Stander and a young Swiss actor, Kurt Kreuger, who played Rex's secretary and the imagined rival for his wife's affections in the film.

Rex played a famed conductor who, believing that his wife is having an affair with his secretary, imagines while conducting various concert pieces different ways of executing the perfect murder in order to punish the lovers. He then attempts to reproduce these plots in reality, with quite different and chaotic results.

Preston Sturges' method of production was much more social than Rex had hitherto experienced in Hollywood. It was a style which agreed with the actor who quickly established a firm working relationship and solid friendship with the director who was no less enamoured of Rex than Rex was of him. Kurt Kreuger recalls,

'Sturges was a little bit infatuated with Rex Harrison. Although he was a terribly intellectual man and a very autocratic man, he did pay a little heed to the stardom of the day; and he catered a little bit to the star because Rex had this imperious attitude.

'Rex got on well with Sturges – he catered to Sturges and Sturges catered to him.'

Sturges chose the way in which he would make a film and he would accept no interference from the front office, as Kreuger continues,

'Sturges at the time had such power because his last movies at Paramount had made a lot of money and he was the only producer-director-writer who had the strength to almost bar Zanuck from the set. Zanuck didn't want to have any fights with him or want to disturb, so he just stayed away and didn't come on the set at all, although he was always on all the other sets.'

It was like a small, enclosed world on the sound stage where *Unfaithfully Yours* was being made, and Sturges organised the entire shooting day in such a way as to keep the team as a close unit. Kurt Kreuger explains this,

'Preston Sturges treated the entire company like a stock company. I was under contract and so as a contract player you were more or less forced to be on the set every day whether you were used in a scene or not – just in case the scene changed.

'Sturges was also a restaurateur at the time. He had a very famous theatrical restaurant called The Players and so he didn't want the actors to go and lunch by themselves. So we all sat at big tables and Sturges presided. We always dined all together, with excellent catered food.'

While *Unfaithfully Yours* was still in production Carole Landis returned to Hollywood and gossip about the couple quickly reappeared as they continued their romance. The affair was becoming more and more widely known and towards the end of the film's three-month shooting schedule Rex found himself increasingly challenged by the press about the relationship. One journalist approached him on the set and asked him outright about the truth of the rumours concerning Landis and himself, but Rex laughingly dismissed any suggestion of an affair. Lilli was also approached for her comments but she denied the truth of the rumours stating firmly, 'Carole is *our* friend.'

But if Lilli defended her husband and marriage in public it was not through ignorance of the true situation. With Carole's return to Hollywood Rex had finally confessed all to his wife and she had decided that she would go to New York as soon as she had completed the film to which she was committed, in the hope that in her absence Rex would sort out his muddled private life.

Carole still found it impossible to get film work in Hollywood and one of the few offers she did receive was to play the lead in a tent-show production of Elmer Rice's play *Dream Girl*. It was to be produced and directed in North Hollywood by Ross Hunter, a young film actor making the first steps, with his partner Jacques Mapes, in the newly-chosen career which would ultimately lead to his becoming one of Hollywood's major independent

producers. Carole accepted the part but Hunter quickly
realised that he had chosen the wrong star to head his
production, as he recalls, 'There was a line in the play
where she says, "I'm a virgin." When she said that the tent
fell in, so we asked if we could replace her with Virginia
Grey, who was Clark Gable's perennial girl friend. So we
did this and Rex called me and wanted to know why we
had let Carole go. I remember saying, "I have no comment." Rex was not very happy with that.'

This incident alone did not bring about Carole's dis-
missal. The main reason for her being replaced was that
she was unable to keep her mind on the play and Ross
Hunter found it impossible to carry on with her in the
production, as he explains, 'She kept rehearsing but her
thoughts were not with us. She was much more interested in her gigantic love affair with Rex Harrison than
she was in anything else. She was absolutely insane over
him – and he was wonderful to her. They figured that
nobody knew about their great romance, which was
ridiculous because Carole was really smitten by this man.
She was absolutely head-over-heels in love with him.'

Rex would visit Carole at her home on Capri Drive in
West Los Angeles, which was only a few minutes away
from his own home on Mandeville Canyon. These discreet visits were only ever witnessed by Carole's maid,
Fannie Mae Bolden, who even today has no doubt that
her mistress was genuinely in love with Rex. 'She would
make me so mad because he would be eating his food and
she would just sit there watching him. And he would be
eating just like a dog, eating like it was going out of style.'

While Rex was filming, these visits would occur during
the evening, but with the completion of *Unfaithfully Yours*
and with Lilli's departure for New York, the couple were
able to see much more of each other than had previously
been possible. Rex was thrown even closer to Carole,
whether he wanted it or not, and his wife's action can be
seen as designed to bring matters to a head. Lilli's withdrawal took away the protective screen of supposed

domestic bliss which had given Rex the opportunity to see his mistress without too much fuss. The shield that Lilli had provided was being increasingly penetrated by the enquiring press but by her departure Lilli had made her position clear, and the next move would have to be Rex's. Whether or not he would return to her was a calculated risk. Lilli recalled her position. 'He kept it hidden – apart from Landis. He always made it quite clear that we belonged together and his tenderness, his affection – which was very great – I never missed until Landis. That threw me totally.'

While Lilli was in New York, staying with her sister Hilde and her husband, Rex, with no immediate film commitments after *Unfaithfully Yours*, would often spend the entire day with Carole, swimming or playing tennis and returning to her house for meals which Fannie Mae would cook for them, as she recalls,

> 'I would go into the kitchen and close the door and they would go in the living room. I could hear the music playing; it seemed like they were having a drink and having a lot of fun. He would call to say what time he would be there for lunch and come around from where he lived every day for lunch and dinner. The only time I saw him was when I would call them in for their meal. I would always serve lunch out on the patio. I would take it out there and speak to him and then when they had finished I would go out and bring the dishes in.'

Fannie Mae was devoted to her mistress and still remembers her with affection. 'Carole was always nice to me. A very sweet person – more like a friend. She seemed very happy-go-lucky all the time.' However, she remembers Rex with little regard, 'I think he was kind of snooty. There were a lot of people who didn't like him. I hated him because he would come in demanding things; he would want to know where his towel was, where this was and who had been using that . . .'

Carole's obsession with Rex was extreme and she took numerous photographs of him which she developed herself in the dark-room which she had in the house. These pictures were then put on display so that the house resembled a shrine to her lover. Fannie Mae recalls that, 'she had pictures of him all over the wall,' and that the house was full of photographic equipment and cameras which were invariably pointed in the direction of her beloved Rex.

For Carole, Lilli's departure from California must have appeared to be the first victory in the gradual process of winning Rex entirely for herself, and his frequent presence at her home must have convinced her that she was making headway. Beyond being in love with Rex, Carole was also sorely in need of a protector of some kind. Opportunities for work in Hollywood remained practically non-existent for her and she found it increasingly difficult to meet her financial commitments. She had run up considerable debts and in an effort to reduce the financial pressure she had put her house up for sale. Professionally, the only glimmer of hope was the possibility of returning to England to make two further films. Otherwise her whole future seemed to depend upon Rex.

Rex remained in contact with Lilli by telephone, calling her every morning, but with his wife in New York, Rex no longer had any excuse for leaving Carole to return home. He found himself trapped in a corner from which he could see no easy escape. Carole quite obviously expected Rex to divorce Lilli and marry her, and her love for him was mixed with the desperate realisation that beyond Rex she had no real hope of resolving the mess her life was in. Approaching thirty and with a film career that showed little chance of reviving itself, she was becoming increasingly convinced that she was washed-up. Now, more than ever, she felt it was time to settle down with the right man and have children of her own.

But if Rex was her choice as the key to future happiness
and security, she had picked the wrong man. His attractions were obvious and he was certainly different from
any other man she had met. Not only was he English,
which automatically meant 'class' in Hollywood at that
time, but he also reinforced this with an air of sophistication and good breeding. Rex, knowing Carole to be a
carefree girl, had not entered into the affair with her with
any serious intent, and could not have expected this
intensity to surface in Landis. Rex did not want to lose the
stability that his marriage to Lilli gave to his life, and he
never regarded Carole as a threat to the marriage. But for
Carole the affair meant much more and Rex found it
increasingly difficult to extricate himself, to the extent
that, with Lilli's departure, it really appeared that his
marriage might be over. More than anything else, Lilli's
action in retreating to New York had served to demonstrate to Rex exactly where he stood. Not only could he
see what life without Lilli and Carey behind him would
be like, but he could also see that Carole was waiting in
the wings to replace Lilli as Mrs Rex Harrison. Rex had
lost the opportunity to cool the affair off with a certain
degree of ease because Lilli's action made it plain that Rex
would have to decide where his future lay – a fact of
which Carole was equally aware.

But if Rex knew how deeply embroiled he was, he was
still infatuated enough with Carole not to break from her
when she was so accessible to him. He seemed to be
behaving just as Carole might have hoped once Lilli had
gone. He was seeing her more frequently and only
seemed to be confirming his continued interest in her.

The whole messy situation had to come to a head, and
Rex was to be the unwitting instigator. It so happened
that Rex was given a copy of Maxwell Anderson's new
play *Anne of the Thousand Days* to read. Rex's friend,
Broadway producer and agent Leland Hayward, intended to produce the play in New York and wanted Rex
to read it and consider playing the part of King Henry

VIII. Not only was it a marvellous acting opportunity, but it also seemed to offer the chance to step back and draw breath in order to consider what he should do next regarding the Landis affair. It would be a convenient enforced separation as it would mean his going to New York for a considerable period of time. Rex was excited about the Anderson play and when he drove over to Carole's home on the evening of July 4th to have dinner with her, as was his usual practice, he brought the play over with him.

It was a clear Sunday evening and the two of them sat down to dinner alone, with Carole dressed simply in a frilly white blouse, a black and white checked skirt and gold sandals. Being Independence Day, Carole had spent the day at a swimming party and was in very gay spirits. Rex showed Carole the play and told her of his intention to accept it, explaining about the necessary separation that would occur. Carole was not the only person with whom he wanted to share his enthusiasm. Rex left her shortly after nine o'clock, an unusually early time since neither of them was filming the next day, and went on to see Roland and Nan Culver at 750 Napoli Drive, the home of Gladys Cooper which they were renting while she lived in her other house next door. Rex stayed with the Culvers until about one-thirty in the morning, talking mainly about the Anderson play, after which he returned home to Mandeville Canyon and went straight to bed.

Even today, Fannie Mae Bolden vividly recalls her feeling of foreboding as she stepped off the bus at the Riviera Country Club and made her way up the road to Carole's house on the corner of Capri Drive on the morning of July 5th.

'On my way up to the house I had an awful feeling. Something told me that something was wrong. I went to the front door where I always went in but it was locked, so I went around to the back door, which was open. So I went in and when I got inside it seemed like I just froze. I was so nervous about something and I didn't know what it was.

'I went on in and the table was full of food and dishes from when they had dined that night of the fourth of July. I cleared up everything and went into the living room. All her cameras and diaries and portfolios were on the table and I dusted them all off. Then the 'phone rang and I answered it. Atwater Kent was calling to invite Carole to a party and I told him "I'm sorry, Miss Landis isn't up yet."

'And then after a while Rex called and I said, "I'm sorry, Miss Landis isn't up yet." He said, "She isn't?" I said, "No."

'Then a few minutes later he called back again and I said, "Well, she's not up yet." He said, "Well, you tell her that I'll be a little late."'

Rex had got up at half-past nine that morning and had called Carole's home at eleven o'clock just before Leland Hayward called at his home to drive him to Maxwell Anderson's house to discuss the play. Rex would say later, 'I rang her in the morning about eleven o'clock because I had a luncheon date with her.'

It was not until half-past two in the afternoon that Rex found another opportunity to ring Carole. Fannie Mae continued, 'In the meantime, something told me to go upstairs.' She walked up the stairs to a bedroom in the house where, as she says, 'you could look clean through into Miss Landis's room.' She recalls what she saw when she looked through the window:

'I could see her lying there and I thought to myself that she didn't look like she had any life in her. When I started to reach for the door to turn the knob it seemed like my hand froze and wouldn't let me open it, because she always told me, "When I need you I will call you on the phone downstairs so you won't have to

run upstairs to see what I want." When I saw her there
I went on back downstairs. I was so nervous.'

Fannie Mae went back to her cleaning and then returned to the kitchen, as she continues,

'I kept my clothes on to clean up and then went to put
my uniform over them. And then I looked towards the
back door and saw Mr Harrison standing there. I said,
"Mr Harrison, are you looking for me?"
    "Yes, Fannie Mae. Have you been in Miss Landis's
room at all?"
    "No, I have not."
    "Well, I think she's dead. Let's go up."''

Rex had previously entered the house unnoticed and
found the body. Now accompanied by Fannie Mae, he
walked up the stairs once more to Carole's room. The
body was lying in the bathroom and to get there they had
to pass through Carole's bedroom, decorated in crimson
and yellow, to her dressing room. Fannie Mae says that
when they entered the room, 'He ran to the bed and he
got this note and he started to holler, "Oh darling, why
did you do it? Why did you do it?"'
The letter, written in pencil on her monogrammed
stationery, had been carefully perched among some
cologne and perfume bottles and was addressed not to
Rex but to 'Dear Mommie'. It read,

'I'm sorry, really sorry, to put you through this, but
there is no way to avoid it. I love you, darling, you have
been the most wonderful Mom ever and that applies to
all our family. I love each and every one of them dearly.
Everything goes to you. Look in the files and there is a
will which decrees everything. Goodbye, my angel.
Pray for me – Your baby.'

Rex and Fannie Mae then entered the bathroom where the body lay next to a cupboard. Her head was resting on a brown leather jewel box, while in her left hand she was clutching a satin ribbon on which was written the Lord's Prayer in gold lettering. Under her right hand was an envelope on which was written in her own handwriting, 'Red – quick – 2 hours. Yellow, about 5. Can take two.' Inside the envelope was a single sleeping pill. In a deposition he gave to an informal enquiry requested by the coroner, Rex stated, 'I felt her pulse. It must have been purely my imagination, but I thought there was a little beat.'

Understandably Rex was confused and in a state of shock at this terrible discovery. He did not want to believe that Carole was dead, beyond hope of revival, and his first instinct was to get a doctor to her as quickly as possible. Rex recalled in his autobiography that he and Fannie Mae both looked for Carole's private telephone book in order to get in touch with her doctor, 'It was by the bed and I went through it. I knew Carole had quite a number of doctors but she hadn't spoken of them by name; by looking from A to Z I hoped to find a name I could identify as a doctor's. When I couldn't, I got into my car and drove home as fast as possible to get the private telephone number of my own doctor.'

Fannie Mae, giving her version of these events, claims that they went downstairs again and that Rex said to her, 'I'll go and notify some of her friends.' Poor Fannie Mae was at a loss as to what to do. She continues, 'Rex didn't call anybody. He didn't call the coroner, the police, or anybody. He just walked on out.' In desperation she ran outside to get help from the residents of the house which backed onto Carole's. She saw the man who lived there swimming in his pool and attracted his attention. She told him what had happened and he immediately got out of the water and jumped over the fence dividing the two properties. He and Fannie Mae went into the house where he called the coroner and the police. With those two calls the news of the tragedy quickly spread, as Fannie Mae recalls, 'In a few minutes there were so many newspapermen there. I didn't know how they got there so fast.'

Meanwhile Rex was hurriedly making the five-minute drive from Carole's house to his own. Upon his arrival he immediately telephoned his doctor but, it being the day after Independence Day, discovered that he was away. He finally managed to track down the doctor's assistant who told him that it would take him at least half an hour to get there. In desperation Rex rang the Culvers, finding only Nan at home as Roland was out playing golf. She suggested that he telephone St John's Hospital and the police. As Rex recalled, 'I reported to the hospital and the police that I'd found Carole and that I hoped she wasn't dead but that she needed assistance immediately, and asked them to go right to the house.'

Rex then rang Nan Culver again to tell her what he had done and she and Judith Fellows, an actress friend of the Culvers, offered to accompany him back to Carole's house. Fannie Mae could not recall their names but verified that, 'Rex Harrison came in with two tall European women when he got back.' In Nan Culver's company, Rex was able to regain some kind of composure and to bolster himself for the further inevitable ordeal which was to come and which would so soon burst upon him. He knew that the gossip columnists would be only too pleased to see him squirming at the centre of such a scandal.

When Rex and his two companions arrived the police and fire brigade were already there. Attempts had been made to revive Carole but these failed and her body had already been taken to the morgue. Upstairs was a friend of Carole's, Mrs Florence Wasson, who had once been Carole's stand-in. Fannie Mae recalls that she was in the back room, 'She came out and said to me, "Fannie Mae, Miss Landis said in her note to you to see that the cat is taken to the vet and his leg seen to."' Fannie Mae thought the note rather strange, as 'there was nothing wrong with the cat.' Rex had also seen the note which in itself was unimportant, but the peculiar events surrounding it were to provoke rumours of further undisclosed notes having been left by Carole.

Rex remained at Carole's house while Detective Captain Emmett Jones and Detective John M. Laymen, the two police officers in charge of the investigation, questioned him about his movements. He then returned home and, anxious for someone to talk to, rang Leland Hayward who immediately drove over. Soon after Hayward's arrival reporters and photographers completely surrounded the house; Rex, trapped inside, adamantly refused to see them.

Rex now felt the full enormity of the tragedy and was unable to comprehend that Carole had taken her life. As he explained, 'I was totally bewildered by the fact that, except for showing mild concern that I might be going to New York, Carole had given me no warning whatsoever of how she felt. I hadn't realised that she had been many times before at the end of her tether, that there was so little stability in her life, and that, as I learned later, she had already attempted to take her life on previous occasions.'

Leland Hayward supported Rex, acting as a shield from the prying outside world, answering all telephone calls. Rex used to telephone Lilli each day in New York. He had already made his call to her before he had discovered Carole's body but now, as Lilli claims in her autobiography, Rex telephoned her a second time and told her what had happened and asked her to take the next flight to Los Angeles, which she agreed to do. Lilli later reiterated her version of these events:

'He rang me every morning, and he had already rung me and we had spoken. But two hours later there was again a call from Hollywood and I said to the operator, "No, I had it already. It's a mistake."

"No, another call."

'It was early afternoon and Leland Hayward was on the 'phone. He said that Rex was there and had something to say to me. Rex then came on the line,

"Something terrible has happened. Carole has killed herself. Come at once."'

In Rex's version of the tragedy, in his autobiography, Lilli read about Carole's suicide in the New York newspapers and caught a night flight to Los Angeles, although at the time he was quoted in the *Los Angeles Times* as saying, 'Immediately after her death . . . I called Lilli in New York and she flew home.' In any case, Lilli was due to arrive in Los Angeles at six o'clock on the following morning.

In the meantime, Leland Hayward stayed close to Rex through the rest of the afternoon and into the evening. Late that night, Rex managed to get out of the house unseen and went to the Culvers' house, where Roland Culver had made a fortuitous discovery earlier that evening. Shortly before his death Culver recalled that day,

'After my golf on the day of the tragedy, I had invited Willard Parker [a Hollywood film actor] and the assistant golf pro to come and have a drink with us at six o'clock. They duly arrived but for some reason parked outside our front gate . . . This gate, and this front door, was seldom, if ever, used. It was our custom, and that of our guests, to enter the house by the side entrance, where there was a large drive leading to the garage with plenty of other parking space . . . There they discovered two small cases, and a note fixed to one of them to Rex. The note and the cases were from Carole. She had clearly dumped them there in the middle of the night before her death, where they had remained all day without being discovered. Had the press thought of querying Rex's statement that he had been with me the previous evening, as he had been, and paid me a visit, they would doubtless have entered the house at the front door and been the first to discover the note and the cases, which Rex explained to me contained all their most intimate possessions, letters, photographs and presents that Rex had given Carole. It was bad luck on the columnists. They missed that scoop.'

Rex was relieved to have these personal items in his possession as they represented the only solid proof of his emotional entanglement with Carole Landis, and with Lilli's timely arrival early on the following morning he hoped that he would be able to ride the storm and keep up the appearance of a stable marriage.

In the early hours of the sixth of July, an unsuspecting Los Angeles press missed the further scoop of the arrival of Mrs Rex Harrison. Following a 3 a.m. stopover in Chicago, Lilli's flight arrived at Los Angeles airport on schedule at 6 a.m. She was met by Leland Hayward who took her to a lounge in the airport and filled her in on the complexities of the situation. Rex remained at the house, where he had managed a fitful night of sleep after being given a shot by the doctor to help him rest. Hayward explained to Lilli what she could expect, warning her that the house in Mandeville Canyon was surrounded by reporters and photographers and that Rex had had to barricade himself inside the house until the police arrived, in order to prevent the press from breaking in. As Lilli and Hayward drove up to the house they were suddenly engulfed by the press, and it was only after Leland got help from two policemen that they were able to escape from them and get safely into the house.

It was an emotional moment as Rex faced Lilli for the first time since the tragedy. Lilli had travelled nearly three thousand miles across America to stand by her husband and show a united front against the prying newspapermen.

Rex was busy destroying as much as he could of the

contents of the suitcases that Carole had left, as Lilli recalled, 'Carole put all the letters and the photographs into a suitcase. The next morning, when I was already there, Rex burned all the letters in the grate. The photograph albums couldn't be burned so easily so Harry, Rex's valet, and I burned them later in the garden when Rex was already in New York.' In the meantime, the photograph albums had to remain discreetly in the house. Legal advisers arrived from both Twentieth Century-Fox and Warner Brothers, where Lilli had been working, and they immediately took charge.

Clearly the major problem was what to do regarding the press outside, who remained adamantly within the grounds. They would obviously not leave until they had had some kind of response from inside, and so it was decided that it would be sensible to grant them an interview with the provision that they all dispersed afterwards. In any case, with rumours flying about Rex's involvement with Carole Landis, it seemed a good idea that Rex and Lilli should present themselves to the world as the happily married Harrisons as soon as possible and thereby perhaps stamp out the gossip and innuendo that was rife in the film capital.

The couple stepped outside and, standing before the front door, prepared to answer questions. Lilli quickly dismissed any allegations of a romantic attachment between Rex and Carole. 'I heard gossip of romance between my husband and Carole, but I don't think there was anything serious in it. They were just good friends.' She also denied that she and Rex were estranged and added, 'I am terribly upset over her death. We have been friends for years.'

The interview over, the reporters and photographers left the grounds and Rex and Lilli were left to spend the rest of the day in the house conversing with their lawyers. In the evening Rex received a telephone call from New York from the mother of Dick Haymes, the popular crooner who had been a Twentieth Century-Fox contract artist and an intimate friend of Carole's in the past. Rex spent some time talking to Mrs Haymes and it was then that he discovered that Carole had attempted suicide on several occasions in the past. On these previous occasions Carole had taken sleeping pills but had always telephoned Mrs Haymes in New York, allowing enough time for the latter to call a doctor. On the night of July 4th Mrs Haymes had been out celebrating until late and although she had found a message that she had had a call from Los Angeles in her absence, she did not return the call because of the hour.

It is possible that Carole was only intending to draw attention to herself and bring Rex round to her. But, if this were true, she made a major miscalculation – it was a public holiday and people were not so easily contactable and, whatever her actions on that night, she finally slumped down in the bathroom and died.

On Wednesday July 7th Rex and Lilli announced that they would be leaving Los Angeles for New York, bound for England. However, that evening the chief deputy coroner telephoned Rex and told him to keep himself available until the coroner was satisfied regarding the case.

Carole's funeral had initially been planned for the Thursday, but the burial permit was not issued in time. There was no suspicion of foul play since all the evidence clearly pointed to the fact that Carole had committed suicide. What still worried coroner Ben Brown was that he could not find a motive for suicide which completely satisfied him. Talking to the press he said, 'All her other acquaintances have told us that up until the time of the dinner with Rex she seemed gay, cheerful, undepressed. We want to know what, if anything, happened that would turn her thoughts to suicide at that time.' Carole's fourth husband, W. Horace Schmidlapp, had by now arrived in Los Angeles and was feeding the fires of the press with his statements. He told them, 'I have heard rumours today from several sources that another note was found. If that is true, I would like to know to whom it was addressed, and what it contained, and what has happened to it.'

Rex had already made assurances that he would be glad to remain in Los Angeles for as long as he could be of help and Lilli publicly stood by her husband, saying, 'We shall go to her funeral no matter how long it may require us to stay here. After that, I shall go wherever my husband, Rex, goes. If he returns to England, I shall return with him; if he stays here, I shall stay.'

An 'informal inquiry' was called for Thursday, July 8th at 2.30 p.m. in coroner Brown's office. Rex, accompanied by his attorney Judd Downing, arrived at the office at the appointed time and was confronted by a barrage of blinding flashbulbs and the sight of hundreds of onlookers anxious to catch a glimpse of the key figure in the story.

Once in the office, Rex's attorney told Brown that his client would answer the questions put to him in the form of a written deposition, which would be read into the record. The hearing was delayed for an hour while the document was typed at Downing's Beverly Hills office and rushed over. Before the deposition was read the coroner reiterated that there was no question but that Landis's death was suicide and he thanked Rex for voluntarily appearing to answer questions. Under oath Rex denied that he knew the motive for her suicide or of the existence of a second note. That Roland Culver, in his autobiography published in 1979, specifically mentions a note from Carole addressed to Rex being affixed to one of the two cases left outside his house by Landis remains an isolated statement and whether Culver recalled this correctly or only imagined it thirty years later can probably never be fully resolved, but it remains a curious, inexplicable statement which stood unremarked in Culver's remaining lifetime.

In the deposition Rex stated that he and Lilli were 'great friends' of Miss Landis and that her death was a tragedy which should not be clouded by sensational innuendos. He described the events of their dinner together on that last evening, 'We discussed the script of a new play and I was also hoping to be able to help her return to England to make a picture. I have influence with producers there.' He claimed that no argument occurred between them and continued, 'I think we had one Scotch and soda before dinner, but nothing during or after dinner.' When he left to go to a friend's house just after nine o'clock she was 'perfectly sober'. He explained that he remained at his friend's house until about one thirty in the morning and then went home to bed. He then reiterated the story that he had already told the police of how he had risen at nine o'clock just before Leland Hayward called by to drive him to Maxwell Anderson's home. When he returned at three he called again and, still being told by the maid that Carole had not yet arisen, he drove round to the house and found the body. He said that he never knew her to take sleeping pills. When asked if she had discussed her business and financial difficulties he said, 'Yes, she told me she had certain financial embarrassments and difficulty in meeting the bills. But she did not seem unduly depressed.'

Fannie Mae Bolden also attended the hearing and recounted her version of the events of the morning of July 5th. Today, she recalls that afternoon in the coroner's office. 'I met Rex Harrison down there. He was on one side and I was on the other. I didn't even look over there because I figured he had done something wrong to her for her to do that.'

Mrs Wasson also came to the stand and told of the second note regarding the health of the cat and confirmed that no suicide motive was given in this note.

Coroner's chemist R. J. Abernathy confirmed that Carole was the victim of a lethal dose of barbiturates and that his examination disclosed the presence of five milligrams of seconal. He added that blood tests showed twelve per cent of ethyl alcohol, three per cent under the level generally marking intoxication.

Rex was called again to the witness stand to elaborate on some of the answers in his written deposition. Deputy coroner Ira Nance asked him, 'Did she express any worry over the future?' Rex replied, 'I don't think she was entirely happy with her career.' No other suicide motive beyond this offered itself and there was nothing more to be done. Closing the enquiry, coroner Brown said, 'I have gone to the limits of my authority.'

Nevertheless, the press reported rumours of financial problems and unhappiness in love as the cause of Carole's suicide and that she had been negotiating the sale of her home and had asked her studio for an advance on her salary for her next film in order to clear some of her debts.

With the enquiry over, Carole's funeral was finally held on Saturday, July 10th at the Church of the Recessional at Forest Lawn cemetery. Douglas Fairbanks recalls the preparations made by Lilli for the occasion: 'Lilli called my wife up to ask what she should wear and whether she should wear black. My wife said, "You don't wear black to your husband's mistress's funeral. You should wear dark blue." And she didn't have a dark blue dress and she came over and borrowed one from my wife because at that time they had a similar size figure.'

At the funeral, one thousand five hundred people filed past the open coffin in which Carole's body lay, dressed in her favourite evening dress – a strapless blue chiffon gown – while in her hands she clutched a matching blue orchid. The pallbearers included actors Cesar Romero and Pat O'Brien. Bishop Fred Pyman, who officiated at the ceremony, said of Carole, 'She was a regular trouper and I don't think the Almighty would judge her too harshly.'

It was a grotesque Hollywood funeral dominated by ghoulish fans and, once again, the unremitting flashbulbs of the numberless press photographers who surrounded the church. For the onlookers it was more an opportunity to see their favourite film stars arrive than to pay tribute to the tragic death of a sad twenty-nine-year-old girl. In death, Carole Landis proved to be a far more popular attraction than she had ever been in her career.

In retrospect, Lilli generously said of Landis, 'She obviously was, quite apart from having been a call-girl once, a very nice woman and obviously very much in love with him. A senseless death at the age of twenty-nine.'

Rex and Lilli left immediately after the service, leaving through a side door before the coffin was closed and carried to its freshly dug grave. As the Harrisons drove away from Forest Lawn, the crowd pushed and shoved each other to get a better view of the coffin being lowered into the ground. Once the grave had been filled in, some of them even ripped away the flowers that had been lying beside the coffin, keeping them as a morbid memento of the occasion. Fortunately, Rex did not see all this, but what he had seen remained an experience which would taint his view of Hollywood for many years to come.

6

THE TRAGEDY of Carole Landis gave the gossip columnists all the ammunition they wanted against Rex, particularly the Hearst newspapers which were very anti-British at the time. If they hoped to drive Rex out of town, however, he robbed them of that satisfaction, having already agreed to go to New York to appear in *Anne of the Thousand Days*. With the pressure on Rex and Lilli continuing, Roland Culver encouraged them to take a break from everything and get away. About a week after Carole's funeral they left Hollywood to stay for a few days at Del Monte Lodge with the Culvers. Rex and Roland spent the days playing golf while Lilli and Nan wandered about the Monterey Peninsula. Culver commented in his autobiography, 'I think the change did them both good. I hoped so.'

The Landis suicide upset Fox's plans for the release of *Unfaithfully Yours* – hardly the most tactful title in the circumstances. They had planned that the film should open at Grauman's Chinese Theatre with a dazzling premiere, but with Rex's name a little sullied by the press it was decided simply to slip the film out without too much fuss. In consequence, what might have been one of Rex's most successful Hollywood films was blighted.

Rex's performance included an interesting glimpse of his abilities as a slapstick comedian. The highlight of the film is a protracted scene of visual humour in which Rex causes progressively more chaos in attempting to prepare his apartment for the perfect murder of his wife. What had seemed in his imagination to be a plan which would run as smoothly as clockwork, in practice only results in him wrecking the room. The carefully paced scene has some marvellous moments, although as a whole the viewer is perhaps too aware of the contrived nature of the sequence for it to be totally successful. This rather shaky balancing of a more sophisticated humour with broader slapstick comedy ultimately makes the film a disappointment and, whether the Landis tragedy had occurred or not, it is doubtful that *Unfaithfully Yours* would have been the successful film that Rex needed. Preston Sturges was already past his peak; his hand as a director no longer seems so firm. He died in 1959.

When Rex and Lilli returned from their brief holiday with the Culvers they did not remain in Los Angeles for long. On August 12th 1948 they boarded a TWA flight for New York and went on from there to Paris where Lilli was to make a film. Rex planned only to return to New York when required to begin rehearsals for *Anne of the Thousand Days*. At Los Angeles airport waiting newsmen asked the Harrisons to comment on rumours of their impending separation. The denial was total, and in unison. It was, they insisted, 'Certainly not true.' Rex and Lilli gave no indication that they were planning to leave the West coast for good, although only three days after their departure an announcement appeared in the *Los Angeles Times* which suggested otherwise. '1948's Finest Auction Event by Catalogue' was hardly discreet, being dominated by a picture of Rex on one side and Lilli on the other. The text explained that the sale would include 'furnishings from the Home of Mr and Mrs Rex Harrison (Lilli Palmer). Renowned Motion Picture Stars.' It concluded, unconvincingly, 'Mr and Mrs Harrison are redecorating their Mandeville Canyon home in the furnishings they have recently received from England, hence this sale of their furnishings.'

Rex claims that Fox gave him leave of absence to appear in *Anne of the Thousand Days* while Lilli asserts that he bought himself out of his contract. That Rex was not to work for that studio again for fifteen years indicates that the contract was terminated, an arrangement desirable for both parties.

The Hollywood press refused to let the Landis affair fade away and continued to attack Rex even after the incident ceased to dominate the front pages. Gossip columnists accused Rex of being unfeeling towards the dead woman, assuming that his rigid silence on the matter indicated indifference rather than good taste. What the Hollywood columnists, particularly Louella Parsons and Hedda Hopper, wanted and expected from Harrison was a public confession of his grief over Carole's death and a few tears. They got neither. Nor did Rex go to them like a penitent schoolboy, which might have prompted them to welcome him back into their fold.

Rex saw that the only way to keep his sanity was to leave Hollywood and he was fortunate that Leland Hayward and Maxwell Anderson remained staunchly behind him, still insisting that he should play Henry VIII on Broadway. The trip with Lilli to Paris proved to be the best therapy, and while Lilli worked on the film *Hans le Marin* with Jean-Pierre Aumont, who also wrote the screenplay, Rex was escorted around Paris by Aumont's brother-in-law Jean Roy, a Resistance war hero, who managed to keep the actor from brooding. Far from being indifferent to the fate of Carole Landis, Rex was tortured by her tragic death and a nagging feeling that he might have been able to save her.

Lilli's work completed, it was time for them to travel to New York for Rex to begin rehearsals for *Anne of the Thousand Days*. Deborah Kerr had originally been approached to play Anne Boleyn but when she proved unavailable Joyce Redman, fresh from the Old Vic's brilliant seasons at the New Theatre in London and the Century Theatre in New York, was chosen for the role. She recalls her first meeting with Rex Harrison. 'I met him at the first rehearsal. He was a terribly attractive man with wonderful manners, which you don't get an awful lot in the theatre. He was absolutely charming and always behaved marvellously with me. Everyone said, "Oh, watch out – he'll do this, he'll do that." But I never had any trouble whatsoever.'

Rex was understandably wary of the reception that he would receive in New York. Joyce Redman recalls Rex's attitude during rehearsals. 'It was naturally a big comeback for Rex, especially after all the bad publicity he had had with the Carole Landis thing. He was nervous; he didn't know how he was going to be received. I heard someone pointing out to him during rehearsal one day, "Bad publicity is good publicity – the best. As long as they are talking about you."'

Rex immersed himself in his work, trying to ignore the barbs that were still being sent from Hollywood. As well as this pressure from outside, rehearsals were unexpectedly fraught. The play, originally written in three acts, proved more coherent in two, and the opening had to be delayed on account of various problems with the scenery. The set changes proved to be totally unworkable, as Joyce Redman continues, 'The scenery was on a round and it didn't work properly. It had to be thrown out at great cost and Jo Mielziner was brought in to make one set.' In the resulting tension, 'Rex and Leland Hayward had terrible rows. I remember once Rex and Leland had a screaming match with Rex saying, "I'll sue you!"'

The original director was Bretaigne Windust who had just directed Bette Davis in two films, *Winter Meeting* and *June Bride*. He was sacked and replaced by H. C. Potter, another film director, who had guided Loretta Young through her Oscar-winning performance in *The Farmer's Daughter* the previous year and who now set about trying to restore some balance to the company. Joyce Redman remembers the efforts made to save the play, 'Potter was extraordinarily nice and I liked him enormously and thought he was a great director. I think he did some good things. And they brought people like Joshua Logan in;

they do this all the time when they haven't got faith in their own integrity.'

Despite the pressures Joyce Redman recalls that Rex came through it admirably. 'He was absolutely marvellous. He took the whole thing in his stride and had he looked more like Henry he would have been absolutely phenomenal. His face was never padded – only his bulk – which was a shame.'

On arrival in Philadelphia, where the play tried out, Rex gave an interview from his room at the Warwick Hotel. Having bottled up his feelings regarding Hollywood's recent treatment of him, he now took the opportunity to air his views on the film colony.

'So far as I am concerned Hollywood is done with. It took me three years to find out that I don't like anything about it, but I'm a big boy now and know the facts of life. Hollywood and I have no future in common and I don't know if Hollywood has any future of its own at all. It's top-heavy in its internal and financial economy; it is so egocentric it doesn't know the rest of the world exists, and its social life is one of simply incredible, preposterous boredom.

'It was, I think, the terms on which life is personally conducted in the film world which finally fed me up. It's all the same party in a different room, over and over and over. The caste system, based on the hilarious thesis that his salary is the index of a person's worth, is more rigid than anything India ever dreamed of. Hollywood's whole little world is geared to the studio salary list and unless your friends are in your brackets, you can't afford to know them. Me, I've had enough of it.

'I had been an actor all my life until I fell into the film mantrap where I had no business, and now I'd like to resume my bowing acquaintance with the legitimate theater. This is my first gesture in that direction and I hope there will be more. Besides, I hear great things about the film industry in England and France, where although they may never achieve the resources or technique of Hollywood, there is at least some trace of intellectual integrity and idea of what realism means.

'One of the great handicaps from which American films suffer is their inhibition by various minority pressure groups, religious organisations and special causes, many of them with no validity or possible reason for existence. By the time a film has been conditioned to the special prejudices of all these specialised cranks there is very little left of it at all.'

While much of Rex's outburst was valid, the editor of the *Hollywood Reporter* leapt to the defence of the film capital and launched a fresh series of personal attacks on Rex Harrison by the press, which his provocative action was bound to produce:

In all the years we have been covering the Hollywood front, we don't remember any actor, foreign or domestic, who breached so many rules of good taste in his conduct among his fellow workers, as did Mr Rex Harrison, the British actor, during his over-two-year stay in our midst. Consequently the pop-off uttered before the press of Philadelphia the other night is a little tough to take, particularly where it now appears doubtful that Mr Harrison will ever be given another Hollywood assignment. However, this situation pre-dated his blast at our town and its people.

Quoting part of Rex's attack, the editor described it as,

A dribbling from the big mouth of an actor, who should now realise that through his own actions he's washed himself up here, as he will be washed up ANYWHERE he goes should he continue the ingratitude he displayed while he was in Hollywood receiving the finest treatment that any visiting artist could be given . . . We doubt that Harrison's exposé of Hollywood will add to

his public appeal, nor will it contribute anything to the
success of the play he is doing for New York audiences.
We rather guess that he will soon be on his way back to
his dear old Britain, which is welcome to him . . .
We've had him and certainly want no more of his kind.

A further attack came from New York where journalist
Frank Conniff supported an outraged Hollywood. 'The
ripe scent of decadent grapes clings to the sour blast actor
Rex Harrison has trumpeted in the general direction of
Hollywood as a well-flushed chattel in the cinematic
vineyards . . . the British thespian has nudged the same
plaintive theme sounded by so many Hollywood failures
before him.' Quoting Rex's description of Hollywood's
social life being one of 'simply incredible, preposterous
boredom', he attacked Rex even more deeply,

Mr Harrison's last statement represents the height of
civilised ennui, considering that this ultimate contact
with Hollywood's 'social life' landed him before the
coroner during the investigation of Carole Landis's
tragic suicide. One might expect a man to share many
emotions in such a situation, but boredom is hardly
one of them . . . even his most ardent fans concede that
the chief factor responsible for Rex Harrison's troubles
in Hollywood was a fellow named Rex Harrison . . .
The suspicion arises that Mr Harrison discovered his
phobia against all things Hollywood only after his own
waverings had trapped him in trouble. The feeling of
distaste may be mutual, and I think Mr Harrison is
acutely aware of the fact . . .
Well, now we've got Rex Harrison. New York has
won him. I suppose we can expect a similar shredding
when he travels 3,000 miles farther and reaches his
native England.

Hedda Hopper summed up the hopes and belief of the
press more vividly and concisely when she added her

contribution, 'Rex Harrison's career is as dead as a mackerel.'

Meanwhile, *Anne of the Thousand Days* opened disastrously in Philadelphia in November 1948 with nothing in the production coming together; it seemed that if the press were out for Rex's blood he was being served up *'en croûte'*.

The clouds were not only gathering on Rex's professional front. While he rehearsed, Lilli returned to Los Angeles. Any pretence that the Harrisons were merely taking a leave of absence from the film capital was forgotten as Lilli put their Mandeville Canyon home up for sale. But the selling of the house proved more difficult than had been anticipated, and when a sale was finally agreed the house was sold at eighty-five thousand dollars, a loss of about thirty thousand dollars to Rex and Lilli. But they had resolved to leave Hollywood and they wanted no delays to keep them tied to the place for any longer than necessary. But if this loss was accepted by the Harrisons, it was unfortunately compounded. Their business manager pointed out that although the house had been sold, the mortgage had to be paid off. Furthermore, Rex and Lilli also owed large sums in back taxes. Their income had only been estimated over the previous two years, as was the common practice at the time, and the final tax demand, once calculated, amounted to thirty-five thousand dollars, to be paid in weekly instalments. Lilli left Hollywood for New York owing money rather than taking out the substantial sum that she and Rex had hoped for, and aware that neither of them could afford not to be working for a considerable time to come. Hollywood had taken its revenge.

Before her departure Lilli had one other task to accomplish. Carole Landis's photograph albums, which had previously proved too difficult to destroy, were still in the Mandeville Canyon house and clearly could not remain there. In a final act, Lilli and Rex's valet, Harry, burned them in the garden.

If Hollywood was now closed to the Harrisons, Rex's position in England was not particularly welcoming either. His alimony debts to Collette were such that she had appealed to the British courts, claiming arrears amounting to twenty-eight thousand dollars, as well as an entitlement of twenty-four thousand dollars a year maintenance. In an attempt to clear up his debts to Collette, Rex had made several payments in November, but his former wife now brought another action against him as he had not paid enough to clear what he owed.

When Lilli returned from Los Angeles her first concern was to find somewhere to live in New York, which seemed their likely future home. While Rex was performing in the out-of-town tryouts of *Anne of the Thousand Days* in Philadelphia and Baltimore, Lilli found a modest apartment on Central Park West and Carey, who was already showing signs of being a very bright boy, was admitted into the Lycée Français, a French-speaking school which was felt to be the most suitable for him. Throughout Carey's childhood Rex and Lilli always managed to keep their son far from the spotlight of their public lives.

Lilli had also been offered the chance to make her Broadway debut in a play by Jean-Pierre Aumont, translated for New York under the title *My Name Is Aquilon*. Aumont, a close friend of the Harrisons', would also be appearing in the play which was produced by the Playwrights' Company and Leland Hayward.

When Rex came into New York after the tryouts he at least returned to some semblance of a home life. Unfortunately, he had little to be confident about concerning the play which doggedly refused to take off and seemed to be heading towards inevitable failure. Rex badly needed a success. He just could not afford to be out of work and such was the worry of this that he developed a stomach ulcer, was admitted to hospital, and the New York opening had to be delayed.

The Playwrights' Company felt compelled to come to Rex's defence. They issued a statement claiming that Rex was being treated unfairly and that far from being unprofessional he was 'one of the most reasonable, understanding and talented players ever.'

The opening was now set for December 8th, and what seemed like a certain failure became an almost unanimous triumph. 'For some unknown reason', recalls Joyce Redman, 'on the first night all the strings pulled.' The play's stage manager, Scott Jackson, recalled, 'Rex just seemed to pick the play up in his arms like a baby – and carry it away with him.'

Most critics hailed the blank verse drama in glowing terms and Rex was highly praised for his performance. Ward Morehouse of the *New York Sun* wrote: 'His Henry is regal, and commanding-brusque, vain, lusty, humorful, a ruler given to anguish, self-analysis, to strutting and to roaring, but a man who is capable and likeable for all his bestiality,' while the play itself was described as 'robust and vivid'. Most reviewers noticed that Rex had managed to humanise his character, bringing to life a vital, vulnerable man rather than presenting a broad caricature of indulgence and gluttony, with another critic praising a 'penetrating performance that conveys the good humor, the boyish charm as well as the coarseness and cruelty of this perplexing monarch.'

E. Mawby Green, reporting for *Theatre World* in England, pointed to the play as one of the few productions that season which seemed, 'certain of staying around any length of time.' Of Rex and Joyce Redman he said: '. . . as Henry VIII and the second of his odd assorted wives, the ill-fated Anne Boleyn, . . . they make a brilliant team, pitting their passion against each other with heroic grandeur that so befits their royal character . . . His [Maxwell Anderson's] verse sings across the footlights sharp, clean, vivid and dramatic.'

Rex achieved a great personal success, displaying his talent and artistry, and it was to those – rather than rumour, innuendo and vindictive press – that the audience responded. He was more a victim in the eyes of ordinary people, and his courage in facing this pressure and still proving himself to be a remarkably fine performer could not but help win the public over to his side. Rex was gratified by the warmth of the reception he received and the crowds of people who would wait outside the stage door of the Shubert Theatre to applaud him as he left after each performance.

To cap this change in his fortunes, Rex received the 1948 Antoinette Perry Award (or 'Tony' as it is more familiarly known) for best actor. If Rex felt that justice had prevailed, the moment was made even sweeter by a marvellous twist of irony. The person who presented him with his award on that triumphant evening was no less than Hedda Hopper, who only months before had declared Rex's career to be 'as dead as a mackerel'.

Lilli's Broadway debut proved less spectacular than her husband's glorious return. *My Name Is Aquilon* had been a success in Paris but any worth it might have had was lost in translation. Lilli went through the same agonies as Rex when the play opened in Philadelphia, but it remained stubbornly lifeless and only survived for four weeks on Broadway. Rex had, meanwhile, settled into a long run and was beginning the slow process of replenishing the familial coffers.

Professionally Rex had achieved a notable success, but his marriage had never really recovered from the severe jolt that Rex's liaison with Carole Landis had given it. While there was no-one else in either of their lives, the marriage seemed more and more to be just a professional convenience. The efforts of Roland Culver and Jean-Pierre Aumont had little lasting effect. Rex himself recalled their marriage at this time, 'Our relationship . . . remained uneasy. For a while after coming back to me, Lilli had felt she was doing the right thing, the correct thing, and she had been wonderful. As time went on, recriminations naturally set in. I don't blame her at all, but it made life extremely uneasy and unhappy. Still, we struggled on.'

During this period much of their free time was spent with the Vincent Astors or, at weekends, with Maxwell Anderson and his wife who lived on Centre Island in upstate New York. Among those who lived in the same road were Helen Hayes, Kurt Weill and Alan Jay Lerner, who first met Rex at this time. 'Rex used to come up to Max's house at the weekend and we used to play a penny poker game. I saw them frequently and many times Lilli would stay over an extra day and I would give her a ride into New York with their little boy.'

Lerner, who was working on a musical with Kurt Weill, recalls a conversation one day when they were walking along the road:

'Kurt Weill said, "You know what I would love you to do, Alan? I would love you to do a proper English version of *The Threepenny Opera*."
   I said, "Who could play Mack the Knife?"
   And he said, "Rex."
   "Rex doesn't sing," I replied.
   "Yes he does."
   "How do you know?"
   He said, "I just know. He sings well enough for that."'

Nothing came of this proposed venture but, as the two men continued walking, Alan Jay Lerner viewed Rex in a new light. It would be some years before he was able to approach Rex with a proposition, but when he did it would be to collaborate on the high point in the careers of both men.

Rex continued in *Anne of the Thousand Days* until the traditional two-month summer break from the end of June. Money was still short for Rex and Lilli but they managed to scrape together enough to take a holiday, hoping that it might improve matters between them. At the suggestion of Lilli's former lover, Rolf Gérard, who now worked as a theatrical designer in New York, the couple decided to go to Santa Margherita on the west coast of northern Italy. Neither of them felt totally confident that a holiday together would be successful if they travelled alone, so they asked Gladys Cooper's daughter, Sally, and her stepson John Merivale, to accompany them.

Once in Italy, Rex and Lilli travelled along the coast by motorboat exploring the villages around the area within the Ligurian Sea. On one of these trips they discovered Portofino and were quickly captivated by its sleepy charm. So impressed was Rex that he made another trip there to explore it further, this time accompanied only by the boatman. The two men climbed up the hill behind the port and sat down at the top. The view from this spot was so breathtaking that Rex immediately resolved to buy the site and build a house. During the Second World War the Germans had demolished a house on the site so as to erect a gun emplacement there, taking advantage of the incredible view. All that now remained was the concrete platform on which the gun had stood, while the hillside around it had grown wild with neglect. Rex initially planned to pay for the land and the building of his house with money that he expected to receive for appearing in an Italian film. When that project fell through he and Lilli agreed to appear in a British film, *The Long Dark Hall*, a thriller scheduled to be made during the summer break from Broadway in the following year.

When they returned to New York Rex reopened in *Anne of the Thousand Days* while Lilli began preparations for her second Broadway appearance. Despite the failure of *My Name Is Aquilon*, Lilli herself had received mostly favourable notices and as a result she was now offered the part of Cleopatra in a new production of Shaw's *Caesar and Cleopatra*, opposite Cedric Hardwicke. On this occasion Lilli scored a great personal success and Mr and Mrs Rex Harrison were the toast of Broadway.

Anne of the Thousand Days resumed its run at the Shubert Theatre for only six weeks. It closed after two hundred and eighty-six performances, but due to the numerous setbacks and difficulties which had beset the play at the beginning, the production had not made any money, despite its reasonable run. As a gesture to Leland Hayward, Rex agreed to take the play on tour through the Mid-West and Canada.

Lilli stayed in New York, continuing her personal success in *Caesar and Cleopatra*. She persuaded Rex to join in a Sunday night charity performance in aid of the American National Theatre and Academy at the Ziegfeld Theatre on 29th January 1950. Rex appeared in Bernard Shaw's playlet *The Dark Lady of the Sonnets*, written in 1910 for a performance in aid of funds for establishing a National Theatre. Rex played William Shakespeare opposite Lilli as the Dark Lady, under Cedric Hardwicke's direction. Other contributors to the evening included Ruth Gordon, Raymond Massey, Ethel Barrymore and Jack Benny.

Rex now received an offer which indicated that it was not only Kurt Weill who felt he had a serviceable singing voice. Richard Rodgers and Oscar Hammerstein had adapted *Anna and the King of Siam* into a musical which they had called *The King and I*, and had clearly been impressed by Rex's portrayal of King Mongkut in the film. But Rex had committed himself to *The Long Dark Hall* in England and had also been asked to appear in the London production of T. S. Eliot's *The Cocktail Party* which was enjoying a successful run on Broadway with Alec Guinness. Rex reluctantly refused the Rodgers and Hammerstein offer leaving the path open to Yul Brynner to score an enduring triumph. Brynner repeated his role in the film version five years later and played the role on stage with continued success right up to his death. Rex's telegram to Brynner on the opening night read, 'The King is dead, long live the King.'

For *The Cocktail Party* Rex returned to England alone to begin rehearsals in April, joining a cast which included Margaret Leighton and Ian Hunter. Just before his departure, he made his acting debut on American television in *The Walking Stick*. His only other television appearance had been as a guest on *Saturday Night Revue*, again for NBC.

Rex travelled to England by sea. He was to play the Unidentified Guest in Eliot's poetical 'comedy', the psychiatrist figure who, with his team, leads the other characters into greater awareness of themselves and of others, and of their roles in life. Eliot presents a disturbing, bleak vision in which only two ways of life are possible. You can either accept and face your own and other people's limitations and lead life within the bounds that this awareness entails, or you can break free and devote yourself more selflessly to the human condition (as Celia, the character played by Margaret Leighton, does by nursing plague-stricken natives and dying in that cause). Whatever the chosen path, each only represents a varying degree of loneliness, and life becomes a matter of coping with that state by one means or another without ever conquering it. Eliot presents the social animal as only outwardly social: people are really more concerned with their own conception of themselves and similarly construct their view of the character and role of any other person only to suit themselves, interpreting other people within their own demands of that person and caring nothing beyond that.

It is an enigmatic play which prompted great debate as to its true significance. In the original production at the Edinburgh Festival before its New York run, Alec Guinness and Irene Worth emphasised the ethereal, abstract elements of the play, following the metre of Eliot's blank verse. But Rex and Margaret Leighton were inclined to approach it in a naturalistic style, which prompted some division among the critics when the play opened on May 3rd 1950 at the New Theatre in London, following its tryout at the King's Theatre in Southsea the week before.

Those who preferred the Guinness interpretation included the critic for the *Daily Telegraph* who wrote,

T. S. Eliot's *The Cocktail Party* when first produced at the Edinburgh Festival last year, gave me one of the most satisfying emotional experiences of my playgoing life. On the material plane it was puzzling at many points, but that somehow did not matter.

Few of the questions which were then raised are answered in the London production . . . Alec Guinness made the psychiatrist who is the play's central character a dedicated, possibly supernatural, being; and passages in Eliot's text seemed to bear him out . . .

There is no such suggestion in Rex Harrison's earthy playing of the Unknown Guest. He is no more than an eccentric scientist who has formed certain members of his London acquaintance into a sort of underground movement for bringing unhappy people out of their troubles.

He ended by echoing a famous beer advertisement of the time as he wrote, 'Which is right? Both readings will have their devotees, no doubt; but I am very certain that mine is, as they say, a Guinness.'

A. E. Wilson, of the *Star*, on the other hand, was full of praise for Rex. Being more reserved in his reaction to the play's pretensions, Rex's approach seemed to him to strike the right balance. He wrote:

But if the play does not enlighten it entertains and sometimes amuses, for it has frequent flashes of witty phrase as well as poetic expression. It is delightful to see the long absent Rex Harrison again. With his clear precise utterance, his amused quizzical air and his personal charm, he gives peculiar distinction to the part of the psychoanalyst.

Other critics saw the London production as more manageable for the average audience:

As now performed, the play seems to be clearer and more human . . . Alec Guinness played the doctor as a tight-lipped, chin-up, remote, exotic figure; Rex Harrison brings him right into the glossier end of Harley Street,

and described the first night as 'London's most brilliant theatrical occasion since the war'. Lilli, who had just returned from America, having finally completed her successful run on Broadway as Cleopatra, was in the audience. Rex was left in no doubt as to the emotional effect of the play, as he recalled, '. . . at the end of each performance the audience would sit numb and silent for quite a time before breaking into applause, and after they had filed out I used to go back to my dressing room and stare at myself in the mirror, feeling that I'd been sitting for several hours in a tepid bath.'

With Lilli's return, following their enforced separation, and their pleasure in planning the construction of their new home in Portofino, the state of their marriage appeared to have improved. Beyond this, they were now about to appear together in a film for the first time since *The Rake's Progress*. However, *The Long Dark Hall* was not an auspicious reunion. Rex had been too anxious to secure the finance to begin building their Portofino home to look at this proposed film with his usual care and his negligence proved regrettable. The film, an inferior thriller, remain one of the worst in his career. Shooting began at Nettlefold Studios in Walton-on-Thames on July 10th. Directed by Reginald Beck and Anthony Bushell, it had a screenplay by American writer Nunnally Johnson based on an Edgar Lustgarten novel. The cast also included Raymond Huntley and, in a small part, Tom Macaulay, Rex's friend from the time when they had both been struggling young actors in London in the early thirties and had shared a flat together. By the time it opened – almost unnoticed – in London the following February, Rex and Lilli were firmly established in a

Broadway hit – John Van Druten's comedy *Bell, Book and Candle*.

Rex and Lilli had been looking around for possible plays and it was Lilli to whom *Bell, Book and Candle* was submitted. The play centred on Gillian Holroyd, an attractive young witch living in Murray Hill in present-day New York, who casts a spell over a handsome publisher, Shepherd Henderson, so that he falls in love with her. This act is done out of revenge against an old college friend of Gillian's, but her scheme backfires when she finds that she is in love with Henderson herself and consequently loses her magic powers.

Margaret Sullavan, as well as Lilli Palmer, had read the initial script and had turned it down, thereby prompting its author, John Van Druten, to withdraw it. However, Irene Mayer Selznick, daughter of Louis B. Mayer and former wife of film producer David O. Selznick, asked Van Druten if he would allow her to read it. Irene Selznick had been making a name for herself as a Broadway producer, not least for the enormously successful first production of Tennessee Williams's *A Streetcar Named Desire*, with Marlon Brando and Jessica Tandy. After such an auspicious debut, Irene was at a loss as to what her next venture should be, but upon reading *Bell, Book and Candle*, felt that this was it, although she wanted certain changes in the script. In particular, she felt that the acts of witchcraft in the play should be toned down so that they were not so realistic as to spoil the essential lightness of the piece. This newly-modified script was again rejected by Margaret Sullavan, as well as Claudette Colbert. Lilli Palmer, however, said yes.

The casting of the principal male character, Shepherd Henderson, still remained. The role had been turned down by just about every suitable actor, feeling that the Gillian Holroyd character so dominated the play that the part of the publisher remained too obviously a secondary role. Recognising this problem, Van Druten, who would also direct, set about strengthening the Henderson part, while Irene Selznick nursed hopes that Lilli might be able to arouse Rex's interest in playing the part.

During their summer break, while overseeing the building of their home in Portofino, now well on the way towards completion, Rex was finally persuaded. He had been working on a play called *The Next Lord Chase*, for production in England, but finding that his inspiration was not being fired he agreed to appear in *Bell, Book and Candle*, although only for three months. As a result he had to forgo appearing in a film which was to prove memorable for another distinguished British actor. Anthony Kimmins had written an original screenplay entitled *The Captain's Paradise*, concerning the adventures of the captain of the Gibraltar ferry who has a wife at home and a mistress in Tangier. Kimmins had fashioned the role of the captain with Rex in mind, but as the eventual star of the film, Alec Guinness, says, 'I was lucky when it was found that Rex wasn't free to do the film and it came my way.'

Although Rex and Lilli had starred in successful Broadway runs during the previous season, *Bell, Book and Candle* marked their first appearance on stage together (barring their one-night appearance in Shaw's *Dark Lady of the Sonnets*) since *No Time For Comedy* in London in 1941, when Lilli had appeared in a supporting role before they were married. Now, as husband and wife, they would appear opposite each other, a combination which fulfilled Irene Selznick's wildest hopes.

But despite her enthusiasm, Irene was 'scared to death of Rex Harrison, who had a reputation for being difficult.' When Rex and Lilli arrived in New York to begin rehearsals Irene's fears at first seemed to be justified, as she recalled:

'Rehearsals didn't take off at a great clip. Everybody was intimidated by Rex, John included. Rex, meanwhile, groped around as though he had never read the play. It took John a few days to figure out what he was up to. Rex would worry a single line over and over, writhing and shuddering, oblivious to everything else, until he got it just right. It was the purest concentration John had ever seen and the results were brilliant. John may have been finicky but Rex was meticulous. It became obvious that these two urbane Englishmen understood theatre the same way.'

Lilli became acutely aware of her own shortcomings when matched against her husband, finding it difficult to play light comedy, particularly in a foreign language. She said in an interview just after the New York opening, 'We rehearsed scenes we'd do together for this play, and that was a rare delight. Rex is an old hand at comedy, and I'm a newcomer, so he really worked me. We rehearsed when we ate, when we walked, when he shaved and when I dressed. He can bring any scene to life the minute he steps into it.'

With the rest of the cast, Jean Adair, Scott McKay and Larry Gates, Rex and Lilli began the out-of-town tryouts in New Haven where the play still did not work as well as was hoped. Moving on to Boston, following some minor alterations and a script change at the end of the second act, the play settled down. When the company reached New York, opening at the Ethel Barrymore Theatre on November 14th 1950, Rex and Lilli were greeted enthusiastically by the public and critics alike, despite certain reservations about the play. The critic for *Variety* wrote, 'The couple, as a sort of junior Alfred Lunt and Lynn Fontanne, play with deft, disarming assurance, providing the principal vitality to a whimsy that starts engagingly, but presently fades into innocuous banalities,' a view which John Chapman, in the *News*, shared, '. . . most of it is good, naughty fun and Miss Palmer and Mr Harrison play it lightly and delightfully . . . The first two acts are the best, and by the third act, when Miss Palmer has been reduced to mere humanity, Mr Van Druten seems to have run out of invention. But there is enough in the whole play, what with the acting and some nice, smart lines, to make *Bell, Book and Candle* a very enjoyable seance.'

The love scenes played by Rex and Lilli were commented upon by both critics; *Variety*'s critic described them as being 'played with diverting realism', while John Chapman wrote, in rather more down-to-earth style, '. . . Mr Harrison and Miss Palmer fall into clutches and onto couches with such ease, and do such real meat-and-potatoes jobs of kissing, that it is reassuring to know that they are married in real life. Most co-stars don't like each other that much.' The *New York Times* described it as 'completely enchanting – a wonderfully suave and impish fancy' and it was the key-note of all the reviews that the charming playing of Rex and Lilli made the evening such a success. *Bell, Book and Candle* joined a vintage Broadway season that already boasted such productions as *Call Me Madam* with Ethel Merman and *South Pacific* with Mary Martin.

Rex was happy to be working with his wife and he said at the time, 'It's ideal . . . When Lilli works and I don't, she comes home exhausted and I want to go out. Now we're both exhausted together.' Publicly and privately Rex and Lilli's marriage appeared stable and happy. In their New York apartment, along with Carey and his new governess, Mademoiselle Mayer, they had the housekeeper, Charlotte, and Rex's valet, Harry. Playing in *Bell, Book and Candle* all through the week, Rex and Lilli had very little time to themselves, but away from the theatre they tried to devote as much time as possible to Carey. On Sundays they would take him out and, whenever possible, would spend the weekend out of the city with friends. Carey, after initial difficulties at the Lycée, was now fluent in French, having had the additional benefit of a French governess.

Rex and Lilli could look forward to their first holiday together in their newly completed home in Portofino the following summer and intended to leave for Italy after

June 2nd 1951, which marked their final performance in *Bell, Book and Candle*. Irene Selznick was fully aware that they would not play beyond that date and had solemnly promised not to plead with them to stay, even though the play was still showing to capacity houses.

During their run in the play Lilli even found time to appear in her own television show, produced by Charles Kebbe, a television director and the husband of Lilli's sister Hilde. In this fifteen-minute chat show broadcast every Thursday in New York, following its first appearance on January 4th 1951, Lilli would entertain the viewers by singing, talking and interviewing friends. On the first show she described her only meeting with George Bernard Shaw, just prior to appearing in *Caesar and Cleopatra*, and she played a recording of his voice. She followed that with a recital of a poem by the Greek poet Euripides and ended with a discussion on ghosts in Britain with actress Pamela Brown. At a time when most television fare was trivial and gossipy, Lilli's show was hailed as refreshingly witty and literate, prompting the show to be extended to Chicago and Philadelphia with plans to expand further and cover the full CBS network. As a result Lilli's fame spread. Her stage and film appearances had exposed her to only a limited number of people and the public at large only really knew her as the wife of Rex Harrison. Now she became a familiar face in people's homes, and she ensured the show's continuing quality by devoting many hours a week to preparing each programme.

However, Lilli's increasing activity prompted a feeling of restlessness in Rex. Never comfortable being alone, Lilli's new commitment and the effort it required on her part left Rex unwillingly neglected. Lilli's work regimen became so intense that she had less and less time for her husband. She began writing scripts herself in what little remained of her time and her life became even more awesomely organised than ever before.

Lilli allowed herself nine hours sleep a night and then

filled Monday to Saturday with occupations of some kind, mainly, as she admitted herself, for commercial reasons although she painted for pleasure when time allowed. Sunday was reserved for Rex and Carey, although even there her will to organise herself surfaced. As a mother she was stern but devoted, as she explained in an interview at the time.

'I love children when they're newly born, still steaming as it were, but when they get to be two or three I can be just as bored and irritated by them as if they were boring adults. That's why I made an agreement with my son while he was still a baby. I told him, 'I shall give you a wonderful childhood, as I had myself: but in return I shall demand *complete* obedience. Every order I give, I shall explain, but you must obey me at once' . . . As a result, I have never had any trouble with Carey . . . When I tell him it's time for bed he never whines for five minutes – he *goes* to bed. Discipline? I've never had to use any. I really think that, at seven, Carey's a highly civilised little human being.'

The difference in Rex's and Lilli's temperaments was always commented on or noticed by their friends and is exemplified by their behaviour together in a restaurant. While Lilli would give her order to the waiter instantly, Rex would agonise over the menu for ten minutes before making an uneasy decision. In terms of hobbies they also tended to go their separate ways, with the exceptions of riding and tennis. Rex's great passion remained fishing, which Lilli hated. This conflict was, however, solved by Lilli accompanying her husband armed with her easel and paints so that she could occupy herself with her painting while Rex fished. Even their musical tastes remained distinct, with Rex's devotion to swing and jazz music continuing while Lilli preferred classical music.

The impression that prevailed at this time was that Lilli wore the trousers both at home and abroad, although she would always deny it. A friend has a vivid memory from this period of the Harrisons together. 'She always seemed to be irritated or mad about something and he was always explaining. I have a sort of mental image of Lilli yelling and Rex jumping.' But if people tended to point out the character differences between the Harrisons and thereby question the stability of the marriage, it was a topic on which neither Rex nor Lilli would be drawn, both insisting that all was well between them and that their common love of the theatre was more than enough of a bond.

Situated fifteen hundred feet above sea-level, the house at Portofino was just below the crest of the hill so that it did not mar the sky-line, and consisted of two wings which ran parallel with the side of the hill it nestled in. Labour being cheap in Italy at the time, the limited amount of money that Rex and Lilli had to spend on the house proved adequate to provide them with a very comfortable home and they spent an idyllic summer planning how to develop the surrounding land which allowed plenty of room for vineyards and gardens. Portofino was still an undiscovered little fishing village at that time, with a population of about eight hundred. But with the arrival of Rex and Lilli all this began to change. During their first summer there the Harrisons entertained Benita and Ronald Colman, and Alexander Korda's yacht could be found moored in the harbour.

At the end of the summer, Rex and Lilli travelled to London where Laurence Olivier offered them the opportunity to play together again on Broadway in Christopher Fry's *Venus Observed*, a modern comedy in verse, which Olivier himself was to direct. Olivier had commissioned the play directly after the enormous success in London at the Globe of Fry's *The Lady's Not For Burning* with John Gielgud as Thomas Mendip and Richard Burton and Claire Bloom in their West End debuts. Olivier had appeared in the role of the Duke of Altair in this new play which marked his first production as actor-manager of the St James's Theatre, opening on January 18th 1950 and running for seven months. Olivier now offered Rex the Duke and Lilli the role of Perpetua, the daughter of the Duke's agent. They were pleased to accept. There could hardly be a more auspicious vehicle in which to return to Broadway.

Meanwhile, the Harrisons had to fulfil another commitment. A few months after they had opened in *Bell, Book and Candle* Stanley Kramer had asked Rex and Lilli to appear in his film version of Jan de Hartog's *The Four-poster*, which was to be made in Hollywood. They had agreed, although not without considerable thought since Rex was still disdainful of the treatment that he had not long before received in the film capital.

Kramer also felt twinges of doubt, especially after the unfavourable reaction in Hollywood when he announced the casting. He went so far as to telephone Rex and Lilli's New York agent to ask him to find out if Lilli would be prepared to make the film opposite an actor other than her husband. The answer was firmly 'no'.

Rex's return to Hollywood was not altogether triumphant. *The Four-poster* was neither a major production nor did it strictly involve a major Hollywood studio, Stanley Kramer being essentially an independent producer who specialised in modestly budgeted films and whose most notable success had been the Western *High Noon* which had brought Gary Cooper his second Oscar. In 1951 Kramer had been forced, for financial reasons, to ally himself with Columbia Pictures, although working as an autonomous unit under the studio banner. He was a pioneering independent producer but unfortunately his productions at this time were not generally the sort to attract a mass audience and most of them lost money even though tightly budgeted.

The production schedule was unusually short, beginning on 17th September 1951 and lasting only three weeks. Rex and Lilli based themselves in a rented house on the ocean at Santa Monica. The method of production was decidedly unorthodox, more suited to a theatrical presentation than to a film. Every scene was fully rehearsed and then the film was shot straight through, a practice which did not help Rex and Lilli to deliver performances that completely satisfied them. Both the actors and technicians remained in a continual state of confusion since it proved almost impossible to recall all that had been planned and rehearsed, and Rex later described the filming as 'a horrible experience' due to the lack of opportunity to prepare for a scene once shooting had started.

No attempt was made to expand the play for the cinema, the entire action taking place in the bedroom of John and Abby Edwards, tracing their life together in eight episodes from their wedding night in 1897 to the death of the surviving partner forty-five years later. Any action outside the bedroom was presented in the form of cartoons drawn by the UPA studio (creators of Mr Magoo) with Rex and Lilli shown in caricature form, presenting a long cruise on which the couple embark, conveying the growth of the neighbourhood and such major events as the First World War, in which they lose their son. The couple also have a daughter and, at one point, Rex's character goes off with another woman, but none of these other characters is introduced to the audience. *The Four-poster* was that rare cinematic breed – a two-hander.

The film was tolerably well received by the critics but was by no means a great success. And Rex's involvement precluded him from a more interesting production. Gabriel Pascal had been preparing a film version of Shaw's *Androcles and the Lion*, to be made for Howard Hughes at the RKO studios in Hollywood. As Pascal's original choice to play Julius Caesar, Rex had signed to play the part before starting work on *The Four-poster*; however, Pascal's project suffered various set-backs (including the replacement of Harpo Marx with Alan Young in the part of Androcles) and by the time it was ready to

go before the cameras Rex was committed to Stanley
Kramer. Maurice Evans, the British-born actor more celebrated on Broadway, replaced him.

During their stay in Hollywood, Rex and Lilli spent
much of their time with old friends, among them the
Ronald Colmans, the Tyrone Powers and the Douglas
Fairbankses. Unlike the press, the Hollywood establish-
ment did not ignore them. Jack L. Warner invited them to
an elaborate party in honour of Charles de Gaulle's
brother, Pierre. Here Rex introduced Lilli to a tall young
Argentinian actor named Carlos Thompson, who was a
friend of and had acted with Juanita Sujo, a contemporary of Lilli's as a drama student in Berlin. While Rex went
his own way, Lilli and Carlos Thompson enjoyed a
pleasant evening talking about their mutual friend.

Following completion of *The Four-poster* Rex and Lilli
headed East to prepare for *Venus Observed*. Since Broadway was becoming a regular destination for the couple
they decided to take a mortgage on a small flat overlooking the East River, near Gracie Square, rather than continue to rent accommodation. Life settled into the pattern
established during the run of *Bell, Book and Candle*. Lilli
began another season of her television show and the two
of them went into rehearsals for *Venus Observed* under the
direction of Laurence Olivier. Harrison and Olivier, who
had not previously worked together, struck up a good
working relationship despite certain conflicts over their
separate interpretations of the role of the Duke, a natural
occurrence, particularly since Olivier had only recently
played the role himself. But any slight disagreements
only encouraged a creative atmosphere and Rex found
Olivier, 'a marvellous director [who] gave me a great deal
of help.'

Rex's role as the Duke of Altair perfectly suited him. He
played a man who, having reached middle-age, decides
that it is time for him to marry. It is a lyrical piece, rich in
imagery and light humour and Rex enjoyed the challenge
of another verse play, although one that was totally

different from *The Cocktail Party*, with its much sparer lines. Unfortunately, the Broadway production was presented under less than ideal conditions. *Venus Observed* is an intimate play requiring a small theatre, like the St James's, to bring it across at its best. The Shuberts, who were producing the play in New York, insisted on putting it into the enormous and totally unsuitable New Century Theatre, where it remained despite the pleas of Rex and Olivier for a smaller theatre. This added the further complication that the sets, designed by Roger Furse for the London production and brought over to New York, had to be adapted to fit this far larger stage.

The company moved to Philadelphia on February 7th 1952 for the play's out-of-town tryout and then returned to Broadway where they opened on February 13th. Despite the difficulties of the verse dialogue, both for the actors and the audience, the play and Rex's performance were generally favourably received. *Variety*'s reviewer wrote:

> Whether or not he [Rex] fully understands everything Fry is getting at, he gives the impression of doing so. And what's more important, he gives the playgoer the illusion, however temporary, that he too grasps what it's all about . . . Nearly always it is saved by Harrison's magnetic, elucidating performance in the principal role.

John Chapman, in the *News*, wrote of the play;

> It is the best and most enjoyable of the Fry pieces I've seen and is deftly performed by a company which includes Rex Harrison, John Williams, Lilli Palmer, John Merivale, Hurd Hatfield and Eileen Peel.
> . . . Right now I am in no mood to quibble over what Fry was driving at all the time; the main thing is that *Venus Observed* is literate, prankish, often frolicsome, generally entertaining, imaginative and frequently

beautiful in its poetry. It is a fantasy, but as it is directed by Laurence Olivier and played by a good cast, it has a down-to-earth quality . . . Harrison and Miss Palmer speak their portions lightly and brightly and are, as always, very attractive stage people.

The production, although it clearly had much of worth in it, was not destined for great commercial success and it closed on April 26th after only eighty-six performances.

With only a short period before Rex and Lilli would be making what was to become their customary pilgrimage back to their haven in Portofino, Rex did not embark on another project, although Lilli continued to present her television show, preparing it with her customary thoroughness.

Rex and Lilli led an active social life in New York, being invited to many of the most important parties of the season. Among their acquaintances were the Duke and Duchess of Windsor. The Duke now drifted around the higher social circles of the world, often hiring himself out as a guest to the highest bidder among those who wished to bask in the remaining glow of his slightly tarnished royalty. And when Rex and Lilli, along with eight-year-old Carey, journeyed back to Portofino, the Duke and the Duchess of Windsor were among their visitors.

In that summer of 1952, Roland and Nan Culver joined the Harrisons as their house guests and Ronald and Benita Colman once again made a welcome appearance. When the Windsors moored their hired yacht in the harbour Rex and Lilli invited them to dinner. They arrived accompanied by their own guest, Woolworth heir Jimmy Donohue, a close confidant of the Duchess. Rex and Lilli were aghast at the Windsors' insistence on total recognition of royal status, and their refusal to allow any lapse in protocol even when they were entertained in a private house. It was an attitude which made it uncomfortable not only for their host and hostess, but also for other guests. The Duke expected other guests to stand when he did and, in greeting him, he expected a curtsey from the ladies present and a nod from the gentlemen, a formality which Benita Colman, who was staying with Rex and Lilli at the time, resolutely refused to comply with. Since the Duke had renounced the throne he had therefore, in her view, lost any entitlement to such singular treatment. The Duke's insistence on sitting at the head of the dining table was only reluctantly conceded by Rex, particularly since such a formality was often nullified by the Duke's previous insistence on handing round a tray of hors d'œuvres, an action that struck Rex as singularly unbefitting a royal personage, whether the possessor of a throne or not.

At the same time as the Windsors' visit, Greta Garbo visited Portofino accompanied by her constant escort, George Schlee, the wandering husband of the famed Russian-born couturier Valentina, who often designed for Lilli. Garbo and Schlee spent a great deal of time up at the villa, enabling Rex to get to know this fascinating woman quite well. He discovered her to be very shy and inclined to changing moods which could appear without any warning. Rex would occasionally walk with her as she wandered about the farm tracks behind the villa, enjoying their conversations together while admiring her great beauty.

Garbo had by this time retired from the screen for over ten years but the myth that she had created around herself still flourished. Far from wanting to be alone, Garbo simply wanted to choose with whom she would spend her time, and Rex and Lilli were among those whose company she enjoyed. The Harrisons entertained an almost continuous stream of guests during that summer, their other visitors including John Gielgud, Mary and John Mills, and Jean-Pierre Aumont who now found Rex and Lilli staunch supporters in his own time of need, having lost his wife, film star Maria Montez, in the previous year, from a heart attack at the tragically early age of thirty-two. Aumont recalled his visits there in his autobiography and presented an acute picture of Rex and Lilli together there:

> 'Each summer Lilli Palmer and Rex Harrison invited my daughter and me to Portofino . . . Lilli was as precise and controlled as Rex was dreamy, naive, and impressionable . . . I can never keep from laughing when I see my friend Rex billed as "sexy Rexy". I can believe that he is sexy. His numerous conquests have proved it. But after seeing his day-to-day life for five summers in a row, I think of Rex more as a little boy, often stammering, throwing tantrums and hiding in corners so that he can do what has been forbidden.'

For Aumont, Rex is a man of conflicting passions which continually battle with each other, '. . . a grand egotist, delightfully tyrannical, in love with himself as Napoleon was with Bonaparte, drunk with independence, then pausing abruptly in the midst of one of his escapades to think of the wife he has just abandoned, crying and ashamed of his own feelings . . .'

Despite the success of their Portofino home, one problem had proved insurmountable. The house was built in a marvellous position overlooking the harbour, but no one had really considered how to reach it. Such inaccessibility was part of the attraction. The local authorities refused to grant the Harrisons permission to build a proper road right up to the house, preferring the mule track which was already there to remain. As a result, the last leg of the journey up to the villa had to be negotiated in an old army jeep which remained the only vehicle other than a mule which was capable of traversing the primitive track successfully. Despite this drawback it was a true home for Rex and Lilli and by now had even acquired a name, 'San Genesio', after the little-known patron saint of actors, an idea suggested by Sir Max Beerbohm, the expatriate author and humorist, shortly before his death.

While at Portofino, Rex had an offer from the Theatre Guild of New York to appear in Peter Ustinov's new comedy *The Love of Four Colonels*. The project interested him and he agreed to travel to London to see the production in which Ustinov himself was appearing at Wyndhams Theatre with Moira Lister. There was also a part in the play for Lilli and having seen Ustinov's production, Rex decided to accept the Guild's offer on behalf of both of them. Rex was also engaged to direct the play which was a comedy concerning four Colonels – American, British, French and Russian – based in a four-power zone in Germany, who are persuaded by the Devil, disguised in a black cloak, to accompany him to a deserted old castle where they are each given the chance to awaken a Sleeping Beauty. Each Colonel sees the Beauty as the ideal of his own country: the Frenchman sees her as an eighteenth-century courtesan, the Russian as a brooding Chekhovian heroine, the Englishman as an Elizabethan virgin and the American as a gangster's moll in a down-at-heel night club, with each sequence parodying respectively Restoration comedy, Chekhov, Shakespeare and modern American drama. The play ends with all four Colonels having failed to awaken the Beauty.

Prior to embarking on rehearsals for *The Love of Four Colonels*, Rex and Lilli made another television appearance in New York when they appeared together in the first show in the *Omnibus* series, written and presented by Alistair Cooke for CBS TV, and broadcast on November 9th 1952. In this first edition of what was to become a long-running and successful series dealing with the arts which continued until 1956, the program included extracts from *The Mikado*, an adaptation of a William Saroyan story, as well as a short play written by Maxwell Anderson entitled *The Trial of Anne Boleyn*, derived from his play *Anne of the Thousand Days*. Rex reprised his interpretation of Henry VIII, this time playing opposite Lilli as Anne Boleyn.

On all fronts, whether it be film, stage or television

work, Rex and Lilli were appearing almost exclusively as a team. They even made a guest appearance as themselves in a film entitled *Main Street To Broadway* made for the purpose of promoting the theatre. In this flimsy tale of a young playwright's attempts to succeed on Broadway Rex and Lilli were seen walking along 44th Street discussing a three-decker sandwich and the problems of eating it. The other guest stars included Tallulah Bankhead, Ethel and Lionel Barrymore, Mary Martin, Rodgers and Hammerstein, and John Van Druten, but despite their participation the film quickly disappeared.

The Love of Four Colonels opened on January 15th 1953 at the Shubert Theatre in New York with Rex playing the Devil to Lilli's Beauty. The cast also included Larry Gates, Leueen McGrath and Robert Coote, who played the English Colonel, while Rex had chosen Rolf Gérard to design the settings and costumes.

Personal tragedy struck Rex during the play when his mother died. His father had died three years before and his mother had already suffered three heart attacks. When the telegram came informing Rex of her death he showed no outward emotion, but for him it was the greatest possible loss for he had adored her. Whether it was linked or not, from that moment on Rex never smoked another cigarette although previously he had been getting through six or seven packets a day, rarely finishing a cigarette but invariably with one in his hand.

Under this cloud, Rex carried on working and when the play opened it was in a considerably altered form from the London production. Rex had asked Ustinov to make certain changes and had excised forty-five minutes from the play's running time in order to structure it into two acts as opposed to the three in London. Some reviewers felt this was detrimental to the play but, despite some reservations by the critics as to the play itself, Rex's debut as a director was a modest success and as usual his performance was singled out for praise. The reviewer in *Variety* wrote, 'If there was any doubt of it before, *Colonels* should establish Harrison as the most expert and ingratiating light comedian today . . . he picks up the show from his initial entrance and gives it an electric quality whenever he's on thereafter.' The critic for the *Herald Tribune* saw the play as a 'light-hearted, random, and often quite puzzling improvisation' and he continued,

It is also a fairly chaotic conceit, ideologically muddy, structurally ragged, furiously unselective . . . The over-all tone is uneven and perhaps still unformed: there are awkward shifts between revue-sketch humour and the elegance of good manners comedy . . . This reviewer found himself tiring of its increasingly frantic burlesques a good while before the final curtain.

But Rex's contribution was singled out as among the rewards of the evening,

There are . . . adroit performances from Rex Harrison and Lilli Palmer as Devil and Sleeping Beauty. Mr Harrison has a good bit of fun with his impersonations of a battered jailbird, a gouty Parisian cuckold, and a tongue-twisting Elizabethan fool. His more casual moments are perhaps unduly mannered – there is a heavy dose of artifice in his lolling over a conference table – but in the evening's later moments he pops his head through a theater curtain with rakish cajolery and brightens many a faltering line.

Rex's performance earned him the Resistol Gold Hat Award in February 1953, while Ustinov received the Critics Award for Best Foreign Play of 1953. The play continued until the Broadway summer break, closing on May 16th after one hundred and forty-one performances.

The summer was again spent at Portofino where Rex and Lilli's house guests were now Robert Coote, John

Merivale and also Noël Coward and Graham Payn, who remained at the villa while Rex and Lilli attended the Venice Film Festival for five days, where Lilli received the award for Best Actress for her performance in *The Four-poster*, which had finally been released late in 1952.

For the first time, their lifestyle in Portofino showed signs of division. Rex was beginning to grow tired of the continual social life of large dinner parties, the key-note of their stays there, feeling rather out of gatherings where Italian or other foreign languages were often spoken. Even the Duke of Windsor would go into a corner with Lilli and speak German with her and sing German songs. For this particular summer, Rex purposely invited Robert Coote and John Merivale in order to provide himself with the type of company in which he could relax. Lilli, able to speak several European languages fluently, was in her element with their dinner parties but as Rex explained in his autobiography:

> I needed a little buffer, and these two friends of mine provided me with a change of pace. They both enjoyed the good things in life, but not necessarily in a social milieu. The three of us would go off to the port, drink far too much and laugh a lot, it was all very impromptu. Then we'd go back to the villa for a circumspect dinner. Since Lilli didn't drink, and was no companion to those who did, I tended always to invite friends of a cheerful disposition to stay.

Rex and Lilli were back in New York in September, reopening in *The Love of Four Colonels*. They had returned via England, to take Carey to his new school at Sunningdale in Berkshire. Rex felt that it was necessary for Carey's education as a proper Englishman that he should attend a boarding school and the arrangement seemed to him to be much more practical and beneficial for his son since he and Lilli were so often travelling around due to their work commitments. He explained in an interview at the time, 'He's not so alone. Lilli's mother and sister are both in London and I daresay they give more time to the boy than we ever could.'

A month after the reopening of *The Love of Four Colonels*, with business below expectations, it was decided to take the play out on a six-week tour, to Hershey, Pennsylvania, then Pittsburgh, Detroit, Toronto and finally two weeks in Washington.

After the tour Rex returned to Hollywood to appear in a film version of Sir Walter Scott's *The Talisman*. Following the tremendous success the year before of Metro-Goldwyn-Mayer's version of *Ivanhoe* and their follow-up film *Knights of the Round Table*, which had proved equally popular, Jack L. Warner decided that he would mount a swashbuckling adventure film of his own. *The Talisman*, budgeted at the then large figure of three million dollars, would be shot in the new Cinemascope process. Rex was cast as Saladin, joining a company which included George Sanders (as King Richard), a young Laurence Harvey, Robert Douglas and Virginia Mayo, with David Butler as director.

Before filming began Rex flew to Hollywood for make-up tests and wardrobe fittings, following a short rest after the end of the tour. For the film Rex would have his hair dyed black and his skin tone darkened, as well as sporting an artificial beard and wearing elaborate jewelled costumes which weighed over forty pounds. With the tests completed to everyone's satisfaction, Rex returned to New York on December 1st to begin rehearsals for a Theatre Guild television show in which he and Lilli would be seen together in an adaptation of H. M. Harwood's play, *Man In Possession*, which had been a great success for Leslie Banks in London in 1930. Broadcast for ABC TV's US Steel Hour on December 8th, it had Rex, as a bailiff's emissary, competing for the affections of a young widow, played by Lilli, with his brother, played by Robert Coote.

Rex and Lilli returned to the West Coast the day after

the broadcast. In Hollywood they rented Errol Flynn's luxurious home on Mulholland Drive for the duration of the shooting. Flynn had originally been considered for the part of a dashing Scottish adventurer in *The Talisman* but years of hard living had taken their toll and he was no longer reliable enough; the role went instead to Laurence Harvey. Instead, Flynn was away in Europe. Now a washed-up shadow of his former self, Flynn was forced to seek employment in mediocre adventure yarns, beginning the last phase of his career before finally falling victim to life-long self-abuse through alcohol and drugs. Rex and Lilli brought their own cook with them from New York since she was familiar with their particular tastes, but otherwise they left the running of the house to the Flynn servants while Lilli occupied her time by taking art lessons.

Much of *King Richard and the Crusaders*, as *The Talisman* was now called, was filmed on location at the Warner ranch at Calabasas and at Salton Sea on the California/Arizona border, sixteen miles east of Yuma, with a break over Christmas, enabling the Harrisons to spend the holiday with Ronald and Benita Colman at Santa Barbara.

Rex and Lilli had one interesting television offer at this time when they were asked if they would consider appearing in a series based on the popular radio comedy show *Halls of Ivy*, which had starred the Colmans as a college dean and his wife. The Colmans had been offered the series first but Ronald Colman had turned it down. Rex and Lilli, surprised by this approach, promptly told Colman, registering their amazement that he had decided against appearing in the series himself. Colman's reaction was both astonishment and anger and he immediately contacted the producer and insisted that he would be doing the series along with his wife.

As a married acting couple, Rex and Lilli were on a par with Ronald Colman and Benita Hume and so it was natural that they were thought of as a suitable replacement for the Colmans. But though they saw themselves as a similar theatrical partnership, Rex Harrison and Lilli Palmer could not lay claim to the renowned position of such eminent couples as Alfred Lunt and Lynn Fontanne, Laurence Olivier and Vivien Leigh or even, in the future, Elizabeth Taylor and Richard Burton, who were individually of equal importance as actors. In the case of the Harrisons, only Rex was in this league and it was his eminence which enabled him to elevate his wife into a theatrical partnership for three plays on Broadway, one in London and two less-than-successful film appearances.

King Richard and the Crusaders was not turning out to be Jack L. Warner's answer to M-G-M's swashbuckling successes, as the production was ill-served by a decidedly second-rate script and some unfortunate casting. Virginia Mayo was nobody's idea of an English lady but after her appearance in Warner Brothers' *Captain Horatio Hornblower* she was regarded by the studio as a suitable choice. Rex himself was outrageously miscast and, in particular in scenes where he attempts to seduce Virginia Mayo's Lady Edith, he becomes ludicrous.

Filming in the desert proved arduous and Rex also experienced discomfort from having to play many scenes sitting cross-legged. Abdullah Abbas, the resident studio masseur – who also helped Rex with the pronunciation of his Arabic lines – had to be called on to the set one day to give Rex a rub-down after his knees had buckled as he attempted to stand after a long cross-legged set-up. The problem was finally solved when the studio installed a whirlpool bathtub off-stage to enable Rex to restore the circulation after shooting a scene.

Despite these discomforts, Rex still found time to co-operate with the studio's publicity department, trying valiantly but in vain to justify the bad decision to appear in the picture, as he enthused over his role as Saladin. 'Certainly I'm happy to be playing a swashbuckling role like this. It gives a man an opportunity to show his versatility – and virility too, I might add. These boudoir shenanigans are all right, of course, but a man likes to be known as something of a he-man, you know.'

After an end-of-shooting party in his and Laurence Harvey's honour at Robert Douglas's San Fernando Valley home Rex and Lilli returned to New York. Once again Rex left Hollywood without having distinguished himself – but this would not be his last association with the film capital. He would return again and as a bigger star than before.

Before his departure Rex, in an interview, gave his recipe for a happy marriage presenting the Hollywood columnists with yet another picture of a healthy and secure relationship between Lilli and himself:

'The husband's career must always come first. Fortunately for our marriage Lilli and I see eye to eye on the matter of blending marriage and careers. We enjoy working together in the cast of a film or play, but we have never been separated nor do we intend to be, by the demands of Lilli's separate career. Lilli is first a wife and mother, a very good one, I might add, then the artist.

'The professional wife who places her career before her marriage is incomprehensible to both of us. Marriage between two persons in the same line of work can and should be ideal, if the wife never forgets that her career is secondary to the marriage. Lilli and I have a perfect understanding on this matter, so there's no reason why we shouldn't go on being happily married until we're both tottering in senility.'

Rex's statement was somewhat punctured by the fact that he next planned to make a film in England, while Lilli intended to make one in Germany. Lilli felt that being apart from each other for a couple of months would do them good and show how much they really needed each other. Meanwhile they crossed the Atlantic together. As Rex felt increasingly restless with life in New York – he had no ties to keep him there – they decided to sell their apartment and return to England. It was not only the country of his birth, but Carey was there too. Meanwhile, Rex and Lilli first had to undergo their first extended separation. They would be apart for a couple of months before life could resume its normal pattern.

7

ON THEIR return to England, Lilli immediately flew to Munich to make her film, while Rex reported for work on *The Constant Husband*, a comedy being made at Shepperton Studios about an amnesia victim who is arrested and put on trial at the Old Bailey when it is discovered that he is married to six different women. Made by Frank Launder and Sidney Gilliat, the team responsible for *The Rake's Progress*, the film was to change the destiny of Rex's personal life and, once again, throw his marriage to Lilli into confusion.

In a film with no fewer than six attractive young leading ladies, it would have been more surprising if he had not indulged in extra-marital activities with one of them but, in this case, Rex was to fall passionately in love with the beautiful actress who played one of his wives – a society photographer – in the film.

At twenty-six Kay Kendall was tall, dark and strikingly attractive. She was also lively, talented and sophisticated and adored by everybody who knew or worked with her. Rex was immediately attracted. Her sister Kim remembers:

'Kay said to my mother one day, "You've got to come out for dinner tonight. We're going to Les Ambassadeurs. Rex Harrison wants to take me out for dinner and I want you to come with us." And mother said, "Wonderful. I'd like that."

'So they went out for dinner, and afterwards my mother said, "You know, darling, this man is absolutely madly in love with you!" Kay said, "Oh really mother! He's twenty years older than I am, and he's got a concave chest and he's going bald."'

However, as shooting on the film progressed Kay's opinion of Rex changed and Kim Kendall says, 'She fell for him because he does have that fabulous charm.' She recalls, 'Kay asked mother to go out for dinner again and mother happened to mention that Rex was looking a little tired and Kay said, "Tired? Have you ever seen a man in such marvellous condition. Look at that bearing!" She really was madly in love with him.'

Kay Kendall was born Kay Justine Kendall McCarthy on May 21st 1926 to Gladys and Terry Kendall at the seaside resort of Withernsea, near Hull in Yorkshire, her mother's home town. Her grandmother was the celebrated Marie Kendall, who was topping the variety bills of music-halls all over England alongside the great stars of the late Victorian era, such as Marie Lloyd, George Robey and Little Tich. Marie Kendall had married a Canadian, Stephen McCarthy; however when her son, Terry, formed a dancing team with his sister, Pat, and began touring the variety halls, they chose to retain their mother's illustrious name and were billed as 'Pat and Terry Kendall'. They scored their first notable West End success in Noël Coward's 1925 revue *On With the Dance* for Charles B. Cochran, and Terry particularly delighted audiences as Valentin the Boneless Wonder, a part Coward created especially for him. Tall and darkly handsome in the Jack Buchanan mould, he was employed in all aspects of the musical theatre and worked a great deal in pantomime. In later years, Kay would delight friends with stories of her father and told them that as a stand-up comedian, his big turn was to take off five or six pairs of pants in front of the audience, before turning around to reveal the Union Jack on his backside.

Coming from such a background, it would have been more of a surprise if Kay had not gone into showbusiness. When war broke out in 1939, she and her sister Kim, who was two years older, were evacuated to a convent in Scotland. Meanwhile their parents were divorced and early in 1940 the two girls decided to return to London to pursue theatrical careers of their own, and were first employed in a chorus line at the Shaftesbury Theatre. After two years of similar work they decided to combine as a dancing act, 'Kim and Kay Kendall', and toured in troop shows all over England as well as appearing on the variety theatre circuit. Kim says, 'As young children we were very close because we just adored each other.' They were not entirely successful and in 1944 Kay began looking for extra-work in British films. She was actually employed on Gabriel Pascal's mammoth production of Shaw's *Caesar and Cleopatra* with Vivien Leigh and Claude Rains, while Kim embarked on an ENSA tour. The turning point in Kay's career came the following year when the comedian Sid Field, together with Hollywood director Wesley Ruggles, picked her to appear opposite him in his eagerly-awaited screen debut, *London Town*. The film did not give her career the boost for which she had hoped as her beauty, style and wit were not used to full advantage and, along with the film, she was slated by the critics. Crushed by her failure she left England and spent the next two years with various repertory companies entertaining the troops in war-torn Germany and Italy. Returning home she tried to revitalise her film career, but was offered nothing better than minor parts in second features. Her sister recalls: 'She was always depressed and was going to jump out of the window, and by the thirteenth time we used to open it and say, "Help yourself!"'

Kay finally achieved fame and popular recognition after her appearance in *Genevieve* in 1953, in which she proved herself a skilful comedienne. Before beginning work on *The Constant Husband* she had appeared in *Doctor in the House*, which starred Dirk Bogarde, a very good friend of hers.

Before meeting Rex, Kay's name had been associated with a number of men. Through her liaison with Sydney Chaplin, Kay became especially close to Oona, Charles Chaplin's wife, and stayed with the couple often. Her romance with William 'Bill' Hanson, the brother of James, later Lord Hanson, was especially tragic. Princess Lilian of Sweden, Kay's closest friend, recalls: 'Tragedy seemed to be the abiding link between Bill Hanson and Kay. They were the same age almost to the day, and Bill died of cancer at thirty-two – the same age as Kay when she died.' Kay was also involved romantically with Prince Carl Johan of Sweden and James Sainsbury, scion of the Sainsbury family, founders of Britain's legendary grocery chain. Kim Kendall recalls: 'James [Sainsbury] used to take her out all the time. Kay said that he wanted to marry her and they almost got as far as the altar, but one or other got cold feet before the wedding. Any man just absolutely worshipped her – they just adored her.' Her carefree life-style and her off-beat sense of humour contributed to her public image as a fun-loving girl, determined to enjoy life to the full. Kim says, 'She used to give these marvellous parties and there was no furniture and yet she would have champagne and caviar and they would have orange boxes to sit on.'

During the shooting of *The Constant Husband* Rex and Kay had become deeply involved but Rex, at least, did not expect their affair to last and, with the film completed, he prepared to leave for Italy. In June he was back with Lilli in Portofino. Her husband's restlessness made it quite clear to Lilli that another woman had entered his life and she could not have been totally surprised when, after only one week at the villa, he announced that he was returning to England himself to collect Carey from boarding school and bring him back to Portofino for the holidays.

Back in London, Rex immediately contacted Kay and they spent a few days together before it was time for him to return to Italy with his son. They vowed that they were parting forever, resigned to the fact that they had no future together.

Summer at Portofino followed the standard pattern, with Rex and Lilli holding open-house at their villa for numerous friends and acquaintances. One of their guests was Hugh Beaumont who was presenting them in the London production of *Bell, Book and Candle* in the autumn – a project to which they had committed themselves before Rex had met Kay. As Rex was also directing, it gave them the opportunity to discuss the play in a leisurely atmosphere, in preparation for the rehearsals which would begin as soon as they returned to London. With Rex replacing the author at the helm, it would clearly take on a different look and this time spent with Binkie Beaumont was invaluable to secure a proper perspective which would be satisfactory to John Van Druten as well as to Rex. Although engrossed in preparations for the production, Rex could not stop thinking about Kay and was noticeably distracted.

Kay had accepted an invitation from her friend, Elinor, former wife of Baron Henri de la Boullerie, and was spending some time at her home in Geneva. Also house-guesting with Elinor was her half-sister, Carol, the estranged wife of playwright William Saroyan, with her young children Aram and Lucy. Kay and Carol struck up an instant friendship and Carol, who was later to marry Walter Matthau, found in her new friend a very special closeness. Not only did Kay possess a great appeal to men, but likewise to women. Kitty Carlisle Hart, who was to know Kay well when her celebrated husband Moss Hart directed Rex in *My Fair Lady*, says of her: 'I was extraordinarily fond of Kay. She was one of the most special human beings I have ever known – very special. She was so lithe, so pretty, so appetising-looking and so funny!'

Carol Saroyan, a vivacious and independent blonde, has recently been the subject of a memoir by her son, Aram Saroyan, entitled *Trio*, about her long friendship with Oona O'Neill Chaplin and Gloria Vanderbilt. In the book, Aram refers to Kay when she first met his mother, as the 'beautiful, rather melancholic young English film star'. Both single and both 'original', the two women began to call each other 'wifey'. Arranging for her son to stay with Oona and Charlie Chaplin in Vevey and her daughter to remain with Elinor, Carol and Kay took off for London where Kay was instrumental in helping Carol obtain work dubbing her voice in English for the heroine of an Italian film comedy, for which she made 'quite a bit of money'. The friendship between them was to last until the end of Kay's life and Carol was able to repay her friend several times over with her support during the next few turbulent and tragic years.

Leaving London, the two women returned to the Continent and finally made their way to St Jean-de-Luz on the west coast of France, where Kay became so desperate to see Rex again that she persuaded Carol that they should go to Italy instead. One evening shortly after, while dining with friends, including the Duke and Duchess of Windsor, at a restaurant at the port, Rex was informed that someone wanted to see him urgently. Excusing himself, he went to investigate and found that the message had come from Kay who was waiting for him at a nearby café. She explained that she had been passing through by chance, and that she and Carol had booked into the Hotel Eden in the neighbouring town of Santa Margherita. Rex felt a mixture of joy and apprehension at seeing Kay once again, knowing that they were treading on very dangerous ground in attempting an assignation right under Lilli's nose, but he felt powerless to stop himself. Over a drink, he swiftly made arrangements to meet Kay at her hotel early the next morning, after which he returned to the restaurant to rejoin the dinner party, before his absence began to cause comment.

Bright and early the following morning Rex drove to Santa Margherita to see Kay. He told her that he was spending the afternoon on the Earl of Warwick's yacht and invited her and Carol to come along, even though Lilli would also be present – and extended the invitation to include dinner afterwards up at the villa. If they thought they could conceal their relationship they were quickly disappointed and, in hindsight, Rex has admitted the folly of his actions which only served to create a highly-charged situation, embarrassing to everyone present. Watching Rex with Kay, Lilli knew that she was looking at the woman who had been occupying her husband's thoughts all summer, and she recalled the moment of realisation in her autobiography. 'All at once, there it was. In the open, clear as daylight. The impact hit me full force.' The other guests could not fail to recognise that Rex and Kay were more than just friends, and Binkie Beaumont in particular, as the producer of *Bell, Book and Candle*, was concerned about the possible consequences.

The next day attention switched to Carol Saroyan who was struck down with appendicitis and had to be rushed to hospital in Rapallo. Kay immediately left for Switzerland to collect some clothes and personal effects for her friend, although not before arranging to meet Rex in Milan. Their secret now out in the open, Rex threw all caution to the wind, jumped into his car and drove to Milan. Kay was waiting for him and they proceeded to Genoa where they enjoyed a few days together, while a bewildered Lilli was left to think about the future. She had been offered the lead in *Anastasia* on Broadway, and saw it as an ideal opportunity to escape from another ugly situation with Rex. She tried to persuade Beaumont to release her from her contract to appear in *Bell, Book and Candle*, but he would not hear of it, being convinced that Rex would come to his senses.

A week later Kay returned to Carol Saroyan's hospital bedside, while Rex went back to the villa to find that Lilli had already left for London and was staying in a suite at the Connaught Hotel. Rex followed her there, to honour his contract to direct and star in *Bell, Book and Candle*. As rehearsals began the other members of the cast were aware of the tension between the Harrisons, and the actress Athene Seyler, who was cast as Miss Holroyd, recollects, 'It wasn't a happy engagement for me. It was unfortunate – this poor dear man who was not behaving very well. One was rather aware that there was a strain and one knew the gossip about Kay Kendall, so that didn't make for a happy company. I never saw Rex or Lilli at all, except just to play with. They were very remote.'

Before opening at London's Phoenix Theatre, they played the Opera House, Manchester and Athene Seyler particularly remembers the culmination of their engagement there when, together with the Harrisons, she boarded the night train to London. 'Coming back from Manchester on the sleeper – mine was next door to theirs – I could hear them arguing and quarrelling the whole way. They kept me awake from Manchester to London. It never stopped!'

The critics' verdict on the play, after the first night at the Phoenix on October 5th, was mixed, although all agreed that it was a very entertaining evening by virtue of the high quality of the acting. The *Times* declared: 'Mr Harrison's comedy seems to have gained with the years in sharpness and firmness of touch, and his performance as the worldly cynic in a wonderland of witches is from first to last delightful in its incisiveness and resource.' The play settled into a very successful run, although the private lives of the two principals deteriorated rapidly, and Lilli moved out of their hotel suite to an apartment nearby in Mount Street. Rex met Kay whenever he could and they regularly had supper together after the show; their affair became such common knowledge that one wag referred to the play as *Bell, Book and Kendall*. Kay even attended a matinee performance, which provoked a strong reaction from Athene Seyler: 'I thought it was bad taste on everybody's part that she should come in front to watch Rex and his wife playing together. Everybody knew that she was in the theatre. It made me very uncomfortable.'

If Athene Seyler felt uncomfortable, the whole engagement was agonising for Rex and Lilli. Rex's love for Kay stunned all other emotions within him and he could not comprehend the principles involved, being unconcerned that his marital status stood in the way of a complete union with Kay. That Lilli was able to continue working in the play is even more astonishing, and by doing so her humiliation was complete. She sought advice from friends, including Noël Coward, but they could offer no solution to her predicament. After talking to Lilli, Coward wrote sadly in his diary, 'Rex Harrison has fallen in love with Kay Kendall and is breaking Lilli's heart.'

Kay, too, suffered emotionally during the long run of the play. She was deeply in love yet had to bear the frustration of not totally belonging to Rex. Her sister says: 'I know Kay was desperately keen to get married, although Rex was not. She had never married before. She'd had a lot of wonderful romances but never marriage and I think she just suddenly thought that this was it – apart from the fact that they had so much in common and her being crazy about him. She was the one who put the pressure on him.'

Not only were the cast and company at the Phoenix Theatre witnesses to the trouble between the Harrisons; whenever they rowed at the theatre they could be heard in the street outside and admirers, waiting for them at the stage door, were often treated to the sound of Rex and Lilli yelling at each other before emerging to greet their public.

Tied to the play, with six evening performances and two matinees a week, the only day on which they were not in each other's company was Sunday. Lilli often visited Carey at Sunningdale and would take him out for the day, while Rex would generally spend the day with Kay in the countryside, most frequently at Beel House, Dirk Bogarde's home in Buckinghamshire. On one particularly memorable Sunday the late Diana Dors and her first husband, Dennis Hamilton, invited their friend Kay to bring Rex along and spend the day with them at their home at Bray on the River Thames. Kay arrived with Rex in his chauffeur-driven Rolls Royce, and the two couples drove together in Miss Dors' Cadillac to a very elegant hotel in the nearby village of Cookham.

On the short drive there Rex became angry when Kay brought up the subject of marriage, and Miss Dors vividly recollected Rex saying: 'Oh come along, Mousey! For God's sake, don't let's start all that bloody nonsense again.' She said, 'This rattled Kay. And, despite his obvious annoyance, she made matters worse by fawning around his neck, begging him to say he loved her. It was all done with a general air of half-amusement, but the conversation came to a very unamusing and sudden stop when Rex clouted her in the ear!' In the restaurant the argument became extremely noisy, and Miss Dors recalled that Rex kept telling Kay to 'Shut up!' and complained that it was like being out with 'an untrained puppy dog'. Finally, 'having been told to shut up for the hundredth time, Kay lost her temper and screamed at Rex, calling him a very unladylike name.' The restaurant was briefly silenced by Kay's sudden outburst, but fortunately they then finished their meal in peace. Afterwards, it was suggested that they all go for a trip on the river in their motor-launch, but in the boat Kay again brought up the subject of marriage with the same reaction from Rex. Diana Dors remembered, 'Suddenly, in a fit of madness, Kay, who could not swim, threw herself into the water, which left Rex with no alternative but to jump in and pull her out. There was a terrible scramble back on the boat, and we made for home for a hot bath.'

Back at the house they sat around in bath towels chatting together until Diana told a story which offended Rex. He promptly stood up, followed closely by Kay, and went in search of his clothes. Dressing hurriedly, they then climbed into the waiting Rolls Royce and were driven away by the chauffeur, without even stopping to bid farewell to their hosts.

Early into the run of the John Van Druten play, Rex's services were already being sought for a projected musical version of George Bernard Shaw's *Pygmalion*. The successful Broadway musical partnership of lyricist Alan Jay Lerner and composer Frederick Loewe had been considering it for some time as a promising vehicle to follow their successes with both *Brigadoon* and *Paint Your Wagon*, and for the part of Henry Higgins, the irascible professor of phonetics, Lerner had immediately thought of Rex. He telephoned Rex from New York and asked if he, along with Frederick Loewe and their producer, Herman Levin, could come over and discuss the project with him. Although remaining non-committal, Rex made no objections and in early January of 1955 the three men arrived in London. They wasted no time in contacting him, and Lerner said, 'We telephoned Rex and made an appointment to have supper with him after the show. When we all trooped backstage to see him, there was an unmistakable strain and *froideur* in the air,' and he recalled, 'After visiting Rex I stopped in to see Lilli, who greeted me with distinct reserve.' They soon discovered that the Harrisons were estranged and that after each performance they would go their separate ways, Rex to his hotel suite and Lilli to her apartment in Mount Street. Lerner remarked, 'This rather prickly situation was covered in a cloak of secrecy so large it could be seen for ten miles.'

From then on Lerner made a point of avoiding contact with Rex at the theatre, as he felt, 'It was a little difficult going to see Rex in the evenings while he was doing the play with Lilli because I knew her so well and felt a little embarrassed about it.' At the time Lerner was married to the American film actress Nancy Olson, who travelled to London with her husband. She recollects, 'It was the first time that I had met Rex. I found him very English – the perfect image of the English gentleman. He was also ideally Henry Higgins: he was very independent, very opinionated, very judgemental, very male and arrogant –

but in the best sense of the word. He knew who he was.'

In Frederick Loewe's room at Claridge's Hotel, Harrison sang one verse of 'Molly Malone', to the composer's piano accompaniment, which was enough to convince them that Rex's voice was perfectly adequate for the role. The problem was to convince Rex Harrison. Lerner and Loewe had brought with them to London the five songs which they had already written for the show. Two were to be sung by Higgins and they played them for him, but Rex was not impressed, as Lerner recalled, 'Rex hated them both. We knew it because he immediately said, "I hate them".' Lerner says, 'The minute I played them for him I knew it was wrong. Somehow he gave me the style – I can't explain why – but I suddenly saw how it should be.' Although they convinced Rex that the songs already written would change dramatically as the show began to take shape, he was still full of misgivings and would not be hurried into making a decision. To take, at the age of forty-seven, the lead in a new musical show was a complete departure from anything else he had done, and he was understandably cautious. He also felt that Leslie Howard's performance in Gabriel Pascal's film version of *Pygmalion* was the definitive one and it was only after Lerner and Loewe arranged for a screening of the film that Rex was convinced that perhaps he could give the role something that Howard had not. Rex vacillated over their offer, reluctant to be parted from Kay while he was rehearsing in New York and unsure that it would be a sensible move in his career. He could see the advantage of putting some distance between himself and Lilli, but Lerner says, 'We talked it out and talked it out, but he couldn't make up his mind.'

In the meantime they went about securing the rights to *Pygmalion* from the Shaw estate, as well as enlisting Cecil Beaton to design the costumes and Stanley Holloway to play Alfred Doolittle. Finally, after having been in London for five weeks, Lerner received a call from Rex one Sunday morning suggesting that they meet him for a walk in Hyde Park. They walked around the park for three hours, Lerner and Loewe desperately trying to keep pace with Rex's long strides as they listened to him weighing up the advantages and disadvantages of the project. Finally, Lerner recalled, '. . . all at once he stopped. He turned to us and said, almost out of nowhere: "All right, I'll do it."' Composer and lyricist were overjoyed. Nancy Olson asserts, 'That was the fuel that Alan and Fritz needed at that moment – the inspiration to go back and finish it.'

They reckoned that *Bell, Book and Candle* would close by the spring and accordingly scheduled rehearsals to commence in New York in the autumn. When Lerner, Loewe and Herman Levin left London in the middle of February, Rex set about preparing himself for the most demanding role of his entire career. 'I went to a singing instructor,' Rex said later, 'and I realised in two short lessons that I'd never be able to sing, or it would take me seven or eight years – far too long, so then I gave up the singing lessons.'

Rex then turned to Bill Low, the musical director for *Guys and Dolls*, which was running at the Coliseum, and under his guidance began to make progress. Harrison later acknowledged, 'He really taught me the initial things . . . he taught me how to talk on pitch. And that is what I did . . . I do use the notes, but I speak-talk,' and he continued, 'I picked it up quite quickly, because I've got a sense of rhythm and it wasn't very difficult, and then I worked on my own after that, and I evolved my own technique of doing it.'

Bell, Book and Candle still continued to do brisk business. An incident in the middle of March during a matinee performance attracted some attention. A four-year-old girl crying in the stalls was putting off both actors and audience to such an extent that Rex called a halt to the performance and barked out to one of the attendants in the theatre, 'Have that child removed!' Mother and child were duly asked to leave, after which they were able to continue with the play. It is a very rare occurrence for an actor in the West End – and especially one of Harrison's calibre – to be put in the position of having to stop in the middle of a scene and when asked afterwards why he had taken such a step, he replied, 'Those of us on the stage and the audience too, were being badly put out by the noise. In fairness to everyone I felt that something had to be done.'

Back in New York, Lerner and Loewe continued with the writing of the score, and also worked closely with Herman Levin in gathering together the cast and company. Moss Hart was approached to direct the show but declined the offer, being heavily involved in work of his own, but was eventually so intrigued by what he heard that he was persuaded to accept the task and in so doing undertook one of the most demanding jobs of his entire career. Moss Hart, a giant of the Broadway theatre as both playwright and director, had a wealth of experience on which to draw and they knew that under his firm guidance they could be certain of achieving the best possible results.

With Higgins cast, their next task was to find an actress to play Eliza Doolittle. Initially, there was the exciting prospect of teaming Rex with Mary Martin who, although forty-two, could still have played the part, but she had long since decided not to become a contender and they finally settled on a young English actress, Julie Andrews, who was making her first appearance on Broadway in the imported British musical *The Boy Friend*. Although she had been on the professional stage for six years she had not distinguished herself greatly, and was a remarkably brave choice for the producers to make.

Work on the score progressed well. Lerner wrote in his autobiography, 'In a very short time Higgins and Harrison became interchangeable in my mind, and instead of Rex's vocal limitations becoming an inhibition, his personality and style seemed to clear away fresh creative paths.' Composer and lyricist soon completed the songs,

Rex's family when he was about three years old, on holiday in the Lake District at Bowness-on-Windermere. Rex is third from the left in the front row. Standing in the back row are (from left): Auntie Edith Harrison, Edward Carey, Evelyn Carey, Arthur Carey, Bill Harrison. Middle row: Brenda Carey, Rhona Carey, May Carey and Brian, Eustace Carey and Joy Carey. Front row: Molly Carey, Sylvia Harrison, Rex, Lola Carey (with Bertie the cat), Dermot Carey, Marjorie Harrison, Sheila Carey, Joan Carey, Marcella Carey.

Rex in the Liverpool College cricket XI when he was seventeen. Jack Abel (also in the back row , fourth from the left) has recalled his cricketing prowess.

LIVERPOOL COLLEGE CRICKET XI. 1925.

Back Row: H. D. HAMILTON. E. P. ANDERTON. G. S. ROBINSON. J. K. ABEL. R. S. ORCHARD. R. C. HARRISON.
Front Row: E. B. CLAYDON. G. D. HAMILTON. N. BOASE. K. L. LITTLE. F. DURE.

Terence Rattigan's *French Without Tears* was Rex's first major West End success. Rex Harrison at the head of the table and reading clockwise: Yvonne Andre, Robert Flemyng, Kay Hammond, Roland Culver, Percy Walsh, Jessica Tandy, Trevor Howard, Guy Middleton.

In Shaw's *Major Barbara* with Wendy Hiller and Sybil Thorndike.

In 1940, during the filming of *Night Train to Munich*.

With Colette and Mr and Mrs Victor Saville at a 1938 premiere.

With Lilli Palmer, standing by him as she did for seventeen years.

With Rachel Roberts on the set of *My Fair Lady*.

Rex and Kay at the time of *The Reluctant Debutante*, in a favourite off-set photograph.

A rare photograph of Elizabeth with Rachel.

At the Albert Hall in *Major Barbara*, in the scene in which he was coached by George Bernard Shaw.

With Audrey Hepburn, being directed by George Cukor on the set of *My Fair Lady*.

If for no other part, Rex will be remembered for Professor Higgins in *My Fair Lady*.

With his sixth wife, Mercia, whom he married in 1978.

'I'm an Ordinary Man' and 'Why Can't The English' and, as they had promised, flew to London so that Rex could hear them. To their relief he approved, and began rehearsing them immediately. Another reason for their visit was to arrange a lunch so that Rex could become acquainted with his leading lady, who by now had completed her commitment to *The Boy Friend* in New York. They were aware that Rex had grave doubts as to the wisdom of casting so young and inexperienced a girl in the part, and the meeting was intended to dispel those doubts. However, he would remain convinced that his initial feelings were correct for some time to come. Herself daunted at the prospect of being teamed with Harrison, Miss Andrews has said, 'I was shaking at the thought of working with him – one heard awful things about Rex, how rude he is and all that.'

At around this time, Rex began to wonder if he had done the right thing in agreeing to appear in a musical, and Lerner recollects, 'Rex had one moment in the spring when he began to be uncertain, but that passed.' He was working a particularly heavy schedule at the time as, in addition to appearing nightly on-stage at the Phoenix Theatre and preparing for *My Fair Lady* during the day, Rex had also agreed to direct another play for Hugh Beaumont in London. Binkie had seen André Roussin's comedy *Nina* in Paris with Elvire Popescu and had bought it for Edith Evans. She disliked the play, a three-handed soufflé concerning a standard romantic triangle of wife, husband and lover, but accepted it nonetheless, perhaps intrigued by the prospect of having Rex Harrison as her director. One can only assume that Harrison, likewise, only agreed to direct the play because of the opportunity it afforded him of working with the great Edith Evans, although he also suspected that Hugh Beaumont, who was very fond of Lilli, hoped the challenge would take his mind off Kay and his muddled private life.

With Arthur Barbosa, his old friend from the Liverpool

Playhouse days, engaged to design the settings, rehearsals began at the Theatre Royal, Haymarket. But from the start there were difficulties as it became increasingly apparent that Edith Evans was unhappy both with the play and the casting of David Hutcheson and James Hayter respectively as her lover and husband. Whenever Rex took the stage to direct her she would tell him that she wished he were playing opposite her – an exciting stage combination never, unfortunately, realised. Work progressed satisfactorily but when they were in Liverpool for the opening Rex received the news that Edith Evans had suffered a total nervous breakdown. The performance that night, with her understudy going on in her place, and in front of an audience which included the play's author, André Roussin, was a disaster. Rex, who had been given the night off from *Bell, Book and Candle* to attend, felt ashamed, blaming himself for Edith Evans's breakdown and his inexperience as a director for the failure of the play. Returning to London the following day, he re-cast the role of Nina with Coral Browne, and replaced David Hutcheson with Michael Hordern, but they lacked the drawing power of Edith Evans. The play opened at the Theatre Royal, Haymarket on July 27th, but closed after only forty-five performances.

Rex continued with preparations for *My Fair Lady*, and submitted himself to Cecil Beaton's expert judgement on his costumes for the show. Beaton took him to his own tailor, and recalled,

'Rex is a perfectionist and demands minute attention . . . He is like a dog with a rat and will worry details at enormous length. If given the opportunity, he will work himself up into a state of alarm. . . . I cannot say that Rex is the easiest boy in the class. But he has good taste and knows when something is not right for him. If it is wrong, he can become wild. One morning, he ripped off in anger his first-act long coat because it was tight under the arms, The seams split and the expensive stuff was frayed. The "strait-jacket" was thrown to the floor.'

Lerner again returned to London with two more songs for Rex, which he liked. Harrison also took the opportunity to suggest his old friend Robert Coote for the role of Colonel Pickering – an idea which was accepted wholeheartedly. The only cloud on the horizon was the continuing success of *Bell, Book and Candle* which, despite predictions that business would fall off after the spring, was if anything doing better than ever. Rex's contract with H. M. Tennent stated that before he could leave the play the returns had to drop below a certain figure for two consecutive weeks. They never did – and it became clear that an arrangement would have to be made with Hugh Beaumont to negotiate Rex's early release from the play to enable him to start rehearsals in New York. It was finally agreed that the play would close at the Phoenix Theatre in November – but in return H. M. Tennent received a cash settlement, in addition to the rights to present *My Fair Lady* in London. It was both a clever and a lucky position in which Beaumont had found himself, and using it to all its advantage he secured what was to be the most spectacular financial success ever achieved by the H. M. Tennent organisation.

Lilli, meanwhile, had found solace from her troubled private life in the arms of the handsome Argentinian film actor, Carlos Thompson. Her friend Noël Coward, to whom she had introduced him, wrote in his diary afterwards: 'Lilli is now over her miseries about Rex and is now madly in love with Carlos and so she is alright for the time being.' She had received an offer to appear in another film in Germany and, still anxious to extricate herself from *Bell, Book and Candle*, she finally persuaded Beaumont to release her from what had already been a twelve months ordeal. On September 21st her part was taken over by Joan Greenwood and that evening marked not only the end of the Rex Harrison–Lilli Palmer stage partnership, but also the conclusion of their life together, for this time there would be no reconciliation. Although Lilli was now gone, *Bell, Book and Candle* continued to play to packed houses and finally closed at the Phoenix Theatre after a total of 484 performances.

When the play closed at the Phoenix Binkie Beaumont sent it out on tour, engaging Robert Flemyng to take over from Rex who agreed to rehearse his successor in the role. Flemyng and Harrison had appeared together in *French Without Tears*.

Esmond Knight, who had replaced Wilfrid Lawson in the play, recalls a conversation he had with Harrison late one evening at the end of the run. Sitting in Rex's car, the two men chatted for a few minutes before they parted, and Knight recollects that Harrison confessed to having certain doubts about the project to which he was now firmly committed, and told him, 'It's absolutely unknown. It will probably be a terrible flop. We've got this little girl called Julie Andrews. I mean, nobody knows anything about her at all. Nobody knows whether she is any damn good or not.' He then began reflecting on his personal life and Esmond Knight distinctly remembers him saying, 'It's very extraordinary, but this is the first time in my life that I can remember that I am free of a woman.'

Although Harrison has a reputation for being absentminded, he was perhaps thinking of the long period when he would be parted from Kay while he was rehearsing *My Fair Lady* in America, as Binkie Beaumont had arranged for her to follow Joan Greenwood in the long provincial tour of *Bell, Book and Candle* when Miss Greenwood left the cast after Christmas. It was said that Beaumont had deliberately cast Kay in the part to ensure that she would not divert Rex's attention during the critical rehearsal period in New York. Although rehearsals did not begin officially until January 3rd, 1956 to allow the English cast members to spend Christmas at home, Rex arranged to fly over early so that he could

begin work with Lerner, Loewe and Moss Hart. A tearful
Kay Kendall saw him off at the airport, knowing that she
would be parted from the man she loved for almost four
months as he went to tackle the greatest challenge of his
career.

Alan Jay Lerner admired Harrison's total dedication to
his craft, and he later remarked, 'Every genuinely great
star with whom I have worked is a star not only because
of talent, but because he works harder than anyone else
and his sense of perfection, which is deeper than anyone
else's, demands more of him.' In the first week of the new
year cast rehearsals began at the New Amsterdam
Theatre on Forty-Second street with a complete read-
through of the script. Rex felt that Higgins got lost in the
second act and it was decided to put in an additional song
for him, which Lerner and Loewe began working on
immediately. During the first week of rehearsals Moss
Hart devoted every evening to Rex and the staging of his
numbers, in order to give him confidence for his first
venture into the musical field. By the second week,
Lerner and Loewe had completed the extra song for the
second act, 'Why Can't a Woman Be More Like a Man',
but its addition caused a rift between Rex and his long-
standing friend Robert Coote, as the song interrupted
Pickering's telephone call to his friend Boozie in the
Foreign Office. In his autobiography Rex said, 'There was
a great deal of the telephone call left, but it was less of a
tour de force, and I think Bob found it hard to forgive, as
anyone might have, the way we had broken into a good
moment. For a long time our old friendship was
strained . . .'

From the start Harrison had been noticeably irritated
when Julie Andrews walked into the theatre practising
her scales and by her nervous habit of laughing in his face
when he was immersed in playing a dramatic scene with
her, and he recalled, 'I always asked her why she
laughed, and she never did tell me.' By the end of the
second week of rehearsals Rex was not the only one who

began to doubt whether she was capable of playing Eliza, and Moss Hart took the drastic step of dismissing the company for two days while he concentrated on bringing her performance up to standard. Kitty Hart says, 'He rehearsed Julie alone on the stage and he pasted the part on her. She had the wit to grow into it and make it her own.'

Lerner says that, 'Rex worried about everybody', while Cecil Beaton referred to him as 'a martyr to indecisions and doubts'. He would keep a copy of the Penguin edition of *Pygmalion* by him at all times so that he could refer to the original play if one of the speeches in the script did not ring true. Lerner recalled that, at least four times a day, Rex would shout out, 'Where's my Penguin?', so that he could satisfy himself that Shaw was not being tampered with by the Americans. Eventually Lerner bought a stuffed penguin from a taxidermist and when Rex next barked out, 'Where's my Penguin?' had it wheeled out on-stage. Rex laughed along with everybody else and kept it as a mascot in his dressing room throughout the run of the show. Harrison's meticulous study of the character of Henry Higgins as written by Bernard Shaw in *Pygmalion* was, of course, the method of a very great actor approaching a part, although he would later pay tribute to Lerner's masterly lyrics. 'What is marvellous and wonderful about Alan Lerner is that he was able to catch the absolute quintessence of Bernard Shaw.' Singling out 'Why Can't a Woman Be More Like a Man', he remarked, 'I think it was so marvellously clever of Alan Lerner to have condensed into this quite short number, so many violent feelings that men have had about women,' and he continued more generally, 'The content of the songs appealed to me enormously as they did, I am sure, to many, many men. In "Ordinary Man" and "Why Can't a Woman Be More Like a Man" I think that Alan Lerner more or less summed up the character of Henry Higgins.' Of Shaw's philosophy in the play he said, 'I think he was expressing his own views very largely. I think that Shaw, first of all, was very interested in the English language and the phonetics problem and his own alphabet, which he was trying to invent. This was part of the play. And I think he was also a woman-hater . . . although he was married, I think he was a firmly established bachelor! And he was writing about that. I think it is Higgins, very closely allied with Bernard Shaw, as a character. And Eliza Doolittle, which was written for Mrs Patrick Campbell, was a figment of his imagination. He used the flower girl motif really to express the whole idea about pronunciation and his own feelings about women.'

Interestingly, Nancy Olson, who felt that Rex was ideal for Higgins, says: 'Alan's relationship with Rex was much closer than with Julie. I don't think Rex was truly interested in women the way many men are. I felt that he did not feel comfortable with women. He was never flirtatious with me – he had a great friendship with Alan which was very important to him.' As rehearsals got well under way, Cecil Beaton recalled that Rex appeared to become increasingly agitated. 'Rex was by now extremely tense: never having appeared in a musical before, and doing something so utterly different, he felt he could not rehearse enough.' Beaton remembered that long after the company were lying down in a state of complete exhaustion, Rex would still doggedly be repeating phrases from his songs over and over until he was satisfied that he felt comfortable with them. Beaton claimed that when the time came to rehearse the scene in which Eliza throws Higgins' slippers in his face, theatre and reality became confused and 'the entire chorus applauded from the stalls'.

Although Cecil Beaton conceded that Rex was right to ignore the impatience of the thirty or more chorus girls in his drive for perfection, he also admitted, 'Rex's continuing egotism upset me to such an extent that only by a miracle was I prevented from making an ugly scene.' Moss Hart was much more sympathetic about Rex's behaviour. 'The key to Rex is he's not a frivolous man . . . What he achieves he gets from digging, digging. Once I discovered this, I could forgive him a good deal,' although even he had to admit, 'There were tremendous rages and stalkings off during rehearsals.'

One such potential crisis loomed when, after four weeks of rehearsing at the New Amsterdam Theatre, the whole company was scheduled to go up to New Haven to rehearse for a week at the Shubert Theatre prior to the opening. Early on Rex had made it quite clear that he had no intention of standing on-stage with Julie Andrews while she sang 'Without You', and had told Lerner, 'I'm not going to stand up there and look like a cunt while this young girl sings a song to me!' Moss Hart, adept at handling such conflicts, advised Lerner, 'Say nothing. I'll rehearse Julie,' and told him, 'You can't argue about that. In the theatre you can only have one fight with an actor – and that's the one you have to win. If you start having arguments every day then it becomes a way of life and it means nothing. We'll just rehearse it until the moment comes and you have to put the blocks to him and you have to win it.' Moss Hart waited until they were on the train to New Haven before he brought up the issue again. Lerner says,

'Moss sat down next to Rex and said, "Now, this is the schedule when we get up to New Haven." Rex looked and saw "Without You" and he said, "I'm not doing that."

'Moss replied, "Well, I think you should at least give me the courtesy of seeing how I would like to stage it – because the song is going to be sung, don't make any mistake about that. It's going to be sung! Now you can walk off-stage while it's being sung and walk on again when it's over, but you will look like the biggest horse's arse in the history of the theatre. So I would suggest you at least come to the rehearsal and see how it could be staged."'

Rex agreed, although Lerner says, 'Fritz and I fixed the ending so he comes in and says, "I did it. I did it. I said I'd make a woman and indeed I did", so that Julie wouldn't get any applause and that made him feel a little more comfortable.'

Arriving in New Haven on Monday, rehearsals continued in preparation for a special preview performance on the Saturday, preceding the official opening the following Monday. By Friday the lighting and scenery had been arranged to everyone's satisfaction, and that evening was put aside for the first orchestra rehearsal. Kitty Hart recalls,

> 'I had warned Rex that when you rehearse a musical you rehearse with a piano and you hear the melody all the time. When you have the first orchestra rehearsal it is very confusing because you hear all the various musical instruments, but you don't hear the tune. So for someone who is not a trained musician it is very confusing, and it makes you very nervous until you get used to the sound of the orchestra.'

What Kitty Hart had told him was true and when he attended the rehearsal he was thrown into panic, although Moss Hart reassured him that at the dress rehearsal the following afternoon he could rehearse with the orchestra for as long as he wished. However, on the Saturday Rex still felt disorientated and Lerner recollected: 'Late that afternoon, with the house sold out and a fierce blizzard blowing, Rex announced that under no circumstances would he go on that night. He needed more time to rehearse with those thirty-two interlopers in the pit.' Unable to persuade Rex to change his mind, they were reluctantly forced to arrange hourly bulletins on local radio networks informing ticket-holders that because of 'technical difficulties' the performance that night had been cancelled. Rex felt that with the whole of Sunday to rehearse he would be ready to tackle the official opening on the Monday night, but the situation changed dramatically when, in spite of the foul weather and the radio announcements, by six o'clock that evening hundreds of people were already lining up at the theatre. Rex still adamantly refused to appear, and Nancy Olson says, 'He just went to pieces and locked himself up in the dressing room. He was terrified.'

Backstage there was total confusion as the house manager, furious at the predicament he had been put in, loudly cursed Rex. It seemed that nothing would persuade Rex to change his mind until, an hour and a half before the curtain was due to go up, Rex's agent arrived. Nancy Olson recalls, 'He pounded on the dressing room door saying, "Come out! Come out! You'll never work again, Rex! You've got to do this!"'

Rex agonised in his dressing room before deciding that, even if he gave a performance that meant the end of his career, he owed it to the other members of the company to go on. He unlocked his dressing room door and prepared for the performance, although he admitted in his autobiography, 'I don't think I've ever been as frightened before or since in my life.'

At 8.40 p.m. the curtain rose to a full house, the expectant audience unaware of the drama which had just been played out behind the scenes. Once on-stage Rex regained confidence and after the thunderous applause which followed 'Why Can't the English' he began to relax. Stanley Holloway said, 'From the moment the curtain rose I felt that we were on a winner. You could sense the cordiality coming up from the audience in waves. There was an electricity in the atmosphere. You realised that everything was falling into place. Yet oddly enough, it wasn't till the interval that I was gripped by that completely sure feeling that this was a terrific hit.'

It was past midnight when the final curtain came down, but the audience stood and cheered. Afterwards Rex's dressing room, which only hours before had been a place of refuge, was flooded with friends and admirers, all eager to congratulate him on his brilliant performance. He could now look forward to the rest of the week in New Haven, followed by four weeks at the Erlanger Theater in Philadelphia. They would finally open in New York at the Mark Hellinger Theater in mid-March. During the tour the show was shortened, an extended ballet sequence was excised, as well as two songs: 'Come to the Ball', sung by Higgins, and 'Say a Prayer for Me Tonight', sung by Eliza, and later re-used by Lerner and Loewe in their film musical *Gigi*.

While he was in New Haven, Rex received a visit from Lilli, who wanted to marry Carlos Thompson. After the show she went back-stage to Rex's dressing room and, when the crowds had disappeared, stayed behind to ask if they could now divorce. Lilli recalled the conversation that took place between them, alone in Rex's dressing room: 'He wouldn't hear of it. He said, "How can you want to marry a man younger than you are? In any case, we belong together and we have our son and our work." We stayed in that dressing room until the early hours of the morning, but all he would grant me then was a separation because he was absolutely certain that, as he called it, this "thing with Carlos" would come to an end. All I know was that I wanted a divorce and he wouldn't give it.' Their private lives would continue in an uncertain limbo until fate took a hand in the most dramatic way, forcing Rex, within the next six months, to make the most difficult and painful decision of his life.

From Philadelphia word-of-mouth spread that a surefire hit was on its way to New York, and on the opening night at the Mark Hellinger Theater on March 15th extra police had to be called out to cope with the crowds of sightseers who had gathered outside. Inside the auditorium the air was electric. The triumph was even greater than anticipated, and everyone involved with the show shared in the plaudits which were heaped upon it. For Rex Harrison it was the crowning achievement of his entire career – a definitive characterisation which firmly placed him among the ranks of the legendary Broadway stars. Mary Martin, giving her view of Harrison's performance, states: 'You don't have to be able to sing to do musical comedy. Great actors can do it. But there is none like Rex – the timing, the perfection. He was wonderful.' Nobody is better qualified than Miss Martin to judge a performance in a musical, for she had been one of the great stars of this particular art form and, as such, her judgement is all the more flattering and absolute.

Among the admirers crowding into Rex's dressing room after the show was T. S. Eliot who, when asked by Harrison if he had enjoyed the evening, replied: 'I must say, Bernard Shaw is greatly improved by music.'

The press on the show was ecstatic. Walter Kerr of the *New York Herald Tribune* acclaimed it 'a miraculous musical', and wrote of Rex:

Mr Harrison's slouch is a rhythmic slouch. His voice is a showman's voice – twangy, biting, confident beyond questioning. His leaps over the fashionable furniture are the leaps of a true enthusiast. But most of all Mr Harrison is an actor, he believes every cranky, snappish, exhilarating syllable of the Alan Jay Lerner lyric he is rattling off, and a fourteen-carat character simply crashes its way onto the stage.

Richard Watts, Jr of the *New York Post* felt:

It would be difficult to say too much in praise of Rex Harrison and Julie Andrews, who have the leading roles. They would be first rate if they were appearing in a straight *Pygmalion*, and they have, in addition, a brilliant skill for musical-comedy playing. Mr Harrison has just the right arrogant charm for the role of the monstrous phonetics expert, and he has never shown himself a more skilful comedian.

Charles Laughton, pressed for his comments, was quoted as saying, 'In all my theatre experience I've seen only a handful of performances to match Rex's. He makes every man in the audience laugh at himself and every woman laugh at the man beside her', while Noël Coward could not fault it: 'Rex Harrison and Julie Andrews are wonderful, the score and lyrics excellent, the decor and dresses lovely and the whole thing beautifully presented.'

Rex was the toast of Broadway, and every newspaper journalist in the country was eager to talk to him – among them Hedda Hopper. Expecting to find him in a more accessible and forgiving mood after his overwhelming success in the show, she made a foolhardy attempt to see him in his dressing room, only to have the door slammed in her face before she could even set foot inside. With queues of people outside the theatre all night hoping to obtain tickets for the hottest show on Broadway, Rex had no need to waste his time with her.

In addition to an apartment in Manhattan, where he could rest between shows on matinee days, Rex also rented a luxurious house on Long Island from Michael Phipps, the polo player. In April he was joined there by Kay Kendall who, having completed her tour with *Bell, Book and Candle*, flew straight over to be reunited with him. During the four months they had been apart they had, according to Kay's sister Kim, 'spent thousands of dollars on long-distance telephone calls'. Overjoyed to be with Rex again, Kay refused all offers of work, including the opportunity to appear as Queenie in a CBS television production of *This Happy Breed*, to be directed by Noël Coward himself. On Long Island she was also able to see her sister again, who was living there with her husband, George F. Baker, an influential New York banker. Kim says of Harrison: 'I thought he was a real egotist but he was always very pleasant and, of course, my late husband was very social so he was always on his best behaviour. Rex liked him very much . . . Rex had a lot of "social friends" like Michael Phipps, Jock Whitney and all these kind of people – they all adored him.'

Rex and Kay Kendall made a striking couple, and Kay soon won the hearts of Rex's many friends in New York. Lerner wrote in his autobiography, 'Rex is a man of charm and the unexpected. The most idle remark can suddenly produce a tempest of vituperation that flashes and thunders and passes like a summer storm,' but by all accounts he had met his match with Kay. Kim Kendall says, 'She knew how to handle him; she could really cut him down to size. She would say, "Come along you stuffy bugger" or something like that to him – which he was,' while Nancy Olson remembers witnessing some spectacular arguments between them. 'When Rex and Kay had a row it was with great humour and with tremendous style. It was like a contest to see who could be the most outrageously nasty, but with an undercurrent of such amusement with it all and tremendous fun. It was not lethal venom – but theatrical venom. They played the part well and they enjoyed their own performances tremendously.' Openly living with Rex, Kay told one reporter, 'Rex is the most wonderful of men. Impossible, of course, but wonderful.'

Having suffered from anaemia for most of her life, Kay would also have spells when she would feel very tired. She often looked pale and Nancy Olson recalls one occasion when she and Alan Lerner went backstage to see Rex so that they could all decide where to go for supper. She says, 'Kay suddenly sat down and looked in the mirror and said, "God, I'm so pale. Look at the circles. I have no energy. I'm absolutely tired all the time."'

As a child she had been sickly, and when she and her sister were dancing in London together she would tire easily; she had also told Kim that when she was filming a scene for *Genevieve* in which she had to push a car out of a ford, she had been haemorrhaging badly. In spite of her history of delicate health she would always perk up because of her tremendous spirit and determination to enjoy life to the full for as long as she could. Living with Rex on Long Island, she was able to enjoy the hectic social life as well as taking advantage of the more relaxing pleasures of long walks along the coast with Rex or boat trips on the Sound.

In August *My Fair Lady* was forced to close for two days when both Rex and his understudy came down with laryngitis, and then, the understudy having recovered, Rex and Kay flew to Bermuda where they spent a week in the sun while he rested his voice.

Rex had only signed an initial contract for nine months, but since the show was such a hit and was now being billed as 'the musical of the century', he was easily persuaded to continue playing Higgins, and agreed to stay with the show until the end of the following year. Rex remarked in later years,

'The stage production was wonderfully exciting because you had the feeling, which you don't always have in the theatre, of audience expectancy. And you felt this kind of electric buzz in the audience before you came on every night. And in the afternoons at matinees. And this kept you keyed, this kept you up more than anything else. It was no difficulty to think about how much the audience was expecting . . . It was in the air. It was in the atmosphere, and it was electric. Every performance we gave.'

Kitty Hart affirms, 'I never found him to give less than his best. On the stage he is a god – there is nobody like him.' Lerner, on the other hand, says that there were days when Rex seemed to be walking through the show, but he would merely tell him before he went on the following night that an important celebrity was in the audience and Rex's performance would brighten up once again.

By the autumn, after almost a year in the show, Rex was feeling exhausted and arranged to have a routine medical check-up at the Harkness Pavilion in New York; he was accompanied by Kay who had lately begun to suffer severe headaches and was also feeling tired. Dr Atchley, who had been the Harrisons' family doctor for some time, telephoned Rex a few weeks afterwards and asked to see Kay again so that he could make some additional blood tests. Miss Kendall duly kept the appointment and they heard nothing for a further few weeks until Rex received another call from the doctor, but this time he asked Harrison to come and see him.

Christmas was approaching and, weighed down by a strong sense of foreboding, Harrison decided to wait until the holidays were over, after Kay had left for Hollywood to start work on a film at M-G-M. For their first Christmas together, he and Kay were joined by her great friends Dirk Bogarde and Tony Forwood, who came over from England to spend the festive season with them at the Long Island house. They brought with them as a gift for the couple a pair of pug dogs who were immediately christened Woolsack and Higgins, the former named in honour of Rex's brother-in-law, David Maxwell-Fyfe, now Lord Kilmuir, the Lord Chancellor. Bogarde has recalled that Christmas of 1956 as a particularly happy one, all enjoying each other's company once again, as well as the sight of the two puppies leaping around, the house crammed with cards, and a huge Christmas tree piled with presents. They were invited to a constant succession of parties, and Bogarde noticed that Kay would occasionally slump exhausted into a chair with a glass in her hand although, considering their hectic life-style, he was not totally surprised.

After the holidays, Kay left for California where she was to appear in her first Hollywood film, *Les Girls*, with Gene Kelly and Mitzi Gaynor under the direction of George Cukor. Only then did Rex make an appointment to see his doctor. Kay rang from Los Angeles that night and told Rex that the studio had found her a gloomy apartment which she did not like, and he told her to call a cab at once and check into the Beverly Hills Hotel.

Between a matinee and an evening performance, Rex finally made his way to the Harkness Pavilion where he was shown into Dr Atchley's consulting room. The doctor explained his position: he did not know Kay's family so could not talk the matter over with them, but Kay had told him that she wanted to marry Rex. Before proceeding further, Atchley told Rex that if he were to disclose the true nature of Kay's condition Rex would have to accept the full responsibility for what he heard. Making no secret of his love for Kay, Rex asked the doctor to continue, and was horrified to be told that Kay was suffering from myeloid leukaemia and would be dead within three years.

Myeloid leukaemia is a cancer of the blood-forming organisms in the bone marrow, which prevents victims from producing their own blood cells. To compensate for the absence of newly-generated cells, blood transfusions eventually become necessary, initially at two-monthly intervals but then more frequently since their effectiveness decreases as more cells are destroyed. Rex was told that Kay would suffer fluctuating ill health, until the final stages of the disease when there would be an accelerated deterioration in her condition. He asked Dr Atchley if anything could be done and was told it could be controlled to some extent by the use of drugs, but they would be palliative measures only – the disease remained incurable.

A dazed Rex Harrison returned to the Mark Hellinger Theater for the evening show, having made up his mind that Kay should never know the horrifying sentence under which she was living. But one person he would have to tell was Lilli. Though in love with Kay, he was still married to Lilli, and decisions for the future would have to be made now that circumstances had altered so radically. Rex immediately wrote to Lilli in Austria, where she was skiing with Carey, and asked her to come to New York as soon as possible. Lilli arrived promptly and she and Rex went together to see Dr Atchley who explained to her the appalling illness from which Kay was suffering. They agreed on the overriding need for a speedy divorce to enable Rex to marry and look after Kay. It would be a heart-breaking task.

After the meeting with Dr Atchley they returned to The Plaza Hotel where, Lilli recalled

'Rex said, "I cannot do it. You know how I feel about death. I cannot do it."

'I told him, "Well, you've got to consider it like a war mission. You've got to do it."

'Rex said, "I could only do it if I knew that you would come back to me and that there is some light at the end of the tunnel."

'I said, "But I'm going to marry Carlos."

'Rex then replied, "Well you can – you can. And when you get that out of your system, then you can come back to me because we belong together."'

Lilli admitted, 'I pledged myself to come back to him,' and that Rex said to her, 'If you change your mind, don't let me know.'

Kay had arrived in Hollywood before filming on *Les Girls* had begun and, talking to George Cukor, discovered that the part of her boyfriend – whom she eventually marries in the film – had yet to be cast. She suggested Leslie Phillips having enjoyed his performance in *On Monday Next* by Philip King, a comedy about a British repertory company, at the Comedy Theatre in London six years before. On her recommendation, Cukor sent for Phillips and, after testing him, gave him the part. He was to prove a good choice as both an actor and a friend to Miss Kendall during her enforced separation from Rex.

Kay, who was being predicted as the next Mrs Rex Harrison, was invited to parties by Gary Cooper, James Mason and Minna Wallis – the sister of producer Hal

Wallis – and all were entranced by her charm and viv-
acity. In Rex's absence, Kay was escorted by Leslie Phillips, although he was well aware that Harrison was
suspicious of other men's attentions towards her. 'Rex
had his eye on everybody, but I was safe because I was
married at the time. It was a brother-sister relationship
between Kay and myself.' At these parties he recollects,
'Kay didn't stay late because she had to work. She wasn't
an all-night lady. She always wanted to leave early but I
never knew why – she was always in good spirits.'
Phillips remembers one occasion when hostess Minna
Wallis pressed her to stay longer to which Kay's retort
was, 'I'm going to bloody well leave!'

'She often couldn't come to work. She didn't always
look well, but people said that she was playing about,'
continues Phillips, who states that Kay was excused from
the dance rehearsals and would watch from the sidelines,
and then expertly step in when the sequences were
filmed. In common with most other actors who have
been directed by George Cukor, Phillips recalls that
unless you had a certain position or stood your ground,
the famed director could be the most devilish bully. Kay,
although obviously ill, had a vibrant, strong personality
which was both appreciated and admired not only by
Cukor, but also by her equally difficult co-star, Gene
Kelly. Phillips says, 'Kay brought warmth onto the picture, and that refreshing quality that she didn't give a shit
for anybody. She didn't kow-tow.'

It is unlikely that those working on the film failed to
realise that something was wrong with Kay. She was
given special privileges, sitting out during rehearsals and
receiving phone calls from Rex at the studio. And their
suspicions would have been confirmed when Kay was
given time off to coincide with Rex's two-week holiday
from *My Fair Lady*, which he spent in Hollywood.

Leslie Phillips confirms, 'They had a break in the
middle of filming and shot around her for a couple of
weeks.' As far as he knew, it was Cukor who had been

responsible for this unprecedented gesture, but Dore Schary as head of the studio, and producer Sol C. Siegel, would have concurred.

Before Rex left for his holiday a problem arose over his replacement. Actor's Equity objected to the casting of the Irish actor, Edward Mulhare, because of his alien status, and refused to sanction his appearance as Higgins. In retaliation Herman Levin threatened to close the show and sue the union for damages, which led to the personal intervention of Mayor Wagner of New York who persuaded Equity to grant their consent, after which Rex was free to leave. Rex had arranged to share a house in the film capital with his old friend Terence Rattigan, who was in Hollywood writing the screenplay of his play *Separate Tables*, and Kay, who had been staying in the Beverly Hills Hotel, moved in with them. Although Rattigan was not happy with what he called 'the swimming pool and star-value protocol general hysteria' of Hollywood, he was a true friend to Rex at just the time when he most needed support. The playwright recalled,

'It was a particularly mad and happy time. If Rex seemed strained at moments I put it down to the fact that *My Fair Lady* was an extremely tiring show and he needed the rest. And if Kay said she was tired and needed to lie down some afternoons, and not come out with us, we just let her get on with it . . . Kay had elegance, charm and was quite outrageous. With all her prep school jokes she had great style. Throughout all their time together her love for Rex was unwavering.'

Lilli, meanwhile, was putting into action what had been agreed in Dr Atchley's consulting room and on February 4th flew to Juarez in Mexico to file the divorce petition, Rex being represented in the proceedings by his friend and lawyer, Aaron Frosch. Lilli charged incompatibility and stated that a reconciliation was impossible.

Under the petition she was to gain custody of twelve-year-old Carey and would retain a half-share in the house at Portofino, but otherwise requested no alimony settlement.

The divorce petition was kept secret until Lilli had returned to Europe and Rex was on his way to Hollywood. Asked for her comments by press reporters in London, Lilli expressed a poor opinion of Englishmen as husbands. 'Let's face it, Englishmen don't like women, at least not in the way that Italians or Frenchmen do. Englishmen don't ever really look at a woman. The greatest compliment Rex could ever pay me was to say that being with me was as good as being with a pal.'

Immediately the petition was filed, Rex became officially engaged to Kay and celebrated the occasion with a hamburger-and-milk lunch party at her dressing room on the set of *Les Girls* at the Metro-Goldwyn-Mayer studios in Culver City. Back in Hollywood, Rex also became embroiled in the party circuit and, ten days after their engagement, was involved in an unfortunate incident at the home of producer Charles Feldman. Attending a party there with Kay and Terence Rattigan, there was an ugly scene just after midnight when Frank Sinatra strolled out onto the patio for a breath of fresh air, and was joined there by Kay. Rex had been looking for her and when he found them together on the patio he asked Kay what she was doing. She replied that she was admiring Sinatra's shirt and asking Rex's opinion said, 'Isn't this a beautiful shirt?' Rex, gritting his teeth, reluctantly admitted that it was and flippantly asked Sinatra its colour, to which the singer is reported to have replied, 'It's just an old shirt. An off-white, sort of yellow.' Rex took offence at the remark and slapped Sinatra, which brought some guests over to investigate, and witnesses stated that the singer stood, biting his lips, with his fists clenched at his side and growled, 'It's still yellow', whereupon Rex slapped him a second time. Controlling himself, Sinatra walked away and rejoined his friends inside, telling them that he had no intention of taking advantage of Harrison, whom he felt hadn't the slightest idea of what he was doing. Sinatra was known to be able and willing to use his fists if the need arose and Rex was lucky to have escaped so lightly. One of the singer's friends told the press: 'Frank could've busted him in half with one hand. What annoyed him most was that Harrison thought he was trying to make time with his girl. But Frank cooled off after a while and laughed it off.'

The same could not be said for Harrison, as Rattigan recalled, 'Rex went off into the night and we found him walking the streets of Beverly Hills.' Kay had also left the party, so Terence Rattigan went in search of them both. 'When I rounded the two of them up, we went off for the weekend to stay with Bing Crosby in Palm Springs. Crosby brought Sinatra over and he and Rex shook hands. Sinatra said, "He could have gone on hitting me all night – I admire the man so."'

Leslie Phillips felt that the whole incident was a complete misunderstanding and says, 'Sinatra was nice to people and Kay was outgoing. Rex got the wrong idea. She adored Rex and wouldn't risk anything.' Shortly after, when Rex returned to New York to resume playing Higgins, he was greeted by the sight of a pair of boxing gloves hanging on his dressing room door, placed there by the girls in the chorus.

When Kay had completed *Les Girls* Rank requested that she return to England to appear opposite Dirk Bogarde in *Wyndham's Way*, which was scheduled to begin shooting at Pinewood studios in April, but she refused, preferring to return to New York to be with Rex.

On April 21st, at the eleventh annual Antoinette Perry Awards, Rex was awarded the Tony for the Best Performance in a Musical by an Actor in 1956. (It was his second Tony, his previous win being for his dramatic performance in *Anne of the Thousand Days*.) *My Fair Lady* was also prominent in other categories and, in addition to being awarded the Tony for Outstanding Musical of the year, four additional Tony awards were given to others connected with the show: Moss Hart, director; Cecil Beaton, costume designer; Oliver Smith, scenic designer and Franz Allers, musical director.

Now Kay was back in New York, they moved into a large boathouse on Long Island Sound belonging to Jock Whitney, the American ambassador to Britain, and Rex bought himself a speedboat which he would take out every day. When Kay did not feel well enough to accompany him, he would throw his rods and tackle into the boat and go fishing. Although Kay continued to suffer occasional severe headaches and bouts of listlessness, there was no need for any form of treatment; Rex kept her blood level under surveillance with regular tests, telling her that they were necessary to keep a check on her anaemia. Otherwise Kay was still possessed of remarkable energy and vitality and it was hard to believe that she was dying.

In June they made final arrangements to marry, alerting the press of their intentions when Rex went to the Municipal Building in New York to obtain a licence. The following day the papers carried an announcement of their forthcoming marriage, although they were unable to give the date or location for the ceremony. Rex had selected the Universalist Church of the Divine Paternity at Central Park West and 76th Street and the ceremony was to take place on June 23rd after the evening performance of *My Fair Lady*, feeling that such an unlikely time for a marriage ceremony would ensure their desire for complete privacy. When Kay invited her sister to be their bridesmaid she told her, 'Don't wear anything too fussy because the press know that we've taken the banns out.'

Rex asked Aaron Frosch, the only other person to whom he had confided the seriousness of Kay's condition, to be his best man. Kay's parents were unable to attend, being in England, although Margaret Leighton, who had been their guest at Christmas and was appearing on Broadway in Terence Rattigan's *Separate Tables*, was invited to join the select wedding group. On the appointed evening, Kim and her husband sat out front and watched the performance, observing that Rex was obviously agitated. Kim recalls the scene just before the show-stopping number 'The Rain in Spain' where Rex says to Eliza, 'I know your nerves are as raw as meat in a butcher's window'. 'Rex got it all the wrong way. He didn't know what he was doing.' As the final curtain came down they made their way backstage to join Rex and Kay as they prepared to leave for the church. Kim says, 'They were so nervous – the pair of them.'

They were dressed as inconspicuously as possible; Rex was wearing his glasses and a plain grey suit while Kay had on a simple beige dress with a baboushka on her head. At eleven-thirty they left the theatre and drove the twenty blocks to the church where liberal clergyman Dr Charles Potter was awaiting their arrival. Dr Potter began the marriage service when the small wedding party had assembled, but had to call a brief halt because he was being distracted by Kay's intermittent giggling and weeping. Kim recollects, 'Kay was roaring with laughter and the poor minister said, "Miss Kendall, if you don't stop – if you can't control yourself, I really can't go on with it."' After Rex gave her a reassuring pat, Kay settled down and the service was able to continue, although both bride and groom were still in an obvious state of agitation, and when the minister asked them to 'join right hands', Rex stuck out his left. The short ceremony over, according to Kim, 'There was a flash of a camera as the columnist Earl Wilson had crept in to take pictures inside the church. So, of course, there was more hysteria: "Oh, how terrible! The press! The terrible press!", and they dashed out and I was left to pick up the document to say that they had been married.'

It was after midnight when they all reassembled at Orsini's for a wedding breakfast, and Kim says, 'Kay cried all the way through it.'

A week later Rex arranged for a second service, held in

the garden of Leland Hayward's Long Island house, with flowers, guests and photographers. Rex felt that Kay had not been entirely satisfied with their midnight marriage in Manhattan, and knew that this was the kind of wedding that she had always wanted. Although, because of Rex's continuing commitment to the show with five months still to run on his contract, they could not go away on a honeymoon, their remaining months in New York were happy ones.

Rex's only other professional engagement was in a ninety-minute CBS television special entitled *Crescendo*, which was broadcast in September. Ethel Merman, who was then appearing on Broadway in *Happy Hunting*, was also scheduled to appear but at the last minute walked off the show amid rumours that she and Harrison had had a difference of opinion. In reality she was dissatisfied with her participation in the show, so Julie Andrews and Stanley Holloway were asked to replace her, singing a medley of songs from *My Fair Lady*, having insufficient time to prepare anything else. The key figure in the show was Harrison, playing an Englishman on a visit to the United States who is entertained with examples of all kinds of American music, although one reviewer felt, 'Rex Harrison was cruelly abused. He was employed only as a narrator, albeit under the guise of being an English visitor to American shores. Though ostensibly being introduced to the panorama of American music, on stage he was used merely to give cues. And matters were not helped in the closing moments when he himself sang only a few bars from "I've Grown Accustomed To Her Face" . . . A viewer who expected to see Mr Harrison do some performing could only feel short-changed.' Harrison himself, however, recalled how thrilled he was to be given the opportunity to assist Louis Armstrong in performing 'That's Jazz' on the show, which had been written by Cole Porter for Armstrong, Bing Crosby and Frank Sinatra in the film *High Society*.

Since its opening, *My Fair Lady* had become one of the

most successful shows ever produced on Broadway, and each performance was a great event for its audience, who often booked up months in advance. Kitty Hart says, 'I saw the show many times and at the same point in the show the same thing always happened. In the middle of "The Rain in Spain" when Rex said, "I think she's got it – Now once again!", at that moment the audience levitated three feet and stayed that way for the rest of the show – they took a deep collective breath.'

During Harrison's long stay with the show in New York there had been occasional mishaps, the most notable in May 1957 when a forty-foot-long piece of scenery, weighing several tons, crashed on to the stage behind the front cloth while Rex was performing. Although it missed him, Rex involuntarily jumped forward a few steps and attempted to continue singing. In the confusion the orchestra stopped playing and Rex recited the lyrics until the musicians took up the tune, and the show could proceed. Had the scenery landed only a few feet closer, Harrison would most certainly have been seriously injured, if not killed.

On another evening a chandelier descended during the first act and lifted Harrison's toupée from his head. He had to carry on, trying to ignore what had happened, while the offending chandelier was then raised with his hair-piece attached to it. When the first act was completed Harrison stormed back-stage, demanding that the culprit responsible be brought to him, threatening not to go on for the second act if this was not done. Phil Adler, the stage manager, told him, 'No, Rex, I won't bring him here. He's a brute. You'll insult him and he'll kill you.' Harrison was finally placated by being permitted to telephone Moss Hart and vent his anger to him.

A potentially dangerous incident occurred when a madman rang up the theatre one night and claimed that he had placed a bomb in the stalls, timed to explode while Rex was performing 'Accustomed to her Face' at the end of the show. The management searched the theatre but could find no such device and they decided to continue with the performance. Rex was not told of the threat until after the final curtain had descended.

Except for such incidents the show had a fluid and comparatively happy 750 performances with Harrison as Higgins. On his last night, December 2nd, Kay made her only appearance on the American stage when she persuaded the stage manager to allow her to change places with the actress playing the Queen of Transylvania in the first act, with Moss Hart as her escort, and in the second act she appeared as Mrs Higgins' maid. After the performance Rex gave a party on-stage for all those who had been involved in making the show the greatest success of his life. On the expiry of his contract on December 2nd, Rex was replaced by Edward Mulhare. Julie Andrews and Stanley Holloway also left the Broadway cast at the same time, as all three principals had been engaged to open the show in London in the following spring.

Rex and Kay immediately set off for a holiday, boarding the *Queen Mary* bound for Cherbourg. When they disembarked in France, Rex told newsmen, 'We want rest, just rest.' He and Kay had signed a contract to appear in a film for M-G-M based on William Douglas-Home's popular play *The Reluctant Debutante*, concerning the last group of debutantes to be presented to the Queen before the practice was abolished, but in the script the English setting had been transferred to America. The veteran Hollywood producer, Pandro S. Berman, suggested Rex and Kay for the husband and wife in the film, and Vincente Minnelli, the director, flew to New York to broach the subject with them. Coming to the end of his contract with *My Fair Lady* in New York, Rex was intrigued by the project and liked the idea of working with Kay once again, and he told Minelli, 'We'd love to do it, but the script is no good.'

Minnelli, who also disapproved of the changes that had been made, assured them that the script would be rewritten, in keeping with the flavour of the original play. To help their tax situation in both England and the United States it was also agreed that the film would be made in Paris, and they were assured that the rewrites on the script would be sent to them in Switzerland. Rex had rented a three-bedroomed chalet in St Moritz, which boasted a spectacular view of the Swiss Alps, for two months, although before they settled in there the couple first went to stay with Oona and Charlie Chaplin in Vevey. Kay was particularly happy to be reunited with Oona. When they went on to St Moritz they were joined by Terence Rattigan.

Unfortunately, what was intended to be an extended holiday before Rex and Kay began work on *The Reluctant Debutante* in Paris was ruined when Kay fell ill. A few months later, Kay said in an interview: 'It was to be our first real holiday. We would climb up mountains and things, and it would be wonderful. That was the idea. And then I fell ill. I had to go to bed almost as soon as we arrived. I became so ill I thought I was going to die. For two whole nights Rex sat by my bed. Whenever I opened my eyes he was there. He got no rest at all.'

Rex called in a doctor and told him the truth about Kay, and she was moved to the clinic in St Moritz. A professor from Zurich who had invented a pill to retard the action of cancer cells came down to see Kay, and after three weeks her blood-count returned to normal. Once Kay was recovering, Rex would go out for walks in the mountains with Rattigan. The playwright, who until then had been unaware of the desperate situation which was facing his friend, was finally let into the secret. He recalled, 'Rex was desperately worried and late one night he told me what had happened. I realised then his courage, his great courage in never being able to let his concern show. He made the last two years of Kay's life the best years.' Rattigan felt, 'Rex's great ability was to feign indifference: when Kay was ill, even desperately sick, he would still go off and play golf with me and be perfectly calm. I have never seen such fortitude.'

While they were still in Switzerland the rewrites on *The Reluctant Debutante* arrived, and when Rex read them he was furious and telephoned Pandro S. Berman in Paris telling him, 'We wouldn't play one word of that lousy script!' Berman had no option but to contact the play's author, William Douglas-Home, in England and ask him to write the screenplay, and a telegram was dispatched urging him: 'Come to Paris tomorrow because Rex won't do the film.'

Douglas-Home had three days to work before Rex was scheduled to arrive in Paris, during which time he managed to untangle enough to enable shooting to begin. Kay, meanwhile, had suffered another set-back in her health when she had cracked a bone in her pelvis in a tobogganing accident and on their way to Paris, they stopped off in Zurich to have X-rays taken. It was not serious but Kay was obliged to lie down until the bone mended. She gave all her pre-production interviews lying on a chaise-longue – and no one, not even Minnelli or Berman, suspected that she could not stand.

William Douglas-Home recalled that when Harrison arrived in Paris he was still seething with anger that the play had been Americanised to cater for the two popular young American stars, Sandra Dee and John Saxon, who had mistakenly been cast as the young romantic leads in this most English of all subjects. Douglas-Home recollects, 'Rex got rather annoyed one night when we were at a restaurant in the Meat Market in Paris. He said that I'd sold myself to the Americans, but Miss Kendall calmed him down, and the next day I received an azalea with a note saying, "Sorry you were there when it happened – Love Rex."' The playwright continues, 'Rex gets angry like that about the script when he thinks it's awful. He's bristly when he's working,' but says, 'The next day I went to play golf with him at Fontainebleau and he sliced his drive through a window of the clubhouse and never turned a hair.'

William Douglas-Home and Harrison soon established

a firm friendship, and the playwright and his wife moved into the Lancaster Hotel where Rex and Kay were staying. He remained in Paris for the filming, working on the script a day in advance of shooting, and he and his wife greatly enjoyed the company of the Harrisons, being particularly enchanted by Kay's eccentric behaviour. On one occasion they were invited for a drink in the Harrisons' hotel suite, and Home recalls:

'Rex was opening a bottle of champagne and Kay was having a bath. The telephone rang and Rex called, "Kay!" and went on opening the bottle. She then came out of the bathroom absolutely stark naked, except for a bath towel around her head, and answered the telephone. It was Sir Gladwyn Jebb, the British ambassador to France, and I clearly heard him say, "Come to dinner next Thursday night." Kay replied, "We work very hard during the week," and he said, "Well, you don't work on Saturdays do you?"

'"No", said Kay, "Rex and I like to dip our finger nails in the gin bottle on Saturday night, if you know what I mean?"

'The Ambassador said, "I understand", and she put down the telephone, waved to us and went back into the bathroom – the most splendid girl in the world.'

Director Vincente Minnelli enjoyed working with the Harrisons and said of Kay: 'She would be raucous and vital and lovable, and when the day's work was over, everyone would want to take her home.' No-one working on the film had any idea that Kay was seriously ill, although Minnelli did say, 'I found Rex wonderfully attentive to her, but gave it no special thought. Kay was equally devoted to him.'

Despite the happy rapport between director and cast the film was not totally successful and was panned by the critics as laborious and contrived, even though Harrison and Kendall provided a few bright moments. The *New*

York Post critic summed it up when he wrote, 'The technical moral is that no performer can rise above his material. The more he struggles the worse he gets mired. Still, there's no one who can go down with the grace of Rex Harrison.'

In February 1958, while they were still filming in Paris, Stanley Holloway, who was working on a film in England, gave an interview to the *Sunday Express* which put Rex in a very unsympathetic light. Regarding his experience of working with Harrison for two years on Broadway, Holloway was quoted as saying, 'Rex and I certainly had nothing in common. In fact, he didn't once come to my dressing room during the two years we were in the show together. Nor did I go to his,' and he continued, 'Well, you know, in *My Fair Lady* Rex really plays himself. For Professor Higgins is arrogant and rude. But charming . . . he's got amazing charm that man. The chorus girls were wild about him.' Asked if Harrison had been popular with the company, Holloway said, 'I can only tell you that when Rex was leaving the show he gave a small cocktail party for the cast and stage hands. Not a single stage hand turned up.'

Rex wasted no time in replying publicly to Holloway's slurs and told reporters in Paris, 'Holloway and the *Express* made me look like a beast. It was such a happy company in New York and everyone got along so well. I didn't even realise Holloway had a gripe.' He stated, 'I've notified my solicitors in London. I have to take steps,' and said that he was quite prepared to sue Stanley Holloway, adding 'Perhaps he'll have to turn over his salary to me at the end of each week.'

Alan Jay Lerner remembers that after Holloway had given the offending interview, 'Rex was fit to be tied and we didn't know what to do because Rex and Kay were in Paris and the press wanted to interview them.' Lerner recalls that when they had completed the filming of *The Reluctant Debutante* and they returned to England for the first time in over two years, 'Rex was behaving as if they were escaping royalty being smuggled into a foreign country. They didn't want to see the press.'

Lerner was completely mystified. 'Stanley eventually apologised and said he was misquoted, which is not uncommon in the British press. There was a professional respect and there was never a moment of disagreement that I knew about when the play was running in New York.' When rehearsals began in London on April 7th for the London opening, Lerner recalls that the men shook hands. *My Fair Lady* had been eagerly awaited in England. The Broadway cast recording of the show had already filtered into the country, and had been selling for enormous sums on the black market for over two years. When the box-office had opened in the previous October at the Theatre Royal, Drury Lane scores of people queued all day long to obtain tickets not only for themselves, but for an assured re-sale at a profit of up to ten times their purchase price. The theatre was sold out for months in advance, and as the opening approached excitement grew to fever pitch and advertisements appeared in *The Times* and other newspapers offering seats for the show. The clever black-marketeers, both professional and amateur, made a large profit.

The high expectations surrounding the show only heightened Rex's doubts about the production. The night before the opening, at Binkie Beaumont's London home in Lord North Street, Rex raged into the small hours about what he felt was wrong. Beaumont, who had known Harrison for many years, knew that it was Rex's way of getting it out of his system and just sat and listened until he collapsed exhausted.

The scene outside the theatre on April 30th was chaotic, with hordes of press photographers trying to spot the celebrities arriving, among them Antony Armstrong-Jones, eager to snap Ingrid Bergman, which he did, Miss Bergman little knowing that she was posing especially for the Queen of England's future brother-in-law. Kay was also in the audience, as well as

Rex's sister and brother-in-law, Lord and Lady Kilmuir; Dirk Bogarde; and those directly involved with the show, including Moss and Kitty Hart, choreographer Hanya Holm and, of course, Alan Jay Lerner and Frederick Loewe. In order to get the show in on time and to avoid interfering with the plot, the management had ordered that under no circumstances were the company to reprise any musical number. It was expected that at important musical first nights one or more numbers would be reprised according to the response from the audience, but they too had been informed in advance that this would not be the case on this particular occasion. Inevitably, as it had done in New York, 'The Rain in Spain' stopped the show, but when it was clearly impossible to carry on, Harrison, Andrews and Robert Coote merely acknowledged the audience's ecstatic response with a brief bow before continuing. Otherwise the show went through without interruption, ending triumphantly with eight curtain calls.

The Times critic wrote:

The individual performances fully live up to the praise already lavished on them in America. Mr Rex Harrison with his light fantastic playing gets a surprising deal of the Higgins professional zeal, social obtuseness, and downright rudeness into the tweedy intellectual . . . Mr Harrison's lack of musicianship has been allowed for by the composer. To say that he speaks Mr Frederick Loewe's songs would be a gross libel: he performs them,

while Caryl Brahms wrote of Harrison's performance in *Plays and Players*: 'His Higgins has all his own preposterously professional charm and personality – his precision of timing and technique. If there is to be an award for the year's most stylish performance, we need look no further.'

On May 5th Her Majesty Queen Elizabeth and His

Royal Highness Prince Philip, Duke of Edinburgh, accompanied by Princess Alexandra, attended a special Gala Performance of the show, although the evening was marred for Her Majesty. Kitty Hart states, 'I don't think she liked it. She had a bit of an upset before the opening and I think it troubled her. Some poor crazy fellow had been found in the Royal Box, not too long before curtain time – he had obviously come in with the cleaners – and I am sure that had upset her. It was unfortunate.' Lerner, Loewe and Moss Hart were presented to the Queen during the interval, and after the show the royal visitors went on to the stage to meet the cast, making it a memorable evening for Rex.

Harrison had agreed to play Higgins in London for one year only, and at first he and Kay rented Lord Warwick's house at Swan Walk, Chelsea. But they had a misunderstanding with the Earl and moved to the Savoy while Kay set about looking for alternative accommodation. She eventually found another house in Cheyne Walk – again in Chelsea – which they both felt was suitable. As had been the case in New York, Rex's dressing room became a focal point for visiting celebrities and friends, eager to congratulate him on his performance. One such visitor was Evelyn Laye, who had appeared with Rex in *Sweet Aloes* on Broadway more than twenty years before when Rex was still struggling to make his mark in the theatre. Having seen the show at that time she feels, 'Nobody has ever matched so clever musically. He was no singer, but gave a remarkable rendering of the numbers within the character.' She says that his performance was 'stunning'.

Margaret Lockwood, another co-star from the past (she appeared in *Night Train to Munich* with him eighteen years before), was amazed at what she saw on stage. 'I thought his performance was one of complete genius. I have never seen such brilliance and timing in my life. I was crying at his genius.' After the show Miss Lockwood went backstage to tell Rex how much she admired his interpretation of Higgins, but she recalls that the dressing room was in chaos.

'Rex had bought Kay a magnificent and very expensive fur jacket which had obviously thrilled Kay enormously. She had worn it to the theatre that evening when she had accompanied Rex and their contingent of pug dogs. As Rex left the dressing room to make his first entrance Kay, shorn of her fur jacket which she had carelessly left in his dressing room, had gone to her usual place in the wings to watch the performance. When they both returned at intermission their brood had completely destroyed the jacket.'

Surprisingly, Miss Lockwood says, 'Kay didn't mind at all and Rex didn't seem to mind either.'

While they were in London Rex engaged a secretary, Edith Jackson, who was to remain in Rex's employment for thirteen years, mesmerised by the way in which he was able to exercise his lethal charm. Rex often told people that he could not live without her and the great help that she gave him, although for her part the period she spent with the actor was less satisfying. She adored Kay, and remembers that Rex would send her to the bank every week to withdraw an allowance of £20 for his wife.

While they were in London Kay would not consider accepting any offers to appear in a film because it would mean that she would never see Rex. She told one interviewer, 'For a film I'd have to get up at six in the morning, and I'd be back home from the studios at seven in the evening. At seven in the evening Rex would be at the theatre, and by the time he was through by eleven I'd have to be in bed to get up again by six the following morning,' and she concluded, 'That is not a satisfactory married life.'

Instead, Kay spent some of her time attempting to find a play that might be suitable for her to appear in, in the West End. As her health became noticeably worse, Dirk

Bogarde, in constant contact by telephone, kept a close watch on her condition, although he was unaware that she was suffering from leukaemia. During the run of *My Fair Lady* Rex was given a week off, which they planned to spend with Prince Bertil of Sweden at his villa at Ste Maxime on the Côte d'Azur, near to St Tropez. Princess Lilian of Sweden had first met Rex with Guy Middleton when they were appearing in *French Without Tears* before the war, and she first saw Kay during the war at a cocktail party given by the American artist Buster Collier and his wife Stevie. The Princess recalls, 'We all adored her. We still do – everyone who ever knew her. She was the loveliest thing I have ever seen and I had more giggles, laughs and best times with Kay than anybody else.'

Just before Rex and Kay were to leave for Ste Maxime Kay had a bad blood transfusion which left her with a high temperature. Rex thought they would be unable to go but the next day Kay recovered completely and Rex recalled that when they arrived at Ste Maxime Kay was as energetic as ever. Rex spent some time playing golf with Prince Bertil, while Kay relaxed. Princess Lilian recalls that she was unaware, even during that last visit to Ste Maxime, of just how ill Kay was. 'I did not know what was wrong with Kay – all I knew was that she was in and out of hospital.'

Back in London, rumours began circulating concerning Kay's health. When the *Star* newspaper rang the Harrisons' house in Cheyne Walk, the phone was answered by Rex's secretary, as Rex was out. The reporter told the secretary of the rumours that Kay was very ill and had leukaemia, and received the firm reply: 'I can't think what gave you that idea. Mr Harrison is out playing golf, and Miss Kendall is undoubtedly carrying the clubs.'

When Rex returned home, the secretary told him of the disturbing phone call she had received that afternoon, and Rex thanked her and told her that she had done the right thing, although he did not confide to her the truth about Kay. She was told of Kay's condition by Terence

Rattigan's secretary and it was not until just before Christmas that Rex told her himself.

Having read a number of scripts, Kay finally selected *The Bright One*, a play about a school-mistress on a cruise who is transformed into a Greek nymph. The author was Judy Campbell, the West End actress who had introduced the song, 'A Nightingale Sang in Berkeley Square'. Rex was not keen on the play, but Kay wanted to appear in it so he did not stand in her way, and he even agreed to direct her, as well as co-producing the play with his old friend, Jack Minster. Rex telephoned Gladys Cooper in Hollywood and persuaded her to appear with Kay as her grandmother.

Fraught with problems from the start, it soon looked as if Rex would be faced with a repeat of the disaster he had had when he had directed Edith Evans in *Nina* at the same time as he was appearing in *Bell, Book and Candle* at the Phoenix Theatre. The opening was to take place at the Theatre Royal, Brighton on November 24th, and rehearsals continued right up until the last possible moment in a desperate bid to get the production into shape, although Rex had to leave late in the afternoon before the first night to ensure that he was back in time for the evening performance at Drury Lane. Kay said, 'It's nearly killed poor Rex. He has been working all day and all night. He's lost weight. Now he's vowed he'll never again direct a play and act in one at the same time.'

The Brighton first night was packed, and the theatre was solidly booked up for its week at the Theatre Royal, but with only two weeks before it was to open at London's Winter Garden Theatre, there was still a great deal of work that needed to be done to make the play more acceptable. On the night, Kay and Gladys Cooper were cheered for their performances and after briefly entertaining well-wishers in her dressing room, Kay rushed down to the railway station to meet Rex who was coming in from London on the midnight train. He arrived with a box of red roses for his wife and she told him all about the reception that the play had been given. But they both knew that in London it would be a different story.

After the Brighton engagement Rex continued working on the show during the day, and on the night before the opening, held a late-night preview, which did not finish until 1 a.m., but it was all to no avail, and after the London opening on December 10th they had to face the verdict of the critics, who disliked the play intensely. After seeing it, Noël Coward wrote: 'I went to see Kay Kendall in a dreadful little play in which she was enchanting and Gladys Cooper magnificent.' The critic from *Plays and Players* who attended the second-night performance wrote:

> Thanks to Miss Kendall's bubbling personality a great deal of charm did in fact emerge. As a Greek nymph in an English botany mistress's clothing the play offered her plenty of scope. But there really were a lot of lines for so few laughs, and a seriously conceived deviation into an off-stage mental home pricked the bubble of charm beyond repair.

Regarding Harrison's contribution the reviewer continued, 'A succession of second-night mishaps made it difficult to gain a fair impression of Rex Harrison's direction.'

As the play reached the second week of its run, Kay fell ill, reportedly suffering from influenza, and was forced to be absent for three days. By the end of the week Jack Minster made the unpopular and difficult decision to close the play on the following Saturday. Kay told the press, 'I think it's bloody awful', and both she and Miss Cooper stated that they would never work for Jack Minster again while Rex, in a statement made the day after the play closed, said, 'The play has not been given a chance. After all, there was only one losing week. That was when my wife was away ill.'

Rex and Kay often spent Sundays with Dirk Bogarde

and Tony Forwood at Beel House, and their hosts became increasingly alarmed by the changes in Kay's health. Bogarde recalled that one day in the summer, when they had all been playing croquet on the lawn, Kay suddenly collapsed and afterwards sat shivering in a corner, drinking a large glass of Guinness and port to revive her. Although it was obvious to all that Kay was ill, Rex continued to keep up the pretence that there was nothing wrong, and tried not to treat Kay like an invalid. Alan Jay Lerner says, 'The thing that was wonderful about the way he behaved was that he never changed. He got angry and he carried on and he behaved just the way he always does because he knew that if he suddenly became all solicitous and not Rex she might become suspicious. He just played Rex all the way.'

That summer Lilli had broken her silence and told Noël Coward, who was staying at Portofino, about the leukaemia from which Kay was suffering. Rex remained in regular contact with his ex-wife, despite her marriage to Carlos Thompson, and she knew of the desperate time that he was having coping with the situation, hardly able to confide in anybody lest the truth should leak out and Kay should hear. Lilli spoke of, 'those dreadful three years in which we were in touch every week, either by 'phone or letter – or both,' and said, 'The letters were desperately affectionate from his side and I had a terrible time because I was very happy.'

After hearing the whole story Coward wrote in his diary:

I am very fond of Lilli but she is certainly in a fine emotional and moral jam – and there were some high-powered tear-diffused heart-to-heart talks. Carlos, her new and charming husband, was in Berlin making a picture. She is still carrying a torch for Rex, although she loves Carlos. Rex never stops badgering her with letters and telephone calls. The poor wretched Kay has apparently got leukaemia and cannot live more than a year or so at the outside! This is a truly horrible situation. She, of course, doesn't know but Rex does, and did when he married her! The poor dear may have behaved badly in the first place when she went bald-headed after Rex but having got her own way she is certainly paying a ghastly price for it.

Lilli said, 'What Noël doesn't record in his diary is that I had a terrible scene with him. It was a frightful scene as we screamed at each other up there at Portofino.' Talking of the fretful time that she went through then, Lilli said: 'It was like sitting on a train racing through the night and you didn't know when it was going to explode. I'm glad I never told my husband because it would have been awful.'

During the run of *My Fair Lady*, Kay became very close to Vivien Leigh and the two women were often seen in the West End together, as Olivier was filming in California at the time. Lauren Bacall became an addition to the group when she came over to England to appear in *North West Frontier*, which was made partially on location in India and at Pinewood studios, and all three actresses often went out together in the evenings. On March 28th 1959 Bacall attended Rex's final performance in *My Fair Lady* at Drury Lane with Kay and remembered it as 'an exciting moving evening. I remember looking over at Kay and seeing tears streaming down her cheeks.'

As the curtain came down, marking the end of Rex's three years in the role, there were cries of 'Speech!' from the audience but Rex ignored them, merely taking his bows along with the rest of the company and retiring to his dressing room at Drury Lane for the last time. His part was to be taken over by Alec Clunes.

Rex said that his immediate plan was 'to laze in the sun and do nothing', intending to travel down to Portofino with Kay, and then on to Paris where Kay was to start work on a new film with Yul Brynner. He did intimate that he was considering appearing at Stratford-upon-

Avon, but was most looking forward to returning to a more normal routine. Kay said, 'I have a hatred of *My Fair Lady* such as nobody else has. I absolutely loathe it. Not as a show, but because it took three and a half years out of my married life. I haven't had a dinner with my husband for years. I'm much more delighted than Rex that it's over with.' Rex told the press that he was glad to have a rest from playing Higgins:

'It's too long to play one part, much too long . . . It's been wonderful but I just couldn't go on doing it any more. I am almost glad it's over. I don't think an audience appreciates exactly what a long, long run means for an actor . . . It is like a lawyer having to plead the same case every day for three years . . . It is like a housewife having to cook the same meal every night . . .',

although he has said also, 'I think if you have music it enables you to do it longer. I think if I'd done straight dramatic roles for three years . . . I'd have gone slightly madder than I did. I think the music does help to keep you fresh.'

As the time had approached for Rex to leave the cast of *My Fair Lady*, after his year-long appearance as Higgins in London, the treatment for Kay's leukaemia became more intensive and it was not unusual for Rex to return home from the theatre in the evening to find Kay in the bedroom of their Cheyne Walk house, undergoing blood transfusions and other help for her worsening condition. Once he had departed from the show, Rex could no longer look forward to the escape of becoming Higgins each day, for now his commitment to his wife in her tragic last six months was total.

It was imperative that they keep busy to avoid Kay feeling that she was being treated like an invalid. She had been disappointed by the failure of *The Bright One* and when she was offered the lead opposite Yul Brynner in

Stanley Donen's comedy *Once More With Feeling*, was excited by the prospect of working in front of the cameras again. The film was to be made in Paris, but before he would make a decision, Rex consulted Dr Carl Goldman, who had been Kay's doctor since she was seventeen, as to whether it would be wise to allow her to work. Goldman agreed with Rex that it would be better for Kay to be given the chance to work again, as it would take her mind off her health, and so it was agreed that she should make the film.

If the insurance physicians had taken even a cursory examination of Miss Kendall, the enlargement of her spleen would have told them all that they wanted to know, and she would not have been permitted to work because of the potential insurance risk. However, Rex would never permit them to examine Kay, as he was frightened that they would tell her the real cause of her increasingly frequent bouts of ill health, having assured her that the blood transfusions she received were because of a recurrence, in a more severe form, of her anaemia. By exercising such deception, albeit out of love for his wife, Rex was treading on very dangerous ground as the studio would have been quite within their rights to charge Rex for any financial loss during production of the film caused directly by her illness.

Shooting on the film began in April, and Kay's condition was quite evident to all who were working on it. Mervyn Johns, who appeared in the film and shared a long scene with her, recalls, 'She was obviously extremely ill – she was not at all well and kept very quiet.' Inevitably, Kay's health cracked under the strain and she was often too ill to report for work at the studio, despite the blood transfusions which were administered at the American Hospital in Paris in a desperate attempt to revive her flagging energy. Moreover, the medication which she had been given in Switzerland was now ineffective, as Kay entered the final stages of her illness.

When Kay was too ill to turn up for work, Columbia

executives, unaware of the poor health of their leading lady, were frantic at the loss of a day's shooting. Rex was in a very uncomfortable situation and when, towards the end of May, she was absent a third time and the production closed down completely for the rest of the week, he felt obliged to make a statement. He lamely claimed that he was responsible for passing on a cold to Kay which had then developed into bronchitis, and he assured the studio that she would be able to return to work after the weekend. Everything possible was being done for Kay to enable her to fulfil her commitment to Columbia Pictures, but she was not responding and on the Saturday morning it was decided that Kay would have to see Dr Goldman at the London Clinic. The studio tried to charter a plane to London but it was not possible and Rex was forced to book them onto the train from the Gare du Nord to connect with the night ferry to Dover. Before they left he explained, 'Kay has been running a temperature for the past few days. A heavy cold turned into bronchial pneumonia. She is a little better today but on our doctor's advice is going to London for treatment.'

They arrived early the next morning at Victoria Station and Kay was leaning heavily on Rex's arm as he guided her to a car which was waiting to drive them to the London Clinic. Once there, Kay was swiftly settled into a room after which Rex left to book into the Connaught Hotel and eat a hurried lunch, before rushing straight back to the Clinic. News of their dramatic return to London spread fast and speculation was now mounting in the press about the seriousness of Kay's condition, but Rex continued to brush aside these rumours. The confusion was made worse when conflicting statements regarding her health were given: Rex claimed that his wife was suffering from congestion of the lungs, a spokesman from the Clinic said that she had bronchitis, while Dr Goldman said that she had anaemia and would be out of the hospital by the end of the week.

Kay's aged grandmother, the music hall star Marie

Kendall, was extremely concerned about her grand-daughter and told reporters, 'We've been so anxious. We don't know much about her illness.'

Fortunately, Kay responded well to the treatment she received at the Clinic and she persuaded Dr Goldman to allow her to return to Paris to complete the film and, four days after she was admitted, she was discharged, although she still looked pale and was noticeably thinner. Within a week she was once again working in front of the cameras.

Rex would meet her at the end of each day's shooting, having spent the day either playing golf with Sydney Chaplin or planning with Irene Selznick his next Broadway appearance. Jean Anouilh's latest play, *Hurluberlu* had just opened in Paris and Irene Selznick was interested in buying the property for presentation on Broadway. She had persuaded Rex to go and see it with a view to his taking the lead in the English version of the play in New York. He had welcomed her invitation and, having seen it, was most interested in her proposition.

Doggedly and by sheer determination Kay was able to complete *Once More With Feeling* although Dr Goldman had twice had to fly out to Paris to attend her and administer heart stimulants to give her the energy she needed to keep going. As soon as shooting was completed Rex took her to Portofino where she brightened up, and in an interview over the telephone she told one journalist: 'I've never felt fitter', and denied rumours that her health would prevent her from working again, saying 'Only death in my sleep would stop me from making another film.'

Soon afterwards, however, they were on the move once again. As the July heat in Portofino became unbearable Rex took Kay to St Moritz. From their hotel in Switzerland Rex explained: 'We just couldn't stand the heat any more. We were dying for a breath of fresh air,' and he assured the inquisitive press that Kay was fine and would be accompanying him to New York in

September, when he would be preparing for the Anouilh play and his wife was to appear in a television spectacular. In the middle of August they returned to Portofino, where Rex's son, Noel, had arranged to meet them; Noel was accompanied by his wife Sarah, whom he had married the previous March in London.

Back in Portofino, Kay's condition deteriorated rapidly and it was decided that she would have to be admitted to the hospital in Rapallo. Dr Goldman travelled down to see Kay there and insisted that it was imperative that they return to the London Clinic where Kay could be properly attended. The journey by train from Italy to London was a nightmare for Rex and Dr Goldman as they tended Kay, who lay helpless in their compartment. By the time they disembarked from the ferry at Dover Kay was too weak to stand. Two seamen had to carry her off the ferry in a canvas chair and, without going through Customs, she was taken straight to their reserved compartment on the Golden Arrow bound for Victoria. At the station Rex once again walked her slowly to a waiting car, supporting her around her waist, reassuring her that all was well. She was unable to walk properly, and her feet barely touched the ground.

Arriving at the Clinic, Kay stood at the door for a moment before going up to her fourth-floor room, and told the waiting newsmen, 'I'm just here for two days.'

Rex again booked into the Connaught Hotel, but kept a vigil at her bedside. In the middle of the week Kay's condition worsened and Rex took a room adjoining hers in the hospital so that he could be by her side day and night as she was given blood transfusions in a desperate attempt to revive her. At 11.30 a.m. on Sunday, September 6th the hospital issued a bulletin, admitting that Kay was 'gravely ill'. On the Saturday, Kim Kendall had read in the newspaper that her sister was very ill in the London Clinic. She says, 'I got through to the Clinic and said, "I want to speak to Mrs Harrison, and they said, "I'm so sorry". I said, "You've got to let me speak to somebody – this is her sister calling from America" and they told me that Mr Harrison would be there at a certain time and I called back and I spoke to Rex and he said, "Don't worry, dear, she's all right – nothing to worry about, she'll be all right."'

By the time the hospital had issued their bulletin on the Sunday morning, Kay was in a coma from which she would never wake, although before she lost consciousness, she had whispered to Rex, 'I love you with all my heart.' At 12.30 p.m. Kay Kendall died at the age of thirty-two. So ended the life of a young woman who had, in such a short time, achieved the film stardom she had sought so strongly and, more important, a loving marriage with her celebrated husband. She had been wed little more than two years but, for her, they had been the best and most precious years of her life. Her death left a void in the lives of her many friends whose love and admiration for her great courage endure to this day.

Rex personally telephoned friends and relatives to give them the news, telling them that she had passed away very peacefully. When Marie Kendall heard the news of her grand-daughter's death she wept and said, 'I think dear Rex deserves a medal. None of us realised that Kay was dying. Kay was so obviously happy with Rex. Oh, how I adored my darling. Poor Rex. He must be heartbroken. In each other they found such happiness. How tragic they should have to lose it so quickly.'

Kay's father, Terry Kendall, says, 'I have always been so grateful to Rex for the happiness he gave Kay. Rex was wonderful during the comparatively short period of their marriage. Kay adored him.' He adds, 'Naturally Rex is controversial but I have always found him considerate and friendly, even after Kay's passing.' And Princess Lilian says, 'I know Kay wanted stardom all her life. She used to come home and tell us, "I've got no talent – I should marry and have children." Kay always wanted to be another Carole Lombard – she always carried a little photograph of her around in her wallet. She was her idol, she adored her. It is so sad that this brilliantly talented and beautiful girl had only three years of stardom.'

While Rex was still at the Clinic he wrote a final letter to Lilli telling her what had happened. Lilli was in London herself, having come over to care for her dying mother, and Rex gave the letter to his secretary, telling her to take a taxi and deliver it to Miss Palmer directly. Lilli said: 'It was a heart-rending letter written from the London Clinic on the day of her death. As long as he knew all was the same: "Are you true to your vow?"'

Rex finally emerged from the Clinic at 3.20 p.m., dressed in a dark suit and wearing a trilby hat. He looked exhausted as his friend Dr Goldman drove him away in his car, and when the doctor returned shortly afterwards he said: 'I believe Rex is going off somewhere to be completely alone. His sister, Lady Kilmuir, will join him and help to comfort him. He has come through such a lot. Now he must face life without the woman he has loved so much,' and continued, 'It has been a long and difficult strain for him. Now it is over and he is completely broken up.'

Rex stayed with his sister, Sylvia Kilmuir, and her husband while friends took charge of the arrangements for the funeral. Harrison requested that no flowers be sent, asking instead that donations be given to the Imperial Cancer Research Fund. Mr Arthur Dickson Wright, the treasurer of the fund, and vice-president of the Royal College of Surgeons, announced the launching of a Kay Kendall Memorial Fund for research into leukaemia, while the Variety Club of Great Britain pledged their support with an annual donation of £5,000.

The private funeral was held on September 9th at the eighteenth-century parish church of St John in Hampstead, picked by Harrison because beside it ran one of his and his late wife's favourite walks. Only family and close friends attended, including Kay's father, Lord and Lady Kilmuir, Noël Coward, Vivien Leigh, Laurence Olivier,

Terence Rattigan, Lauren Bacall, Gladys Cooper, George Cukor and Dr Carl Goldman.

Rex entered the church through a side door near the altar, accompanied by his sons, Noel and Carey; his head was bowed as he took his place next to the plain oak coffin, bearing a simple brass plaque: 'Kay Harrison, died 6th September 1959. Age 32', on top of which were six dozen red roses with a card: 'For my beloved – Rex'. After the ten-minute service the coffin was taken to the churchyard, where Kay Kendall was laid to rest in Actors' Corner, under the shade of two larch trees, between the grave of Herbert Beerbohm Tree and that of George du Maurier and his son, Sir Gerald du Maurier. After the funeral rites were performed Rex was the last to leave the graveside, supported on either arm by his two sons. A very saddened Rex said that his life was ruined and he confided to Binkie Beaumont that he wanted Lilli back, telling him, '. . . after all she is my wife.'

8

IN ATTEMPTING to pick up the pieces of his life, Rex Harrison characteristically turned to the only remedy he knew – work. As the routine of *My Fair Lady* had enabled him to survive what he referred to in his autobiography as 'without doubt the worst and the best years of my life', so he hoped it would again prove to be the answer. Before Kay's death he had considered appearing with her in a production of *The Taming of the Shrew*, and there had also been the possibility of their both appearing in the film version of *The Grass is Greener* with Cary Grant and Deborah Kerr, but Rex must have known that neither project was possible.

However, he still had the Jean Anouilh play, now translated by Lucienne Hill and given the title, *The Fighting Cock*, and within a week of Kay's funeral he was engrossed in preparations for the Broadway production. During discussions with Irene Selznick and director Peter Brook over casting, the French actress Odile Versois was summoned to London, but the part eventually went to director Peter Brook's beautiful actress-wife, Natasha Parry, who had recently excited a great deal of favourable comment after her appearances at the Shakespeare Memorial Theatre (with what later became the Royal Shakespeare Company).

During these early days of working on the production in London, Irene Selznick and Peter Brook had a disagreement which resulted in Irene's withdrawal from the project. Her departure caused Rex to pause and consider his own continued involvement, but he chose to remain with the play, although in retrospect he would regard his decision as 'a hideous error on my part'. Rex was, however, grateful to have the various problems associated with putting on a new play to occupy his mind, and he spent a great deal of time working with Brook at his Kensington home.

Lilli's reply to his letter from the London Clinic had dashed any remaining hope that she would return to him, but if support from her was not forthcoming, he was at least surrounded by family and friends eager to help bolster up his spirits. After staying with the Kilmuirs for a short time, Rex gratefully accepted Terence Rattigan's invitation to come and stay at his home in Sunningdale, where he was able to continue working with Peter Brook on the play. Rattigan remarked on his friend at this time: 'There was at first about him a certain contentment, gaiety even, as well as relief that the strain was over at last. And this feeling was right because he knew he had done everything a husband could do for his wife – and more. Although there was an appalling gap, he had no regrets.'

On September 27th, Rex's first grandchild, Cathryn – the daughter of his son, Noel – was christened at Hampstead Parish Church but, reluctant to appear in public, Rex did not attend the ceremony. In the same church, less than three weeks before, he had attended his wife's funeral.

Anxious that Rex should not brood too much over the events of the past months, Rattigan suggested that they should travel together down to the South of France for a few days before Rex embarked for New York to begin rehearsals. There he would be able to learn his lines while Rattigan intended to write a play. The two men arrived in Nice on September 30th where they were met by Rex's Bentley which he had arranged to have brought up from Portofino. Although Rex spent many hours working on his script and playing golf with Rattigan, he also took long solitary drives in his car through the spectacular

Riviera countryside, haunted by memories of the past '. . . my philosophy of tomorrow left me. For me, there were no tomorrows, there was only yesterday,' he wrote nearly fifteen years later.

Returning to England, Rex made preparations for his trip to New York. He would be accompanied by his secretary, Edith Jackson, and his elder sister Marjorie, who would remain there with him for a month. Kay was to have gone with him and their intention had been to cross the Atlantic by ship, but now Rex was eager to arrive in New York as swiftly as possible and booked a flight from Heathrow airport. Before boarding the plane he told reporters, 'I want to get there and get started', and speaking candidly of his feelings after his wife's death, he said,

'I can't think of anything more worthwhile than those three and a half years when I was with Kate and was able to help her. They were not years of agony, because she gave back so much . . . as she gave to everyone who knew her, particularly to me. I do not regret those years – and I would go through them again. Every day was a fresh day and she helped to make it wonderful. How could I be in anguish during those years?

'Now, of course, I am in the depth. But one cannot give up and stop. So I must go on. And work.'

Collette, who had never remarried, was at the airport with Noel and his wife, to see him off. When he had departed she told reporters: '. . . he is lonely. As soon as Kay died he plunged into this new play. It has really saved him – so I'm grateful.' In the years since their divorce Collette had remained in contact with Rex, but spent much of her time in the Swiss resort of Klosters where she ran a small boutique. Their son Noel, now married after leaving the army, where he had been a champion skier, was beginning to find a special following at the newly-fashionable Blue Angel nightspot in

London's Soho, singing to his own accompaniment on the guitar. He had inherited much of his father's charm and good looks.

In New York Rex threw himself into rehearsals with the company, which included his close friend Michael Gough, who had been with him during the last days of Kay's illness and was sharing a flat in Sutton Place with him during the run of the play. Other members of the cast included Arthur Treacher and Roddy McDowall, while the sets and costumes were designed by Rolf Gérard, the great love of Lilli Palmer's life before she had met Rex.

After rehearsals, the play opened on November 16th for a two-week tryout at the Walnut Theatre in Philadelphia where the local press were complimentary but by no means ecstatic. Although the play had provided Rex with an escape from his grief, it became apparent that, in accepting it, his professional judgement had been at a low ebb. The character of the 'General', an idealist of a bygone age who pathetically tries to preserve a code of ethics out-of-step with the time in which he now lives, was too closely modelled on France's General de Gaulle to have much significance for its American audience to whom de Gaulle was then scarcely known. In imitation of his character's real-life counterpart, Rex had chosen to wear heavy make-up including a false nose, which obscured his well-known features, but the audiences at the early performances in Philadelphia were unwilling to accept him in this way and Rex gradually dispensed with the false nose and heavier make-up, opting instead for a short military-style hair-cut. Rex's secretary, Edith Jackson, was aware of the tremendous amount of effort that he was putting into the play and felt that, although barely mentioning her name, he was obviously missing Kay a great deal. He had no-one to go back to at the end of the day to give him confidence and felt her loss all the more.

When the play finally opened at the ANTA Theatre in New York on December 8th, Rex's performance was praised, but the play was received less enthusiastically. Walter Kerr of the *New York Post* wrote: 'What M. Anouilh has rather wistfully written, and what Mr Harrison is playing with such restless vitality, stirs now and then into a lively ping-pong game of ideas', but he felt that the play, 'lacking a clear core around which its glistening flying saucers can soar, comes to seem fragile and thin before its philosophising is done! The fragments are tantalising, and by now we must all have learned not to discuss an Anouilh play on the basis of a single production. But for all the lively nuance, the heartbeat is lacking.'

The play limped on, but the theatre-going public were not keen about seeing the Rex Harrison they had last acclaimed as Henry Higgins in a play in which they found little of relevance. For the first time in years, Rex found himself playing to half-empty houses, and *The Fighting Cock* finally closed on February 20th after only eighty-seven performances. From his spectacular success in *My Fair Lady*, which was still playing to capacity business, Rex's professional career dipped as dramatically as his personal life, and in a very short time he was floundering. His guest appearance on a television special celebrating *The Fabulous Fifties* at the end of January, in which he performed a supposed recreation of his nervous and halting attempts to sing in front of the *My Fair Lady* orchestra for the first time, was just another reminder of past glory.

Rex at least found some consolation in the company of a young actress who was just embarking on a successful Broadway career. Tammy Grimes, from Lynn, Massachusetts, was twenty-six years old when she met Rex at a party in New York during the closing days of the decade. She had made her New York debut in 1955 as a replacement for Kim Stanley in *Bus Stop* and was now starring in Noël Coward's *Looking After Lulu*. In her personal life she had just separated from her husband, the Canadian actor Christopher Plummer, by whom she had a daughter,

Amanda. By a strange coincidence, Tammy had met Rex for the first time some years before, at the age of nineteen, when he and Lilli Palmer had been appearing in Boston in *The Love of Four Colonels*. The Harrisons had frequently played golf at the Country Club in Chestnut Hill, which was managed by her father, and Tammy had always remembered seeing him one day at the club: 'He had on a yellow sweater and looked absolutely wonderful.' She had even waited back-stage for him, to get his autograph.

'There was a kind of immediate attraction between the two of us. He was an exciting man to be around,' Miss Grimes says of their meeting seven years later in New York, but she also detected a change in him since their last meeting. 'He was very alone and very saddened. He was still in a state of grief and I think I just came along in his life when he needed someone. I felt as if I were important to him and that I made him happy,' although she adds, 'One just knew that he was thinking about Kay a lot.'

Tammy remembers Rex as 'a very generous man', but also that 'he had a bit of a temper and was very possessive' and once admitted: 'I once remember escaping from an hotel, just to be on my own, to take a walk in the park . . . He never loved his women, he adored them. I always felt like a jewel in a bright box, something to be displayed and admired.' She also remembers the thrill of walking on his arm, and watching the effect he had on other people. 'Walking down the street with him was like walking down the street with the President of the United States. Everybody said, "Hello, Rex", and he would smile and touch his hat.'

While Rex was appearing in *The Fighting Cock*, Laurence Olivier came over to New York to direct Charlton Heston in *The Tumbler* by Ben Levy, which was to open at the Helen Hayes Theatre at the end of February. Olivier had just separated from Vivien Leigh and they would be divorced in the following May, and Rex often invited him to dine at Sutton Place, where Miss Grimes would act as his hostess. She was not, however, as punctual as Rex would have wished and recalls one dinner party attended by Olivier: 'I was late and Rex banished me. He said, "You don't have to bother to sit down!" It was Larry who saved me and said, "No, no. You can't do that."' But Tammy says 'Rex was angry because I was always late, so he bought me a Cartier watch to make me stay on time.'

In March Rex returned to television, in an NBC 'Ford Star Time' production, *Dear Arthur*, from a Ferenc Molnar play which boasted a screenplay by Gore Vidal from P. G. Wodehouse's adaptation of the original play. But, even with a cast which included Hermione Baddeley, it proved to be a grave disappointment when it was broadcast on March 22nd. Jack Gould of the *New York Times* deplored what he saw: 'The formidable charms of Rex Harrison were regrettably dissipated last night in a sixty-minute item of strained sophistication,' and continued, 'In telling the story of a highly attractive scoundrel who concocts an imaginary husband for his designing daughter, the TV playlet only intermittently suggested the Molnar touch in dealing with the sexes, conventions and love,' although he did add: 'Rex Harrison was as urbane as ever.'

Rex's next offer came from Hollywood: to play opposite Doris Day in *Midnight Lace*, a thriller based on a little known play, *Matilda Shouted Fire* by Janet Green. The producer, Ross Hunter, had flown to New York to see Natasha Parry in *The Fighting Cock*, having heard that she might be perfect for a supporting part in the film. He signed her on the spot, as well as engaging Roddy McDowall, but it was only when he was flying back to California – with still no leading man cast – that it struck him that Rex would be ideal casting for the part of Doris Day's husband, and when he arrived back in Los Angeles he immediately telephoned Rex and offered him the part. Rex was intrigued by the prospect of playing a suave villain in a film which was basically an updated re-working of the *Gaslight* theme, with Rex as the husband, pushing Doris Day's rich heiress towards suicide in the hope of securing her fortune for himself and his mistress, played by Natasha Parry. The supporting cast was also impressive and included Myrna Loy, Herbert Marshall and John Gavin.

Rex flew out to California while Tammy Grimes remained in New York, although they continued their romance over the telephone, talking to each other every day. In Hollywood Rex dated Eloise Hardt, an actress he had met when Kay was filming *Les Girls* at M-G-M in 1957. Of Kay Kendall, Miss Hardt says, 'She burned herself out – she couldn't stand reality. Everything was on a high-wire. She had it all – but for such a short time,' and on this occasion she had a chance to get to know Rex further, which led her to the conclusion: 'He was a better friend than a beau for a girl. You were married to him, but he wasn't necessarily married to you. He was charming, irascible, and had a vile temper.'

To celebrate Rex's fifty-second birthday in March 1960, Eloise threw a party for him and recalls: 'Producers, directors, actor-types were invited – nice people in the business – and he hated everyone.' In the middle of the party, he selected the prettiest girl there – a dark-haired actress – and a writer friend of Miss Hardt's, and 'as he could not do anything alone' took them both to The Daisy, a popular night spot on Rodeo Drive. Eloise says, 'That was the end as far as I was concerned.' Rex was also briefly reunited with Lilli, who was in Hollywood for *The Pleasure of His Company* in which she was co-starring with Fred Astaire. They lunched together in Beverly Hills one day, and Lilli was shocked by what she saw. She told Rex's secretary afterwards, 'I've never seen Rex looking so unhappy', but was advised that he was playing with her emotions.

As work on *Midnight Lace* neared completion, Rex was joined by Tammy Grimes, who flew out to discuss playing the lead in an upcoming musical on Broadway, *The Unsinkable Molly Brown* with producer Dore Schary.

Ross Hunter recalls the making of *Midnight Lace* with affection and says that David Miller was a popular director with his cast. Hunter says that Rex was 'super-professional', and found him the complete antithesis of what he had been told. 'Everybody warned me about Rex. I heard that he was difficult and that he was egocentric, but he was co-operation personified. All those people who kept calling me and warning me saying "You're going to have trouble" – they were all wrong. I truthfully have to say that it was a delight to work with him.

'We really had a tough schedule on this picture and Doris was under a great deal of tension, due to the fact that she lives a part when she plays it and Rex, I know, was quite amazed by the talent of this lady. He liked her very much and was impressed by her wonderful energy – she was always up, and always professional, and always on time.'

As well as for Rex, who was playing a completely unsympathetic part, Doris Day's role in the film was a departure from the heroines of slick romantic comedies on which her reputation was based, and her total immersion in the character had a profound effect on her, as Hunter recalls: 'Doris had to do a scene where she is trying to prove to Rex that she is not lying and that someone is either trying to drive her insane or kill her. I remember that she was so great in that scene that she became hysterical and we had to take her home. There was no one more sympathetic than Rex.'

Miss Day herself recalls: 'Rex helped me out of the car,' and she refers to him as, 'A darling, witty man . . . whose sense of humour helped me to keep my sanity balanced throughout the rough part of the picture.'

Unfortunately, the film itself received only a lukewarm reception from both critics and public.

In June Rex returned to New York, where he spent a

great deal of time with his old friends Vivien Leigh and Roland Culver. Miss Leigh had been appearing in a revival of her London success, Duel of Angels.. Now divorced from Olivier, she confided her troubles to Rex who kept a careful eye on her, knowing her depressed and tearful state. Tammy Grimes, who met Vivien Leigh on the many occasions when Rex entertained her to dinner at his flat in Sutton Place, says: 'Rex liked Vivien very much and he was very loyal to her. He gave several dinner parties when she was there and she was very pleased and delighted to be with him. It was a bad time for her and he realised that she was going through a lot of pain.'

The following month Rex returned to London, once more installing himself at the Connaught Hotel, which had so often served as his London home. He was joined there a few days later by Tammy Grimes, and they were often seen together at first nights in the West End. When asked about his association with the young American actress before her arrival in England, Rex stated, 'Miss Grimes is just a great friend of mine. As for marrying again, I have no intention of doing so at present.' Rex met her at the airport when she arrived on July 18th, but she was just as evasive when questioned by the press. Cornered by waiting newsmen as they emerged from a visit back-stage after attending a performance of the hit musical Oliver!, the subject of marriage was again brought up, but Rex replied, 'You will have to ask Miss Grimes about that.' When they turned to her she told them, 'This is not a subject we have discussed. Mr Harrison and I are very good friends, but more than that I cannot say.'

Tammy says that in truth at this point in their romance 'Marriage was brought up, and I considered it very deeply. I loved Rex but I couldn't marry him then. The age difference was quite a lot and I was just embarking on a career. I think that he felt that he needed someone there and that if I was working there would be a conflict. He would have preferred that I had given up my career and gone to be with him.'

During their stay in London Rex was invited by Laurence Olivier to appear in his annual midsummer midnight matinee performance, *Night of a Hundred Stars* at the London Palladium on Thursday, July 21st in aid of the Actors' Benevolent Fund. Tammy Grimes was to have been a programme seller, but Rex intervened and requested that she be permitted to contribute to the show by singing. She says, 'I enjoyed doing *Night of a Hundred Stars*. I shook like a leaf, but I was very honoured to be there.'

At the benefit, Rex appeared as Stephen Harris in *Oranges and Lemons*, a sketch written by Noël Coward for his 1925 revue *On With The Dance*, about two middle-aged women, stranded at a party because of fog, whose bedroom is invaded by two men. Rex and Jack Hawkins played the two intruders opposite Laurence Olivier and Kenneth More in drag. Afterwards, when Rex and Olivier took their curtain call they raised the roof as Harrison presented his co-star to the audience as if he were a prima ballerina, with Olivier performing the deepest of curtsies.

Rex and Tammy discussed going to Portofino together, but on July 24th Tammy returned to New York, where she was soon to begin preparations for her starring role in Meredith Wilson's *The Unsinkable Molly Brown* on Broadway. Just over two weeks later Rex, accompanied by his son Carey, flew out to Italy.

During his visit to London Rex was introduced to George Devine, the artistic director of the recently-founded English Stage Company, based at the Royal Court Theatre in Sloane Square, Chelsea. In the four years since his appointment in 1956, the Company had become the focus for a new wave of theatre, ushered in by their production of *Look Back in Anger* by actor-turned-playwright, John Osborne. This was the first of the 'kitchen sink dramas' whose grim realism and depiction of a new generation of 'angry young men' was a direct challenge to the comfortably-off upper-class heroes of the sophisticated light comedies in which Rex had made his reputation. Initially the great names of the British theatre were wary of the management and 'freedom' of the Royal Court, but the climate changed after Peggy Ashcroft agreed to appear in their production of Brecht's *The Good Woman of Setzuan*, and the real turning-point came when Laurence Olivier collaborated with John Osborne on his next play, *The Entertainer*, which was presented at the Royal Court in 1957. It was a great success and transferred to the West End, at the Palace Theatre.

Despite its reputation, the Royal Court still needed stars to help bring in an audience, and on meeting Harrison, George Devine asked him if he would be interested in appearing in a play there. Rex was enthusiastic when Devine told him of the existence of *Platonov*, a scarcely-known play by Anton Chekhov, discovered in draft form among the late Russian playwright's papers in 1923 and never yet performed in Britain. He had been working on a script with Dmitri Makaroff in the hope of directing the first English-language production and was eager to sign a star for the title role. While Rex was enjoying his brief holiday in Portofino, Devine sent the completed script to him. Rex read the play and accepted the challenge. The earliest known play by Chekhov, *Platonov* was very much a precursor of his later, more polished, work, dealing as it did with his favourite subject, the malaise of provincial life in late nineteenth-century Russia. Platonov is a schoolteacher whose marriage breaks up when he becomes involved with three local women who, bored with their mundane existence, seek excitement and some meaning in their lives through love and passion.

Before starting rehearsals Rex returned to New York where he appeared in a play for NBC television, *The Datchet Diamonds*, in their series of 'Great Mysteries'. At first Rex had been reluctant to take the lead but having already cast Tammy Grimes, the dancer Gower Champion, who was fast becoming one of the most sought-after directors on television and Broadway, sought her aid in persuading Rex to change his mind. She said, 'Oh Rex, wouldn't it be lovely to work together? Can't we?' and he relented.

In New York Rex also attended the first reading of *The Unsinkable Molly Brown* and heard Meredith Wilson sing his score for the cast. Miss Grimes recollects: 'Rex thought it was good but knew it would be a big problem. He wanted to marry me but it didn't make him terribly happy that I was involved in a musical that, if it were a success, would mean that I would have to stay in New York. He asked me, "Do you really want to be a star?"' Rex proposed again, but Tammy says, 'I couldn't because I thought the careers would get in the way and he wouldn't like the separations. It just wasn't meant to be and so we stopped seeing each other.'

By the time *The Unsinkable Molly Brown* opened at the Winter Garden in November Rex had returned to England and was appearing in *Platonov,* but he knew of the triumph that Tammy had scored in the show. She says, 'Rex was very proud of me and sent me three dozen red roses.' For her performance she won the Tony award as the Best Actress in a Musical. Reflecting on the end of her romance with Rex she says: 'I was just unhappy that I made him unhappy because I truly did love him. He was wonderful to me – something very special in my life. He swept me off my feet, but he was very possessive, very strong and very much of a loner. He needed me too much.'

Rex, aware that his career had reached an impasse, hoped that the pioneering atmosphere of the Royal Court might revive his fortunes. Asked why he had accepted the offer to appear there at a salary of £60 a week when he had considerably more lucrative offers, he replied,

'Why am I doing this? Because it's about time I had a stab at Chekhov, because I think this is a wonderful play. I suppose the obvious thing after *My Fair Lady* would have been to go into another musical. But I never like doing obvious things. I prefer to ring the changes all the time. I like to think that the money I make in films enables me to take uncommercial chances in the theatre.

'Anyway, I'm free to go wherever the next play or film takes me. I'm not married, both my boys have grown up and I have no roots at all except my villa at Portofino.'

Rex could not have known that once again he was to meet someone who would alter the course of his life. She was Rachel Roberts, the thirty-three-year-old actress engaged to play Anna Petrovna – a rich widow in love with Platonov. She had been born in Llanelli, Wales in 1927, the daughter of a Baptist minister, the Reverend Richard Roberts and his wife. Early on she had rebelled against her austere upbringing and after graduating from the University of Wales, where she studied English and French, she forsook her initial ambition to teach and turned instead to acting. After studying at RADA she joined the Old Vic Company and supplemented her meagre income by working as a nightclub singer at the Churchill Club, where she wore eye-catching black net stockings, designed to show off her shapely legs. In 1955 she met and married Alan Dobie, a struggling young actor, and together they scraped a very drab existence in a London council flat. Opportunities had begun to present themselves in films, however, and Rachel had just completed a major role in Karel Reisz's *Saturday Night and Sunday Morning*, set among Nottingham's urban working class, in which she appeared as a dissatisfied wife having an affair with a young man played by Albert Finney, who works in the same factory as her husband. Although not strikingly beautiful in the way that Kay Kendall had been, Rachel Roberts was attractive, with a warm personality and an earthy sexuality which was appealing.

Also in the cast of *Platonov* was Rosalind Knight, the daughter of actor Esmond Knight, who was a friend of Rachel Roberts. She says that for Rachel, 'life was very humdrum, striving and harsh', and that consequently, 'she was slightly depressed'. Rachel had hoped that she and her husband might have been able to have children to give some stability to their marriage but it proved impossible, and she had sought solace by having affairs with other men. She was excited at the prospect of acting with Rex Harrison, who was such a great name in the theatre, and subconsciously hoped that she would make a favourable impression on him. On the first day of rehearsals she was aware that Rex was watching her approvingly and was flattered by his obvious attentions. As rehearsals progressed, Rosalind Knight recollects, 'Rex was always in her dressing room – talking to her, advising and being very sweet,' and asserts, 'No marriage could have survived that onslaught of charm and luxury and wealth. Rex made a dead-set for Rachel from the outset.

'Her marriage to Dobie was not over but Rachel had no misgivings, I don't know how Alan felt – he was a dour, quiet, introverted young man.'

At first Rachel would still go out with friends like Rosalind Knight for coffee at the ABC cafeteria, but gradually Rex began to monopolise her company and would take her out to lunch at his favourite restaurant nearby or invite her to his flat around the corner in Eaton Square. Rex always had a taste for traditional English food, and now found a woman who enjoyed cooking it for him. Rosalind Knight remembers a break in rehearsals when Rachel was preparing a fry-up and Rex said to her:

'Oh, Rach, wouldn't a piece of fried bread be lovely!'
She said, 'Yes. I'll make you some.'

'What? Can you make fried bread, Rach?'
'Of course I can.'

Rachel recalls: 'Rex fascinated me. Underneath the glitter, I saw the widower making a brave attempt to carry on.' Known by her friends as a very demonstrative and forthright young woman, Rachel became strangely passive in Rex's company and, uncharacteristically, fell completely under the spell of his worldly sophistication. Having lived a hand-to-mouth existence for so long, the luxury that he held out to her, in the form of expensive gifts, was like the fulfilment of a long wished-for dream. She and Rex became inseparable as rehearsals came to a close. Rosalind Knight recalls, 'Rex was very awkward to work with. Rachel would go round to his flat on the pretence of hearing his lines – and she probably did hear them – and cook them tasty meals. She had a completely down-to-earth, working class approach to life. Rex had no training in the niceties of domestic life – he just had servants.'

Platonov opened at the Royal Court Theatre on October 13th for a limited run of six weeks. Caryl Brahms in *Plays and Players* wrote:

There can be no doubt that *Platonov* . . . is by a master writer, poet and humorist; nor can there be any doubt that the early play lacks the mastery of the later plays. But there should be enough in *Platonov* to please most thinking playgoers most of the time.

First there is the game of tennis which Mr Rex Harrison plays with his lines – the restless, split-second volleying of phrases. Beneath the shambles of his hirsute and lined exterior there lies the wary pacing of the panther. I do not know whether his performance could be bettered. I would like to see Mr O'Toole take this part before committing myself on the point. And also, possibly, Sir Donald Wolfit. Somewhere north of

Sir Donald and south of Mr O'Toole lies the climate of Mr Harrison's Platonov, almost too good to be true.

The role of the bearded Platonov was a triumph for Rex. The Court played capacity business throughout the whole of its limited season reaffirming Rex's tremendous drawing power with the public in the right part. The experience restored his confidence after the disappointment of *The Fighting Cock*, and for his performance he shared the *Evening Standard* Best Actor of 1960 Award with Alec Guinness, who won for his portrayal of T. E. Lawrence in Terence Rattigan's *Ross*. Rachel Roberts was given the Clarence Derwent Award as the Best Supporting Actress of the year for her interpretation of Anna Petrovna.

When the show closed Rex asked Rachel to return with him to Portofino and stay at his villa. Rosalind Knight says 'The way that Rachel was treated by Rex made her feel she was just not in the same league with the rest of us. Rex completely swept her off her feet. She thought she could cope with him, feeling that with her Welsh background and her strong opinions, she could cope with anyone at all.' Leaving her husband alone in their council flat, Rachel allowed Rex to take charge completely. They took the Golden Arrow to Paris, where they stayed at the Lancaster Hotel, and for the last leg of the journey they boarded the Rome Express to Santa Margherita, from there going to Portofino. Rex delighted in Rachel's infectious enthusiasm for the Italian hideaway and they spent a relaxed and happy time together, with Rachel basking in the reflected glory of her association with Rex.

The couple remained at the villa over Christmas, and were joined in the new year by Rita Hayworth and her husband James Hill, who came to discuss a new film which they were producing in Spain the following month. Rex had agreed to play opposite Rita Hayworth, but he was to regret his decision almost immediately.

Although *Platonov* had clearly demonstrated his popularity with the theatre-going public, Rex was uncertain of
himself and his future career and had mistakenly listened
to the advice of his agent who recommended that he take
the money offered to him by film producers while he still
could. Rex's acceptance of *The Happy Thieves* appears
wildly inconsistent behaviour on his part, after having
worked for a paltry salary of £60 a week at the Royal
Court, and in retrospect he put it down to his own
'sloppy professional judgement'.

Rex and Rachel arrived in Madrid, where the film was
to be shot, in the middle of February 1961. During
production they lived in a large eighteenth-century
house in the old part of the city, and Rita Hayworth and
James Hill often dined with them in the evenings. But
despite the rapport which existed between Rex and Rita
the film was not a happy experience, made worse by the
precarious state of the Hayworth/Hill marriage. The
working atmosphere on the film reflected Rita
Hayworth's worries about her career and her marriage.
At forty-three she had passed her peak as a star and *The
Happy Thieves* was a tawdry attempt to stay at the top. The
marriage to James Hill (her fifth) was in a bad way. That
she was depressed was not surprising, and it communicated itself to Rex, who blamed himself for getting
embroiled in such a second-rate project. Rachel was
blinded by the surface trappings of Rex's success and his
seemingly effortless life-style. She could not appreciate
the insecurities which were plaguing Rex, a man of
fifty-three who only three years before had been at the
very pinnacle of his fame, but now found himself working on a film which could, he believed, irreparably damage his standing as a serious actor.

Confused and unhappy at Rex's apparent change in
attitude towards her, Rachel was anxious to get away for
a while and decided to take a brief trip to London. There
she was greeted by the news that she had not only been
awarded the Clarence Derwent Award for *Platonov* but

had also been named best British film actress of 1960 for her performance in *Saturday Night and Sunday Morning*. When she telephoned Rex in Spain to share the good news it was like a slap in the face to him, serving only to enhance the fear that his own career was on a downward trend, through his own misjudgement, while Rachel was just beginning to receive acclaim for her acting abilities. However, when Rachel returned to Madrid they were happily reunited.

Rex also received a telephone call from Tammy Grimes who was in Rome. 'I called him and he was happy to hear my voice and he said, "I've found another bird." I said, "I'm so happy for you."'

Miss Grimes believes, 'Without a woman in Rex's life, was not to be. He always had to have *that* woman.'

During filming in Madrid Rex also had to contend with the newspaper reporter who had exposed his alleged feud with Stanley Holloway during the New York run of *My Fair Lady*, and now persuaded Rita Hayworth to give an interview on the set. As is customary, Rex was informed that this journalist would be on the set the following day, and he immediately made it known that he could not possibly be present during the man's visit. Rita Hayworth, in deference to her leading man's feelings, naturally cancelled the interview.

The Happy Thieves turned out as disastrously as Rex had feared. It was slipped unannounced into the London Pavilion in March 1962 without even a press showing, although an un-named *Daily Mail* critic, dwelling principally on Rita Hayworth, gave a clear indication of the film's merits in which Rex played an art thief attempting to rob the Prado museum with his glamorous accomplice:

> I suppose it is my own fault. They didn't want me to see this film. But I insisted. And what I think they did not want me to see was the sad, sad collapse of the enchanting Rita Hayworth.

She scarcely looked pretty. Her voice was shrill, hysterical and harsh. And she over-acted disastrously. But I don't give up hope. Rather than despair of Miss Hayworth, I blame the film-makers. After all, a director who allows Rex Harrison to appear on the screen with a cut on his forehead two minutes before he receives the blow which caused it, must be held responsible for making so little of Rita Hayworth.

After the film's completion Rex, accompanied by Rachel, returned to Portofino, although they were obliged to leave when Lilli arrived with her husband. They moved on to Richard Burton's house at Celigny, where Alan Dobie called by unexpectedly, demanding that his wife come back to him. Rachel drove off with her husband but returned to Rex shortly afterwards, unable to face the prospect of resuming the life she had known before Rex had taken her under his wing. From Celigny they continued to Geneva before returning to Portofino where Rex invited Rachel's parents to stay with them for a couple of weeks, an invitation which they gratefully accepted.

The beginning of July found Rex back in London, negotiating with George Devine to appear in another production for the English Stage Company, while Rachel was working on a film and also finalising her divorce from Alan Dobie. The play which Rex selected, *August for the People* by Nigel Dennis, would be directed by Devine and there was a part for Rachel.

When her divorce came through Rachel told Rex at once, but he was engrossed in discussions with George Devine, and appeared indifferent to the news. In *August for the People*, a peculiar play to have caught Harrison's interest, he played Sir Augustus Thwaites, who is forced to open his stately home to the public despite his feelings of disgust at the idea. Muddled in intent, it presented an unsympathetic picture of the landed gentry with the character of Sir Augustus denouncing democracy as a dirty word; Rachel played the part of his mistress.

The play was not as happy an experience as *Platonov*. Rex and Nigel Dennis took a dislike to one another on the first day of rehearsals when Dennis lectured the company on the meaning of his play and his motivation for writing it. Expecting to have the first read-through of the play with the rest of the cast, Rex was in no mood to hear the playwright's opinions on his own work before they had even had a chance to begin working on it; the cast's intelligence was being insulted and Rex told George Devine that he would not attend rehearsals if Nigel Dennis appeared again.

By the time they reached Newcastle, where the play was to have a week's tryout before opening at the Edinburgh Festival, Dennis had already walked out on it. The play had originally been intended for a six-week season at the Royal Court from September 12th, and if successful, would then transfer to the West End, but its reception in Newcastle did not fulfil expectations, and now even its Royal Court season was in jeopardy.

At this point Rex was put in a difficult position. He received an offer to play Julius Caesar in Twentieth Century-Fox's *Cleopatra*, with Elizabeth Taylor in the title role, to be directed in Italy by Joseph L. Mankiewicz from his own screenplay. A major production, with Richard Burton as Antony, it was clearly an opportunity he could ill afford to turn down. Shooting on *Cleopatra* was, however, scheduled to begin on September 18th, six days after *August for the People* was to open in London, and Rex would be required shortly after that date.

The whole company waited on Rex's decision but while negotiations were going on Rex would not discuss it. Devine, who knew that the play was doomed without Rex's involvement, enlisted the aid of Laurence Olivier, one of the English Stage Company's most staunch supporters, who, on the night of August 30th, travelled to Newcastle to discuss the matter with his old friend.

Rex refused to make any comment to the press who badgered him relentlessly about his intentions. Another member of the company, Hugh Latimer, recalls Rex asking him one evening to walk with him back to his hotel and, although puzzled by this request, he agreed. 'No sooner had we got out of the stage door than he was set on by reporters who said, "Are you going to leave the show and go to Rome? Are you going to do *Cleopatra*?"' Rex had no intention of answering any questions and used Latimer as a buffer – he then walked off briskly in the direction of his hotel. By the time they reached Edinburgh, it had been accepted, albeit reluctantly, that Rex would be leaving the play soon after it opened in London. He told the press in Edinburgh: 'I originally contracted to do the play for six weeks. Now we have decided to go on for two weeks at the Royal Court Theatre, London, after the festival. Then I will go to Rome for a month for the film and when I come back we will revive the play for another season.'

When the play opened in Edinburgh on September 4th *The Times* critic called it a 'Satire that fails to hit its target', and when it reached the Royal Court on September 12th a second reviewer for *The Times* commented: 'Mr Rex Harrison's playing is at once light and forceful, but he is handicapped by a great many clever ideas which would fit together better on paper than they sound when thrown into stage dialogue.'

Time magazine, putting their own interpretation on the reasons behind Rex's withdrawal from *August for the People*, claimed that the actor was concerned that his association with a play in which he had to denounce democracy as 'disgusting' might jeopardise his chances of being included in Queen Elizabeth's next Honours List, and quoted him as having said, 'I don't want to be in anything subversive.' But whatever the truth, the wisdom of Rex's decision was borne out by the play's public and critical reception. The cast could not reasonably have expected it to run past its six-week engagement at the

Royal Court, but, says Hugh Latimer, when the play ended its shortened run at the Royal Court, 'We were all given five weeks' salary.'

Rex has also stated that one of the conditions of his leaving was that he help finance the next production at the Royal Court Theatre, although he would never again work with George Devine or the English Stage Company. Within a couple of days of the play's closure Rex flew out to Rome, having told reporters at the airport, 'I will probably be away about six months.'

Producer Walter Wanger approached Elizabeth Taylor about playing Cleopatra in 1959 and she accepted the role for a reputed fee of one million dollars plus five per cent of the gross. Laurence Olivier was offered the role of Caesar but declined, whereupon – as early as May 1960 – Rex Harrison's name was put forward, much to Miss Taylor's delight. However, by the time work began on the film in England in September 1960 Peter Finch had been cast as Caesar and Stephen Boyd as Mark Antony, with Rouben Mamoulian directing.

Taking advantage of the British government's Eady levy, which offered financial incentives to foreign film producers to work in Britain, Twentieth Century-Fox decided to film at Pinewood, where they constructed an enormous outdoor set of Cleopatra's Alexandrine palace. From the start production was hampered by the gener- ally dull English weather and persistent rain, while dissatisfaction with an ill-prepared script, compounded by the frail state of Elizabeth Taylor's health, added to the problems. Miss Taylor had fallen ill soon after arriving in England which necessitated shooting around her for much of the time. With tension mounting, the director, Rouben Mamoulian, resigned and was replaced by Joseph L. Mankiewicz, who was also engaged to write a new screenplay. With Mankiewicz at the helm optimism returned but it was short-lived when Miss Taylor's health deteriorated further and what had been diagnosed as Asian flu developed into staphylococcus pneumonia. The actress developed breathing difficulties owing to congestion in her lungs and an emergency tracheotomy was performed.

For the following two days she was critically ill, and was kept alive on a respirator. She did then begin to regain strength but, aware that the star would need time to recuperate, Spyros Skouras, the President of Twentieth Century-Fox, closed down production of the film, rescheduling it to begin again the following September. Ten minutes of footage had been shot – at an astounding cost of over five million dollars – none of which could be used. Fox's recent output had been unsuccessful and the company needed to regain the confidence of the industry – and its backers – and convince them that a potential blockbuster was in the pipeline.

The revised plan was to film *Cleopatra* on location in Italy and Egypt with interiors at Fox's Hollywood studios, but because of a lack of available space it was decided at the end of June that the entire film would be made at Cinecittà studios in Rome. Also, as a result of the many delays, both Peter Finch and Stephen Boyd were unable to continue, and rapid negotiations began to secure their replacements. Richard Burton was signed to play Mark Antony, after Fox paid fifty thousand dollars to buy his release from the Lerner and Loewe Broadway production of *Camelot*. By the end of August, with the script incomplete, no costumes, and the sets still under construction in Rome, Mankiewicz begged Skouras to delay the starting date once again to enable him to finish the screenplay and over-see final preparations at Cinecittà. But faced with pressure from Fox's board of directors, he had to get on with the job of making the film. He told Skouras that even a ten-week delay would be nothing compared with the financial madness of shooting the film without prior knowledge of what sets, costumes and actors would be required for the second half of the film, but his protestations fell on deaf ears. Walter Wanger wrote on August 13th: 'We are being forced to begin shooting next month so Skouras can keep the Board of Directors quiet and because of the starting date on Liz's contract.' Skouras' only concern was, 'For God's sake, get something on film!'

It was at this late stage that Mankiewicz and Wanger began once again to pursue Rex, whom they both felt would be ideal as Caesar. By September 11th negotiations had been finalised, giving Rex, according to Wanger, 'ten thousand dollars a week plus expenses, a car and driver and co-star billing.' While still appearing in *August for the People* in London Rex had dutifully begun costume fittings, but after viewing the tests in Rome Mankiewicz called Irene Sharaff, who was designing Elizabeth Taylor's clothes for the film, and pleaded with her, 'Look, you've got to help us. Rex can't look like that. Do something!' Miss Sharaff recalled, 'Without the fine tailoring of Savile Row, Rex's figure was not impressive. The Roman costumes with tunics and short sleeves exposed the weak points: narrow shoulders, long thin arms, spindly legs.' She set to work and designed Caesar's costumes in such a way that they were ideal for both the character and the actor.

The day before shooting was scheduled to begin, Wanger gave a disccuraging report on the state of preparation: 'JLM is writing in longhand every day, laboring over the script, trying to get it as near right as possible. We are waiting for the costumes to be completed and fitted. Of the sixty sets needed only one is ready. Every day that we are not before the cameras costs us sixty-seven thousand dollars in overhead. So, tomorrow – ready or not – we start the picture.'

That day, Rex, anxious to discuss his role with Mankiewicz but unable to meet him, as he was still feverishly writing the screenplay, was taken to lunch by Wanger, who recalled: 'Rex had done a great deal of reading about Caesar. He wanted to discuss the part and his concept of it and he wanted to be reassured that his thoughts coincided with ours.' He continued, 'A terribly serious, meticulous man and a great artist, Rex, like most of the actors in the company, wanted to feel a part of the entire project and to believe he was important to it.'

The first day of shooting for Rex was Cleopatra's entry into Rome, one of the spectacular set pieces in the film. Standing in the massive reconstruction of the Roman Forum built for the production, and surrounded by thousands of extras, Rex was understandably nervous. 'It was frightening. Scared the hell out of me. I blew my lines.' Although by the following day he had settled in and all went well, over the next few months the film was plagued with troubles which sent the budget spiralling upward. Fox made continual attempts to reduce the enormous expenditure, and on one memorable occasion Rex returned from a brief visit to Rachel in London – where she was making *This Sporting Life* with Richard Harris – to find that his luxurious trailer had been taken away and he had been installed in a much smaller dressing room above one of the sound-stages and, in addition, his Italian chauffeur was up in arms because the studio had refused to pay his wages. Never a man to take anything lying down, Rex sprang into action and called Wanger on the telephone, demanding that he and Sid Rogell, the executive who had authorised the changes, meet him in his dressing room at once.

Rogell, a physically impressive man, and what Wanger called 'an outspoken man', found that he had met his match when faced with the wrath of Rex Harrison. Before he started Rex warned Rogell, 'I treat my servants better than I am about to treat you', and then proceeded to administer the worst dressing-down that Wanger had ever heard in his life, telling Rogell that he would not report for work until his trailer was back and his chauffeur paid. Rex concluded the interview by pointing his finger at Rogell and saying, 'You are now dismissed.'

The hapless executive was visibly shaken by what he

had just been through and immediately complied with Rex's very definite instructions. News of the confrontation spread rapidly and when Rex walked out on the set ready for work, happy that his demands had been adhered to, he was vigorously applauded by the cast and crew.

Throughout the making of *Cleopatra* Rex and Rachel met in London or Rome as often as the shooting schedules of their respective films allowed. By the new year they had decided to marry and in January Rex was observed collecting a marriage form from the British Consulate, but would give no indication of when the ceremony might take place. 'This is only a preliminary enquiry, you may say, into the technicalities of marrying Miss Rachel Roberts,' he informed the inquisitive press.

It was not until two months later that the banns went up outside the Consulate announcing the forthcoming marriage of Reginald Carey Harrison and Rachel Dobie. The ceremony, in Italian with the aid of an interpreter, was set for noon on March 21st at Genoa Town Hall, and both were given time off from their busy working schedules for a brief honeymoon in Portofino afterwards.

The couple arrived at the Town Hall in a white Fiat, to be greeted by hundreds of photographers and press. As they stepped out of the car a scene of total pandemonium was unleashed. Sr Paolo Macchiavelli, who was to conduct the marriage service, showed them into the registry secretary's office but the crowd of *papparazzi* outside were intent on accompanying them. There was a great deal of undignified pushing and shoving as the pressmen tried to squeeze into the tiny office, and at least one potted plant was sent crashing to the floor. As Sr Macchiavelli was brusquely knocked aside the registrar flung up his arms in despair, while Rex pleaded with the intruders to leave. Furious, he threatened to call off the wedding, which sent Rachel into a flood of tears; walking outside into the corridor, he was confronted by an even larger mob, but at this point the registrar beckoned him into his own office and, declaring a 'state of necessity', decided that the wedding had to be held behind closed doors, although this was contrary to Italian law which said that marriages had to be conducted in public. Even this emergency measure did not prevent the more determined among the *papparazzi* from slipping past the British Consul, who was making a vain attempt to keep them out. After being chased around the registrar's desk they were eventually ejected. The ceremony could then proceed and shortly afterwards Rex emerged smiling with Rachel, his fourth bride, on his arm. They stepped into the waiting Fiat and sped off to Portofino where they transferred to the army jeep and, having paused to smile for the press awaiting them there, drove up to the villa.

After a brief honeymoon Rachel had to report back to continue work on her film. Rex accompanied her to England, returning to Rome a couple of days later, but soon after, they were reunited when Rachel arrived in Italy on another flying visit. Their reunion did not pass without incident, as a misunderstanding occurred at the airport. Anxious to greet her husband, Rachel dashed through Customs and failed to notice that she had been requested to halt. Stopped by officials, she refused to return and follow the proper procedure as she was only carrying a handbag. Rex came over to investigate and soon found himself involved in a noisy argument with Customs officials which resulted in their both being taken to the Customs Inspector's office, where the Inspector claimed he was insulted. Walter Wanger recorded: 'They said some things which were not flattering to the Italian government and the Italian people – something one cannot do in Italy. They would have been jailed for the night except for the consideration of the Italian officials.' After being detained for three hours Rachel and Rex were permitted to return to the villa Rex was renting on the Via Sebastiano at the foot of the Appia Antica. An official representative from Fox issued a statement to the press: 'It was just a language problem. The

Customs men did not understand English. The Harrisons did not understand Italian. And the Customs men could not understand that Mrs Harrison had no baggage.' Rex was charged with having 'insulted a public official' – an offence carrying a minimum sentence of six months in Italy – but the case was dismissed after he apologised in court two days after the incident.

Rex was tied up with *Cleopatra* well into the first half of 1962. Fox's losses for the previous year had been calculated at forty million dollars, half of which was attributable to the film. By the end of May there was pressure from executives to wind up production as swiftly as possible, which meant cancelling filming of the Battle of Pharsalia in which Caesar defeats Pompey. When Rex heard this he called Wanger and offered to underwrite himself the costs of staging it, believing it necessary to open the film intelligibly. The producer felt it was a 'magnificent gesture!'

Fox finally filmed the battle, although on a much less elaborate scale than originally intended – at their own expense. By mid-June Rex was free of any further commitment to the film and retreated to Portofino for a well-deserved rest. The finished film was a fiasco, with the exception of Harrison's contribution which earned him an Academy Award nomination. In retrospect, the actor would regard Caesar as his most satisfying film role.

Rex was glad to settle back into the leisurely pace of life at the villa: getting up at twelve, having lunch down in the port, walking along the quayside with Rachel, drinking in the Gritti Bar and dining at the villa in the evenings. In August Elizabeth Taylor and Richard Burton, having finally completed *Cleopatra*, joined them at Portofino and stayed as house guests for a few weeks. Rachel appeared quite happy to forsake her career to devote herself to the role of Mrs Rex Harrison. Talking of their future together Rex said, 'Rachel and I would love to have children. Rachel would be quite content to become a full-time housewife. But I can't let a talent like hers be completely submerged in domestic chores. So we've settled on the policy of her making just the occasional appearance.' He concluded, 'The happiest married men I know have a wife to go home to, not to go home *with*', a view with which Rachel concurred. 'Marriage to Rex has made me discover that there are far more important things in life than acting . . . Living with Rex is far more fun than having a career in a film factory.'

Over the summer Noël Coward came to stay with them for a couple of days and tried to interest Rex in appearing as the Prince Regent in a musical version of *The Sleeping Prince* which he had written with Harry Kurnitz – eventually entitled *The Girl Who Came to Supper*. Rex was intrigued by the idea after hearing Coward play a couple of songs from the show, but remained noncommittal. His mind was on something else.

In September 1962, *My Fair Lady* had closed on Broadway after 2,717 performances over five and a half years. Jack Warner, who was in the audience on the first night in 1956, had been determined to make the film version, and after lengthy discussions with CBS he concluded a deal in which he agreed to pay them five and a half million dollars for the rights. Under the terms of the deal the rights were leased to Warner Brothers for a seven-year release period after which they, and the ownership of the film, would revert to CBS. Within these seven years Warner also contracted to pay five per cent of the gross to the Shaw estate from the outset and agreed to divide the profits equally with CBS after they had exceeded twenty million dollars.

Incredibly, when Jack L. Warner, who personally produced the film, began to assemble his cast he did not favour Rex Harrison for Henry Higgins and first approached Cary Grant who declined, telling him, 'Not only will I not play Higgins, if you don't put Rex Harrison in it, I won't go and see it.' Still not convinced about Rex, Warner discussed the possibility of Peter O'Toole with the film's prospective director, George Cukor. From Switzerland, where he was staying with Noël Coward at his home at Les Avants, Cukor contacted Steve Trilling, Warner's production manager, informing him that O'Toole had spoken to Alan Jay Lerner about the role. He wrote: 'I hope O'Toole was liked. I think he's our man. If you want a test made I agree with you, it should be done in California. If not – I'd do it in London – that is *if* he'll make the test at all. I think he might. He really wants the part. He's great.'

O'Toole himself publicly expressed very positive feelings about playing Higgins, declaring: 'I'm exactly the Professor Higgins type. Very Shavian. A bit violent with blonde hair and blue eyes. Basically, Professor Higgins was a bully.'

With the publicity given to Warner Brothers' interest in O'Toole, Rex confided his fear to Alan Jay Lerner that he would not get the part. 'Rex was terribly worried he wouldn't get it and I said, "Don't worry. You're going to get it because I'm going to turn everybody down until there is nobody left but you." Rex said, "Are you sure?" and I said, "I'm absolutely sure because I'm not going to approve anybody but you."'

Lerner explains, 'I didn't have the right to select the leading man, but I had the right of approval so I kept disapproving everybody until finally Warner came round to Rex.'

Warner Brothers opened negotiations with Peter O'Toole, but his demands were far too high and he lost his chance. Rex kept checking with Lerner and finally he was rewarded when Warner and Cukor offered him the role which, in all fairness, was his entitlement. On October 25th 1962 it was officially announced that Rex had been signed to play Henry Higgins in the film version of *My Fair Lady*. As Eliza, instead of Julie Andrews who Warner felt did not have sufficient box-office appeal, he cast Audrey Hepburn who could not sing, which fact alone made her casting quite astonishing; he said that her name on the marquee would guarantee at least five million dollars at the box office. Miss Hepburn's standing at this time not only secured her top billing, but also a salary far in excess of that paid to Rex.

The only other member of the original stage production signed by Warner was Stanley Holloway, to recreate his part as Alfred P. Doolittle. Wilfred Hyde-White took over from Rex's friend Robert Coote as Pickering, while Gladys Cooper was cast to play Mrs Higgins with Jeremy Brett as Freddie. Work on the film was scheduled to begin at Warner Brothers' Burbank studios in August of the following year. In the meantime, Rex travelled to Paris in November where he met Noël Coward to decide whether he was still interested in appearing in *The Girl Who Came to Supper*. He declined and the role of the Prince Regent eventually went to Jose Ferrer. On to London, where he agreed in the new year to make a full-length recording of *Much Ado About Nothing*, with Rachel and an all-British cast, produced for the Shakespeare Recording Society by Caedmon Records, a New York-based company. It was Rex's first attempt at Shakespeare since his walk-on in *Richard III* in 1930. He played Benedict under the direction of a thirty-four-year-old New Yorker, Howard Sackler, who would gain distinction as the author of the play, *The Great White Hope*. Rex and Rachel then returned to the villa at Portofino, which he now owned outright. Lilli recalled, 'He had married Rachel Roberts and he had received my letter that I could not come back to him. A year or two had passed and he sent me a letter saying that Rachel Roberts had so fallen in love with the place that she wanted to own it all outright. So then I thought, "Well, it's only cement and stones and we have a lovely home, Carlos and I. Why hang on to it? Let them be happy."'

Rex's only working commitment before he travelled to Los Angeles in the summer was in February when he had to go to Almeria in south-eastern Spain to re-shoot the Battle of Pharsalia for *Cleopatra*. Fox had rejected the cut-price version shot in Italy the previous year. Rachel accompanied Rex but their stay in Spain was marred by an incident in Madrid, after the sequence had been shot, when he and Rachel were stopped by police for crossing the street against a red light. The language barrier blew out of all proportion what would otherwise have been a petty incident, and they were taken to Madrid's central police station for questioning, and only released three hours later when the British Consul arrived. Incensed, Rex announced that he would never set foot in Spain again, and left for Portofino immediately.

In the late spring Rex finally set off for California, stopping off on the way in Paris, where Rachel received news that her father had suffered a stroke and she rushed to Wales to be at his bedside. Fortunately he was soon out of danger and she rejoined Rex in Paris. They sailed from Cherbourg to New York in the *Queen Elizabeth*, accompanied by Rex's Rolls-Royce which, once in America, he had driven across country to await them in Los Angeles.

Apart from going to the latest Broadway shows, Rex's time in New York was also taken up with the unnecessary nuisance of instigating proceedings against Twentieth Century-Fox over their publicity for the forthcoming *Cleopatra*, which emphasised Taylor and Burton in an obvious attempt to capitalise on their highly-publicised romance.

Rex also dined at the White House with President John F. Kennedy, afterwards joining the President and Jacqueline Kennedy for a night-cap.

On May 24th he and Rachel settled into the Bel Air Hotel in Los Angeles, and while Rachel began looking for a suitable house for them to rent during their extended stay in California, Rex reported to the studio for wig and costume fittings. Before beginning rehearsals Rex made a brief trip back to New York to attend the gala premiere of *Cleopatra* on June 12th. Although the film was heavily criticised, praise for Rex's performance was unanimous; *Variety* said, 'Rex Harrison is superb as Caesar. His are the film's most brilliant lines, and something is lost with his assassination.'

By June 17th Rex was back in Los Angeles to start book rehearsals for *My Fair Lady* with the whole cast, under the supervision of George Cukor, followed by preparations for the musical numbers. By August 13th they were ready to begin principal photography. The original intention had been to post-dub all the songs for the film, but Rex was horrified to hear this, never having been trained as a singer. To add weight to his case Rex said that he rarely performed a song the same way twice, which would cause difficulties when he came to match his voice to the playback. As a result a concealed microphone was developed to allow Rex to sing his numbers 'live' in exactly the same way as he had done in the theatre. This technique also enabled him to bring out certain laughs in the lyrics which it had been impossible to do on the stage. Cukor said, 'He needed the intimacy of this technique with the camera for them.'

Only those directly involved with the production were permitted on the set. An inter-office directive stressed: '. . . because of the various temperaments involved in the production, it is necessary *all* MFL sets be restricted during the entire production.' To facilitate this, additional police were posted.

Rex said, 'The only danger I felt myself was that I would give what is called a "stagey" film performance'. Over four years after he had performed the role on-stage for the last time at Drury Lane, he expertly adapted himself to the film medium. George Cukor was enthralled by Rex's supreme craftsmanship, and Cecil Beaton recorded the director's reaction while Rex sang 'Why Can't the English' repeatedly for the cameras without a single error: 'During these long takes Cukor swayed backwards and forwards with a wide, beatific grin on his face.' Beaton thought, 'This surely was Rex at the very peak of his career.'

Rex appreciated the way in which Cukor worked,

concentrating on bringing out the best performances possible from his cast. Harrison said, 'He doesn't really bother with the camera too much. He has a man who actually more or less picks the shots for him and then he works very closely with the actors and watches the actors very closely as they perform and doesn't really care so much for the technical part of it.'

Cukor's way of working certainly brought out the best in everyone, and Rex would recall that there was 'an electric feeling about the whole production' throughout filming, as they were aware that a great film was in the making. Under Cukor's firm guidance the three-month shooting schedule was completed perfectly, the only major flare-up of temperament occurring between the director and Cecil Beaton, who had been engaged to repeat his successful collaboration with the show as both costume and production designer. The two disliked each other intensely and their enmity came to a head when Cukor banned Beaton from the set.

As far as Rex's Eliza was concerned the story was very different from the theatre. Audrey Hepburn sums up the relationship between herself and Rex in five simple words, 'I love and respect him', while he himself referred to his co-star as a 'lovely lady. Truly a lady. Very, very few actresses are ladies.' Both enjoyed the experience of working together, although the same could not be said for Mona Washbourne, who was brought over from Britain to play Henry Higgins' housekeeper, Mrs Pearce. She shared many scenes with Rex. 'I didn't like what I did know of him. He was very rude to people.'

Rex's total professional concentration has often caused offence. He once explained, 'I think about the job at hand. My nerves take me into a sort of state of being aloof and distant. It seems to me a waste of effort to go around being sociable all the time . . . Off-stage I can be far from charming. I am acid. Acid. I have a direct tongue and I say what I think is the truth and I don't give a damn for the consequences.'

Rex completed his scenes on December 9th, and early in the new year was able to see a rough-cut of the film. Cukor and Jack L. Warner were present at the screening and all were thrilled with the result, having caught the excitement and style of the original show, and immortalising Rex's brilliant performance.

Audrey Hepburn gave as good an account of herself as possible within her almost non-existent musical skills, although she had tried to sing the score herself. Alan Jay Lerner confirms, 'She's a lovely girl and through most of the picture I thought she was wonderful, but it was just a pity: she tried like the devil to sing it. She had a singing teacher and I went out six weeks early to work with her,' but she finally had to give up her attempt, and her singing voice was dubbed by Marnie Nixon. As with his performance on the stage, Rex gathered the whole of *My Fair Lady* to his bosom and created for the screen, as indeed for the theatre, one of the most brilliant and compelling performances ever seen.

For Rachel the six months spent in Hollywood while Rex was making *My Fair Lady* were to mark a drastic change in their marriage. Rex would recall: 'Rachel was restless and unhappy. I think she could enjoy the fleshpots as much as I, but felt a deep need to earn them. She had burning ambition, great talent and enormous energy, and she felt she was wasting her days when she was not working.' In the film capital Rachel was a distinctly minor celebrity in the shadow of her husband, who was carrying the weight of a multi-million dollar film on his shoulders.

Shortly after their arrival in Hollywood Rachel told Louella Parsons: 'It's a very challenging place – makes you face up to yourself. Everyone in the world, whether he admits it or not, wants to get on. And if you really want to get on in films you must come to Hollywood to do it.'

This Sporting Life opened in New York to excellent critical reviews, and Rachel was highly praised for her

performance. This added fuel to the regrets which were
boiling up inside her, and led to the first serious conflict
between her personal and career ambitions. Because of
her inability to drive, Rachel was tied to their rented
home at 9554, Hidden Valley Road and began to flounder
in the atmosphere of rich indolence. Visits from her
parents and her long-standing friend Lindsay Anderson
gave her some company during the day while Rex was
hard at work on *My Fair Lady*, but did nothing to curtail
her gnawing dissatisfaction with her life. She would later
write: 'Rex upset my life, not just because he was so
self-centred, not only because he'd lived and loved so
much more than I had, but because of something in me
that didn't want just to be a man's wife.'

In Hollywood, the brightest moments for Rachel were
the weekends they spent with David O. Selznick and his
wife, the film star Jennifer Jones, at their Beverly Hills
home. Although she and David got on very well
together, Rachel's sense of inferiority among the people
with whom her husband was so at ease socially caused
her to drink heavily and her behaviour often became
unruly. Rex felt a mixture of disgust and embarrassment,
and Rachel became aware that he was beginning to show
interest in other women. She would recall, for example,
'Rex would leap up at the bidding of Romy Schneider.'

One happy addition to their lives was Homer, a French
basset hound they acquired from a litter in the San
Fernando Valley, to whom they would both become
equally devoted.

During the filming of *My Fair Lady* Rex was approached
by Twentieth Century-Fox to play Pope Julius II in
the screen version of Irving Stone's best-selling novel
The Agony and the Ecstasy, based upon the life of
Michelangelo. Charlton Heston had already been cast
in the leading part for the film which was to be shot
entirely on location in Italy in June 1964.

Laurence Olivier and Spencer Tracy had initially been
considered for the role of the Pope, but both had de-

clined; Tracy by this time was a very sick man and Olivier was committed to the National Theatre. Rex was then approached and expressed interest and was finally signed in November for what was a particularly large fee, a quarter of a million dollars. Fred Zinnemann was asked to direct the picture, but after he too declined, Carol Reed was approached and accepted this daunting task, which would reunite him professionally with his old friend Rex Harrison for the first time since they made *Night Train to Munich* in 1940.

As there were six months after the completion of *My Fair Lady* before Rex was due to report for work on *The Agony and the Ecstasy*, he and Rachel decided to return to Europe. Stopping off in New York en route, Rex fortuitously met Carol Reed and discussed their future project.

Aboard the S.S. *Leonardo da Vinci*, Rex and Rachel sailed from New York to Italy once more, disembarking at Naples and making their way back to Portofino for a short holiday. In Italy the news came through that they had both been nominated for an Academy Award, Rex for *Cleopatra* and Rachel for her performance in *This Sporting Life* – only the second time in the Academy's history that a husband and wife had been nominated, (Alfred Lunt and Lynn Fontanne were the first, for their parts in *The Guardsman* in 1932). Like the Lunts, neither won the Oscar, but in Rachel's case the nomination was further proof of the career she had forsaken to be Mrs Rex Harrison.

Because of the success of their film *The V.I.P.s*, producer Anatole de Grunwald, writer Terence Rattigan and director Anthony Asquith had decided to follow up with the story of a Rolls-Royce and its various owners, to be entitled simply, *The Yellow Rolls-Royce*. Rattigan wrote the story in three episodes, each one designed to team two major stars. Ingrid Bergman, Shirley Maclaine, Alain Delon and Omar Sharif were signed for the film, and to star in the first episode Rattigan created the role of the

Marquess of Frinton for his old friend, Rex. Because of the short shooting schedule involved, the actor was able to accept the offer to appear in what promised to be a prestige production.

There was increasing friction between Rex and Rachel as his working schedule began to fill up for months ahead and she began to rebel against the prospect of another six months of idleness while her husband was filming. It was a grave disappointment to Rex that he had not found a wife who was content just to be with him.

In London, where they returned in March to allow Rex to prepare for the film, Rachel was offered the lead in Lionel Bart's new musical *Maggie May*, to be presented by impresario Bernard Delfont. Despite initial protestations that she did not want to be separated from Rex for what would be a considerable time, she finally accepted the part. Rehearsals were to begin while Rex was filming in Italy.

Shooting on *The Yellow Rolls-Royce* began at the beginning of April at M-G-M's Elstree studios. The film's first episode was set in 1932 and Rex played the role of the Marquess of Frinton who purchases this special Rolls-Royce for his wife, played by Jeanne Moreau, only to discover that she is being unfaithful to him, which prompts him to dispose of the car. The South African-born actress Moira Lister, who appeared in the first episode as Lady St Simeon, had been looking forward to working with Rex. She says: 'We were called in to rehearse and I realised the kind of man he was and I was very, very disillusioned. He gave me and my role absolutely no consideration at all. He just sat down and with a pencil he crossed out half a dozen of my lines, without the graciousness of saying, "Terribly sorry, but the scene's too long." He just said, "We are doing this!"'

Although Rattigan was present as Rex made the cuts, Moira Lister recalls, 'Terry was a bit in awe of him and he didn't say very much. He just stood by. He was obviously very keen to keep Rex happy.'

Although she felt that Rex must have had good reason to reduce her lines, she says, 'From that moment my admiration for him as a person went out of the window. I was terribly hurt that he had done it in that way. I think Rex just felt he was the star and therefore everything should be done exactly as he wanted it.'

Moira Lister goes on to recall an occasion when Rex was presented with a Rolls-Royce, which Rachel came down to the studio to inspect. She had known Rachel before her marriage to Rex and says,

'I saw the most fantastic transformation in her, because she had been a really down-to-earth girl and had never worried what she looked like. She always had a pretty face but she was very "avant-garde" before she met Rex. From being that kind of person she became the highly glamorous, superbly-groomed, beautifully turned-out, expensively-dressed and bejewelled wife of Rex Harrison. She was wreathed in furs and looked extremely glamorous – which was a totally new Rachel.'

While working on the film Rex began making notes for a proposed autobiography, about which he remarked: 'I want it to be outspoken, though if you are controversial you may offend people.' Whatever progress Rex made at this time, it was to be another ten years before his autobiography was published.

At the beginning of June Rex began work on *The Agony and the Ecstasy* in Italy but, unfortunately, the film was not the happy professional reunion with Carol Reed that Rex had hoped for, and he began to wonder why either of them had ever become involved in the project in the first place. His relationship with his co-star was particularly strained. At the start of production Charlton Heston noted, 'Rex Harrison . . . will not be an easy man to work with. Perhaps he's insecure over who has the best part, which is understandable.' A professional rivalry developed during the three months of shooting, as both men were anxious to impress their own personalities on the film. Rex wrote in his autobiography that Heston, '. . . very politely and very nicely made me feel that it was extremely kind of me to be supporting him,' while Heston noted that Rex's contribution as the Pope was 'worth all the megrims', and when he came to edit his working journals for publication he wrote of Harrison: 'Rex is a very gifted performer. He also has the temperament of a thoroughbred racehorse . . . highly strung, with a tendency to snort and rear and kick at the starting gate.'

Today Charlton Heston says, 'I admire Rex enormously as an actor and feel he gave a remarkable performance as Pope Julius', although Rex has been more acid when reminiscing about his co-star on this past collaboration. He said recently: 'Very assuming fellow, thinks the world is his supporting cast.'

Rex had been understandably excited at the prospect of tackling so unusual a part as that of the 'Warrior Pope', a pontiff who was as much at home on the battlefield as in church. However, the script chose to concentrate in tedious detail on Michelangelo's daunting three-year task of painting the frescoes for the ceiling of the Sistine Chapel in Rome, at the expense of exploring further the exploits of Julius II in defending the Papal States. The film was popular with neither critics nor public, and the Pope's frequent pleas to Michelangelo, 'When will you make an end?' could equally have been uttered by the audience. Bosley Crowther, reviewing the film for the *New York Times*, referred to it as, 'not a strong and soaring drama but an illustrated lecture on a slow artist at work.'

While Rex was making the film in Italy, Rachel began rehearsing *Maggie May* in London. Her behaviour was so erratic it was rumoured that Judy Garland, who had expressed great interest in the show, would stand by to take over should it be necessary; as it was, Miss Garland did make recordings of four songs from the show.

A week prior to the show's opening in Manchester,

Rex flew over from Rome on a brief visit to see his wife. Peter Roberts, a production manager for the Bernard Delfont organisation, was present at the dress rehearsal and recalls, 'Rachel was on the stage and Rex was in the dress circle and the director, Ted Kotcheff, gave Rachel a move and suddenly a voice out of the darkness said, "I wouldn't do that if I were you, darling". It was the voice of Rex Harrison. The whole rehearsal came to a halt. Ted Kotcheff was furious and Rex was asked *not* to attend rehearsals in future.'

During the four weeks *Maggie May* played in Manchester Rex was there for much of the time, but when it opened at the Adelphi Theatre in London on September 22nd he was conspicuous by his absence. The first-night audience included Noël Coward, Judy Garland, Anthony Perkins, Rosalind Russell, Peter Sellers and Brian Epstein, making it a star-studded occasion. The combination of Rachel Roberts and Lionel Bart certainly succeeded in drawing the public, and Rachel remained with the show for nearly seven months.

With Rachel committed to the show, Rex attended alone the world premiere of *My Fair Lady* in New York on October 22nd. The film was a triumph for all concerned, and Rex accompanied Jack L. Warner, Audrey Hepburn, George Cukor and Cecil Beaton to further openings in Chicago and Los Angeles, before returning to England at the end of the year. He also heard that the New York Film Critics had voted him the Actor of the Year for his performance in the film.

On December 30th Rex attended yet another premiere, this time for *The Yellow Rolls-Royce*, at the Empire, Leicester Square, where he was accompanied by Terence Rattigan. The film was a record-breaking success, and, with the release in America of *My Fair Lady*, Rex's stock rose dramatically. He could now command half a million dollars a film, plus a share in the profits.

On January 21st 1965 *My Fair Lady* had its Royal Premiere at the Warner Theatre, Leicester Square in the presence of Princess Alexandra and Earl Mountbatten of Burma. Beforehand, Audrey Hepburn and Jack L. Warner joined Rex to host an all-day session with the press. The film was rapturously received by both press and public alike, and in Rex's particular case *My Fair Lady* now joined *Cleopatra* at the Dominion and *The Yellow Rolls-Royce* at the Empire, giving him a triumvirate of films playing simultaneously in the West End.

Just before its London premiere it was announced that Georgia Brown would replace Rachel Roberts in *Maggie May* in March. Due to their long separations, Rex and Rachel's relationship was suffering considerable strain, something which Rachel was uncomfortably aware of, as she explained: 'I have had leave of absence from my marriage for too long. I love Rex. I have to be with him. It's as simple as that.' Rex said at this time, 'We are looking for a production in which we can play opposite each other. Preferably for a very long time,' and spoke of appearing in a television adaptation of *Platonov* with Rachel. It would be some time before Rachel completed her commitment to *Maggie May*, so Rex returned to New York to discuss some of the numerous projects which had been submitted to him for his consideration. Upon his arrival he learned that he had been nominated for the Academy Award for his performance in *My Fair Lady*.

After so much activity Rex was to spend a whole year sifting and sorting out what to do next; he chose to bide his time, unwilling to commit himself to anything for the time being. He spoke of a return to the theatre, which he had neglected since *August for the People*, and claimed to be seriously considering taking a year off from films to head his own repertory company which would present plays in both London and New York. Inevitably there were attempts to lure him into appearing in another musical, and he was briefly involved in the intriguing prospect of a musical version of Cervantes' *Don Quixote*, for which W. H. Auden was writing the lyrics, but when the poet was taken off the project Rex lost interest, and

Cervantes' classic novel was eventually made into the musical, *Man of La Mancha*. Rex also considered appearing in musical adaptations of *The Scarlet Pimpernel* – a role he had always wanted to play – and *Goodbye Mr Chips* for which Terence Rattigan was writing the screenplay. Again Rex turned them both down, and in the latter case the part finally went to Peter O'Toole. Rex also admitted to having considered appearing at the National Theatre in London, under the directorship of Laurence Olivier but it proved to be impossible. 'I've discussed one or two things with Larry but he doesn't like to disrupt it with visiting stars.' Rex was also offered roles in two major films: Lord Cardigan in Tony Richardson's remake of *The Charge of the Light Brigade* and Noah in *The Bible*, to be directed by John Huston.

When Rex returned to London he took part in a charity television show, entitled *Golden Drama*, in aid of the Actors' Orphanage, which was broadcast live from the Queen's Theatre on January 31st 1966. Others taking part included Laurence Olivier and Noël Coward, who appeared in extracts from plays from sources as diverse as Shakespeare and Rattigan; Rex contributed by singing 'I've Grown Accustomed to Her Face'.

When Rachel left *Maggie May* she and Rex returned to Portofino to attempt to settle back into a routine of married life more to Rex's liking. At this time, Rex made some very strong and decidedly chauvinistic comments about his views on marriage: 'I vowed never to fit into the life of some woman. She has to fit into mine.'

'What I need in a wife is a companion, someone who understands my work. An actor has no routine, no security. His life is nomadic. He has bursts of working, bursts of preparing, and times when he's not working at all. The routine of a stage actor sounds so lovely – all day off and work a few hours at night. But it's not so.

During the day you're preparing mentally for the night's performance. You need a companion who shares that time with you, stays up for dinner after the theatre. I suppose that's why I marry actresses . . . I really believe the world would be a happier place if women stayed home. If we start from that premise, we would figure out a way for them to enjoy being home. Some women still do, you know. Bless them. A woman shouldn't compete with her husband. She should get behind him and help advance his career. And that's true in all walks of life.'

While they were in Portofino Rex invited the playwright Robert Bolt to stay with them at the villa. Rex was interested in playing Charles II and was hoping that Bolt, who had come to prominence in 1960 with *A Man for all Seasons* about Sir Thomas More, would write a play for him on the subject, but the project, like so many others, did not materialise.

In March Rex and Rachel travelled to Gstaad and at the end of the month, accompanied by their basset hound Homer, they boarded the *Queen Mary* for New York, where Rex was presented with a Humanitarian Award in recognition of his various charity works, particularly with the March of Dimes. Rex has always lent his services to worthy charities with a minimum of publicity.

The Harrisons then proceeded to Los Angeles for the Academy Award ceremony at the Civic Auditorium, Santa Monica on April 5th 1965. For his performance in *My Fair Lady*, Rex was honoured with the Oscar for the best performance of the year by an Actor in a Leading Role, one of the most richly deserved awards in the Academy's history. Rex was presented with his statuette by his co-star in the film, Audrey Hepburn.

Interestingly his stage Eliza, Julie Andrews, was similarly honoured at the same ceremony for her performance in the film *Mary Poppins*, which she had made for Walt Disney after Jack Warner rejected her casting as

Eliza in the film. *My Fair Lady* won a total of eight awards, including Best Film and Best Director for George Cukor – surprisingly his first and only Oscar.

Shortly after the ceremony Rex and Rachel flew to New York. They were met at the airport by Alan Jay Lerner, stayed at his home in Oyster Bay, Long Island and then proceeded to the St Regis Hotel in Manhattan, where Rex received a surprise visit from Joseph L. Mankiewicz, who brought with him a suitcase filled by an enormous screenplay in which he hoped to interest Rex. The as-yet unfinished treatment, based loosely on Ben Jonson's *Volpone*, was entitled *Mr Fox of Venice*, but would finally reach the screen as *The Honey Pot*, after going through numerous title changes during production.

The central character was the supposedly wealthy Cecil Fox, who calls the three most important women in his past life to what they understand to be his death-bed, with the intention of watching them scramble for his fortune. Mankiewicz interpreted and performed various scenes from the comedy in Rex's hotel room, and succeeded in arousing the actor's interest. Mankiewicz's enthusiasm was infectious and prompted Rex to make a hasty and perhaps ill-considered decision to lend the weight of his name to the project. Although the material was clearly intriguing, the haphazard manner in which it was presented to Rex should have given him an indication of the lack of restraint with which Mankiewicz had put his ideas on paper, but the writer-director had managed to persuade him to take the lead, and left the hotel after promising Rex that he would contact him as soon as he had produced a working screenplay.

Arriving back in Italy, clutching his well-deserved Oscar, Rex was even more of a local celebrity and at a noisy ceremony was made an honorary citizen of Portofino, the once-sleepy village which was now firmly on the tourist map, in no small part because of Rex's association with it.

Frequent guests at the villa during this time were Rex's

son Noel, his wife and their two children, Cathryn and Simon. Simon Harrison retains vivid memories of one of their visits to his grandfather. 'We went to stay with him in Portofino – mother, father, Cathryn and myself. I can't have been more than three. I remember his speedboat, his jeep and his basset hound, Homer.' He continues,

'There was an incident in the house which was quite traumatic at the time. I was wandering around like three-year-olds do, just exploring on my own and I found my way into his bedroom. I found a bidet – I'd never seen anything like it before, but it looked like a sink made for a three-year-old, so I put the plug in and filled it up. I was absolutely fascinated and I got all his clean underwear and threw it all in and started washing it, thinking I was being terribly useful. But then my grandfather came in and kicked me up the bum. I couldn't understand what I'd done wrong, but it's the physical memory that lasts. I think he was just annoyed I'd got into his clean clothes.'

Simon also says: 'I remember being rather frightened of Rachel with her great deep voice. I remember thinking that she was terribly loud and frightening.'

In the late spring Rex discussed the possibility of making an NBC television special, tentatively titled, *The Paris of Rex Harrison and Rachel Roberts*, to be directed by Lindsay Anderson, along the lines of similar productions which had featured Elizabeth Taylor and Sophia Loren, but Rex eventually decided against it.

In May, Rex sailed to Cannes, accompanied by Rachel and the ubiquitous Homer, in his luxurious new cabin cruiser *Henry*, which flew the Italian flag and the pennant of the RAF Yacht Club. Rex was invited to be on the panel of judges for the 1965 Film Festival. Relations between the Harrisons were turbulent and Noël Coward, who was in Cannes at the time, recorded having a 'brief encounter with Rex and Rachel', noting tersely: 'Rachel noisier than ever.' The English comedian, Lance Percival, who had worked briefly with Rex in *The Yellow Rolls-Royce*, was also there and recalls seeing them at the Carlton Hotel and at other locations during the two weeks of the festival. He remembers that he was witness to 'Rachel shouting – Rex shouting – terrible bust-ups all the time.'

The summer was marred by one sad event, the death in June of Rachel's father, whose health had been fragile over the past couple of years.

In July Rachel accompanied Rex to Moscow for the International Film Festival, where *My Fair Lady* was shown at the Palace of Congress in the Kremlin. In Russia, Rex continued to have difficulty controlling Rachel's excessive drinking and erratic behaviour.

When they returned to Italy, Rex received further laurels. He was presented with the prestigious Maschera D'Argento in Rome and won the coveted 'David' – the Davide di Donatello Award which was presented to him at Taormina, Sicily in August.

In September, Rex and Rachel returned to Rome where work was finally to begin on *The Honey Pot*, with Susan Hayward and Cliff Robertson also in the cast. They rented a house on the Via Appia Antica for the five months of shooting, but the whole experience was to prove an unhappy one for all concerned. The film was dogged by tragedy: the Italian cinematographer, Gianni Di Venanzo, died mid-way through production, while Susan Hayward suffered the tragic loss of her husband, forcing her to return briefly to America. Rex would remember Susan Hayward as 'A marvellous woman, that rare blend of beauty and strength. She kept her grief totally private, did her work like a pro, then went home.' In Rome, faced with another extended period of idleness, Rachel was in a depressed state. She had hoped to play Miss Hayward's nurse/companion, Sarah Watkins, in the film but the role went instead to Maggie Smith. During shooting Rachel took an overdose of Seconal and was rushed to hospital, while Mankiewicz did his best to keep the story out of the newspapers.

Throughout the five months spent on the film in Rome, Rex also became aware of a great change in Mankiewicz since they had last worked together, on *Cleopatra*. He found the director a 'changed man . . . far less relaxed . . . much more easily irritable, and less tolerant of everything.'

The Honey Pot was not successful when it finally reached the cinemas. Bosley Crowther wrote in the *New York Times* that Mankiewicz had written and directed 'a sleek and saucy simulation of contemporary high comedy', but 'what might have been a brisk and brazen satire forms into a prolix and slow comedy mystery.' The critic did, however, reserve praise for Rex's lively performance: '. . . the agile Mr Harrison is at his mischievous best.'

Rex hoped to revive his fortunes with his next project, which was being prepared for him while he was making *The Honey Pot* at Cinecittà in Rome. It was to be a film musical based on Hugh Lofting's children's books about Dr Dolittle, a country doctor who decides to administer to animals rather than ungrateful humans, developing the unique ability to converse with them. Producer Arthur Jacobs and Twentieth Century-Fox felt that the books were ideal material for a musical, and they hoped to interest Alan Jay Lerner and Rex Harrison in the project. After talking to Jacobs, Lerner was convinced that the role of the doctor would be perfect casting for Rex and contacted his old friend. Lerner says: 'Rex became very excited about the project but he said, "I'll only do it if you do it."' The two men agreed and contracts were drawn up, but at the last moment Lerner and his partner on the project, André Previn, withdrew. Alan Lerner says, 'When Rex first found out I wasn't going to do it, he said he wouldn't do it either.' However, Fox were able to persuade Rex to continue when, according to Lerner, they 'doubled their offer', ensuring Rex an 'enormous' amount of money for his participation.

With the departure of Lerner and Previn, Arthur Jacobs gave the task of writing both the score and the screenplay to Leslie Bricusse, who had made his reputation with Anthony Newley's *Stop the World . . .* Bricusse recalled, 'The next nine months were absolute misery. The problem wasn't so much in writing it but in dealing with Rex Harrison.' Rex was naturally disappointed by Lerner's departure, and found it hard to adapt to the change. Bricusse said, 'Our relationship at first was extremely difficult – like a headmaster (Rex) and a new pupil (me). I would tell him what I had done and he would say in effect, "Could do better".' Bricusse states that, 'At one time while I was writing it, Rex even had writers of his own holed up secretly in London. He queried everything.'

Filming finally began at the end of June 1966 at Castle Combe in Wiltshire, reputed to be the prettiest village in England. As had been the case for the film version of *My Fair Lady*, Rex sang his songs 'live' for the cameras rather than dub them afterwards, but shooting proved to be fraught by the tremendous problems of working with so many animals. They generally failed to pick up their cues and never reacted as they should. Shortly after the film was completed Rex would remark upon his less sophisticated co-stars: 'To work in close proximity with all those animals for a year wasn't the most pleasant experience of my life . . . They would all be doing their business quite naturally, so we would then have to clear the set, sweep it up, air it, come back and start again.'

Production continued in England well into the summer, but had to be abandoned when the weather deteriorated, making further shooting impossible. Rather than risk a repetition of their expensive misadventures with *Cleopatra* when faced with the same problem, Twentieth Century-Fox moved the unit to Hollywood. Further location work took place at Santa Lucia in the British West Indies, but again they ran into the rainy season and experienced costly delays.

Doctor Dolittle was a disaster for Fox, despite being incomprehensibly nominated for the Academy Award as Best Film of 1967. It is obvious from the style of the integrated songs, and even their individual tempo as the story progresses, that the creators had kept a side-long glance on *My Fair Lady* all the time, but Lerner and Loewe's magic was not just a tough act to follow – it could not be followed.

Massively overlong and aimed too obviously at a juvenile audience, *Doctor Dolittle*, under the unimaginative direction of Richard Fleischer, lacks wit and is curiously dull. As for Rex, for once even his charm is muted: an indication of his own dissatisfaction with a film which was so clearly designed to create for him another *Fair Lady*-type of vehicle – on this occasion teaching animals, rather than humans, how to speak – without the creative talent to bring it off successfully.

Added to the nightmare of making *Doctor Dolittle* was, for Rex, the disturbing state of his private life, as Rachel continued to show signs of suicidal tendencies. She had worked occasionally, including an appearance in a television production of *Blithe Spirit* in New York, but her drinking had not abated and her behaviour became increasingly embarrassing and outrageous.

Noel Harrison had moved to Los Angeles in 1965, and he and his family occasionally saw Rex while he was in Hollywood for *Doctor Dolittle*. Simon Harrison recalls, 'We went over to their house a couple of times during the day and heard some terrible slanging matches between them, but they both used to come out of it looking perfectly normal – as if it happened all the time.'

The Harrisons would also socialise frequently with Richard Harris and his wife Elizabeth, who was one of Rachel's closest friends. Of Rachel, Elizabeth says, 'I used to spend quite a lot of time with her. She used to come up to our house in Bel-Air. She wasn't happy – they were having problems then.'

Richard Harris and his wife were very fond of throwing parties, and would always invite Rex and Rachel. But the social life in the film capital no longer held the same charm for Rex who had witnessed Hollywood during its golden era. He now found it tired and forced, as new arrivals tried to duplicate a way of life lost forever in the changing fashions of the 1960s. At one of Richard Harris's parties, when the guests began to throw themselves into the swimming pool in various states of undress, Elizabeth recalled Rex saying irritably, 'Oh God! It's all so bloody passé!'

In all, the year Rex spent on *Doctor Dolittle* was not a happy one; in his autobiography he admitted that his unsettled personal life and the constant irritations and delays when making the film 'nearly finished me.'

Doctor Dolittle has the distinction, if undeserved, of remaining one of Rex's best-known films. It is unfortunate that Rex, who has achieved such success in so many more worthwhile roles, should be indelibly associated with a part which gave him little opportunity to display his considerable gifts.

After filming was completed, Rex and Rachel left for Europe on the *Queen Elizabeth*. Rex had decided, after consultation with close friends, that the only way that Rachel might be able to lift herself out of her depression was to start working more regularly again. Rex himself had been discussing the possibility of appearing in a film about Casanova in middle-age, from a screenplay by John Mortimer, to be called *Casanova's Homecoming*. The film was to be produced in Europe for Twentieth Century-Fox with George Cukor directing, but instead, at the end of March 1967, it was announced that Rex and Rachel would appear together in a screen adaptation of George Feydeau's farce, *A Flea in her Ear*, scheduled to begin production in Paris in July.

Before shooting began, Rex and Rachel returned to

Portofino, and were faced with a near-disaster when Homer was involved in an accident, as Rachel explained: 'Homer's been ill and in a way it's all Rex's fault. You see, whenever we took Homer for a walk, I'd shout out, "Sit!" if I saw he was about to cross the road. Well Rex thought my shouting sounded a bit common, so I stopped. And one day Homer literally walked under a car.' Fortunately the vehicle was not travelling at great speed and Homer escaped serious injury, although he was operated on for the removal of his spleen.

In the middle of the summer, Rex and Rachel travelled to Paris, with Homer, to start work on *A Flea in her Ear*. Rex had now publically altered his views about his wife pursuing her career: 'I prefer Rachel to work. She *needs* to work. You see, she's got all this Welsh energy!' However, working together on a film for the first time did nothing to reinforce their splintering marriage, as she continued to drink heavily. *A Flea in her Ear* provided no consolation. Directed by Jacques Charon of the Comédie Française – who had directed the play successfully for the National Theatre in London – Rex was cast in the dual role of Victor Chandebisse, a rich Parisian lawyer, and Poche, a drunken porter in a sleazy Paris hotel. Set at the turn of the century it was the usual Feydeau concotion of sex and mistaken identity, but the farce did not translate well to the screen and it was yet another disaster for Twentieth Century-Fox, as well as its star. Darryl F. Zanuck condemned the film as, 'A catastrophe! An absolute bust everywhere.'

After completing the film, Rex was next seen in London when he attended the Royal Premiere of *Doctor Dolittle* in the presence of the Queen. Two days later he was in Paris for the opening there, and was the recipient of the Silver Medal of Honour of the City of Paris. With Rachel, he then flew to New York and Paris to publicise the film.

It was at this time that Rex disclosed the true state of his marriage in one of his most revealing and, at the same time, defensive analyses of their troubled union. 'I am not completely happy. I would hate that. Rachel and I have a stormy relationship but it is wonderful. I think that conflict between a man and woman – a cat-and-dog existence if you like – is essential. But that is what is meant to be. To be in agreement about everything would be utter boredom.'

As he approached sixty, Rex Harrison's successful screen career came to a close when it became clear that the film medium could no longer provide him with material worthy of his talent. This was sadly emphasised when he announced that he would be appearing in Charles Dyer's screen adaptation of his play, *Staircase* about two ageing homosexual barbers in the dilapidated London suburb of Brixton. Rex had not seen the stage production when he was approached by Stanley Donen to appear in the film with Richard Burton. Both actors accepted the challenge; as Harrison stated, 'It was a case of "I'll do it if you'll do it." And I felt I was old enough and rich enough to risk it.'

But by the time the cameras rolled at the Billancourt studios in Paris on September 3rd 1968, it must have been clear to both Harrison and Burton that they had made a dreadful mistake in accepting this distasteful adaptation of an equally distasteful play. Not even the major talents of a Harrison or a Burton could save the enterprise from disaster. During production Rex attempted to keep a brave face, and was quoted as saying, 'Variety is what keeps one's interest in life and it is what keeps the public interested in what you are doing,' but in the case of *Staircase* he was to be proved disastrously wrong.

The *Daily Mail* critic said of Rex's interpretation of Charlie: 'Harrison merely appears to be acting out everyone's preconception of the "mincing" poove', while Vincent Canby of the *New York Times* felt: 'Harry and Charlie are exploited as freaks . . . The two stars seem terribly uncomfortable, and I wonder if the apparent discomfort, conscious or not, isn't meant to call attention to the real distance that exists between the actors and their roles.'

Not surprisingly, the film was a total failure. Although when he attended the opening of *Doctor Dolittle* in New York Rex had declared: 'I never intend to retire. Never,' it was clear that he would have to look for opportunities elsewhere. On April 20th 1969 he was presented with a special Tony award in New York for his unique contribution to the theatre, which must have strengthened his resolve to return to the stage. It was time for change in his life.

Although he had spent a great deal of time working apart from Rachel, they spent the summer together when Rex chartered the *Calisto*, a luxurious yacht requiring an eleven-man crew, and sailed around the Mediterranean, calling at Sardinia, Elba and Corsica. Elizabeth Harris, now separated from her husband Richard, joined them, together with her three children and her brother, Morgan. At the time she believed her friend was happy with Rex, but she would soon realise that this was a misconception.

Reflecting some years later on the time he spent with Rachel, Rex said: 'It had been a long hard struggle since Kay died – a long haul of nine years in which it seemed to me that there had been more dark than light, at any rate in my private life.'

9

ON JULY 23rd, 1969, it was announced that Rex Harrison would be appearing in a play in London's West End for the first time since *August For the People* at the Royal Court Theatre eight years before.

Rex now felt that it was time to return to the stage, and decided to accept the role of Lionel Fairleigh in a new comedy by an untried author, George Hulme, who had submitted a play to Rex entitled *The Lionel Touch*. Rex explained his enthusiasm for the play to the press: '. . . the attractions of this play are that its author, George Hulme, is a newcomer to the theatre – and it is always satisfying to take on a new playwright's work. And the play he has written is very light, very witty. I find that's a rare quality these days.'

The thirty-eight-year-old Canadian playwright had visited Rex at Portofino that summer to discuss the project, just before Rex had left for his Mediterranean cruise, and had stayed for a week at Harrison's expense at the Hotel Splendido, near the house, meeting him every day to discuss the play and having dinner with him on most evenings.

The principal character in the play was based on Lionel Burleigh, an eccentric painter who lived in Chelsea with his common-law wife Vivian and their nine children until his death in 1967 at the age of sixty. In the play, Lionel is an impoverished painter with a long-suffering wife and three children who look on while he attempts to evade bailiffs and a possible prison sentence. Playing Lionel's wife would be Joyce Redman with whom Rex had so successfully appeared on Broadway in *Anne of the Thousand Days* twenty years before.

Rex arrived in London for rehearsals at the beginning of September, while Rachel had already gone to Bath where she was rehearsing at the Theatre Royal for a revival of Edward Albee's *Who's Afraid of Virginia Woolf?* opposite her former husband Alan Dobie, now happily married with three children. Rachel's working with Dobie caused some comment in the press but she was quick to point out that Rex had encouraged her to take on the part and that the Harrisons and Alan Dobie and his wife Maureen were good friends. She explained, 'Not many men would allow the woman they love to team up with her ex-husband. But Rex is generous, unmalicious, strong, kind and tolerant, and this is a measure of his love and trust.'

Alan Dobie also recalls this time: 'Rachel Roberts and I were reunited professionally and to let off a lot of old steam, as the husband and wife protagonists. Rachel did not talk about Rex much as their relationship was a little estranged by then.'

Rumours of a separation between Rex and Rachel had been flourishing since the late spring of 1969 when Rachel had taken a small apartment in Lowndes Square under her own name while making a television film, *The Gaunt Woman*, in London with Lorne Greene. A friend was quoted as saying at that time, 'Rachel is two people. A fine stage and screen actress, she can be warm, amusing, intelligent, very much a lady. In another mood, she can be vulgar, shocking and ridiculous.'

Further suspicion was aroused when Elizabeth Harris, one of Rachel's closest friends, was invited to join the Harrisons, along with her three children, at Portofino that Easter. But still they clung onto the appearance of a stable marriage, even to the pitiful spectacle of Rachel holding a press conference in Bath at which there was pointedly displayed a portrait of Rex, lovingly inscribed to his wife, and complemented by two dozen long-stemmed roses. Rex did actually visit Bath to attend a performance of *Virginia Woolf* after which he, Rachel and Alan Dobie had a meal together in a small café, but otherwise Rex was not in evidence.

Matters would come to a head with Rex's involvement in *The Lionel Touch*, a play which he had great hopes for but which became one of his most unsatisfactory professional experiences. Indeed, so galling was the experience for Rex that his only mention of the play in his autobiography is a cursory note of his involvement in it at the time when he was becoming closer to Elizabeth Harris.

With his marriage to Rachel now on the verge of collapse, it was to Elizabeth Harris that Rex turned for comfort. Elizabeth and Richard Harris had finally been divorced at the end of July 1969 and she had not heard from the Harrisons since their holiday together that summer. However, about a month later she received a letter from Rachel who told her of her plans to appear in *Who's Afraid of Virginia Woolf?* at Bath and that Rex would be in London for rehearsals of his new play.

With Rachel in Bath, Rex, alone in London, was not long in making contact with Elizabeth. He would often arrive unannounced at her home in Bedford Gardens, in Notting Hill Gate, which he sought as a refuge from the misery of his troubled marriage and the new play which was not progressing as he had hoped. Elizabeth kept a noisy household with three fast-growing sons and an ever-open door. It was the sort of bohemian existence that was far removed from Rex's own style of living, but it was a comfortable home in which to relax.

Elizabeth was well aware that Rex and Rachel's marriage was in trouble and Rachel had many times confided to her that she and Rex were getting divorced, but Elizabeth had never taken these claims seriously, particularly as they were usually said in the presence of her husband.

Rex began to visit Elizabeth more and more frequently and the two of them would talk together for hours on end. Elizabeth represented someone whom Rex felt he could approach with his problems because she knew something of the state of his marriage, having witnessed its varying moods at close quarters. But Elizabeth was unprepared for the depth of feeling which Rex, a normally reticent man in such matters, displayed to her, as she recalls, 'I can remember one night he came round in a terrible state. I was having a dinner party and he just came in. I left the people in the dining-room because he was in such a state over Rachel. It was really his concern over Rachel – this was the ironic thing. And he was also not at all well at the time.' Rex was able to let his emotions out when talking to her. Elizabeth had just been through a divorce herself and in many ways they had been in a similar predicament.

So great did Rex's dependence on seeing Elizabeth become that the desire was not to be thwarted even if she was not at home. On one occasion, Rex called at Bedford Gardens and learned from the housekeeper that Elizabeth had gone out for dinner with a party including British film producer Maxwell Setton. Rex found out where they had gone and promptly made his way there, as Elizabeth again remembers,

'He turned up at the restaurant. Unasked, he sat down and so Max obviously said, "Would you like some dinner?"
'Rex said, "No, no. I don't want anything to eat – I'll have some wine."
'So he started to drink a glass of wine and then began to make these terrible gestures at me – pantomime things – and said in a stage whisper, "Don't drink the wine! It's filthy! It's off!" He was an uninvited guest and he was complaining about the bloody wine.'

A similar incident occurred on a further occasion.

'I was having dinner with David Frost and Rex suddenly turns up out of the blue. Again, he'd gone to the house and the housekeeper had told him where I was. I would always tell the housekeeper where I was because I had the children. So he came and joined us at the restaurant; it was, "Sit down. Do join us", and he was complaining, "Why? What did you want to choose this bloody awful restaurant for?"'

Rehearsals for *The Lionel Touch* had indeed got off to a very shaky start, as Christopher Cazenove, who was then making his West End debut with the play, recalls. 'The first inkling that there was a danger area was with the girl who was cast as Rex's daughter. At the end of the first week of rehearsals, she had been turning up as her idea of a "serious" actress – with her hair in a sort of elastic band, glasses and a kaftan. She was told by her agent, would she please wear a short and proper skirt on Monday, which she refused basically – and so Sharon Gurney took over.'

Further trouble seemed to be looming because another of the actors, Christopher Witty, was very tall and dwarfed Rex if they stood next to each other. Christopher Cazenove continues, 'This was a problem and we were all thinking, "Who's the next one to go?" It was the chat going around that Chris was in trouble purely on account of his height. We were all pretty nervous, but anyway he wasn't sacked. The problem was got round by having him coming on stage and being directed to sit at every possible opportunity whenever Rex was on stage.'

A major problem with the production was that both the author and the director, John Gorrie, lacked sufficient experience and so were timid in their dealings with Rex whose massive reputation and imperious manner left them helpless while he went his own way, cutting passages in the play that he did not like and casting only a surface regard towards the nominal director. Rex was not actually unpleasant towards John Gorrie, but there was no proper director/actor relationship, as Cazenove asserts:

'I think John tried once or twice to give Rex a note or two but with so little effect that he gave up after a while. So we got notes, but they were kind of round the back somewhere. It was a big, big chance for John Gorrie and he absolutely rightly and sensibly realised that if he started trying to tell Rex what to do, he would be out on his ear. Anybody could have been out at a moment's notice.'

George Hulme suffered at Rex's hands with the blithe cutting of the script, which not only made the author unhappy but destroyed the fabric of the play. Rex was even making cuts which were against his character in the play but no one had the courage to challenge his over-whelming authority. Cazenove continues, 'Rex did a lot of cutting and mainly the serious stuff. He really cut it from joke to joke, which was odd actually because some-body with his incredible stage craft you would have thought would realise that you need the bits in between to make the jokes really work; otherwise it becomes so lightweight.'

Joyce Redman's role as Rex's wife was one that suf-fered greatly through the cuts that were made, but she chose to accept this, although she herself does not believe that Rex was responsible for the cuts made to her part. 'Rex wasn't like that at all with me. I could have said I won't do it, but I didn't take an acrimonious view. It was not a very good play.' But if Miss Redman accepted the cuts and hid a natural feeling of disturbance, Christopher Cazenove believes that these alterations to the script took away much of the heart of the play. 'The relationship between Lionel Fairleigh and his wife Vivian was nicely written and there were emotional moments and serious moments. Most of these went, which affected Joyce's part quite considerably, although she was such a darling and very sweet about it. But I think she was less than deliriously happy about the whole thing.'

The first night of the play, on October 13th 1969 at the Opera House, Manchester, was not encouraging and Rex was in even more of a state because Rachel had made a surprise appearance, having flown up to Manchester to attend the opening of her husband's new play. By the end of the performance everybody involved was painfully aware that the play was still in trouble, although Rex's personality and experience had kept it from going under completely, as Cazenove asserts, 'He's got this wonderful way; it doesn't matter what he says – he stands there and commands the audience and smiles.'

The producer, John Gale, had organised a big dinner for the cast after the opening night at the Henry V Restaurant, hiring a private room in which the tables were arranged in a semi-circle. Following the performance, the company rushed off to the restaurant, although they were not surprised when Rex did not make an immediate appearance because not only had Rachel come up but also his British agent Laurence Evans and his wife Mary. Cazenove continues,

'We had drinks and dinner was laid out, and we drank and we waited and waited – and no sign of Rex. We knew that it had been less than an enormous success that first night but Rex did eventually appear at the party. He and Rachel turned up together somewhat the worse for a drink or two and, in fact, we then heard later that Rex and Laurence Evans had parted company that evening over a remark that Rex made to his wife.'

Rex had long since entered the realm of international superstar and his affairs, like many others' in the top league, were handled by an eminent lawyer in the United States: in Rex's case, Aaron Frosch of the law firm of Weissberger and Frosch in New York. However, a British theatrical agent was required to be present when, as a major star, he made an important personal appearance, and to handle his day-to-day professional problems. In this particular case, not only the agent but also his wife had expressed opinions regarding the play which were not only unwelcome but were rather ill-considered at such a time. The result was that Rex and Laurence Evans, whom Rex had known well and liked for many years, parted company.

This incident set the seal on the rest of the evening, with no-one recalling it as being anything but a disaster. Rex and Rachel arrived just as the rest of the company were about to start their second course, having given up any hope of their making an appearance. The meal ended without incident, but a strong current of emotion was only just concealed below the surface. The disappointment of the evening weighed heavily on everyone and when the dinner was over and the speeches began, they were in that vein, as Christopher Cazenove recalls,

'John Gale got up and gave a speech and then Rex got up and made a speech. The speeches were reconciliatory in nature and Rex thanked the producer and the author for the wonderful play. Then George thanked Rex for being so marvellous in his play.

'It was all very friendly to start with, but then I remember Rex stood again, this time to reply to George and that George made another speech – and they got worse and worse and worse until they were almost insulting each other towards the end of it. Before it really got too bad, the whole proceedings were brought to a halt.'

After Manchester the play went to Oxford and Brighton before its opening in London and throughout this three-week period there was constant rewriting and re-rehearsing in an effort to get the play into a reasonable state for the West End. Although Rex's relationship with the rest of the company remained amicable, his relationship with George Hulme had broken down completely. With all its problems, Rex was unable to hide his disregard for the play and he no longer cared what he said about it or its author. When Hulme resisted cuts that Rex wanted to make, Harrison simply dismissed him.

When the company arrived at Oxford, following their week in Manchester, Rex was further irritated by the arrival of actor Nigel Patrick who had been invited by the producer to come and see the play and offer some advice and help with it, an act which led to an unpleasant confrontation between Rex and Patrick. Elizabeth Harris was there to see Rex and he escorted her to dinner, where they were joined by Patrick who had just seen the play. Joyce Redman, who was dining in the same restaurant with John Gale and actor Hugh Latimer, who was Rex's understudy, recalls what happened. 'I saw Rex and Elizabeth together and I stopped to say "Goodnight" and suddenly Elizabeth attacked Nigel. The whole thing blew up. Something was said. Eventually we left them to it, but it got very nasty.'

Hugh Latimer also gives his version of this débâcle, 'Suddenly there were voices raised; Nigel Patrick's voice saying, "You couldn't bloody well play comedy!" and then saying the most unspeakable rudenesses to Mrs Harris. There was an almighty row; it went on for about a quarter of an hour and they both left in high dudgeon.'

Elizabeth Harris recalls that Nigel Patrick remarked to Rex that he had previously been offered the part and had turned it down. He expressed surprise that Harrison should have accepted it, a remark which Elizabeth considered most inopportune, particularly as Rex had only a little more than a week before he was due to open in London. It was this that prompted her attack on Patrick. She did not presume to take a professional stand on the matter, but rather defended Rex from what she considered to be an unwarranted and tactless remark.

Hugh Latimer understood Rex's annoyance at Nigel Patrick's presence and was amazed that Patrick had the temerity to advise an actor whose skill and knowledge of comedy left him far behind. Latimer described it as, 'raving mad to bring Nigel Patrick up to advise Rex Harrison.'

Elizabeth Harris was becoming an ever more visible companion to Rex and with Rachel also often turning up, Rex found himself caught in the middle of a difficult and potentially explosive situation. As Hugh Latimer recalls, 'There were frightful scenes and awful shouting. Rachel was unhappy. Mrs Harris was around. The rows were in hotel foyers and places like that and Rachel would shout like mad – and in public.'

The play finally opened at the Lyric Theatre on Shaftesbury Avenue on November 5th. Rachel was escorted to the event by Joyce Redman's husband. Most reviewers were kind to Rex, blaming any faults in his performance on the material he had at his disposal. The pleasure of seeing Rex Harrison once again on a West End stage was clearly a considerable compensation in an unrewarding play. Irving Wardle in *The Times*, summed it up when he wrote,

> This comedy exists strictly for the sake of Rex Harrison . . . The part fits him like a hand-made suit, giving ample scope for his best-loved mannerisms: the offhand charm . . . the foxy guile, and the storms of comic exasperation that hit the eardrums like tearing metal . . . it offers the combination of aristocratic style and renegade values which add up to Mr Harrison's brand of theatrical effrontery.

The play itself was dismissed as trite and old-fashioned, '[it] relies too glibly on the middle-aged comic formula of drawing a flattering contrast between a parent still young at heart and his stuffily humourless progeny.'

Peter Lewis, in the *Daily Mail*, also welcomed Rex back but detected a lack of assurance:

Mr Harrison was uncertain with the joke lines which, though not bad, need all the help they can get in such an artificial, not to say idiotic, situation. Like Joyce Redman, his exasperated wife, and his precociously awful family, he often seemed in doubt whether he was playing for real or for comic effect. The result is a slowness on the ball which loses many a good player a championship.

But if most critics tended to make allowances for Rex and foist the blame for the failure of the production entirely onto the play itself, Christopher Cazenove believes that Rex was instrumental in causing his return to the West End to be such a disaster. 'I don't think it was a great play but I think it was all right, and I do still have the feeling that if Rex had not tampered with the script so much it would have been better than it was. I do feel that was the reason why it didn't work.' Hugh Latimer supports this view to a certain extent, but is critical of Rex agreeing to appear in the play in the first place.

'With all due respect to Mr Hulme, what can you say about a man who chooses *The Lionel Touch*? I know exactly why – because I don't think there's a great deal of critical faculty or choice there and I think that he felt that it was a tremendous show-off part. The play had a lot to say – largely with what the wife said – but when all the wife's opinions were cut out, it was a bit one-sided.'

Cazenove does not, however, regret this opportunity to work with Harrison, 'It was a great experience, an extraordinary experience for us all. I don't think anybody did dislike him. I think everybody that knows him is aware of the fact that he can be, and is, the bastard of all time if he wants to be. Likewise, he's just got this extraordinary charm and talent that makes you forgive him.' In working with Rex Cazenove asserts that there were never any problems between them and that he was, 'always marvellous and absolutely sweet' to him, but Rex would never forget his own position as the star of the production. The two men had to play billiards together during one scene, at which Rex was supposed to beat Cazenove. It was a difficult scene in which the billiard game had to match their speeches:

> 'If the game went wrong, we had to adapt the dialogue to fit. But there was one thing you had to do: you had to be downstage of him. If, as inevitably happened from time to time, it would end up with me being at the top end of the table to do a shot because that was where the ball had gone, Rex would actually stand there and smile wonderfully at me until I got downstage of him before he would carry on. It was all sort of a joke; he never did it nastily. It was always a charming smile, but one knew what it was.'

With the complications in his private life and the disappointing reception by the critics for his long-awaited return to the West End, Rex was understandably down. On Friday, December 12th, his doctor announced that he was suffering from 'general fatigue and over-work' and recommended that his patient should take a rest from the play for a minimum of three weeks. Hugh Latimer stepped in at short notice and by the Saturday matinee performance was appearing as Lionel Fairleigh.

Initially, Rex had intended to enter a hospital, but instead he sought refuge with Elizabeth Harris whose presence in her husband's life Rachel had fatalistically accepted. Elizabeth had been increasingly in Rex's company since the tour of *The Lionel Touch* had begun and Rachel finally telephoned her to find out how matters stood between her and Rex. Elizabeth recalled the incident in her autobiography.

'"Are you in love with . . . ?"

'After a long pause I said, "Yes, I am."

'This time the long pause was hers. Quietly she thanked me for telling her the truth. I felt terrible. I told her I was sorry I had fallen in love with Rex.

'"It happens," she said. Her voice was so flat now, without accusation, without malice . . . There were no adequate excuses. She was my friend and I had fallen in love with her husband.'

A confrontation occurred a few nights later when Rachel turned up at Bedford Gardens and found Rex and Elizabeth there together. It was a trying situation for all of them and they stood around in uncomfortable silence. Elizabeth poured Rex and Rachel a drink, while her sons' dog, Dodger, jumped around her feet excitedly. It was Rachel who finally broke the silence, as Elizabeth recalled,

'"All right, Rex. Make up your mind. Which one of us do you want? You must make a choice. Now."

'Rex took a long desperate look at each of us in turn. Then he pointed to the dog. "I'll take Dodger," he said, and was out of the house like hell on stilts.

'Rachel and I were left staring blankly at each other.'

The whole situation had become too much for Rex and the act of moving into Elizabeth's home to recover himself was a clear sign that Elizabeth had won. But this was no romantic idyll, as Elizabeth remembers, 'He was in my room and I was sleeping up with the children in the nursery. He couldn't stand being alone and so he came round because I had help there at the house. The bedroom was so full of pill bottles and things like that. Rex was suffering from utter fatigue. There was no romance, nothing going on between us then.'

Rex's illness also forced him to withdraw from another project. He had agreed to play Ebenezer Scrooge in a proposed new musical film, written by Leslie Bricusse, based on Charles Dickens' *A Christmas Carol*, replacing none other than Richard Harris, who was unavailable. The role was now taken over by Albert Finney and the film was released in 1970 under the title *Scrooge*.

Rex had also been talking of making a film in which he would play Sir Charles Dilke, who was the subject of an infamous Victorian scandal over his sordid extra-marital affairs. The film was to be based on Roy Jenkins' book, *Sir Charles Dilke: A Victorian Tragedy* but again this came to nothing. Several years before Rex and George Cukor had wanted to collaborate on a film version of Michael Bradley-Dyne's play *The Right Honourable Gentleman*, which had also dealt with Sir Charles Dilke and had been a big West End success for Anthony Quayle, but as with Rex's later proposal, the idea was never realised.

Within a week of Rex's departure from *The Lionel Touch*, the first public admission was made that his marriage to Rachel was in difficulty. On December 19th, 1969 Rex's lawyer in London, Brian Eagles, issued a statement to the press: 'In view of certain rumours that have begun to circulate about his marriage to Rachel Roberts, Rex Harrison has authorised me to announce that he and his wife are living separately and apart.' Rachel was quick to rebuff this announcement when asked for her reaction as she was leaving her flat in Lowndes Square: 'I've just been talking to Rex on the telephone. We are going to be reconciled. He said it has all been blown out of proportion.' Rachel was in the middle of rehearsals for the Christmas show at the Royal Court Theatre, *The Three Musketeers Ride Again*. She carried on as best she could while the press sought her out continually to discover the true situation. Amid this speculation, Rex's lawyer issued a further statement on the following day denying that Rex and Rachel would be reconciled again; 'There is no reconciliation. The effect of the statement which I made yesterday has not altered in any way.' Elizabeth Harris's name was mentioned as having been linked with

Rex's recently, as newspapers speculated on possible reasons for the failure of his marriage.

Thirty-three-year-old Elizabeth Harris's pedigree was impressive. Born Elizabeth Rees-Williams, she was the daughter of the First Baron Ogmore of Bridgend who, before being elevated to the peerage by Clement Attlee in 1950, had been the Member of Parliament for Croydon and held the posts of Parliamentary Under Secretary of State for Commonwealth Relations, Parliamentary Secretary of State for the Colonies, and Minister of Aviation before he lost his seat in the 1950 general election.

Elizabeth had spent a year at a convent school in Switzerland after which she decided, without having any driving ambition, that she would become an actress. She attended the Royal Academy of Dramatic Art in the mid-1950s where her fellow students included Peter O'Toole. Elizabeth's devotion to social gatherings and the life of a debutante daughter of a peer prevented her from making any real progress, although it was as an aspiring actress that she met a young and ambitious Irish actor, Richard Harris, who lived in near poverty in London as he struggled on, directing and appearing in what plays he could.

Elizabeth and Richard fell in love and became engaged when she was twenty and he was twenty-five. After they were married they shared a one-room flat in Paddington for six pounds a week, an existence that was in stark contrast to the marriage itself, which had been an impressive affair at the Church of Notre Dame in Leicester Square followed by a reception at the House of Lords attended by three hundred guests.

Shortly after her marriage, Lord Ogmore organised a birthday gift for his daughter, enlisting the help of the Lord Chancellor, Lord Kilmuir, who was married to Rex Harrison's sister Sylvia. Elizabeth recalls, 'My father wanted to give me a treat for my twenty-first and I said I wanted to see *My Fair Lady*. The only way he could get tickets was from Lord Kilmuir who was a good friend of my father's and he got Rex's house seats and gave them to my father and Richard and I went to see it.'

Richard and Elizabeth's first child, Damian, was born in August 1958 and was later followed by two more boys, Jared and Jamie. Their union was stormy almost from the start and their first separation occurred within two years of the marriage.

Richard Harris struggled on with his career but it was hard for him and his family. In 1960 he gained a part in the film, *The Long and the Short and the Tall* with Richard Todd and Laurence Harvey. During the filming Harris and his wife arranged to meet Laurence Harvey and his then wife, Margaret Leighton, at Alexander's, the well-known Chelsea restaurant, and it was there that Elizabeth caught her first proper glimpse of Rex Harrison who came over to the table where they were seated. Rex talked exclusively to Margaret Leighton, of whom Elizabeth was less than enamoured, although he did not disappoint her at all, as she recalled, 'He was exactly as I had imagined him: handsome, elegant, worldly and so very English. He was also rather frightening. He had an aloof quality about him that was inhibiting. I had the feeling it was better not to speak at all than to say something less than brilliant.'

She met Rex once more at the wrap-up party for *This Sporting Life* in which Richard Harris appeared opposite Rachel Roberts. Again Elizabeth did not find it easy to talk to Rex and it was not until she and Harris went over to Hollywood, where Richard was to appear as King Arthur in the film version of Lerner and Loewe's musical *Camelot*, that she got to know Harrison better. By this time Richard had achieved considerable success; their marriage, however, remained unstable, and their ever increasing quarrels and Harris's sometimes violent behaviour brought her close to a breakdown. She was separated and finally divorced from Richard Harris in July 1969 and the only potentially serious relationship she had before meeting Rex was with actor Christopher Plummer.

Rex returned to *The Lionel Touch* at the beginning of January, easing back into the play after his three-week absence by going over his lines with Joyce Redman in private. At this time Rex confessed to Miss Redman that there was no chance of a reconciliation with Rachel, as she recalls,

> 'He told me that he couldn't cope with her – he simply couldn't cope with her – and that he was going to get a divorce. I said, "I'm very sorry. She's a smashing girl."
> 'He said, "Yes, but I can't take what's going on."
> 'I was very fond of Rachel, but she did have a bad drinking problem.'

Rex played in *The Lionel Touch* for a further three weeks. After the last performance he immediately drove to Luton airport where he and Elizabeth Harris boarded a private jet which was to take them to Tangier, where the yacht *Calisto* was waiting for them. Rex could finally turn his back on what had been without doubt one of the most disastrous years of his life, in which not only *The Lionel Touch* had been a major error of judgement, but his only film for that year, *Staircase*, had received an equally unenthusiastic response from critics. On top of this had come the final break-up of his marriage to Rachel.

Rachel was by now in Los Angeles where she had travelled to appear in a minor film called *Doctors' Wives* in which she played a wife who confesses to having had a lesbian affair and is forgiven by her husband. Still drinking heavily, she sank further when she became embroiled with a black hustler who attempted to introduce her to hard drugs. The divorce settlement with Rex was now in the hands of lawyers and Rachel's friends urged her to hold out for as much money as she could get, while she still hoped that by not asking for too much she would retain some regard in Rex's eyes. In her sad state, the only good thing to happen to her was her meeting with a twenty-three year old Mexican, who had settled in Los Angeles and who was to remain her closest companion for the next nine years – Darren Ramirez.

Rex and Elizabeth departed for their holiday together in the utmost secrecy, hoping to escape the notice of the press. Rex had suggested that they invite some friends along as a further decoy and Elizabeth also brought Jamie and his nanny, while her two older sons remained at their prep school.

Rex felt debilitated by the experience of *The Lionel Touch* and he had resolved to spend the rest of 1970 relaxing and regaining his strength. Looking back, he was painfully aware that his career had slumped badly and that, since he won his Oscar for the film version of *My Fair Lady* he had not been involved in a single project that could be regarded as successful. Rather than rush into just any other play or film, he decided that the best thing for himself and his career was to sit back for a while and to take on more work only when a worthwhile proposition appeared.

Not until their friends and Jamie returned to England after ten days were Rex and Elizabeth alone for the first time. They decided to make for the most remote island that they could find and, following the suggestion of the captain, made for Lanzarote, several hundred miles off the west coast of Morocco. However, finding the island a disappointment, Rex promptly cabled his secretary, who arranged for a private jet to pick them up and take them to Fez, the capital of Morocco, while the *Calisto* was dispatched to Agadir, on the other side of the Atlas Mountains, to wait for them. The couple were in Fez for several days, staying in a luxurious hotel and being escorted around the town by one of the hotel's assistant managers, who showed them the city and its nightlife.

While touring the nightclubs, although Elizabeth was

keen, Rex danced with her only a couple of times, appearing more interested in listening to their guide's account of the history of Fez. As Elizabeth recalled, 'Rex appeared to be utterly engrossed in the political development of the city. Perhaps it was a ruse to avoid dancing with me; my style was dangerously energetic. I can see that now.'

Seeing Rex thus engrossed and Elizabeth neglected, a handsome young Arab asked her to dance, which she accepted; Elizabeth continues, 'It was a mistake. He was an agile fellow and clearly a lovely mover. He saw Rex's fist swinging toward him. Like a shadow, he ducked and was gone. I caught the blow smack on the chin and went down for the count as if poleaxed.'

Rex was immediately bending over her on the dance floor, while a crowd of onlookers stood behind him, '"How awful, darling." Through the enveloping fog I now recognized the anger as well as the concern in his voice. "It was a terrible thing to have done."' Elizabeth tried to reassure him that it was only an accident but Rex was blaming the young Arab, claiming that he had done it on purpose, '"He could see perfectly well that I intended to bean *him* and he bloody well ducked . . . Of course he did it on purpose. He *made* me miss."' Rex had managed to justify his action in his own mind and had made himself the innocent party.

It was not the only incident to occur between Rex and Elizabeth on this trip. Rex planned to drive them both over the Atlas Mountains to Agadir, but Elizabeth did not trust Rex's driving skills, particularly with his blind eye. 'He believed that being blind in one eye was sufficiently compensated for by having double vision in the other eye.' Elizabeth finally won over Rex and she drove them, but he made it clear that he was far from happy in his defeat.

Following this holiday the couple returned to London where rumours of a million-dollar divorce settlement between Rex and Rachel were reported, although Rex chose to remain silent. He decided to take Elizabeth to his beloved Portofino and planned to spend most of the summer there or cruising around the Mediterranean. Elizabeth, however, was none too enthusiastic, feeling that Portofino was too full of ghosts from Rex's past. She felt uncomfortable not only in the villa but also in the port. As she recalls, 'Rachel's shadow was over the port because they loved Rachel there, but Lilli's shadow was in the regimentation of the staff at the villa, the way everything was served and the way there was no casual arrangement for meal times as you felt like it. It was all set.'

But Elizabeth also recognised that if Lilli had instigated this strictly organised regimen, it had remained because it suited Rex.

'I found out also that that is quite Rex as well. I hate that; it was one of the things which drove me to despair: this, "if it's fish it must be Friday" – just so predictable. It's absolutely true that he sent his own wine back. I couldn't stand a three-course lunch, a three-course dinner with the Byford service – just the two of us; and all I want is a sandwich. I don't like to know what's happening next week. I can't stand it.

Most of May and June were spent on their cruise when Rex and Elizabeth were joined by Elizabeth's brother Morgan and his girlfriend. Rex had again chartered the *Calisto*, this time taking her around Italy and along the Yugoslavian coast. At Dubrovnik they met Helen and Trevor Howard, Rex's friend since they had appeared in *French Without Tears* together over thirty years before. The Howards travelled with them as they sailed on to Corfu and the Greek islands, ending an enjoyable holiday in Athens.

Elizabeth had not been able to see much of her children during her extended holiday with Rex, and this was made even more difficult when Richard Harris had his children barred by the courts from visiting Rex's house in Portofino until Harrison had obtained his divorce and was free to marry Elizabeth. Elizabeth cannot recall when Rex actually proposed to her. 'I don't think it was one particular time. We were together for quite a long time before we were married. Rex is a marrying man. I think he only had about two or three days between divorce and remarriage. He doesn't like not being married.'

In order that Elizabeth could be with her children as well as Rex, the couple took a large house at Cap Bénat, near Le Lavandou in the South of France, and during their school summer holidays Damian, Jared and Jamie, then aged twelve, ten and eight, came down to join their mother. Rex prepared for the difficult task of winning the regard of their children, as their prospective stepfather. He did not feel totally at ease with children and it had been many years since he had had even Carey to cope with, let alone three children.

The odds were even more against Rex because Elizabeth's boys did not arrive alone, but with various cousins and friends as was their custom. Rex and Elizabeth also engaged students from Edinburgh University to take care of the eleven children who now populated the house. The result was that at one point there were twenty-two people in the house and Rex's efforts at being a benign stepfather began to wear a little thin, as Elizabeth recalls,

'Let's face it, Rex was never good with children. During that first summer in Le Lavandou there were eleven kids and Pied Piper he ain't! I didn't realise what I was landing him with because every summer we had eleven kids. It seemed to me: you've got three, you've got eleven – what's the difference. Rex was not good with one, let alone eleven.

Jared did a very funny imitation of him. He used to shout at them, "Bugger off, you buggering kids, bugger off!'', so they all used to imitate him then, going, "Bugger off! Bugger off!"'

Damian Harris remembers these outbursts, which the children clearly did not take too seriously. 'He would shout theatrically; he would say, "Buggering kids!" He had standard set phrases for us which meant he was pissed off.'

Unlike his mother, Damian enjoyed some aspects of the set regimentation that Rex demanded in his household. 'Meals were all together most of the time. His meals used to be like an event: three courses and very good wine and good food. It was fun; it made meals like an occasion. We would be round a table and the meals would take a long time – you'd spend two hours at dinner. My brothers weren't into that too much!'

It was with Jamie, the youngest of the brothers and four years younger than Damian, that Rex was closest, as Damian continues, 'He used to get on very well with Jamie. The most affection was between Jamie and him because my youngest brother had this very winning personality. That's what helped him. There was a warmth between them. Jared, at that time, was a little more difficult to get on with.'

Since Rex had been through such a traumatic year Elizabeth felt that he would enjoy the bustle and noise of a large, young family, but the perpetual chaos found Rex exhausted and soon he was asking the local doctor for vitamin injections when he came on one of his bi-weekly visits to the house to deal with the childrens' endless cuts, upset stomachs and summer colds. Rex found his set routine of quiet, civilised living broken down. Different types of music were played by the children throughout the house at the same time and, worst of all, some of the records that were played were those made by Richard Harris, which Rex found alarming, as Damian remembers, 'He would want to take them off and he would hide Dad's records from us.'

Rex Harrison and Richard Harris were total opposites in every way and each fostered a mutual disregard, as Damian continues,

> 'Dad was the antithesis of what Rex was – especially as an actor and a personality. My father didn't like Rex at all; he admired him as an actor but he just didn't much hold with his life-style and the way he behaved.
> Rex didn't really like to talk about my father very much. I think he assumed that deep down Mum still had an affection towards him. In a sense, she still has it to this day, but Rex didn't want to go with it. He wanted Mummy to be his completely and I think my brothers and I being there was obviously a reminder of our father and we tended to behave more like him than like Rex. I don't think Rex held much to my father's acting; it only showed itself as a certain disdain. It was just a complete lack of interest.'

Elizabeth says, '"That bloody Irishman!" would come out quite a few times; that was a favourite expression and he wasn't fussy about when he said it.'

Rex's role as prospective stepfather did not extend to giving the boys pocket money. 'He generally thought he was doing enough as it was. He felt that our father should definitely be keeping us anyway and my father felt that as well.'

Richard Harris kept in regular contact with his children and would ask them how everything was, as Damian continues, 'We didn't really have any bona fide complaints because everything was okay. If we flew out to see my mother and Rex somewhere we would go tourist and my father would complain about that, but he didn't really mean it; he would say, "You should be sending them first class." He would complain to Rex as a sort of joke to get at him and send a lawyer's letter, "They should be going first class."'

The time finally came for the children to return to

England and Rex and Elizabeth went off in different directions. As Elizabeth said, 'That holiday very nearly finished off our romance forever. I returned to London with the children. I suggested to Rex that he go back to Portofino to think things over. He agreed with alarming alacrity.' But their separation was short-lived. Elizabeth had only been back at Bedford Gardens for two days when she received a telephone call from Rex, 'He sounded distraught. "I can't stand it," he said, "All this silence. I can't cope with it any more. I miss you madly and I even miss all those buggering kids."'

Rex returned to London and took a flat in Eaton Square while Elizabeth remained in Bedford Gardens and the two of them divided their time between both homes. It came as no surprise to anyone when Rex and Elizabeth announced their intention to marry as soon as his divorce from Rachel came through.

After his year of inactivity Rex now felt ready to work again but found that little was on offer for an actor approaching his sixty-third birthday. The fashion for explicit sex and graphic violence left Rex as a rather anachronistic figure and he began to consider getting involved behind the camera rather than in front of it. He had been offered a part in a horror film, a fact which dismayed him and only brought home to him even more how far the film industry had sunk. Rex had too much inherent good taste to involve himself in such a shabby project at a time when many great actors from the past were prostituting their names by their involvement in similar projects.

Rex expressed an ambition to produce films and he announced that he would be the executive producer on two forthcoming productions for which he had bought the film rights: *Nowhere Girl* and *Pride of Lions*. The latter was to be an anti-war film about what happens to young people trained to kill, and he envisaged Henry Fonda and his son Peter in the principal roles. Rex presented himself as a man anxious to foster new talent and was reported as being in search of young directors who were 'bright, quick, intelligent in their views.' Rex commissioned the authors David Pursall and Jack Seddon to write a screenplay, but the project was finally abandoned.

With *Nowhere Girl*, based on a novel by Angela Huth, Rex got as far as interesting Shirley Maclaine in appearing in the film which he even planned to direct himself. When asked if he was interested in turning to direction at this time, Rex stated, 'Yes, if I could find something which I felt was right to do. Whether anyone would let me do it is another matter.'

But again, this second project died, falling victim to the disastrous climate within the film industry which at that time was going through one of the worst periods in its history, losing ground rapidly as the film-makers lost touch with their potential audiences.

If opportunities in the cinema, in whatever capacity, seemed to be closed to Rex, he did receive an attractive offer from the BBC who proposed that the actor should revive his performance in the title role in Chekhov's *Platonov* which he had played at the Royal Court Theatre ten years previously. It would be Rex's first major British television appearance, to be broadcast on Sunday, May 23rd 1971 as part of BBC Television's 'Play of the Month' series. The part of the widow, Anna, previously played by Rachel Roberts, was now taken on by Sian Phillips. Produced by Cedric Messina and directed by Christopher Morahan, the play went into rehearsal for five weeks before it was blocked and filmed in two parts over a four-day period in March 1971.

While Rex was rehearsing the play his divorce from Rachel was officially announced, on February 20th. The marriage ended in an uncontested action in Santa Monica, where the grounds for divorce were given as 'irreconcilable differences'. Rachel was reportedly granted a lump sum of thirty-five thousand dollars which was to be paid immediately, as well as ten thousand dollars a year for the rest of her life, although this would be cut to half if she remarried. In addition to this, Rex was also compelled to buy Rachel a house in whatever place in the world that she requested up to the value of one hundred thousand dollars. In the event of Rachel predeceasing Rex, the property would revert to him.

Rachel was quoted at the time as saying, 'I am quite satisfied with the settlement.' Indeed, there was only one point on which she expressed any reservations and that was over who would have custody of Homer, who at the time was in Portofino being looked after by the caretaker. Rachel said, 'Homer is more people than dog and I am sure he broods about being separated from me. I'm asking for his custody, to bring him back to live with me in California.' However, on this point Rachel failed to achieve her wish and Homer remained in Rex's custody. Of her marriage to Rex, she continued,

'I used to be a very good actress. Then I married Rex Harrison, and got lost. I just ceased to exist. We led a very aristocratic life in Paris and on yachts, and in our villa in Portofino.

'But I couldn't live on one more yacht for one more day. I just turned into a vegetable. So I gave it up.'

Since her separation from Rex Rachel had actively resumed her career. After appearing in the western, *Wild Rovers* with William Holden and Ryan O'Neal she planned two television shows and to make her American stage debut in *The Effect of Gamma Rays on Man-in-the-Moon Marigolds* at the Huntington Hartford Theater in Los Angeles.

Rex, meanwhile, continued work on *Platonov*, working hard but remaining somewhat aloof from the rest of the cast. Bridget Armstrong, who appeared in the play, expressed the general opinion of the rest of the cast: 'You don't meet them like that anymore. He's very awesome. He's so far above, and he has a terrific sort of starry aura

. . . We always called him Sir. He was king of the production . . .'

The play had been edited in order to fit into a two-hour slot on television and when it was broadcast it proved to be as triumphant for Rex on television as it had been on the stage. Peter Fiddick in the *Guardian* wrote, 'Here is an actor who – with the face becoming more expressive the older, more rubbery, it gets – becomes even stronger in presence yet retains the elegance of touch for which the matinee idol was somewhat mindlessly lauded. He played the quicksilver range of Platonov's character with apparent ease.' Of the production as a whole Fiddick wrote, 'Director and actors swept through the play with fine confidence,' although T. C. Worsley in the *Financial Times* considered that Harrison, 'makes most of the other actors on the set seem stagey.'

Following *Platonov* Rex began discussing the possibility as his next venture of another collaboration with Alan Jay Lerner. With composer John Barry, Lerner had written a musical based on Nabokov's novel *Lolita*, the story of a middle-aged man's obsession with a twelve-year-old girl. Before they approached Rex, the musical had already had several tryouts but audience reaction had been poor and Lerner and Barry now proposed to rewrite it completely with Harrison in mind. Rex said, 'I'm very fascinated and I'd like to do it,' and went on to explain what attracted him to the project:

'They've got a totally different conception of the theme than the novel and are working to come up with something funny. The great thing with that subject is to keep it in comedy and that's a difficult thing to do. It is a very delicate subject and if it comes off it has got to be amusing. It is a tight-rope walk. If it is not funny then it is absolutely revolting.'

Rex was pleased to be working with Lerner again, knowing that on account of their collaboration on *My Fair*

Lady the lyricist was totally in tune with Rex's capabilities. 'He does know exactly what I can and cannot do.'

It was hoped that the show might be ready for Broadway by Christmas but, regretfully, Lerner and Barry were still unable to produce a revised version that satisfied them and the project was ultimately abandoned, leaving us only to speculate, as with *Doctor Dolittle*, as to how successful a new collaboration between Lerner and Harrison might have proved.

Rex was by now free to marry Elizabeth and they began to discuss possible venues for the wedding. Theirs had been a stormy courtship, each equally possessive of the other and jealous of any previous attachments. As Elizabeth explained, 'The fact is, Rex and I were still recovering from our old heartaches. We were both vulnerable. We really met too soon; there had been no time to become whole again. But by now we had become committed to each other and to our plan to wed.'

Despite the cracks that were showing in their relationship, Rex and Elizabeth decided to get married in America. Rex was not very enthusiastic about a registry office for the ceremony and was confident that it was unlikely that the church would be keen to bless a fifth marriage, so he approached Alan Jay Lerner, who lived in Oyster Bay, Long Island. 'They were going to be married and Rex said, "I don't know where to be married. Could we be married in your house?" I said, "I'd be delighted."'

The wedding was set for August 26th, 1971 and proved not to be without its fair share of misfortunes, as Lerner recalls:

'It was a very funny wedding. My four children were all there – three girls, who were then in their teens, and a much younger boy – and Rex had four or five friends that he'd invited down, whom I didn't know – which surprised me.

'We had a dining-room and we took all the furniture

out and fixed it up a little; we made it very nuptial with
white flowers everywhere. There was a little room off
the dining-room which was a guest-room and Rex and
Elizabeth were in there waiting for the judge to arrive.
And it was terribly funny because the judge turned out
to have been the lawyer from *Murder Incorporated*. The
judge got lost trying to find the house and I kept
opening the guest-room door and handing in bottles of
champagne. And Elizabeth thought she was taking
some stimulant to keep herself bucked up, but she was
taking some other pills by mistake so that, by the time
they got to the altar, the poor thing could hardly keep
her head up.'

Elizabeth remembers her error. 'I took these pills that I
thought would calm me down, but it was a pee-ing pill. I
was pretty desperate to get through the service.'

The bride and groom were, however, pronounced man
and wife and Alan Jay Lerner dispatched them off on
their honeymoon, which the couple planned to spend in
Portofino with Elizabeth's parents and children. 'They
finally got into the car and I gave them another bottle of
champagne to get to the airport. But when they got there,
something happened to the plane and they had to sit in
the airport lounge until about three in the morning.'
Elizabeth elaborates on this, 'That was terrible at the
airport afterwards. There was a delay and so by the time
we got on the plane – on our wedding night – we shared it
with I don't know how many Arabs. And on the plane I
swear there were some goats as well.'

Rex and Elizabeth arrived safely in London and three
days later left for Portofino to begin their rather crowded
honeymoon. Elizabeth was still as unenthusiastic about
the villa as before, particularly as her new husband had
an alarming habit of occasionally getting her name
wrong, something that never happened anywhere else.
Rex had resorted to a simple solution to ensure that these
embarrassing slip-ups did not occur too frequently,

although again it was a solution not without its own hazards, as Elizabeth recalls. 'He was very careful. He called every wife "darling" so that he would never trip up. But he also occasionally tripped up by calling the waiters and other people "darling", which floored the steward on our yacht. He referred to this very nice Robert as "darling" several times. He was playing it safe with the wives and then occasionally it backfired on him because other people suddenly got landed.'

Rex got on well with Lord and Lady Ogmore during their stay and when the newly-weds arrived back in London they both felt confident that this was a marriage that would last. The couple took an elegant six-storey town house in Wilton Crescent, Belgravia and moved in there with Elizabeth's three children.

But if Rex had made a favourable impression on Elizabeth's parents, unfortunately the same could not be said for Elizabeth with Rex's sister Sylvia. She was now Countess de la Warr, having remarried in 1968 following the death of Lord Kilmuir in 1967, five years after he himself had been created an earl.

'Sylvia and I were never exactly bosom buddies. I remember ringing her up about something to do with Carey and I said that I thought she should be more supportive with Rex. And Sylvia said, "I've never been spoken to in this way in my life!"

'So I said, "Well, it's about bloody time somebody starts speaking to you this way."

'I heard her turning to de la Warr, who was nice and I liked, and say, "Oh God! He's done it again! He's married another one of them." Sylvia and I were never exactly close.'

Elizabeth detected some similarities between Rex and his sister but never felt that he was comfortable in Sylvia's presence.

'I think they were very alike but I always thought he was rather nervous of her. She is very sharp; Sylvia is nobody's fool. I always thought that he was never really at ease with her. He was rather impressed that she had been a countess not just once but twice. He would say, "Dame in her own right and countess in her own wrong twice." So I think in a way he was rather proud of her; he respected her and was slightly nervous of her.'

To celebrate their wedding, Rex and Elizabeth held a feather ball for three hundred guests in their new home after which, having deposited Elizabeth's children back at school to start their autumn term, Rex suggested to his new wife that they go on a world trip together, starting at San Francisco, where there was to be a film festival at the beginning of October which included a Rex Harrison retrospective, which he had been invited to attend.

After a couple of days in San Francisco, Rex and Elizabeth flew on to Honolulu staying for just over a week before once again boarding a flight, this time for Hong Kong. Their other destinations included Kuala Lumpur and the Malay Peninsula and finally Bangkok before their return to London and their new home.

Life in Wilton Crescent began to take on a routine and it was Rex who decided what that routine should be. His ideal life-style was the pampered existence of the wealthy with an army of servants to ensure that the huge town house ran like clockwork. So large was the house that a lift had been installed, which made movement from floor to floor considerably easier. But this time- and effort-saving apparatus was to prove a significant centre of disruption in Rex's orderly and sedate household when Elizabeth's boys descended on Wilton Crescent at weekends away from their boarding school. Elizabeth recalls,

'Jared kept going up in the lift and getting it caught. And all their friends would come, about five boys, and their idea of fun was playing with the lift while another lot of them were in it. They would all get in or try to jam the lift while another lot of them were in it. Rex would go berserk. We would have to get the police and the firemen round to get them out. And he would go mad at this, while the grinning faces of a whole group of boys would be drawn up higher by the firemen. Rex would be speechless with rage; he would just storm off. The boys used to take it in their stride. Rex would be so funny. I would be speechless with laughing so much; you just couldn't help but laugh. Only about three should have been in the lift and not only that, they were jamming it between floors with about six or seven of them in it. Rex wasn't cut out to be a father figure.'

Rex sought stability through the timetable that he set for the entire household. Elizabeth had expected that once she and Rex were married she would assume the duties of running their home, but she quickly found that Rex continued to dominate his home just as she had witnessed in Portofino. Rex had established for himself a set pattern of living and he was too entrenched in his ways by now to wish to see it changed. Meal times were precise and he expected his wife to dress formally for dinner whether they had guests or not. As time went on and it became clear that she could decide on nothing to do with the running and furnishing of the house without it first being approved by her husband, she began to balk at the lack of spontaneity that life with Rex held.

Elizabeth attempted to reform Rex and suggest doing things which broke this set pattern, but when she did succeed it was with difficulty and Rex's attitude in defeat would ensure that her victory was hollow. Elizabeth recalls an incident that occurred when she and Rex were in Portofino together. 'I remember coming back one day

from the airport after picking Damian up. It was a lovely
sunny day and I said, "Come on. Let's go to a bistro and
eat outside. It's so gorgeous." Rex said, "We've ordered
lamb chops, soufflé . . ." this, that and the other, and he
was so bad tempered that it ruined going out.'

The accustomed view was always that Lilli Palmer had
been the instigator of this desire for a totally ordered
existence but Elizabeth saw a different side to it. 'It may
not just have been Lilli. I think Lilli and Rex, in that way,
were very well suited because they were both very regi-
mented.' On another occasion Elizabeth and a friend of
hers went with their children to the races with Rex and
while the rest of the group tucked into a simple picnic of
sandwiches and crisps on the grass Rex remained in
splendid isolation in his Rolls-Royce, being served a
magnificent four-course meal on the best china by his
chauffeur, as he watched the races on a portable television which was installed in the car. Rex stayed successfully aloof from the rabble until the end of the day, but
then he was forced to join the queue at the twenty-pence
window in order to collect the children's winnings of the
day. As Elizabeth commented, 'Rex in line for anything –
let alone such bagatelle – is an incongruous sight.'

Rex's home life had more in common with the running
of a plush and exclusive hotel than with most people's
idea of a home and he would behave at meal times just as
if he was in a restaurant. When the butler served wine
from Rex's own cellar he became, in Rex's eyes, no more
nor less than any other wine waiter and would be treated
in the same manner, as Damian witnessed.

'The wine would come up and the butler would open
it. Rex would sniff the cork suspiciously and then the
guy would pour out the glass. And then Rex's expression would start darkening and the butler would start
quivering his knees. Rex would sip the wine and then
he'd go, "No, this is awful. Take it back, take it back!" It
was like it was the waiter's fault – in his own house.

The butler could have said, "But Mr Harrison, you bought this wine", but that had nothing to do with it whatsoever; it was a bad choice on the butler's part – how dare he! And the butler would take the wine back hurriedly, come up with another brand and hope for the best.

'There were quite a few butlers – they came and went – but I think specifically because they didn't get on with Mum.'

Alan Jay Lerner recalls the origins of Rex's well-stocked cellar.

'Rex loves wine. As a matter of fact, when he and Elizabeth got married his business adviser suggested that he go over to the Continent and buy five thousand bottles of new wine to store in his cellar and in about ten years it would be worth quite a bit. I was around when he was moving into Wilton Crescent and I was helping him move in. And I went down into the cellar and saw all the vino that was there. So about three years later I was back at his house and I said, "Well, you must be getting rich with the wine down in the cellar." There was a long pause and then he said, "I drank it." It was all gone, it was supposed to mature down there but he drank up all his liquid assets!'

If life at Wilton Crescent did not always run as Rex would have wished, one great consolation was the arrival of Homer from Portofino. He had had to endure six months' quarantine before he could join his beloved master, which had proved a difficult situation for both of them. Elizabeth Harrison says, 'Rex was upset about that; we both visited Homer – and it was a hell of a long way.' But their reunion was a joyous one. Damian remembers Homer's arrival at Wilton Crescent.

'Homer was the most spoilt dog. He was this huge basset hound who had been around for about fifteen years and was the only person who had managed to stick it out with Rex – and Rex loved him. Actually, talk about how dogs and masters look alike: a basset hound and Rex are perfect. He loved Homer; Homer could do no wrong. The dog would lie at his feet and the brush would be brought in and Rex would brush his ears once a day. Homer was like him – they knew they had soul mates in each other.'

Elizabeth, however, sensed a mutual disregard between Homer and herself.

'Homer was ghastly. He hated women. He would stand in front of the door just as you were ready to go out and trip you up. And you know how basset hounds slobber and have all this saliva: in the morning he would come into the bedroom where Rex and I would have breakfast in bed. Rex's tray would be on one side and mine would be on the other. Homer would come right the way round and slobber all over my breakfast, leaving this spittle all over it, and then he would go round and wag his tail to Rex, who would pat him and say what a good dog he was – and my breakfast was ruined every damn time!

'Homer loathed me. If we were going out, he would stand and wait until I was dressed and then do his slobbering bit; so I would have to run or jump or hide behind the curtain from him.

'I told this to a friend of mine, Peggy Taylor, who had a place in the South of France with her husband Henry. They looked after Homer when we went away once and they had him for about a month. Peggy adores animals and said I was just being unnecessarily difficult about Homer. But when we came back she said, "My God, you're right. Homer is a chauvinist." He did exactly the same thing to her as to me, but he was adorable with her husband Henry.'

Homer was most obedient to Rex but he was not above being deliberately difficult when he was left alone with Elizabeth in Wilton Crescent, as she remembers:

'Homer slept in a basement and would have to go down the basement steps from the morning-room to sleep in his quarters. When I was on my own, Homer would refuse to go down unless I took him down in the lift. He would just sit there, and he weighed a ton so I couldn't move him. So I would have to get the lift and then he would go. Homer was a pretty independent dog because he was left on his own a lot, but Rex did love him.'

Homer's main rival to his claim as Rex's longest-standing friend was Arthur Barbosa, who had known Rex since childhood and who still saw him regularly. Arthur's presence was not welcomed by Rex in every way; he was an uncomfortable reminder to Rex that the sands of time stop for no one, as Elizabeth recalls.

'Arthur Barbosa and Rex were born on the same day and grew up together in Liverpool. Often they would spend their birthdays together and whenever Arthur said, "Oh my God! Another birthday and we're getting so old!" Rex would be infuriated by this and would say, "It's nothing bloody-well to do with it! You were born of old parents. Nothing to do with me at all."

'Arthur would say it deliberately to irritate him and Rex would rise to the bait every time.'

But this issue apart, it remained a long-standing friendship and Arthur and his wife Isobel were welcome and frequent guests. On one occasion, they even went on holiday to Portugal with Rex, Elizabeth and the boys.

A major event that occurred not long after Rex and Elizabeth's wedding was the marriage of Rex's second son Carey. Lilli, whom Rex had not seen for a number of years, would naturally attend her son's wedding, accompanied by Carlos and her sister Irene. Lilli recalled, 'Before Carey's wedding I had seen Rex once or twice in Hollywood and once in Paris – but of course it was so traumatic for both of us.' Elizabeth realised that, with Rex and Lilli both planning to attend the ceremony, it was potentially a very difficult situation, not only for them but also for their son. Elizabeth recalls,

'I said that I didn't think it was very nice for Carey. Lilli and Rex hadn't met for years so I said, "Why don't they all come for dinner as a little present, so that at least the first time that you see each other won't be in the church in front of photographers and everything." So they came to dinner the night before: Lilli, Carlos, Lilli's very nice sister and Carey and his about-to-be wife – his first wife. And I ended up with egg all over my face because Lilli was making conversation with Rex: "Do you remember this? Do you remember that?" and idiot here was sitting there – and you know how somebody can make conversation and exclude you without being deliberately rude. So here it was – memory lane time – and I was a new bride, not best pleased and thinking, "What an idiot! I've organised this whole thing."

'Rex was loving every second of it. I don't think Carlos was that worried because he would have remembered a lot of what they were talking about anyway.'

With the arrival of the new year Rex, who had not worked since *Platonov*, received another offer from the BBC, this time to appear in the title role in an ambitious television production based on the Cervantes classic, *Don Quixote*. Rex's efforts to branch out as a film producer and director had all proved abortive and so he eagerly accepted this new acting challenge. Interest in *Don Quixote* had been revived due to the recent musical version of the book, *Man of La Mancha*, which had run both on Broadway and in London and was now to be filmed with Peter O'Toole and Sophia Loren.

When the forthcoming television version was announced in late February 1972 it was emphasised that the two productions were not rival versions of *Don Quixote*, but rather that the BBC version would follow Cervantes' original novel, while the film version was a recreation of the Broadway musical. The production was announced as being budgeted at one hundred thousand pounds and was to be made in partnership with the American film company, Universal Pictures, in order to split these costs which at that time were huge for a television venture.

The film was to be made on location in Spain and in the months before he was due to depart Rex immersed himself in his preparations for the part as Elizabeth remembers. 'He would never read very much for pleasure but when he did *Don Quixote* he read the whole of Cervantes, which is a hell of a lot. He would read anything if it was something to help him with the part, but he would rarely sit down and relax and find enjoyment out of a good book.'

Alvin Rakoff was to direct the film and the two men went into intensive preparations together on the project. Their meetings took place at the house in Wilton Crescent and Alvin Rakoff recalls their first meeting, in February, at which Rex carefully planned his entrance in order to give himself a psychological advantage over his director.

'On that first meeting I was on my own and I went up to this sort of games room/study in which were displayed Rex's gold disc for *My Fair Lady* and a number of other awards. It was on the top floor and I was shown up there first. I had walked up and then Rex came up in the elevator afterwards. He would make sure that the guest would be shown up first.

'Rex came into the room and I remember being enormously impressed. He was charming, as Rex undoubtedly can be, and debonair, as one would expect from him.'

The two men discussed the forthcoming project and then both read the script, about which the producer, Gerald Savory, was very enthusiastic. However, Rex and Alvin Rakoff were not totally satisfied with this script and decided to enlist writer Hugh Whitemore to go over it with them. The three men set about rewriting the script and simplifying the storyline. Rakoff continues:

'Rex was helpful on that level. At that stage he was lucid and he knew what the story needed. He had both an emotional grasp of what the story needed as well as an intellectual grasp. I always say that *Don Quixote* is the world's best-known unread book; everybody thinks that they know the story but in fact very few do. I read one translation and then another one came out around that time. It's difficult enough to get through one translation but Rex, I think, got through both.

'The meetings were always at the house and were always cordial. I don't think that at that time I ever saw Rex lose his temper.'

They would break for lunch and eat in the dining room in Rex's customary style. 'It was always a grand affair, with Rex sitting at one end of the rather long, narrow table, myself sitting at the other and Hugh usually in the middle. We were always served excellent food and he was always gracious – an absolutely splendid host.'

Elizabeth was not much in evidence while the three men were working and she never joined them for meals or took part in their meetings; Rakoff says,

'I don't think Rex would have tolerated it. He immediately conveys what he conveys on the screen: that he is not a man who would suffer fools gladly or would suffer interference with the script. You had to prove your points with Rex. Some days, like any human being, he was in better form and in better humour than other days, but at that stage, aside from the aura he conveyed of the world star, there was nothing that he did which I could criticise in any way.'

Apart from recording a guest appearance for *The Burt Bacharach Show* at Elstree studios at the beginning of March, in which he and Bacharach sang together, Rex devoted himself entirely to *Don Quixote*. In an interview he gave in March he outlined their intentions for the production:

'What we are trying to do is to show what it was like in sixteenth-century Spain and why a character changes himself into the twelfth century, puts armour on and creeps into knight-errantry. Putting armour on in those days was as strange as it would be putting it on today. They hadn't worn it for two hundred years. In no sense is it a sad story. What I think is beautiful about the character is the way he goes out in the most romantic manner to discover a world which is in his mind. A lot of kids do that now, don't they? They pretend things are not what they are.'

It proved a daunting task to condense the two volumes of Cervantes' *Don Quixote* into a two-hour-long script, but the three men eventually came up with a finished draft which satisfied them.

After all this intense preparation, the film was almost cancelled, as Alvin Rakoff reveals,

'After we had had our meetings and we saw the script we had got from Hugh Whitemore we went on to getting Rex fitted, testing his make-up for the part and all the usual pre-production. The *Daily Mail* had taken pictures of Rex, who looked magnificent in a plastic version of metal armour, and they had a big centre spread on it. Then suddenly the BBC, which was going through an economy wave, announced that they were cancelling *Don Quixote* and I presume they were going to pay Rex off. But he was furious about this and he said, "I'm the fool whose picture was in the paper!" and he threatened to sue them if they cancelled.

'So I was called in by Sir Huw Weldon, the Managing Director of the BBC, who said, "Go and see Rex and try to calm him down. We don't want to get into a suit. And also see what you can knock off the budget." We did knock out a half-hour of the script and two major, and costly, locations went.'

With this problem resolved, the only one that remained was the casting of Don Quixote's squire, Sancho Panza. Leo McKern and Colin Blakely were both rumoured to be possibilities, but it was Frank Finlay who was finally chosen, while Dulcinea was to be played by Rosemary Leach, a decision that Rex was not totally enthusiastic about, as the director asserts. 'I think he thought of his Dulcinea as being a much more glamorous person than Rosemary, but I didn't cast it that way; I cast a very fine actress. Rex accepted that, but didn't like it.'

The film had an eight-week shooting schedule and it was due to begin at the end of May on location on the plains of La Mancha in Spain. A few weeks before leaving for the location Rex and Elizabeth travelled to Portofino to inspect some land which Rex had purchased to enlarge his property. While standing on one of the terraces Rex slipped and fell a considerable distance before landing heavily on his right side. At first he thought he had only suffered bruising, but on the following morning he found it difficult to get out of bed and on inspection it was discovered that he had broken three ribs. It was too late to postpone the shooting of *Don Quixote* since all arrangements had been made, so Rex had himself strapped up and made the journey to Spain as scheduled, accompanied by Elizabeth who recalls with admiration:

'He had a very painful time of it. This is what I really respect: his professionalism. He was in agony and he had to wear armour, which was fortunately lightweight, and he had to ride. He had to drive for two hours from the hotel to the location over very bad roads. He never complained. He used to have to get out of bed by rolling onto the floor and then pulling himself up. He is a superb professional – but he does think that everything and everyone else comes second to his talent.'

Wearing a wispy, white, pointed beard and with his angular frame clad in armour, Rex bore a remarkable resemblance to the traditional image of Cervantes' knight, looking entirely different from his usual, carefully groomed appearance. Rex enthused over his role to the press, 'The character has always appealed to me . . . I've always wanted to play him. How many parts are there in an actor's life which he really wants to play? Not all that many.'

The conditions on the location were primitive and the crew and actors had to endure plagues of horseflies and temperatures of almost one hundred degrees in the remote, almost desert country. Not surprisingly tempers became frayed and Rex was in the middle of it, as Alvin Rakoff says.

'Rex made enemies of a number of members of the unit. He never made an enemy of me, but I was always respectful of his talent and also I kept myself at a distance from him. Not that I was afraid of him; it worked mutually and we both stayed out of each other's way. Rex is probably better off with a shouting director, which I am not, because I think he enjoys a slanging match. Often shouting at an actor upsets them but of course, it couldn't upset Rex.'

Rakoff is quick to emphasise that Rex never rowed with anybody on the set and is mindful that Harrison was in considerable pain. Rex was understandably reluctant to sit on a horse in his condition and once on the animal he found that it was more comfortable to remain mounted for as long as the shooting required him to be on horseback, rather than suffer the agony of dismounting and remounting the horse. He got onto the horse with the aid of a stepladder and between shots one of the crew would hold an umbrella over him in order to shade him from the blazing sun.

Rakoff also took care to put Rex on his horse only if it was absolutely necessary, 'Usually it is his double on the horse. If you look at the whole of *Don Quixote* I would say that Rex is on the horse for less than twenty per cent of it. A lot of his close-ups were done by shaking him back and forth in a chair. We had to make it easy.'

Furthermore, the horse itself was a difficult animal and was treated with the utmost caution. On one occasion Rex almost received further injury due to this particular horse, as the director recalls.

'I remember him cursing and swearing at one of the horse-handlers, who didn't speak English. The man had taken weeks of abuse from Rex and he kept holding onto this rather fearsome horse while Rex kept saying, "Well, lead her round slowly." And the man wouldn't do it. Rex finally said, "Let go of the reins," and, of course, the horse bolted immediately – which is why the handler was holding the reins. Our stunt director, who was fortunately on a horse nearby, grabbed hold of the reins and calmed the horse down.'

Rex tended not to socialise with the rest of the crew during filming, although he and Frank Finlay did enjoy a very good professional relationship. 'Frank Finlay and Rex got on terribly well. Rex kept calling out, "You're a plucky little chap!" because Frank wouldn't have the stunt man when he had to do things like hang upside down from a tree or crash onto Rex who, of course, couldn't absorb the impact, so we got a stuntman to catch Frank.'

After filming Rex and Elizabeth could usually be seen socialising with the film's producer, Gerald Savory, and his wife Sheila, and this foursome always stayed in the same hotel while Rakoff contrived whenever possible to be in one of the other hotels in which the unit was based, although he often dined with Rex and his group. 'His main pal on it was Gerald Savory because they had known each other for a long time and they were of an equal age. I was, as all directors are, very busy at the time. It needed a lot of production help; it was a very difficult shoot.'

Filming was finally completed with a week of shooting interiors at the BBC studios at Ealing, when Rex was able to settle back into his luxurious life-style after the primitive conditions in Spain. Eating became a true pleasure again, as Damian Harris recalls,

'The Rolls-Royce would go out with a specially prepared meal on a silver salver. The wine would be taken out and the guy would serve it to him in his dressing room. The same was true when he was doing a matinee at the theatre. The meal would be specially prepared and sent out to him. He liked baked beans, which didn't seem to go with the image – it seemed a little off-key. They would be served in a silver bowl on a silver tray, with cold chicken or cottage pie or whatever he was having.'

Alvin Rakoff saw both the good and bad sides of Rex during filming and he does not let the negative aspects obliterate the positive side of a very professional actor.

'He is a difficult man, but let me also say that he was magnificent in the part. He arrived on location with three broken ribs and still would be into make-up on time and was never late on the set. There must have been three or four occasions when one had a go at him, but on the whole, when we parted company it was as friends.'

The production was shown amid a great deal of publicity on BBC television on January 7th 1973 and in the United States, on the CBS network, on April 23rd. Critical reaction on both sides of the Atlantic was cautious, with the general feeling that it ultimately did not quite come off. The *Daily Mail* critic wrote after it was broadcast in Britain,

The first half was so promising I hugged myself with surprise and delight. Rex Harrison's Don, gently going dotty, riding off on his solemn and preposterous adventures, Finlay's earthy squire, the dry, brown Spanish landscape, caught with love and reverence the very echo of the original.

But in the second half the production seemed to lose its way, as the *Mail*'s critic continued,

The essence of this great book, its high ironic humour and marvellous manipulation of sanity and madness as between Don Quixote and mankind, became a mawkish dissertation on dreams versus reality.

I became resentfully aware that the style chosen was that of Zeffirelli's over-praised versions of Shakespeare, pictorial elegance first and the words a bad second.

The critic for the *New York Times* saw much good in this adaptation and was inclined to view the casting of Rex in the title part as its essential fault.

> Unfortunately, the production's biggest flaw is the performance of its star . . . His performance is not disastrous. Mr Harrison is too intelligent an actor for that. Perhaps that is part of the problem.
>
> His Quixote is bloodless. Mr Harrison gives every indication of understanding the character, but seems to keep a very proper distance from the dramatic core. Bemused and sympathetic, he stands outside, rarely rising above an expert reading of the role, more suited to the civilized drawing room than the dusty plains of La Mancha.
>
> Apparently Alvin Rakoff, the director, has scaled back the other performances to the subdued level of the production's star. As Sancho Panza, the shrewd rustic, Frank Finlay is earthily convincing but curiously detached. As Dulcinea, Rosemary Leach is superb when given the chance, which is not often enough.
>
> *The Adventures of Don Quixote* is an interesting production . . . it is often intelligent and strikingly handsome. The missing ingredient is a palpable sense of Quixote's fine madness.

By the time that *Don Quixote* was broadcast, Rex was already involved in another project. The failure of *The Lionel Touch* on the London stage had continued to gall Rex and he was anxious to restore the damage that he felt his involvement in that play had done to his theatrical reputation. He wanted a part which would provide him with an opportunity to display his skills and perhaps even give him the chance to broaden his range.

Rex decided on a rarely seen play by the Italian playwright Luigi Pirandello, *Henry IV*, which had only been infrequently performed in the English language and had not been presented on the London stage since 1927, five

years after it was written. Rex himself acquired the rights
to the play from Pirandello's estate and set about organis-
ing the preparation of a new translation by Stephen Rich,
with the help of Clifford Williams, whom he had enlisted
to direct the production.

The play offered Rex one of his most off-beat roles and
he was nervous about the whole enterprise. He was to
play a wealthy Italian who had fallen from his horse and
been knocked on the head twenty years before while
dressed up as the tyrannical eleventh-century German
Emperor Henry IV, whom he had been impersonating
for a pageant. Since that time he has believed himself to
be Henry IV and due to his wealth he is able to sustain
this fantasy, living in a palace decorated to complement
his role and with servants dressed in period costume who
are paid to perform within his imagined world. One of
his former lovers and his old rival for her affections
appear on the scene and are forced to join in this fantasy
while they attempt to discover whether his insanity can
be cured. They have, however, arrived too late because
he has known the truth for eight years during which he
has continued to live out his role as the tyrannical
Emperor for his own enjoyment, having found the present totally unappealing.

Rex chose to take the play first to America, presenting
it under the banner of producer Sol Hurok, planning first
to embark on a sixteen-week tour covering Toronto, Los
Angeles, Boston and Washington, followed by a limited
six-week engagement at the Ethel Barrymore Theatre in
New York, which would mark his return to Broadway
after an absence since his appearance in *The Fighting Cock*
of thirteen years. He hoped then to bring the play to
London in the autumn.

Rex arrived in New York early in December 1972 to
begin rehearsals, staying at the Waldorf Towers, where
he immediately immersed himself in preparations for the
role. Elizabeth and her children, accompanied by their
nanny Rena, joined him several weeks later and, due to

Rex's busy work schedule, were met at the airport by a public relations man to whom Rex had given a detailed description of his wife to ensure that he did not miss her. The PR man spotted them immediately, as Elizabeth recalled.

'He advanced right past me and shook Rena warmly by the hand. "Welcome to New York City, Mrs Harrison," he said with great sincerity. "I recognised you at once. Couldn't miss you after your husband's graphic description."

'I could never see it myself, but the boys had often commented on the resemblance between Rachel and Rena. I could only imagine that Rex had suffered a temporary time lapse when describing his wife.'

Elizabeth witnessed the obvious strain which Rex suffered as he pushed himself further than he had ever before attempted as an actor, and the unfortunate error at the airport was but an indication of the pressure that he had put upon himself. He followed a tough daily routine which would have daunted even a far younger man. He got up at six in the morning and, after bathing, studied his lines in the sitting room until breakfast, which he had at half past eight. Rehearsals began at half past nine and he would not return until six in the evening. He would relax with Elizabeth and the boys before dinner at eight-thirty, after which he would study his script for a further hour before going to bed at half past ten.

The children were with Rex and Elizabeth until Boxing Day when they left to join their father in California, having enjoyed a holiday dominated by Rex's tension over *Henry IV*. Rex permitted himself Christmas Day off from his rigid timetable, so as to join in the festivities with Elizabeth and the boys, and a surprise visitor that day was Rex's first wife Collette, as Elizabeth remembers.

'I met Collette once in New York. She came on Christmas Day for a drink, accompanied by a young fellow. She was an amazing woman; she had hair down to her waist and when she walked in she had no overcoat on even though it was a freezing cold day. Rex had told me that she was very proud of her figure – and she did have a marvellous figure. She wore very tight clothes to reveal it.

'She asked for some champagne which Rex gave her and then for about ten minutes they were talking. Then Rex went to pour her another glass of champagne and she said, "No, no, no! I don't want that. Get a fresh bottle. That will be warm." And to my utter amazement Rex went and opened a fresh bottle. I thought, "My God, I should take some lessons from her."

'Rex was very agreeable towards Collette. He used to see her periodically when he was in New York. I think she usually used to ring him up and he would see her. She was very involved with the Church when I met her; Rex said, "She's gone mad on the Church now."'

Apart from this Christmas break Rex's days continued to be dominated by the rehearsals for the play and as the opening drew nearer he became progressively more on edge, something which Elizabeth had to cope with on her own now that the boys had left for California.

The play opened in Toronto in early 1973 under the title *Emperor Henry IV*. Despite the usual teething troubles it looked as if all Rex's hard work would prove worthwhile. He himself said at the time, 'It is a bloody difficult role, full of ambiguities. One might get one part of the play right one night and another wrong. You never give it all in one piece. This means you cannot settle down into a pattern, but I suppose that's good.'

The company moved on to Los Angeles, opening on January 30th to a rapturous reception from both audience and critics, and playing there until February 17th when the production moved on to the last leg of its tour, playing at the Kennedy Center in Washington for three weeks where it took an incredible quarter of a million dollars at the box-office.

When the play opened at the Ethel Barrymore Theatre in New York on March 29th Rex received the kind of reviews that he had dreamed of but had scarcely dared to expect in the long, agonising months in which he had worked so hard. Douglas Watt in the *Daily News* summed up the enthusiastic response of the critics:

Rex Harrison is giving a bravura performance in *Emperor Henry IV* . . . he plays the title role with the sweep, scope, resonance and an all-around resourcefulness that very few living actors can command. It is an altogether brilliant and delightful piece of work.

Noting that the play had not been performed in almost fifty years, he continued,

That's much too long a lapse, of course, but the fact is that it requires a star performance and one that can evoke compassion for its enigmatic central character, along with a kind of intuitive understanding of his perverse behaviour.

Rex's return to the New York stage was an unqualified triumph and if his aim was to eradicate the memory of *The Lionel Touch* from his mind he succeeded, and at the same time provided himself with one of his most memorable and stunning theatrical roles. Watt ended his review, 'It's high time we had Rex Harrison back on Broadway. He brings sheen, thrust and charm to a 20th century masterpiece.'

Following the end of its limited run on April 28th, Rex returned to London where Elizabeth was waiting for him, having gone on ahead. Rex planned to leave almost immediately for Portofino for a holiday and to get to grips with an interesting new challenge, although he did delay his departure in order to attend a gala preview of *No, No, Nanette* at the Theatre Royal, Drury Lane in aid of the Save London's Theatres campaign. Rex had been disturbed by the number of darkened theatres he had seen in New York and this terrible trend was clearly being repeated in London, where many of the fine old London theatres where Rex had appeared in his long career were threatened with demolition in order to make way for new roads within the capital.

Rex's new project was the writing of his autobiography, which he finally began in earnest, following approaches from Macmillan, the British publishers. He felt that Portofino would be the ideal place in which to concentrate on his book without too many disturbances. He had already begun preliminary work before embarking on the *Henry IV* tour, but now he wanted to devote himself entirely to the task.

Unfortunately, the Portofino villa did not prove to be the ideal location. Both Rex and many of his friends were certainly not getting any younger and the inaccessibility of the villa began to be less a charming quirk of the place and more an increasingly uncomfortable obstacle. Elizabeth recalls,

'He loved the house at Portofino but towards the end it all went disastrously wrong because of this bloody road. Even with the jeep, you always had this five-minute walk with all the luggage. You could never get anything sent up from the port. It was just impossible to run and I think the older he got, the more he realised how cut off he was up there.'

The result was that Rex announced to a delighted Elizabeth that he would like to find a more accessible home and so they began their search in the South of France. Rex had no intention of parting with the villa in Portofino; he still felt a great attachment to it since it remained the only real home he had ever had.

Rex and Elizabeth found a house which appealed to them at Beauchamp on Cap Ferrat, near Nice. It was a charming Edwardian villa with a swimming pool and a garden and it was situated right on the point next to the lighthouse. More important, access could be gained by conventional means. Rex immediately put in an offer, which was just as promptly accepted, and most of the remainder of the year was spent in moving into their new home, while Rex also continued in his attempt to write his memoirs.

Among the visitors to their new home was Rex's son Carey, whom his father suspected, to his horror, of having socialist tendencies, a suspicion that seemed to be corroborated by Carey's travelling down to the South of France on a bicycle, accompanied by his wife. Damian Harris recalls how Rex coped with the situation. 'The big skeleton in Rex's closet was that he had a son who was vaguely socialist. He wasn't socialist at all; he maybe had certain socialist tendencies, which looked glaringly red in Rex's eyes: he planted his own vegetables and made his own wine – as much a socialist as that, although probably economics also led to that.'

The imminent arrival of Carey became a major event and the situation required delicate handling. Damian continues,

'It was like being prepared for the fact that Rex's son is coming – and so be cool. Not us. Elizabeth was preparing Rex: "For God's sake be civil. Just don't do anything to antagonise him." Rex is going, "No, no, no – of course I won't." "Then don't bring up this Communist issue thing." Rex wasn't well founded on the Communist issues, but he would just say, "You bloody Communist!" That was enough; they would never discuss issues.'

After all this build-up, Damian and his brothers were unsure what to expect from Carey, but were pleasantly surprised when he arrived.

'He was very nice. He's a writer and very intelligent. At first it was pretty easy going and after about three or four days Rex was beginning to relax a bit, not being so particular and careful anymore – becoming himself.

'There was this castle quite near the house which looked out on to the Mediterranean. It had been completely run down and there had been some spray painting over it. We were looking at it from the house and one of us said to Rex,

"God, look, that's a wonderful castle, isn't it?"

He said, "Yes." He was mixing a cocktail. "Yes, it is."

I said, "It's completely ruined, isn't it?"

He was going, "Yes, it's probably those bloody Communists." And then he turned round and he said, "Oh, I'm very sorry Carey."

And Carey said, "Oh, that's perfectly all right."

Rex had put his foot in it. Rex is ultra Conservative, very right wing.'

Elizabeth also remembers Carey at this time.

'All the boys liked Carey. He was very nice with them. I think he was very aware, having been in a similar situation with stepfathers and all the rest of it. He was very, very sweet with my children. I think he was close to his mother. Carey really tried in his relationship with his father. I don't think Rex understood about relationships very well – not just with his children, but with anyone. I think he was so single-minded in what he was doing that he never gave that much thought to other relationships at all.'

As Elizabeth's boys grew older, they also began to see a little more of Rex's true character behind the imperious manner. Damian discovered that his stepfather appeared to be rather limited in his knowledge, as his blanket attitude towards socialism revealed, 'He was strange in a sense because from what I could gather, and I was quite young, I wouldn't say that he was a very well-informed person. Everything he knew was instinctive or else it was through his roles. When he would get into a role he would know that role thoroughly – but nothing that didn't relate to it. Then he really wouldn't know much.'

But if Rex's knowledge was limited to that which was necessary for his work, a trait not at all uncommon among actors, including Laurence Olivier, he did receive a well-deserved tribute to his great achievements in theatre and film when he went to Boston University in November 1973, to be presented with the honorary degree of Doctor of Humane Letters. He had previously sent over all his personal memorabilia for the University Library, including letters, scripts and photographs. Boston University had approached Rex on the matter of his papers and he was thrilled to donate them. That these papers went to an American university and not an English one was simply due to the fact that no English universities, to their shame, had ever bothered to ask Harrison for them. Rex wrote in his autobiography, 'I was extremely delighted that America should reward me in this way for all the work I had done both in films and in the theatre in that country.'

It is not difficult to imagine Rex's disappointment that his native country had not honoured his contribution to the acting profession in any way, and well over a decade after he received his honorary doctorate at Boston, he remains unacknowledged by his own country when far lesser performers have received the highest of honours.

Rex and Elizabeth flew into Boston for the ceremony, where they were joined by Rex's British press agent, Judy Tarlo, of the Rogers and Cowan Public Relations organisation, who had arrived there ahead of them. Dr Gottlieb of the University and Miss Tarlo met the Harrisons at the airport in a University car and drove them to the Ritz Carlton Hotel. Judy Tarlo recalls that day. 'We then went to the University where everybody was robed in scarlet gowns. The ceremony took place in the auditorium which was crammed with students, faculty and press. They gave him a standing ovation.'

Dressed in a gown and cap, Rex became Dr Harrison, after which he gave a speech from the podium surrounded by eminent professors from the University. As Rex later said, it 'seemed a long way away from *Charley's Aunt*,' as he nervously delivered his eloquent speech of acceptance, affected by the solemnity and emotion of the occasion.

In the evening, Dr Gottlieb escorted Rex and Elizabeth to a formal dinner at the Algonquin Club, one of the city's oldest private clubs, where thirty members of the University faculty attended. Afterwards, Rex and Elizabeth returned to their hotel suite, accompanied by Judy Tarlo, who recalls Rex's jubilant mood. 'Over a glass of port we discussed what had happened all day, and had lots of giggles. He was very thrilled with the honour.'

On the following evening a large ball was held at the University at which all of Boston society had their opportunity to participate in the honouring of Rex Harrison. Tickets for the ball sold for two hundred and fifty dollars each. After the dinner there were various speeches and presentations, followed by dancing and cabaret. Rex then moved on to a special after-dinner party given by the President of the University, John Silber, which brought to a close two marvellous and memorable days for him.

Travelling via New York, Rex and Elizabeth returned to London and Wilton Crescent, where Rex continued to work on his autobiography. The London opening of *Henry IV* had now been put back to February 1974 and Rex was scheduled to film John Mortimer's autobiographical play, *Voyage Round My Father* with Alvin Rakoff as director and co-starring Wendy Hiller, Edward Fox, Alistair Sim and Lisa Harrow. Rex was to play Mortimer's cantankerous, blind, lawyer father. Filming had actually started in November without Rex, but when he joined the cast he wanted to make significant alterations. He wanted to play his character as not totally blind, much to Rakoff's annoyance. 'It is amazing how he failed to grasp intellectually the need for the father to be blind. His argument was that actors' eyes are one of their main tools. It was an enormous bone of contention and the more he rehearsed, the more he wanted to see. As usual, Rex started this niggling thing.'

Unfortunately, the production ran into financial problems and was closed down after two weeks on location and six days, shooting at Elstree studios. Hope remained that the production might be re-started early in the new year, but nothing came of this and *Voyage Round My Father* was not filmed until 1981, when Rakoff produced, as well as directed, an entirely new production with a new cast. Laurence Olivier now played the father, providing him with one of his most memorable parts in recent times and showing that Rex had lost a marvellous opportunity.

In the midst of all this Rex was finding the writing of his memoirs a daunting task and with the approach of the London opening of *Henry IV* he suffered a renewal of his nervousness over that too. As a result his marriage to Elizabeth was undergoing severe strain; Rex was always a worrier over whatever project he was involved in, but now the writing of his book and the performing of the play became insurmountable tasks in his eyes and his gloomy mood affected the entire household. Elizabeth recalled,

'As the weeks passed, he became more and more removed from me. It is strange how an atmosphere quickly communicates itself: instinctively friends stopped calling; the children no longer drifted into rooms where Rex might be. The whole relationship between Rex and the children, which had been affable and relaxed, underwent a disturbing change: they began to call him sir; they stood up whenever he entered the room. Sometimes I even found myself standing up when he entered the room.'

Judy Tarlo recalls how Rex's personality would alter when he was working, more so at this time than ever before.

'He always wanted to discuss the trauma and the hard work that he was going through to get the part right and he always went through agony. He never felt that any role he undertook was going to be right or that the play was going to work. As long as I knew him, he had the same fears that a young, unknown, untested student would have. He went through the jitters on whatever he was doing – even writing his own book, which he thought wasn't going to work. That was the worst time to even discuss anything or approach him on anything because he was totally immersed and involved – and worried. It was his nature to worry and, therefore, there were always traumatic times with whatever project it was. It was because he cared so much and really wanted to make it work, but he never had any clear feeling inside himself that he had made the right decision.'

Rex's work on his book was doubly hard because he had to start from scratch, as Miss Tarlo states. 'I don't think he has kept any real or serious record of what he has done.' His method of getting the book down was one not uncommon among those without previous writing experience, as Miss Tarlo explains. 'He dictated into a machine at Wilton Crescent. Then the editor would go through it and come round to discuss different aspects and sometimes try to get more.'

With Rex's marriage in serious trouble and the tension between Rex and Elizabeth's children at home, the Christmas of 1973 did not seem to be the ideal occasion on which to present to the world a glimpse of a united and loving family, but that is exactly what occurred. Rogers and Cowan arranged for a photographic session on Christmas Day at which Rex's grandchildren, Simon and Harriette, were also present, although his eldest grand-daughter, Cathryn, was not available to attend.

Cathryn had not exactly endeared herself to Rex several years before when she had been interviewed by the press on the set of her first film, *The Pied Piper of Hamelin*, in 1971 when she was just eleven years old. When asked about her famous grandfather, she had said, 'The difference between grandfather and myself is that I am going to be a *serious* actress.' She further compounded her foolishness by stating, 'He'll write when he sees me in the film and probably criticise, but then I will write to tell him what I think of his movies.' She added that she thought that Rex's performance as Julius Caesar in *Cleopatra* was, 'the funniest thing I've ever seen.' Although the girl was very young, her comments hurt her grandfather and he made sure, in a letter, that his feelings were made known to her.

A photograph taken on that Christmas Day ultimately appeared, not surprisingly, in Rex's autobiography, picturing a happy, laughing family surrounded by presents and with Rex displaying his most benign and paternal smile. The truth was somewhat different, as Elizabeth asserts. 'I can tell you that all the children loathed every minute of it. The picture was a put-up.' Simon Harrison recalls the occasion.

'The press were there to photograph the family scene at Christmas and I met Elizabeth's three sons. My first impression was that they were terribly obnoxious but we all posed for the photographers while Elizabeth and Rex played around bursting balloons and that sort of thing, trying to make us kids laugh and not take it so seriously.'

Early in 1974, Rex began rehearsals for *Henry IV*, this time with an entirely new cast, including Yvonne Mitchell; only Clifford Williams and Rex remained from the American production. Rex and his director had restored certain passages in the play which had been cut from the American version, which provided an additional challenge for Rex.

Following an approach from Rex, Bernard Delfont was to present the production in London and it was set to open at Her Majesty's Theatre on February 20th for a limited season. Rex and his director continued to enjoy an excellent professional relationship, as Peter Roberts, of the Bernard Delfont Organisation, recalls. 'Rex and Clifford got on very well. Rex would confide in him over his problems about the play. To him Clifford Williams was the key; they clearly had a great understanding and sympathy between them.'

While Rex was rehearsing, Elizabeth decided to travel to California for a few weeks, staying with actor John Ireland and his wife Daphne while she attempted to restore her shattered nerves. She felt the need to get away from her husband for a short time, hoping that their marriage would survive this crisis. Indeed, so anxious was she to believe that all could be well once again that she decided to return to London after less than a week. She described her husband's attitude when she returned. 'By now Rex had accepted that there was something seriously wrong with me as well as with our marriage. He was anxious to keep everything quiet. His attitude toward me now was both sympathetic and defensive.'

Elizabeth decided to stay at the Berkeley Hotel for a week before returning to Wilton Crescent, and Rex visited her every day while they attempted to resolve their differences. Rex agreed to give his wife more control of the running of the household and also accepted that she needed to be able freely to invite her friends to Wilton Crescent. She had become increasingly aware that as Rex Harrison's wife she led a closeted and isolated existence in which she felt totally redundant, with nothing to occupy her. She had even discovered that the almost total lack of a proper social life was no accident.

'I remember bumping into Angela and Kenneth More one day in Harrods and they said, "Oh, we're seeing you tonight."

I said, "No. Why?" and they named somebody's party. I said, "We haven't been invited," but they replied, "We know you have."

I said, "Well, I haven't heard anything about it."

'When I spoke to Rex later he said, "I don't know anything about it", and denied all knowledge – and didn't take me to the party.

'This happened quite a few times and Rex would never tell me about the invitations. The invitations would come to the house and the secretary would open them. It was only afterwards that I realised how cut off I was from people. I just thought people didn't want to see us.'

The problem was that Rex had reached the age when he was happier just to relax at home, something which Elizabeth had not anticipated during their courtship. Judy Tarlo says,

'Elizabeth was very social and wanted to entertain and go out a great deal. It is very difficult to marry a man older than yourself who has a very definite pattern of life that he does not wish to alter. He altered it to a large degree for Elizabeth. They gave balls, such as their fabulous feather ball; they did things very grandly. But Rex enjoyed peace and quiet.'

But all these differences seemed to have been sorted out and Elizabeth moved back into Wilton Crescent, although Rex's opening, and most probably innocent, remark upon her arrival was ominous; he explained about a new addition to the household staff, 'I have engaged a splendid couple . . . I'm sure you'll find them satisfactory – although I don't expect you will be staying very long.'

The male member of this couple, a large, humourless Spaniard, was to be the new butler and he quickly earned the name 'A Butler' from Elizabeth's boys due to his habit of announcing himself as such when he answered the telephone. 'A Butler' took his role very seriously and Rex clearly believed him to be a very lucky find. Now, instead of waiting for his breakfast to be brought to him in bed, Rex would get up and put on his silk dressing gown before the butler arrived. As Elizabeth commented, 'Rex had become a master worthy of A Butler. It was a rewarding relationship and made them both very happy.'

This mutual regard between servant and master did not, however, extend to Elizabeth and the boys and it seemed that Elizabeth had returned to a worse situation than before, as she recalls.

'A lot of things of Rex's I can see as funny now, but at the time it wasn't that funny – like that bloody A Butler. He was such an appalling snob and Rex was such an appalling snob. They were made for each other. I went to take some fruit out of the bowl and A Butler said, "No, no. That is for Mr Harrison's dinner." Forget me. And when I complained to Rex that night he said, "Quite right. It was mine." He would compliment the man that he was doing a good job. Mrs Harrison didn't come into it.'

Damian Harris also recalls A Butler in less than glowing terms. 'He was completely fawning – but he believed in it. He was the servant and Rex was the master; that was the relationship. He always used to complain about us going up and down in the lift and Rex would give us complete bollockings.'

Elizabeth was only waiting for the right opportunity to give A Butler his notice, although Rex displayed a remarkably high level of tolerance regarding his butler's behaviour, which made it harder than she expected, and when he finally did leave it was of his own accord.

Meanwhile, Rex opened in *Henry IV* in London on February 20th and, as in New York, he received some of the best notices he had ever had in his entire career. Robert Cushman wrote in the *Observer*, 'Mr Harrison is almost a great actor – who fits, by a truly Pirandellian irony, into hardly any of the great parts – and his wit, authority and vocal resource are to be treasured.'

The play's limited run ended on May 18th 1974. It had not proved as great an attraction with audiences as it had been in America, as Peter Roberts reveals. 'In New York the play was a great success. Here it was an artistic success. The business was very good but it was not capacity; it was not sold right out as it was in New York.'

While Rex played in *Henry IV* each night, he was by now in the final stages of his autobiography, which he had continued to work on during the day. One wet Wednesday morning, having reached the final chapter, Rex went to find Elizabeth. Before he could plan the chapter he had to get something clear in his own mind and so he went downstairs to confront his wife. Despite feeling a little awkward, Elizabeth recalls that he came straight to the point, asking her: '"I want to know what your intentions are." I said, "Why particularly today?" "Because I've reached the last chapter and I want to know how to finish the book."'

Rex had to know whether Elizabeth would still be with him when the book was published and would write the ending accordingly. Elizabeth says, 'I was appalled because at that stage I was very, very unhappy.' She clearly convinced him that she intended to remain with him because the final pages of his autobiography are laden with tributes to her and the book is also dedicated to her, although as Elizabeth states, one other name was seriously under consideration for the dedication page. 'Rex couldn't decide whether he was going to dedicate his book to Homer or to me. He had great difficulty deciding that. I was very surprised that it was me. In fact, I didn't know until I saw the book that it was going to be me.'

With the closing of the play Rex left immediately for the Continent amid press reports that he was leaving the country as a tax exile. The stricter tax regulations which had been brought in by the Chancellor of the Exchequer, Denis Healey, and the Labour Government, forced Rex to comply with the tighter restrictions on how long he could stay in Britain without paying ridiculously high taxation. The press, rather than attacking him for his departure, were sympathetic to his predicament.

Elizabeth was to follow on later in June, feeling that the separation meanwhile would do them both good. Rex still had his homes in Europe, at Portofino and Beauchamp, and planned to divide his time between these two.

Elizabeth met Rex in the South of France and they spent the first part of the summer there. They had a successful holiday together and all seemed well again between them. But then Rex decided to spend the remainder of the summer in Portofino. The difficulty of accessibility to the villa was not the only problem. The picturesque little village of Portofino was no longer the great attraction it had once been with the rich and famous, and yachts now tended to by-pass it for other, more fashionable, resorts. The local attitude may have contributed to this. Where they had previously welcomed such residents as Rex, people were now less approachable and appeared uneasy. Even Rex's gardener and caretaker of the past ten years, a thirty-eight-year-old Sardinian, Amando Marongiu, showed the same surly characteristics, as Elizabeth quickly noticed, although Rex seemed oblivious to any change.

It was not until Rex began to notice that his jeep was

not always available to him that he decided to question Amando. Previously there had been an arrangement whereby the gardener used the jeep in the morning to bring up the provisions for the household and then Rex had it for the afternoon. But now Rex often found that it was nowhere to be seen all through the day. Amando's reaction to Rex's querying the breakdown of the arrangement was totally unexpected. He suddenly let out a torrent of abuse towards Rex and began threatening him with a knife. Elizabeth states, 'The gardener said to Rex, "I'm going to cut your heart out!" You can't get much more vulgar than that.' Amando then drove off in the jeep while Rex stood in speechless amazement.

Rex resolved to deal with this situation through the law, but it quickly transpired that the village had fallen under the influence of the local Communists and he was fighting a losing battle. He realised that he would have to leave the villa; incredible demands were made on behalf of Amando and his wife in an agreement made out by the local Communist party, and Amando finally departed from the villa with a kind of severance payment amounting to seven thousand dollars.

Following Amando's departure, the rest of the staff also left and Rex and Elizabeth had to fend entirely for themselves. The villa had been Rex's home for a quarter of a century but now he was being forced to leave it. Elizabeth recalls his mood in those final days at his villa, uncertain as to how affected he was:

'You couldn't tell whether Rex was upset, because he had already got the house in France. Once a thing has finished, Rex doesn't ever look back. I think he's quite like that with his friends – and his wives! When it's over, it's over. It's like it never happened. If something appears in the press that he doesn't like, then he doesn't read it – and therefore it didn't happen, it wasn't written. That's how he tackles it.'

Elizabeth's boys were also there at the time, staying in a nearby hotel while the house was being closed down. Damian says of Rex, 'I remember him being extremely distraught about the whole thing, but then he just dismissed it.'

Not only was the move from the house proving difficult, but Rex was also otherwise occupied, as Elizabeth remembers.

'The last day in Portofino was so extraordinary. Richard Kershaw was there doing a profile on Rex with a whole BBC camera crew and there was Rex showing everybody the wonderful view and saying, "Have a glass of my own wine." And the whole thing looks as if it's so serene and heavenly. But behind him, we're moving out; the villa is going to be sold, and nobody would come up from the village to help. We had to leave most of the furniture in the villa because we couldn't get it down. I had managed to get a fellow with a wheelbarrow and his brother, who was very strong, and these two fellows were literally moving us out. They were tripping over the television wires and the lights: all the books, all Rex's clothes, his personal letters, everything was being thrown into sheets and lumbered down the mountainside. All this total chaos going on in the background, and there was Rex saying, "You can see the wonderful view. That's why I decided to buy this place."

'The cameramen are going on as if nothing is happening. Rex didn't recognise any of the things going on in the background even though, if he had turned his eye slightly, he couldn't help but see.'

In those final days Rex was also visited by Terence Rattigan and producer Arthur Cantor, who came to discuss Rattigan's new play, *In Praise of Love* which Rex had agreed to appear in on Broadway in November. He and Elizabeth had seen the play when it had been performed at the Duchess Theatre in London where it had opened on September 27th 1973, with Donald Sinden and Joan Greenwood.

The play, concerning the relationship between a writer, Sebastian Cruttwell, and his wife Lydia who is dying of an incurable disease, was clearly based on Rex and Kay Kendall. In the play the husband and his dying wife both believe that the other is unaware of the seriousness of her illness, with Sebastian behaving as boorishly as ever to conceal his true knowledge from his beloved wife, while she believes that her faked medical reports have deceived him into believing that her condition is improving. A mutual friend uncovers this situation and contrives to reveal the truth to Lydia, who, in finding copies of the genuine medical reports that have been hidden by her husband, realises the true depth of Sebastian's concern. Despite this knowledge, husband and wife continue to act out their deception to the end, still hiding their emotions, but at least confident in the genuine love that the discovery has revealed.

Elizabeth recalls what happened when she and Rex attended a performance of the play.

'We didn't go on the opening night. Terry warned us before we went; he said that he would like us to see it, but he did warn Rex to know that it was based on Kay and himself and, therefore, that he would understand if Rex didn't want to see it if it was too upsetting.

'Rex saw it and wanted to play it. If he was upset, he didn't tell anyone.'

Rex's decision to do the play did not improve matters with Elizabeth. She realised that she was caught in a difficult situation; to object to Rex's participation in it might have appeared to be motivated by unattractive reasons. 'I was in an impossible position. Our marriage was too fragile to bear too much truth.' Elizabeth had never actually met Kay Kendall herself. 'I only knew what Rex told me about her and he always portrayed it as the great love affair.'

When Rex and Elizabeth left Portofino for their villa in the South of France Rex began his preparatory work for the play. With Kay Kendall's spirit hanging over them so heavily, and Rex being constantly reminded of her as he worked, it was inevitable that his present marriage crumbled even more. What improvements had occurred during the first half of the summer had vanished and, not surprisingly, when Rex left for New York to begin rehearsals, Elizabeth remained behind and travelled instead to London.

Although they kept in contact by telephone, absence from each other did not improve matters, and when Elizabeth travelled to New York to attend the opening of the play it was only to keep up appearances.

'At that time Rex and I weren't getting on that well, so I didn't go out there very much. I went out about two days before the opening. Rex said he wasn't going to open unless the play was cut; he had been having this long fight with Terry. As far as I know, the battle was because he felt her part was too long and I said, "Well, it's her tragedy."

'"What the hell do you mean?" he said.

'I said, "Well, she's dying."

'"Absolute rubbish. Absolute rubbish!"'

Elizabeth's only other visit to New York during this time had been a short visit in the middle of October to attend Frank Sinatra's Main Event concert, recorded for television at Madison Square Garden. Sinatra had invited Rex to attend with Elizabeth and when Rex explained that his wife was in London, Sinatra sent Elizabeth a return ticket to New York. The invitation had been prompted by a letter that Rex had written to Sinatra when he had been ill during the run of *The Lionel Touch*.

'At Bedford Gardens, Rex was lying watching Sinatra perform on television and he was so moved by his performance. Rex was very down and he wrote to Sinatra to tell him how much pleasure it had given him and how much it gave him a lift and the will to go on. Sinatra acknowledged the letter and when we next bumped into him in Claridges, he invited us to a party. After that there was a good rapport between Sinatra and Rex.'

However, Sinatra's invitation led to a further rift between Rex and Elizabeth.

'Sinatra was marvellous. He invited us and he paid for my ticket over and gave us wonderful ringside seats. And I was looking forward to going to the party afterwards, but Rex said that he didn't know where it was. We drove around and I was furious. We never went; I never found out how to thank Sinatra. We just didn't turn up. I couldn't believe it. Sinatra had been so generous and so kind to us. We went back to the hotel and we had another flaming row.'

Elizabeth flew alone to London, and not long after her return she received a panic-stricken call from the caretaker at their home in Beauchamp. It was to lead to a staggering discovery for Elizabeth, who was already becoming progressively more disenchanted with her marriage. She recalls,

'I was in Wilton Crescent and Rex was in America and I got this call telling me that there had been a break-in and would I come over and find out what had been taken. The caretaker and his wife had been through the house and they couldn't find anything missing.

'When I got there, the caretaker, who was very fond of Homer, was in a terrible state; he said, "Somebody is trying to kidnap Homer!" And all trailed across the

garden were Rex's veterinary reports on Homer, which
had been picked up by whoever had got in there. There
was nothing taken. They had left money, all the things
they would usually take. So I was having to put all
these papers back. We had just left Portofino and all
Rex had done was to empty the contents of his desk in
Portofino into a sheet, tie it up, and undo the sheet
and throw them all back into a draw in Beauchamp.
Now they were all thrown over the floor.

'As I started to put the letters back, I looked at one of
the letters on his own distinctive blue paper; I thought,
"I'm sure I've got that in London." And then I saw
another letter and it was: "I realise how upset this
makes you, and that makes you, and the other makes
you." I thought, "Christ, I know I've got that in
London." Then I saw another letter: "This is absolutely
the last time that you'll ever have to ask me not to do
. . ." And I thought, "I'm going mad! I know I've got
these letters in London, because he had been writing to
me from America."

'Then I looked at the top and it was, "My darling
Rachel" instead of "My darling Elizabeth." And it was
verbatim. I think he had a sort of round-robin that he
sent to all his wives, because he knew what they were
going to complain about. He obviously did a sort of
stereotyped letter and then he would just top and tail
it. It was in his own hand. Either we all complained
about the same things or he got so used to hearing it
that he had them all ready.'

In London *In Praise of Love* had consisted of a double bill of
two short plays, *Before Dawn*, an inconsequential burles-
que on *Tosca*, and *After Lydia*, the two-act play partly
based on Rex and Kay. However, for the New York
production it was decided that *Before Dawn* should be
withdrawn and *After Lydia* be extended into a full-length
play, with its title being changed to *In Praise of Love*.

Rattigan had developed pneumonia, caught while

campaigning for the Liberal Party for a General Election, and so was unable to attend the rehearsals for the New York production in October. He eventually arrived in the United States just before the New York opening. However, on seeing the play for the first time during its tryout in Washington, he found that changes had been made about which he had not been consulted.

To Rattigan's horror, Rex was playing Sebastian for sympathy as soon as the curtain rose, sneaking a look at Lydia's medical report almost immediately in order to convey his true concern about her health. In doing this, the whole construction of the play was damaged because it was Rattigan's intention that the audience should believe that Sebastian is really as boorish towards his wife as he appears, so that the revelation that he knows the true circumstances should have its full dramatic impact. Only then should the audience realise that he has been behaving in this manner in order to conceal his awareness from her.

Rattigan was angry at this shifting of the balance of the play and there was some friction between him and Harrison. Rattigan failed to excise Rex's alterations and this caused a rift which lasted until Rattigan's death in late November 1977. Rex's leading lady, the American actress Julie Harris, says she knew nothing of the trouble between Rex and Rattigan. Her first meeting with Rex had promised well, after her initial doubts that she would be too unsophisticated for his taste. 'When I first met him he was very charming and very kind to me. I had the feeling that he was looking forward to working with me in the rehearsal period.'

However, once they began rehearsals Miss Harris saw a different Rex Harrison.

'I found him very businesslike as far as the acting went – and a perfectionist. But I thought, "I've never met anyone who is so self-centred." I never got to know Rex and, curiously, the basic difference in us as human

beings was very good for the play, because the character that Terence had written was very homey and not
sophisticated – a girl who came from a different background – and that contrast in us was very good.

'We never talked outside the theatre; he never
wanted to get to know me because he had a different
lifestyle. He never gave that a chance.'

Rex's reticence may have been partly explained by publication of his autobiography in London in October.
Amid rumours in the press of difficulties between Rex
and his publisher, Macmillan, the book appeared to
generally dismissive reviews, and when it was published
in America, by William Morrow, it received a similar
reaction. The *New York Times* book critic began,

On the basis of his performances, I have always
imagined him to be a most sophisticated person –
worldly, articulate, ironical, perhaps even a bit cynical.
But now, after reading *Rex: An Autobiography*, I find he
is nothing of the sort. He seems to have kept intact a
personality that has very little resemblance to his professional image. One of his favourite words, for example, is "fun" and what he means by it is not very
different from the dictionary definition. Even acting,
he says, is fun . . .

On Rex's treatment of his love-life in the book, the
reviewer was equally caustic, 'It is difficult to tell whether
he is gentlemanly or inarticulate when he refers to one of
his affairs as "doing a lot of mad things and having fun."'
He finally dismissed it with: 'I felt that serene, uncritical
satisfaction one gets at the end of a good, sentimental,
G-rated film that frankly invites you to regress.'

Rex may have felt some embarrassment at Elizabeth's
absence from his side after the high praise he had
lavished upon her in the closing chapter of the book. Julie
Harris recalls this situation:

'His wife was in London a lot of the time and I think he was feeling the pull of that. His book had just come out where he said Elizabeth had given him his life back and I think as the run went on he must have been feeling that she wasn't giving him his life. I only supposed that their marriage was under some strain because she was so much in London and not with him. And he needed somebody to be with him.'

Rex remained a solitary figure, distant from everyone, as Julie Harris continues: 'He's like a lord and there's a caste system. You don't associate with the underlings. That's the difference between us. I feel that in the theatre we are all a family – the whole company.'

The question of Rex's clothes for the role proved a long-running problem. Theoni V. Aldredge, who was in charge of costumes, endeavoured to meet Rex's requirements, as Julie Harris remembers. 'Theoni was trying to get the right clothes, but she never could. Everything she bought was the wrong thing and so Rex ended up using his own clothes, which are so beautiful and right and perfect. Theoni said, "He's absolutely impossible!"'

Rex's wardrobe has always been of great concern to him and he is satisfied by nothing but the best. His suits are from Kilgour, French and Stanbury of Savile Row, his shoes from John Lobb's in St James's Street, and his silk shirts are handmade by Turnbull and Asser of Jermyn Street. Indeed such care does he take of his clothes that his shirts are returned to Turnbull and Asser for laundering, even if Rex is in New York.

The pre-Broadway tryouts began on November 2nd when *In Praise of Love* played for a week at the Playhouse in Wilmington, Delaware, before moving for three weeks to the Opera House at the Kennedy Center in Washington. It opened in New York at the Morosco Theatre on December 10th.

Though Rattigan was critical of the alterations, perversely *In Praise of Love* received much more favourable reviews in New York than in London and had a longer run. Only one critic noticed that Rattigan's play had been interfered with: Holly Hill, in the *Educational Theatre Journal*, wrote, 'Rex Harrison's performance distorts the character which Rattigan created, and the critics' praise for this distortion exposes their inability to distinguish between acting and writing.' She continued by declaring that it was a 'misrepresentation of Rattigan's work.'

The play closed at the end of May 1975, after one hundred and ninety-nine performances, compared with the one hundred and thirty-one given in London. Indeed, the New York production, says Julie Harris, could have continued for even longer. 'People liked the play very, very much. We ended when we could have still gone on, but Rex didn't want to go through the summer. It was to be over by the end of May.' There would be no recasting of the leading role. 'Who would you find to take over from Rex? People do come to see him. He is a great star. I loved working with him; it was just thrilling.'

Elizabeth had only stayed for a few days in New York when she came over to attend the opening of the play. The marriage remained difficult and she returned to England to spend Christmas with her children. She made one more trip to New York in January, but despite a more promising start the situation between them worsened once again and after a few days Elizabeth was on her way back to England. Their separations were becoming more frequent and even when Rex had finished the run of *In Praise of Love* he flew straight to the South of France, while Elizabeth remained in London where she had now taken an apartment in Belgrave Place.

Following a further attempt at a reconciliation in July 1975, when Elizabeth joined Rex in the South of France, she instructed her lawyer to sue for a divorce on the grounds of 'irreconcilable differences'. They had been married for four years.

Rex was reportedly deeply distressed by this turn in events and he sought refuge and comfort at the home of

Leslie and Evie Bricusse in St Paul de Vence rather than remain alone in his villa in Beauchamp. Elizabeth explained her reasons for finally deciding to divorce Rex. 'I still loved him and he loved me, but we were simply destroying each other.'

The press reported that sixty-seven-year-old Rex was desperate for a further reconciliation with Elizabeth and that he was writing letters and making frequent telephone calls to her in England. But Elizabeth stood her ground and refused to enter into any communication with him. Today, she recalls the situation. 'There was no bitterness, there was no fighting about it, and actually, when the chips were down, he behaved very well. It was all decided that it was over and that we would be better friends if we were not married.'

Even after he had recovered from the initial shock of his wife actually leaving him, Rex continued to divide his time between his own villa and that of Leslie Bricusse. He was now discussing the possibility of appearing in Bricusse's proposed new musical, *Sherlock Holmes* in which he would play the Baker Street detective. It was hoped that the show would open in London in the following year but, as with so many projects that Rex has toyed with over the past decade, it was finally shelved.

Rex had by now become embroiled in a controversy surrounding his autobiography, providing him with further aggravation on top of his anxiety over the collapse of his fifth marriage.

In 1973 Lilli Palmer wrote her autobiography in her mother tongue, German. Having decided that it would not be an exposé of the later, turbulent years with Rex she omitted the saga of Rex and Kay Kendall. She did, however, choose to chronicle in considerable detail her ex-husband's affair with Carole Landis.

On its publication in Germany, under the title *Dicke Lilli – gutes Kind*, it received critical acclaim and became an instant bestseller, although it must have left its public still hungry since no account of their stormy marriage had yet been published by either Rex or Lilli. To ignore the Kay Kendall situation was foolish, since neither Lilli nor Rex had ever been able to hide any of the tumultuous events in their life together from an intensely curious and relentless press and, through them, the public. Her action also acted as the catalyst to an ugly row with Rex, which once again linked their names in newspaper headlines.

Lilli was astonished and hurt by Rex's autobiography. She recalled,

> 'I wrote to him at once and said, "Would you please put those dreadful things right that are in there."
> 'And he said he wasn't interested in putting anything right. I wrote back and said, "I warn you that if you do not, then in the English version of my book I will put an extra chapter in and tell the truth, because I don't want to appear an idiot, sentimentalising our marriage when, according to you, I never really existed." He didn't answer.'

Lilli felt that Rex had relegated her to a very minor place in his life and had ignored her in many instances, as she explained.

> 'Read about Portofino: *we* bought the place and built the house. It was at least my house as well as his. He makes *alone* a film called *The Long Dark Hall* – we both did it and got paid the same money. Have you noticed how he describes how we met: "a bond was forged" – you will never find the word "love" anywhere. And when Kay came into our life he wrote, "Lilli was upset and cross." He did all of this on purpose – pushing me out.'

Lilli determined to write the extra chapter for her book. At a press conference in New York in September 1975, to coincide with the English-language edition of her autobiography, she condemned Rex's account of his affair with Kay Kendall and the circumstances surrounding it as 'fantasy'. Lilli stated,

'Although he fell in love with Kay, Rex was not prepared to give up his marriage to me. But when the doctor told us about her condition I said to Rex that he must marry her. He went ahead on the condition that we would remarry after her death, and he wrote me a letter every week during that period. I still have them as proof of the arrangement. When I read Rex's account of the marriage in his autobiography I realised I had to set the record straight. He opened a can of worms.'

Rex was in London for an emergency dental operation when Lilli's autobiography appeared in America, under the title *Change Lobsters and Dance*. He was quick to condemn the allegations that Lilli made concerning Kay Kendall and told the press at his own conference,

'Without wishing to engage in verbal combat with Miss Palmer, the facts speak for themselves. I never went back to Miss Palmer. Furthermore, the reason that I did not elaborate on our marital problems was because of Carlos Thompson, to whom Miss Palmer was married at the time I was married to Miss Kendall. I consider to have done so would have been in the worst possible taste. That anybody should take the trouble, just to sell a book, to try and denigrate a dead woman, and a much beloved woman by all the world, is totally incomprehensible to me.'

Lilli's retort followed quickly; she was reported as saying, 'We kept in touch writing weekly for three years. I have kept his letters. I have told the absolute truth in my book.' Carlos Thompson also came to the support of his wife, stating that Rex's remarks were a 'total misstatement of fact.' He confirmed that he had read the letters and added, 'It is implicit in Lilli's story that Rex married Kay because he had no choice and the proof is in the letters.' Lilli could see only one way of stopping the escalation of their public feud, 'I took one letter and sent it to our lawyer and he wrote to Rex and said, "You'd better stop and not say another word or you'll be in court for defamation."'

In 1985, shortly before her death, Lilli still emphasised that she only reluctantly wrote of the Kay Kendall affair. 'He forced me to write it. As far as I was concerned I wouldn't have mentioned it. To this day, in all the sixteen German editions there is not a word of Kay Kendall. It is a deeply tragic story.' However, Lilli was still anxious that those events of so many years ago would, once and for all, be dutifully correct. Of Rex she said, 'I have read in an interview that he says that his best point is that he is a liar – but never to himself. I understand what he means. It is also the devastating honesty and insight that he has occasionally. But I would say that he sets little store by the truth, which, in all its implications, is a dangerous thing to have.'

With Rex's marriage to Lilli Palmer and Kay Kendall caught up in the middle of this very public dispute, his marriage to Elizabeth Harrison came to an end on December 16th 1975. In a fifteen-minute hearing in the London Divorce Court, Deputy Judge Miller decided that the marriage had 'irretrievably broken down because of Mr Harrison's conduct' and granted a decree nisi to Elizabeth Harrison, then aged thirty-nine. Elizabeth, dressed in black, was quoted afterwards as saying, 'I'm relieved it's all over. I have no plans to remarry.'

Proof that she and Rex harboured no bitterness towards one another following the divorce is given by Elizabeth who recalls, 'We got on very well after we were divorced. He spent Christmas with me in my flat in Belgrave Place and, because there was no sort of tension then, we could laugh about the things we used to laugh about.'

After Christmas, Rex travelled to Los Angeles where he was to film a series of commercials for a new car from Dodge Motors, directed by Hollywood veteran Mervyn LeRoy, (prompting Rex to remark, 'If you're going to do it, you might as well do it properly'). Rex reportedly received a million dollars for his participation in these popular commercials and at this time he also lent his face to magazine advertisements for Cutty 12, Blended Scots Whisky. Darren Ramirez, who was still continuing his erratic relationship with Rachel Roberts, recalls meeting Rex at this time,

'When Rex was doing the commercials out here we met and had dinner a few times with Rachel: once in Rachel's flat on Doheny Drive, where we were joined by my mother. Another time it was at a brunch one Sunday and then we had dinner at the Beverly Hills Hotel, where he was staying. Rex would see Rachel every day. At that time I was still living at my house at Hutton Drive on Coldwater Canyon and she was living on Doheny Drive and we were not together again yet.'

Of Rex's behaviour towards him, Ramirez adds, 'He was always very nice – always very, very warm.'

Rachel had just enjoyed a hugely successful run in Alan Bennett's *Habeas Corpus* at the Martin Beck Theater in New York, in a production which also featured Richard Gere. Her success in this resulted in a lucrative offer to appear in *The Tony Randall Show*, a television series filmed in California.

Rex visited Rachel on the set of the television series on one occasion, witnessing the first flights of her enthusiasm for this new venture. Rachel's moods were beginning to become more disturbing, but this was balanced by her pleasure in the memory of her recent Broadway success and her high hopes for her involvement in the television series.

But after Rex's departure, Rachel's moods became

progressively more worrying and even her relationship with Ramirez did not always provide the stability that she sought. She was still having trouble with her drinking and would behave outrageously even after only one drink. The steady working pattern restored her to a certain extent and she enjoyed the team spirit that a long-running television series often has. But her private life remained fractured even after she moved in to Hutton Drive with Ramirez. She would become suddenly restless and fly off to New York, returning a few days later and frequently tearing their home apart in a drunken rage. Ramirez learned to cope with the situation, but coping never really progressed to curing, and Rachel seemed to be spiralling downwards in a gradual but inevitable decline.

10

As HE approached seventy, Rex said: 'I consider myself primarily a stage actor, but one who sometimes makes movies too.' Unfortunately, worthwhile opportunities in films were scarce for a man of his age and he had not lent his considerable presence to the cinema since making the disastrous *Staircase* in 1969. Over the next two years he was to appear in a handful of unworthy films, for the most part in cameo roles which required little time to put on film, but for which he was very well paid. Producers hoped Harrison's name on the credits gave their films a distinction they often did not deserve and lent weight at the box-office.

The first role of this kind that Rex accepted was that of the Duke of Norfolk in Ilya and Alexander Salkind's re-make of *The Prince and the Pauper* by Mark Twain, to be directed by Richard Fleischer, who had last worked with Rex on *Doctor Dolittle*. Completion of his role would require only one week's shooting. The cast included Charlton Heston, Raquel Welch and George C. Scott; the dual role of Prince Edward and Tom Canty, the prince and the pauper of the title who swap identities, was given to Mark Lester, whose career had floundered over the years since his appearance in the title role of *Oliver!*, directed by Carol Reed.

Although a large part of the film was made on location in Hungary, Rex's involvement only entailed him working in England at Penshurst in Kent, which was used to represent Hampton Court, and shooting took place in mid-May. Rex appeared in scenes with both Mark Lester and Charlton Heston, who was cast as Henry VIII. It was over ten years since Rex had appeared with Heston in *The Agony and the Ecstasy*, but the passage of time does not seem to have mellowed either's opinion of the other. Mark Lester observed that the two men were distinctly reserved with one another, and at a script meeting held at the Spa Hotel in Tunbridge Wells where many of the cast and crew were staying they merely acknowledged one another and made no attempt to converse. Mark says: 'The only time they ever spoke was on-camera.'

Mark Lester looks back on working with Harrison as 'a great thrill', and comparing him with Charlton Heston says:

'There was something about Rex Harrison that was extraordinary – he was something different – the old school of actor. I had all these visions built up in my mind before I met him and they were all perfectly accurate.

'Although I was scared to death knowing I had to play these enormous scenes with him I felt totally calm when I met him. We shook hands and he said, "Nice to meet you." Within two or three minutes he totally relaxed me and I knew the scenes we would be doing, which before had seemed terrifying, would be okay.'

Lester remembers that the shooting schedule was arranged around Rex, who was suffering from a nervous complaint in his stomach, to enable him to begin work after lunch. In the brief time they worked together Lester believes they built up a certain rapport, and that Rex indicated why he accepted the part: 'He did mention about paying for re-stocking his wine cellar up at his villa. He was hoping to get some Château-le-Tour pretty soon after he got back and hinted quite heavily that that might be the reason why he had accepted the role.'

After completing his week's work Rex returned to the South of France, while the rest of the company went off to

Hungary to continue shooting. In the finished film Rex's role filled less than five minutes' screen time, which he invested with as much wit as he was able, and he was further used as a commentator at the end of the film, explaining the fates of the various characters involved.

In July Rex once again acted as host, along with other celebrities including Douglas Fairbanks Jr, at a special gala at the Theatre Royal, Drury Lane on Sunday, July 4th in aid of the Combined Theatrical Charities, as part of the celebrations for the American Bi-Centennial.

He was in England to begin rehearsals for a new play, having decided in the previous February to follow in the footsteps of those, led by Laurence Olivier, who had gone to the Chichester Festival Theatre, and to appear for the first time in his life on an open non-proscenium stage. Keith Michell, then artistic director of the company, had enticed him to the theatre to play the title role in the French farce *Monsieur Perrichon's Travels* by Eugène Labiche and Edouard Martin, to be directed by Patrick Garland as the closing production of the season. Rex described Monsieur Perrichon as an 'immensely conceited, vain, absent-minded Frenchman' who takes his wife and daughter on a holiday in Switzerland in the 1860s to show them the wonders of nature, and where he intends to scale the Matterhorn. The production was lavish, but the reviews were poor.

Irving Wardle of the *The Times* found it, 'full of eyetaking spectacle on the margins and framing a magnetic star, but woefully slack when it comes to character, rhythm, and all the elements that make comedy funny.' Rex's interpretation of this self-important Frenchman needed a different approach: 'Mr Harrison brings his relaxed upper-class comedy style to bear on a vulgarian who above all requires a display of exertion.' The *Daily Mail*'s Jack Tinker wrote:

> Mr Harrison presents us with his North Face and it is not the most easily accessible for his style of comedy.

There is, however, a good reason for his approach. M. Perrichon is a fool. His first trip abroad shows he is not only at the mercy of platform porters, duelling majors, scheming suitors, nature itself, but his own personal vanity. In the play's closing moments, however, he also has the dignity of self-realisation. Mr Harrison clings on to this throughout, mostly at the expense of the fun of the moment.

While appearing in Chichester Rex rented a house in nearby Bognor, where he appeared to be very relaxed and happy. During the run the Broadway producer Elliott Martin, who had presented Rex in Pirandello's *Henry IV*, travelled to Chichester. Having seen the farce however, he concurred with the West End impresarios that it was not strong enough for London or New York. Still anxious to secure an agreement with Rex to ensure his return to Broadway under his own banner and knowing Harrison well, he suggested a production of George Bernard Shaw's *Caesar and Cleopatra*. Rex had always nursed an ambition to appear in the play; he agreed and rehearsals were set to begin in New York in December.

Meanwhile, after the closure of the play in Chichester on September 25th, Rex travelled to Vienna for another re-make of a swashbuckling adventure, *The Man in the Iron Mask* (eventually released as *The Fifth Musketeer*), in which he played Jean Baptiste Colbert, the great statesman at the court of Louis XIV. With a cast headed by Beau Bridges, Sylvia Kristel and Ursula Andress, and a supporting cast including such names from the past as Olivia de Havilland and Cornel Wilde, it was a comically poor attempt to film the classic adventure novel by Alexandre Dumas, with Rex giving a colourless performance as Colbert, and looking uncomfortable in period costume. The film was only grudgingly released theatrically in 1979.

Rex was accompanied on the trip to Austria by Elizabeth Harris, whose autobiography, *Love, Honour and*

Dismay had just been published in England. In it she dealt humorously with her life and two stormy marriages, dedicating the work 'To R.H.'. She recalls that Rex had not approved of his ex-wife writing her memoirs: 'The whole time I was writing he would refer to it as "that bloody book" on one hand and on the other hand he wouldn't admit that I was doing it.' After it was published she says: 'He never admitted really that I had written a book and so he decided he wasn't going to read it. That was his attitude to most things actually. If he didn't read it then it hadn't happened.' Elizabeth states, 'We got on very well after we were divorced', and she enjoyed herself in Austria while Rex was making the film: 'He was very generous; we had a marvellous time.'

One day, on the spur of the moment, Elizabeth suggested to Rex, 'Let's go to Budapest for lunch!' She had been unaware of just how far away it was, but says, 'Rex didn't say no to anything I suggested – before marriage, or after marriage – but during marriage, that was something else.' She remembers another day, when they were having dinner together, 'Rex was eating a peach and I said, "You know, I put that in my book. I've said that the way you peel a peach is positively pornographic." "Oh! Oh!", he said, "So you have written some nice things about me. Well!"'

Rex and Elizabeth returned to London together on December 5th, and Rex then flew on to New York to begin rehearsals on *Caesar and Cleopatra*. Asked at the airport if he had read Elizabeth's autobiography he replied that he had not, but that Elizabeth had promised to give him a copy.

On December 7th Rex began work on the Shaw play, in preparation for four weeks at the Kennedy Center in Washington opening on January 7th 1977, followed by a limited season in New York at the Palace Theatre, where it was advertised to open on February 7th. The American actress Elizabeth Ashley was cast as Cleopatra.

From the start rehearsals went badly, and the British

director Noel Willman was replaced by the American, Ellis Rabb. During rehearsals Rex was noticeably edgy and inaccessible, and when approached by one reporter angrily told him, 'I only have time to talk to my director!'

The difficulties during the tryout delayed the opening at the Palace until February 24th, but its critical reception mirrored the troubles with which it had been plagued from the start, which Elizabeth Ashley would remember as 'a horror show'. Clive Barnes of the *New York Times*, although feeling that Harrison's Caesar was played with a 'charming world-weary urbanity', wrote:

> The difficulty with his performance – and by chance I saw it twice – was that it had more irony than energy, more style than substance. Something of the same could be said of Elizabeth Ashley's Cleopatra. She looked like a dusky Helen but pouted like a St Tropez starlet. Both of them had charm, but it was the kind of charm that bored rather than the charm that charmed.

Jack Kroll of *Newsweek* was even less complimentary: 'Rex Harrison gets by on an indestructible minimum of charm. Elizabeth Ashley snaps and slithers irritatingly, turning Cleo into a cat on a hot stone Sphinx. The most killing thing in the theatre is a squalor of mediocrity that seeps onto a stage when energy is low or ill-considered. So seeps this *Caesar*.'

It was the third time that *Caesar and Cleopatra* had been presented on Broadway since 1949, with Harrison and Ashley following Cedric Hardwicke and Lilli Palmer and the brilliant partnership of Laurence Olivier and Vivien Leigh in this, one of Shaw's less popular plays. The limited season for Rex's attempt proved more limited than had been envisaged, as the show failed dismally and closed on March 5th after only twelve performances, at a loss of £300,000. Faced with the worst disaster in his theatrical career as a major star Rex – publicly at least –

took it philosophically and was quoted as saying: 'I'm old enough, and after all that's happened to me, wise enough too, not to care!'

Rex spent Christmas 1976 with Rachel Roberts and they were frequently seen in each other's company, which fuelled rumours that they might get back together again. While he was working on *Caesar and Cleopatra*, Rex also invited Elizabeth to New York and on one occasion Rachel rang when they were together. Rex was at first reluctant to take the call and Elizabeth recalls, 'I took the phone and I said, "Hi, Rach. This is the woman that dumped him." Rachel said, "Hello love. When are we going to meet?"'

At the time of his appearance in *Caesar and Cleopatra* Rex also became reacquainted with Mercia Tinker, whom he had first met over a year before at a New Year's party in Monte Carlo, where she owned a flat. Tall, slender, dark-haired and superbly well-dressed, Mercia was thirty years younger than Rex. A sophisticated and beautiful woman, she was extremely well-read and spoke French, Italian and Malay. Brought up in Singapore, she had been married to a man who captured animals for zoos, but by the time she met Rex was divorced, a woman of independent means with a coterie of international friends. It was only after they were reunited in New York that their relationship developed. Rex no longer encouraged contact with his ex-wives, and when Rachel telephoned him from California, where she was still appearing on the *Tony Randall Show*, she could tell by his reserved attitude towards her that another woman had entered his life. Rex and Mercia were seen everywhere together, and on his return to Europe she accompanied him. At the age of sixty-nine Rex's personal life had taken another turn.

Mercia accompanied Rex to Scotland where he had agreed to present five matinée performances of readings from Shaw's theatrical criticism for the Edinburgh Festival, directed by Patrick Garland under the title *Our*

Theatre in the Nineties. The *Daily Telegraph* critic wrote, 'Inasmuch as Shaw's criticism can be brought to life by speaking, Mr Harrison's intelligent and well-nuanced speech does that.'

The Edinburgh Festival was also graced by the appearance of Julie Harris in her celebrated portrayal of the poet Emily Dickinson in *The Belle of Amherst*. Julie Harris recalls attending one of Rex's matinees: 'it was extraordinary, it was wonderful', although when she ventured backstage to visit her co-star of *In Praise of Love*, she says, 'Rex was pleased to see me – but distant.'

Departing from Edinburgh, Rex and Mercia travelled to London where they spent a week at the Savoy before leaving for India, where Rex was to make another film, *Shalimar*. In this Indian-American co-production Rex was cast as Sir John Locksley, a successful international jewel thief living in retirement in India. He is the owner of a priceless gem, the Shalimar ruby, and to allay his fears that it might be stolen, he challenges the world's greatest thieves to outwit his elaborate security system. Made simultaneously in English and Hindi, with a cast including John Saxon and Sylvia Miles, it was a crudely put-together caper movie. Rex walked through his part without any apparent interest. Rex accepted the film, which offered the opportunity to visit India with all expenses paid, thinking it unlikely that it would secure a release outside the Indian market. He completed work towards the end of October and, with Mercia, returned to London where they were observed one evening at Scott's, the fashionable Mayfair restaurant, having an intimate dinner together.

December found Rex in Los Angeles. He had been approached by Robert Fryer of the Center Theater group to appear in another play by his favourite playwright George Bernard Shaw: *The Devil's Disciple*. Frank Dunlop directed, taking leave of absence from the Young Vic Theatre in London, with Rex playing the flamboyant but relatively small role of General Burgoyne, who only appears in the third and last act of the play. Rex stayed with the production only from its opening, on December 16th, until January 28th 1978, when it crossed the country to the Brooklyn Academy of Music, where George Rose replaced him as the General. It was the consensus of opinion among the Los Angeles critics that the production only came to life when Harrison finally appeared. Because of a prior commitment to make a film in Israel and Kenya, Rex was unable to remain longer with the play, and three years later he would refer to it as 'not a very good production'.

The same could be said of *Ashanti*, the film he had contracted to make in Israel and Kenya for director Richard Fleischer about which even its star, Michael Caine, would say, 'It was the only film I ever did for the money alone, and I was never so unhappy in my whole career.' Rex appeared only very briefly in the film, as Brian Walker, a violent anti-slaver, while William Holden featured even more fleetingly in this ponderous tale of slave-trading in modern-day Africa.

In March 1978 Rex turned seventy, still cutting a dashing figure with the beautiful Mercia on his arm and dividing their time between New York, the South of France and London.

In May, Ralph Richardson and Celia Johnson opened in *The Kingfisher* in London, a new play by William Douglas-Home, directed by Lindsay Anderson. It enjoyed considerable success, due in no small part to being a craftily conceived vehicle for two senior actors, and once again Rex's New York impresario friend, Elliott Martin, rescued him from a barren period in his career, and offered to produce *The Kingfisher* on Broadway. With Lindsay Anderson engaged to direct, the question immediately arose of a leading lady of a similar age to Rex – particularly as she not only had to be as big a name as Harrison, but would also need the stamina to stand up to his idiosyncracies. Few such actresses remained who would suffer Rex Harrison.

Claudette Colbert's acceptance of the part was a celebration for all concerned. From the old school in Hollywood, she had always been known for her brisk and professional manner, and her insistence on proper etiquette at all times. The prospect of co-starring the names of Rex Harrison and Claudette Colbert outside the Biltmore Theatre was, even for New York audiences, a rare attraction.

Before beginning work on *The Kingfisher* Rex cut his first solo record album, produced in London by Norman Newell, in which he sang in his own distinctive style. Recorded in the summer of 1978, and titled *Rex Harrison: His Favourite Songs*, it included selections by Lerner and Loewe, Irving Berlin, Rodgers and Hart, and Burt Bacharach and Hal David. Rex was also working on an anthology of his favourite poetry and prose about love, to be published in London by W. H. Allen, and when he and Mercia travelled to New York in the autumn he continued to devote some of his free time to making his selection. By this time Rex had made it clear that he and Mercia intended to be married soon after *The Kingfisher* opened on Broadway, although he characteristically refused to give any indication of when or where the ceremony was likely to take place.

The Kingfisher opened in Philadelphia on October 11th, and transferred to Boston before beginning its engagement at the Biltmore Theatre on December 6th. Rex played Cecil, a bachelor novelist who arranges a reunion with an old sweetheart, just widowed after fifty years of marriage, but he cannot make up his mind whether he should finally propose to her after having let the opportunity slip half a century before. Claudette Colbert was cast as Evelyn, and George Rose as Hawkins, Cecil's devoted butler, who fears the destruction of a life-long routine by the appearance of the attractive widow. *The Kingfisher* marked Rex's return to sophisticated light comedy, a genre which he had neglected for so long. *Variety* confirmed that he has lost none of his skills. 'Harrison gives an expertly projected comedy portrayal of the selfish but disarming novelist . . . As usual, his timing and shading of the lines is brilliant.'

After the disappointment of his recent theatrical ventures, Rex was indeed fortunate to have found a vehicle so perfectly tailored to his talents, and with the amazingly youthful Claudette Colbert, settled into a sell-out Broadway run.

It was a time of real contentment for Rex – he had made a great many errors of judgement in the past, in both his private and professional life, but finally looked set to achieve a domestic harmony which had eluded him for so long. When extolling Mercia's virtues to the press he was surprisingly glib: 'She's a wonderful woman, very beautiful, terribly bright. She's at the New School all day. Art, art history, philosophy. She's after a degree, so we will live here for five months a year. Mercia loves learning. It's marvellous to have that kind of drive.'

At her instigation Rex discovered a new passion in his life when he began taking painting lessons one day a week with a New York-based artist, Cliff Enright. Mercia had originally joined him but, lacking the natural talent for it, she quickly dropped out while Rex persevered, finding it 'absolutely absorbing', and would paint whenever he had the opportunity.

Contemplating his imminent remarriage, he remarked: 'After five marriages, I have learned a lot. I used to think actors should marry actresses but now I see that is garbage. Actors should be married to wives,' and speaking of his plans for the future he said, 'From now on I hope to lead a quiet home life with occasional travel for plays and films.'

With *The Kingfisher* firmly launched, Mercia Tinker became the sixth Mrs Rex Harrison at a civil ceremony on December 17th, followed shortly after, at Mercia's request, by a religious ceremony conducted at the Little Church Around the Corner on Manhattan's East Side, early in the new year. Among the select number of guests was Noel Harrison who, divorced from his first wife, had remarried and was now the father of six-year-old twins. For much of his son's life Rex had been as distant with him as his own father had been towards himself, but in later years he began to have a closer relationship with both of his children, and had even helped Noel over some financial difficulties.

Mercia remains an unknown quantity to most people who have met her, whether they be Rex's ex-wives, friends or associates. Her beauty and elegance are always remarked upon, as is a certain aloofness which, in the role of the sixth Mrs Harrison, she has been exceedingly wise to adopt.

The only concern for Rex was the alarming state of Rachel Roberts, whose drinking had reached uncontrollable proportions. She had been attending Alcoholics Anonymous meetings regularly but suffered severe depression, becoming increasingly fixated with the idea that Rex was the only man capable of bringing any happiness or contentment back into her life. Friends of Rachel's have remarked that her conversation would continually return to the subject of Rex, and she tortured herself by retracing, over and over in her mind, the early months of their relationship, trying to discover why it had all turned sour so rapidly. In retrospect, her life with Rex at Portofino became more of a dream than reality and one which she could never hope to re-live. Happily re-married, there was little that Rex could do to help her, although he remained in regular contact and kept a watchful eye on her condition.

Shortly before *The Kingfisher* closed on Broadway on May 13th 1979, it was announced that Rex would recreate his role as Henry Higgins in a revival of *My Fair Lady*. This would follow a national tour of *The Kingfisher*. Producers Mike Merrick and Don Gregory had recently achieved great success with their revival of *The King and I* with Yul

Brynner. Aware of Rex's continuing ability to draw large audiences, *My Fair Lady* was a logical choice as a follow-up. Rex recalled, 'I was actually toying with the idea of doing something else when they turned up with what I can only describe as an astronomical offer.'

In the most lucrative contract in theatrical history, Rex stood to make £1 million a year out of the production, as well as being granted final artistic control 'down to the last nail of the scenery', as he put it. It was more than he could resist and he signed up for two years, to include a lengthy tour of major cities in the United States followed by a season on Broadway, after which it was hoped the production would cross the Atlantic for a European tour, culminating with a final engagement in London. Rex hoped to change the approach of the original production, presenting a more realistic picture of London in 1907 with less emphasis on the stylised costumes of Cecil Beaton. He said: 'It wasn't quite right the first time in 1956. I didn't think Shaw was done total justice. We engaged singers rather than actors.'

With over a year before *My Fair Lady* would actually open, Rex returned to the South of France with Mercia, and took a cruise around the Greek islands before travelling to Amsterdam to work on another film. Originally titled *Mario Puzo's Seven Graves for Rogan*, but eventually released four years later as *A Time to Die*, the film was a poorly-made revenge drama which cast Rex as an officer in the German army during World War II, who later becomes a judge being groomed by the allies as the new Chancellor of post-war Germany. Although receiving top billing Rex appeared only in the film's opening and closing scenes, while the weight of the film was carried by Edward Albert, Jr and Rod Taylor. Asked recently about the film, Harrison was unaware that it had undergone a title change and said: 'I think it just disappeared. It was one of those films which never saw the light of day. I haven't seen it myself.'

The film is Harrison's last to date and since then he has

limited his appearances to the stage, where he still has the opportunity to demonstrate his consummate skill as an actor in leading roles – something which has evaded him in the cinema since the ill-fated *Staircase* in 1969.

After five weeks in Amsterdam, Rex returned to London for the publication of his anthology, *If Love Be Love* in October. He summed up his whole reason for marrying Mercia in the dedication to the slim volume: 'For Mercia – I dedicate this anthology to my beloved wife from whom I have learnt the art of living and loving at last.'

While in London Rex collaborated on preparations for *My Fair Lady* with Patrick Garland, whom he had chosen as director, beginning with the search for a suitable Eliza. He was also curious to see the revival with Tony Britton, Liz Robertson and Anna Neagle which was touring the provinces, and arranged for a group, including himself, Mercia, Alan Jay Lerner, Mike Merrick and Don Gregory, to see the show in Nottingham. According to Lerner, 'Rex hated it' while the lyricist himself says, 'I thought the cast were quite good in it, but I thought the production had been terribly directed.'

At the time Lerner was working on a new musical with Michel Legrand, but received a call from the show's producer, Cameron Mackintosh, saying that he planned to bring the revival into London. 'You can't bring it in like that!' declared Lerner, to which Mackintosh replied, 'Well, if you're unhappy, come over and redirect it.' Lerner accepted his offer and requested four weeks of rehearsals, telling Mackintosh: 'If it's coming in I want it to be good.' Lerner says, 'Rex got very upset with me for doing it. He was auditioning for his production and I was directing the one here. I used to take my lunch hour and go over to the auditions with him and Patrick Garland. I said, "I'm just helping out," but I could tell he was very unhappy.'

Rex knew that should the London revival be a success, it would make it impossible for him to bring his own production into the West End. During his stay in London

Lerner says, 'Rex was appearing on a lot of television programmes and they were talking to him about his forthcoming revival of *My Fair Lady*, and he had it in his contract with every one of those programmes that they were not allowed to mention the revival of *My Fair Lady* here.'

During this time Rex caused a minor panic at the BBC when he appeared on the popular and long-running radio show, *Desert Island Discs*. As a 'castaway' he selected among the books he would wish to take with him Bertrand Russell's *Philosophers of the Western Hemisphere*, a book which, upon investigation, turned out to be completely non-existent. A spokesman for the BBC explained: 'It was Rex Harrison's fault. He was absolutely adamant he'd got the title right. By the time the producer realised the mistake it was too late to re-record the programme.'

Rex returned to America where he was to begin the national tour of *The Kingfisher* in Chicago, although he kept half an eye on the preparations for *My Fair Lady*. American actresses who auditioned for the part of Eliza proved to be unsuitable. 'They all sang beautifully,' said Rex, 'but basically the problem was the dialogue. To speak both Cockney and King's or Queen's English is too much for American actresses. They don't understand the nuances.'

In December the English actress Cheryl Kennedy was finally selected. She had already appeared in a number of West End musicals and Rex was confident that she would be perfect, although he had to fight hard to get her casting approved by American Equity. They were loth to have another foreign artist in the show, since both Rex and 91-year-old Cathleen Nesbitt – who had been engaged to recreate the role of Mrs Higgins which she had played in the original 1956 production – remained British subjects. At the first hearing before the Equity Council Cheryl was rejected, but Rex fought on and when a second hearing was called he personally flew up from

Florida, where he was appearing in *The Kingfisher*, to put forward the argument for an English girl. Despite Harrison's presence the plea was once more rejected, but the case went to arbitration and Cheryl Kennedy was finally granted permission to appear in the show because of 'unique circumstances'.

As soon as the tour with Claudette Colbert was completed, after a final engagement in Washington in March 1980, Rex and Mercia returned to their villa in the South of France. There Mercia placed her husband on a special diet and encouraged him to do sit-ups and yoga so that he would be in top physical condition for what would be a gruelling tour with the show. Rex also visited a nearby spa which specialised in natural spring baths and mud immersion treatment which he described as 'most refreshing'.

Rehearsals began in New York in July, with a cast including Milo O'Shea as Alfred P. Doolittle and Jack Gwillim as Colonel Pickering, and two months later the company were in New Orleans for the first night at the Saenger Performing Arts Center on September 23rd. There was a great deal of excitement in the house packed to welcome Harrison's return to the show, and their reception afterwards seemed to bode well for the success of the tour. However, *Variety*'s reviewer expressed some reservations about the production, particularly the principal performances, and wrote of Rex:

> For most of the evening, he presents a delightful picture of irascibility, egotism and sexism, talk-singing his songs in the effective method he developed for the original production. Near the end, his effect on an audience is affecting as he sings, 'I've Grown Accustomed to Her Face'. But there are several stretches when Harrison doesn't seem to have his heart in his work, resulting in an inconsistent performance that goes through rapturous peaks and uneasy valleys. On the opening night, he made several flubs in his lines

and in 'I'm an Ordinary Man', the complex song in which Higgins spells out his credo.

The reviewer also noted that Cheryl Kennedy, 'some times has trouble keeping her accents straight, and has trouble in the higher parts of her vocal register.' After two weeks in New Orleans, the show began its country-wide tour on October 9th at the Golden Gate Theatre in San Francisco where it remained for a six-week engagement. Rex himself scored a personal success but there was alarming evidence that Cheryl Kennedy's voice was not strong enough to cope with the long and difficult part of Eliza, and reviewers continued to make reference to her inability to perform the higher registers. These criticisms did not prevent the show from being a sell-out, where the main attraction was to see Harrison in the part which he had undisputably made his own.

During the engagement in San Francisco Rex called Rachel and invited her to come up for the weekend and see the show. He was well aware that she was in a state of extreme depression and was still drinking heavily, but as Darren Ramirez confirms, 'She and Rex were very much in contact.' Rex had last seen Rachel in January when he was in New York holding auditions for *My Fair Lady*, but they remained in contact by telephone and he had received a barrage of desperate letters from her. Still hoping for a reconciliation with Rex, and ignoring the fact that he was happily married to Mercia, Rachel jumped at the opportunity to see him again as if clutching for a life-line, although Darren Ramirez feels, 'Rachel knew underneath that their marriage had been very destructive. I think she was sensible enough to realise that they would never get back together again, but she fantasised with the idea right after he divorced Elizabeth and then actually during the marriage to Mercia.'

Her trip to San Francisco was, however, to shatter any illusion that she might have had about winning him back. In an effort to comfort and encourage her, Rex said that he needed her and that she was very important to him, but when she returned to Los Angeles she was faced with the stark realities of her life, and knew that she had been deluding herself with her dreams of recapturing the idyllic early days when she first met Rex. A friend remarked that on her return from San Francisco 'she was very depressed and upset.'

Rex continued to keep a close watch on her, and immediately he arrived in Los Angeles with the show, he called round to see her. On November 24th, the day before she was scheduled to leave for New York to audition for the part of the mother in a stage production of *Lolita* for Frank Dunlop, Rex had dinner with her at the house on Hutton Drive which she shared with Darren Ramirez. When Ramirez returned to the house late that night Rex was gone, but he recalls, 'Rachel was bouncy and she was happy and slightly high.' Having drunk too much that evening, Rachel was in no condition to travel and so delayed her flight until the following afternoon. On November 26th she telephoned Rex to say goodbye as she was taking the four o'clock flight to New York. He wished her luck and then worked with Mike Merrick on the technical rehearsals at the Pantages Theatre in preparation for the opening of the show the following evening. Late in the afternoon he received the shocking news that Rachel Roberts had been found dead at the house on Hutton Drive. Producer Mike Merrick recollects that Harrison was close to tears when he heard: 'He was extremely distressed and very upset.'

Rex spent the afternoon at the theatre, trying to avoid talking to the press who were pressing him for his reaction to the death of his ex-wife, but all he would say publicly was, 'It's a tragedy and I'm extremely sorry.' The cause of death was initially reported to be a heart attack, but three days later a coroner's report confirmed a verdict of suicide. She had taken an overdose of Nembutal and Mogadon, and had swallowed a caustic substance, presumed to be either a weed-killer or disinfectant. To anyone who knew Rachel, her carefully-planned suicide came as no surprise, as Darren Ramirez reflects: 'Rachel used to love life, but at the end she wanted to die so badly.'

The body was cremated privately – with only Darren Ramirez present at the ceremony – and the ashes now rest in a small box at the London home of her close friend Lindsay Anderson. Shortly after her death, Rex contacted Ramirez, who says, 'He wanted to tell me how sorry he was and how much he appreciated me being so kind to Rachel.' More than anybody else the two men knew what it was like to live with Rachel. Ramirez says, 'She was always constantly trying to provoke the people that she loved to see how far she could go. She was like that with her mother, she was like that with Rex, she was like that with me – but not with her friends: with them she was constantly trying to be approved of and constantly trying to please.'

Through yet another stormy passage in his life, which rekindled painful memories of the summer of 1948 when Carole Landis had taken her own life in the same city, Rex continued with the nightly performances of *My Fair Lady*. Mike Merrick says, 'He went on with his work. He was a complete professional – always on time.'

In December Rex was named 'Star of the Year' by the British–American Chamber of Commerce. After a little over three months in Los Angeles the company prepared to leave for Chicago. Business had continued to be very good, but the producers were becoming increasingly concerned about Cheryl Kennedy's voice. She had developed nodules in the throat which not only caused her great distress but also made it impossible for her to sing the score properly, and it was clear to all concerned that she would have to leave the production. Already her understudy, Kitty Sullivan, the wife of Milo O'Shea, had gone on for her while she underwent treatment but Rex did not feel comfortable with her and did not take kindly to the producer's suggestion that she should play all the matinees to spare Cheryl's voice. Mike Merrick says, 'Rex would not hear of it.'

By the time the show reached Miami in the middle of May Merrick and Gregory decided that some action would have to be taken to take the strain off Miss Kennedy. Merrick says,

'Don and I went down to Florida to see Cheryl and we both decided that she just couldn't continue, and we got into our first strenuous disagreement with Rex over that point. We wanted to replace her then, but again he would have none of it and we told him that it was just ruining the show – which it was. A lot of people were complaining that she just couldn't hit those notes. It wasn't fair to her – she was ruining her voice.'

Because of Rex's unhappiness with Kitty Sullivan it was suggested that Nancy Ringham, who was recruited from among the singers in the chorus, should perform the matinees instead. Rex's standby, Michael Allison, had been coaching her privately in the role and when they finally reached Boston in June, Rex agreed to give her a chance. The producer and director were sufficiently impressed but Rex was not and he tried to retain Cheryl Kennedy as long as possible.

After a prearranged holiday of three weeks following the Boston engagement, which Rex and Mercia spent with Claudette Colbert in Barbados, the play was scheduled to open at the Uris Theatre in New York on August 18th. But by the time they were to open on Broadway Cheryl was barely able to sing at all. It was left to Patrick Garland to break the news to her that she would not be going on, while Mike Merrick informed Kitty Sullivan that the management were in favour of using Nancy Ringham. Rex, however, brought forward another girl and suggested they share the weekly performances, but again there were strong arguments between Harrison and the producers. When Cheryl Kennedy was finally

forced to leave the show, it was not only an unfortunate
blow to her, but also to Rex. There was no other leading
lady available who could adequately partner Rex Harrison.

That Rex still would not tolerate the possibility of Kitty
Sullivan taking over upset Milo O'Shea, who considered
Nancy Ringham a totally unsuitable replacement.
Merrick states that Rex 'wasn't very helpful to her', but
by this time Harrison was feeling totally disillusioned.
Merrick says: 'He was tired and he was unhappy and it
was a big demand on him – a man in his seventies doing
eight performances a week. He could hardly wait to get
out. He and I had a number of conversations in Boston
before New York. He wanted to go to New York, but he
wanted to cut the run short.' Rex had also been upset by
the success of the London revival, which had destroyed
his dream of taking the show to England.

The mixed reviews for the New York opening reflected
Rex's loss of heart. The *New York Post* noted that Rex was
tired: 'Even the star of the production is a pale shadow of
Rex Harrison . . . as a septugenarian, he is hardly equipped with the vitality to do full justice to the character he
helped to immortalise.' The reception of Nancy Ringham's performance bore out Rex's own opinion. The *New
York Daily News* commented: 'She gave a thoroughly
professional performance but it was far from electrifying
or even inspiring,' and added, 'her Cockney accent was
inconsistent.'

Alan Jay Lerner says: 'Eliza is a very difficult part to
cast and they found that out when Rex did the revival
. . . I only saw it near the end of the run in New
York – an American girl took over, and you can't have
an American girl play Eliza Doolittle – it's not possible.' The show finally closed on November 29th 1981.
In the final analysis, without an equal Higgins and
Eliza, neither *Pygmalion* nor *My Fair Lady* could ever
hope to succeed.

Reflecting on his experience of working with Rex,

producer Mike Merrick says: 'Sometimes I found it great
fun and sometimes I found it very trying. The thing with
Rex is you have to stand up to him. If he feels you're
weak, you're dead. When he was beautiful he was
beautiful, and when he was difficult he was a pain. A
very difficult man to reason with, he just wouldn't listen
– and the only time I ever got through to him was by
yelling.' On the personal level he says of Harrison: 'The
man is probably one of the most charming, disarming,
erudite, mesmerising, clever fellows around who is great
fun to be with, and a good chum.'

Utterly exhausted after almost a year and a half rehearsing and performing in *My Fair Lady*, Rex spent
much of the next few months in New York, where he and
Mercia lived in their luxurious new flat at 450, East 52nd
Street, in the same apartment block as Greta Garbo –
whom they would occasionally see in the elevator. They
had dispensed with their villa in the South of France and
instead chose to establish a permanent base in New York.
They soon settled into the local community, and regularly attended services at the Episcopal Church of the
Transfiguration at 1 East 29th Street, known affectionate-
ly as the Church Around the Corner, in which they had
been married. Early in the new year Rex and Mercia
became involved in a fund-raising event for the church to
generate cash for urgent restoration work to preserve the
130-year old landmark. Rex hosted a 'guided tour in
words' on January 6th for 150 people, followed by a
cocktail party.

Rex's next professional engagement was in the summer when he agreed to return to England to appear in a
re-creation of *The Kingfisher* in an Anglia Television production, which had been adapted by William Douglas-Home
from his stage play. Rex was partnered by Wendy Hiller
as Lady Evelyn Thornton, reuniting, forty-one years on,
the two stars of *Major Barbara*, with Cyril Cusack as the
butler.

After rehearsals in Chelsea the production went on

location to Hunsworth in Norfolk, where Rex was provided with a comfortable house and a car at his disposal
for the duration of the shooting, although he confided in
William Douglas-Home that he did not think Anglia
Television would be able to afford such luxury.

Wendy Hiller and her husband, the author Ronald
Gow, took a house at Blakeney, on the coast. At a local
public house at the end of the first week's shooting she
overheard one farmer tell another: 'I hear there's a television film being made around here with three old geriat-
rics in it. Why the hell can't they let those people stop
acting when they get to that age?' Dame Wendy turned to
the farmer and said, 'We enjoy it very much!' She then
bought him a drink.

To her great friend Julie Harris she wrote that both Rex
and Cyril were 'naughty!' Julie Harris says, 'I think she
really enjoyed the whole experience.' It was indeed a
happy experience and a happy result. Wendy Hiller and
Rex partnered each other as perfectly as they had over
forty years earlier under the direction of James Cellan
Jones. The finer qualities of William Douglas-Home's
play were spotlighted and Cyril Cusack's performance as
the butler perfectly complemented the two stars.

At this period in his life Rex presented himself to the
press as a much more contented and happy man than he
had ever been before:

'My reputation of being arrogant or difficult is only
held by those who don't take me seriously. But I have
mellowed with age and that, it turns out, is one of the
nicer parts of growing old. What has happened is that I
am happier now than at any other period of my life.
You see, there is nothing more dragging down than
being unhappy in your private life. Having to fight
depression is not an easy thing to do. But with Mercia I
feel very happy and so I am full of energy. The inner
happiness means that everything becomes much more
pleasurable. But that doesn't mean I let myself off

lightly or anyone else either. I still believe in keeping at it and trying for the best there is.'

In 1983 Rex was back in England rehearsing George Bernard Shaw's *Heartbreak House* under the direction of John Dexter. For the part of Captain Shotover, the eighty-eight-year-old retired sea captain, Rex grew a large and luxuriant beard, and was supported by a distinguished cast including Diana Rigg and Rosemary Harris, with whom he had last appeared in Jacques Charon's disastrous film version of *A Flea in Her Ear* fifteen years before. The play opened at the Palace Theatre in Manchester on February 8th, and one critic wrote: 'This is Bernard Shaw at his most pontificating and long-winded – a dreary propaganda piece saved by brilliant performances from Harrison, Rigg, Frank Middlemass and Rosemary Harris.' After a tour of the West country, *Heartbreak House* opened at London's Theatre Royal, Haymarket for a limited run of twelve weeks beginning on March 10th, shortly after Rex's seventy-fifth birthday. Irving Wardle of *The Times* was full of praise for the first-night performance:

> This is the most resplendently cast production that has appeared in the West End for many a day; and it is an unexpected bonus to find that they also make up a company. Rex Harrison's Shotover is full of amazing surprises. Patriarchally bearded and dressed for impotence, he continually erupts into undiminished vigour: but always with the precarious force of senility, his mind suddenly collapsing, or succumbing to unpremeditated pathos. He gathers the play in his hands in the great last act speeches, and then dwindles into an old man slumbering on a bench.

Not since the legendary London production of the play forty years before, with Robert Donat, Edith Evans, Isabel Jeans and Deborah Kerr, had there been a successful revival of this most difficult of Shaw's plays.

After the sell-out London run, Rex and Mercia retreated to St Moritz for the summer and then stayed with Claudette Colbert once more in the Bahamas. Rex and Mercia both enjoyed travelling whenever Rex was not working; Rex said:

'Maybe in years to come, when I'm not working so much, we'll have a home of our own. But at the moment we are happy. I live for the day, and I always have. I earn money for the delight of living well. I couldn't economise by living in a small back room. At one time I had to, and I lugged all my possessions around with me in a suitcase. Now Mercia lugs forty-two suitcases around for me. It's a gypsy's life, and it's exciting.'

In September 1983 Rex began rehearsals for the American production of *Heartbreak House*. Anthony Page took over the direction of the play and Rosemary Harris, who had appeared as Ariadne Utterword in London, now played Hesione Hushabye, the part taken by Diana Rigg in London; Rex had hoped that Maggie Smith would join the American cast in place of Diana Rigg but it proved impossible.

After two and a half weeks of previews, *Heartbreak House* opened in New York at the Circle in the Square on December 7th, once again for a limited twelve-week run which ended on February 5th 1984. The production was a triumph, especially for Rex who was nominated for a Tony award for his performance. The production was also taped for television, and was first broadcast in April 1985. Mel Gussow of the *New York Times* thought, 'Mr Harrison has improved his performance from the Broadway production. At Circle in the Square, he sometimes seemed to be dithering in the background. On television in close-up, he projects both sagacity and humour, giving us a portrait of an artful octogenarian, hellbent on achieving the seventh degree of concentration.'

Rex was now interested in returning to his beloved Haymarket Theatre in London and a search started for another vehicle. The popular and fashionable British playwright of the 1920s, Frederick Lonsdale, had always been a favourite with Rex, and his comedy *Aren't We All?*, originally conceived in 1908 but seen for the first time in its finished form in 1923, was his first choice. The play had last been presented in London in 1953 with Marie Lohr and Rex's early idol, Ronald Squire, under the direction of his old friend, Roland Culver. The role of Lord Grenham would give Rex the opportunity to reaffirm his reputation as the stage's most gifted light comedian, but who should play opposite him? Rex came to the rescue of both management and himself by persuading Claudette Colbert to appear with him once again – bringing her back to the West End stage for the first time since 1928, much to the delight of London audiences.

With a cast which also included Nicola Pagett, Francis Matthews, Madge Evans and Rex's old friend, Michael Gough, they began rehearsals in Chelsea. During this time, Rex talked about the style of light comedy acting, saying,

'Ronnie Squire, Charles Hawtrey, Gerald du Maurier, the men who made it all seem so easy: they made you believe they had just popped into the theatre for a spot of acting on the way to the club. Now that I come to do one of Ronnie's great roles, I realise how right I was to admire him. Lonsdale is not easy to play: I'd rather have Bernard Shaw any day. Shaw worked for his actors: Lonsdale made them work for him. He gives you practically nothing: he wrote in a weird style all of his own.'

Meriel Richardson recollects how both she and Ralph Richardson viewed Rex's work: 'My husband and I admired his work wholeheartedly – he is the last actor able to remind one of how du Maurier and Ronald Squire could hold an audience with seeming ease and affability, and yet with an intensive incandescence. There is no one after him to show us.'

After rehearsals the company travelled to Birmingham for the opening at the Birmingham Repertory Theatre on May 14th, before beginning previews in London on June 12th. The London previews of *Aren't We All?* were a brilliant success, and the whole town was talking about Colbert and Harrison, but on the play's official first night on June 20th, disaster struck Rex. Milton Schulman of the *London Standard* wrote of his performance:

> In his prime, Rex Harrison would have brought to the part of Lord Grenham an insouciant professionalism that would have charmed an audience with its effortless grace. Last night he seemed to lose himself amidst the Lonsdale aphorisms as he time and again confused names, pronouns and meanings so that one waited with bated breath for the next hesitant speech. Fortunately, he was better served by his memory in the play's later stages, and in such casual gestures as his reading of *The Times* or contemplating an unexpected bouquet of roses, one caught glimpses of the superb comic actor Harrison can be.

Jack Tinker of the *Daily Mail* wrote,

> Rex Harrison delivers his lines with a nonchalance which all too often verges on the negligent. During his languid verbal peregrinations around the text, he occasionally bumps into the odd phrase which even Frederick Lonsdale might have recognised as his own. But it scarcely helps director Clifford Williams keep the fizz in an evening which must be as light and frothy as the bubbles in champagne if it is to be one hundred per cent successful.'

Kenneth Hurren of the *Mail on Sunday*, although paying tribute to Rex's considerable professional charm, wrote of the actor's delivery of his lines: 'He has all the best ones and he fluffs or forgets most of them – at least, he did on the first night at the Theatre Royal, Haymarket. Time after time, the cue for a quip hung expectantly in the air like a shuttlecock waiting to be hit.'

This kind of lapse is not uncommon for actors, but Rex has always been prone to being felled by first night nerves. He once said, 'I never look forward to openings. You're always aware the press is out front and the audience never seems to laugh as much as at other performances.' The play was saved in no small way by the alluring and assured presence of Claudette Colbert who, at eighty-one, did not put a foot wrong and was able to lead a shattered cast to an eventual victory.

However, Rex soon regained his confidence and he and Colbert kept the Haymarket Theatre full, thoroughly delighting their massive audience, and the limited season of three months was extended by two months because of the continued demand for tickets.

A highlight of their stay in London was an invitation to lunch with Margaret Thatcher and her husband Denis at Chequers. Rex and David Lean, another guest at the luncheon, were seated at the dining table on either side of Mrs Thatcher, and the other guests included pop singer Elton John and his wife. Rex invited the Prime Minister and her husband to see *Aren't We All?* on August 8th and afterwards he and Mercia entertained them in a private room at the Mirabelle restaurant in Mayfair where they were joined by Claudette Colbert. Margaret Thatcher is not a keen theatre-goer and, as with so many others, it took the powerful teaming of Rex and Claudette to entice her to find time in her busy schedule to visit the theatre.

So great a success had they scored in *Aren't We All?*, in spite of the disastrous opening, that it was decided that, after a brief holiday, Rex and Claudette would take the comedy to Broadway the following spring, this time supported by Lynn Redgrave, Jeremy Brett and George Rose.

During rehearsals Rex caused some controversy over remarks he made in a particularly painful interview with Russell Miller for the April edition of *Vanity Fair* in which, for the first time, the irascible actor showed his age. He explained the fact that he was still working with 'I suppose it is the challenge and the fact that I am still more or less capable of standing up and walking that keep me going.' It was said that Noël Coward had remarked that if Harrison were not such a gifted light comedy actor he would be fit for nothing but selling cars, while Rex's own reflections on Coward were:

> 'I knew him as well as I wanted to know him. Noël was a terrible cunt in many ways, and I never liked doing his plays, because unless you were very careful you ended up sounding just like him. He wrote as he talked. I thought he was a lousy actor, personally – he was so mannered and unmanly. He was much better in cabaret, singing his own songs. But as an actor, he was a joke.'

In the interview Rex finally said to Miller: 'I shiver to think what you have uncovered about me. Of course, the great thing is to be homosexual. Then, no-one can say anything about you – it virtually guarantees discreet press coverage. It is too late for me to change my sexual proclivities, however. *Far* too late.'

Rex's remarks about Coward were not taken lightly by Harrison's peers, and he once again lost friends. Douglas Fairbanks, Jr remarked on Rex's outburst: 'He does things like that I'm afraid – wicked and unnecessary, untrue and indiscreet, tactless and very offensive to a lot of people. I think everybody who knew Noël, and even Rex's friends, were infuriated by it. And people who didn't see it heard about it because it was such a spectacularly bad thing to say. But sometimes he lets off steam like that.'

Aren't We All? opened at the Brooks Atkinson Theatre on April 29th, after previews and, in contrast to the disastrous first night in London, was welcomed by an enthusiastic press, with Rex being dubbed the 'imp of Broadway'. Frank Rich of the *New York Times* wrote: 'With its minimal story, minor aphorisms and stock characters, *Aren't We All?* is guaranteed to evaporate from any theatregoer's mind within fifteen minutes after the final curtain,' but felt that the performances more than made up for the essentially dated play. 'If Mr Harrison's energy level isn't what it was in *Heartbreak House* last season, he's still an impish silver fox who deftly brays his roguish lines while studying *The Times* through a monocle.'

Variety said,

> Rex Harrison is the Pavarotti, Baryshnikov and Larry Bird of English light comedy . . . No need at this point to blow the bugle for Harrison's fascinating technique of deceptively casual comedy. His mastery of timing, inflection and relaxed charm has been pleasing audiences for about fifty years and remains as impressive as ever.
>
> *Aren't We All?* was terribly thin stuff even in 1923 and would be hard to take in an even merely competent production. But Rex Harrison is a lot more than competent and his distinctive gifts make it worthwhile.

Clive Barnes of the *New York Post* declared, 'Rex Harrison is a delight. He should be knighted.'

As had been the case in London, the run had to be extended by popular demand, finally closing on July 21st. In May, Rex and Claudette were presented with a special 1985 Drama Desk Award 'for the continuing pleasure of their company.'

After a two-month rest the indefatigable pair took the

play on tour, starting with a four-week engagement in San Francisco on September 25th, where they once again duplicated their tremendous success with the production. The critic of the *Sacramento Bee* wrote,

If anything could make this fluff worth the drive down to San Francisco and the cost of a ticket, it's Harrison. Age has deepened the actor's distinctive laugh lines and exaggerated his droopy-lidded squint until he looks like a caricature of himself, just right for the unrepentant Lord Grenham. The stage and film veteran breezes through his part with what appears no effort. He is pure style – showing off with a little slip-glide step, milking the best laughs of the evening with impeccable, seamless comic timing.

On then for engagements in Los Angeles, and in Washington DC where in December, during their last week, Claudette Colbert's closest friends, Nancy and Ronald Reagan, came to see the play. An extended visit backstage enabled Claudette to present Rex to the President of the United States and the First Lady.

Upon arriving for their engagement in Los Angeles – a city which had been a backdrop to so much tragedy in Rex's life – he learned that Lilli was also there, being treated for terminal cancer. She needed day and night nursing but Rex said, 'Don't worry about the expense. I'll pay what's necessary.' Rex confided to a mutual friend that he did not expect her to live beyond Christmas, but in fact she died on January 28th 1986 aged seventy-one.

His first wife, Collette, is now being cared for at St Peter's Convent, a nursing home in Plymouth. She had been living in a brownstone house in a fashionable part of New York but had become increasingly ill and was no longer able to look after herself. She was brought back to England to be close to her family, and was admitted to St Wilfrid's in Tite Street, Chelsea, where Sister Peggy recalls, 'She had beautiful clothes and wore them well,' but also says, 'she was very confused.' Her condition worsened and she was moved to the Plymouth nursing home where her sisters, Pat and the Dowager Duchess of Somerset, keep a close eye on her. Collette continually refers to herself as Mrs Rex Harrison.

On March 5th 1986, Rex was seventy-eight. Still young of heart, urbane, sprightly, wickedly attractive and brilliantly talented, Rex Harrison is, as he was sixty years ago, ready, willing and able to work.

Throughout a long and distinguished career, Rex Harrison has consistently given his best to the stage and screen. He is now the only actor of his calibre who has not been honoured by his country, but it is honour enough that today he stands beside Olivier and Gielgud as one of the greatest British actors of the twentieth century, in addition to being a long-serving ambassador for England, whose great talents and presence are welcomed throughout the world.

BIBLIOGRAPHY

Aumont, Jean-Pierre. *Sun and Shadow* (W. W. Norton Inc., New York, 1977)

Bacall, Lauren. *By Myself* (Alfred A. Knopf, New York, 1979; Jonathan Cape, London, 1979)

Baron. *Baron by Baron* (Frederick Muller, London, 1956)

Batters, Jean. *Edith Evans: A Personal Memoir* (Hart-Davis Mac-Gibbon, London, 1977)

Beaton, Cecil. *Self Portrait With Friends: The Selected Diaries of Cecil Beaton 1926–1974* ed. Richard Buckle (Weidenfeld and Nicolson, London, 1979)

Black, Kitty. *Upper Circle: A Theatrical Chronicle* (Methuen, London, 1984)

Bogarde, Dirk. *Snakes and Ladders* (Chatto and Windus, London, 1978)

Braun, Eric. *Deborah Kerr* (W. H. Allen, London, 1977)

Brodsky, Jack and Nathan Weiss: *The Cleopatra Papers: A Private Correspondence* (Simon and Schuster, New York, 1963)

Cochran, Charles B. *Cock-a-Doodle-do* (Dent, London, 1941)

Colman, Juliet Benita. *Ronald Colman: A Very Private Person* (W. H. Allen, London, 1975)

Costello, Donald P. *The Serpent's Eye: Shaw and the Cinema* (University of Notre Dame Press, Indiana, 1965; University of Notre Dame Press: Book Centre, 1966)

Cottrell, John. *Laurence Olivier* (Weidenfeld and Nicolson, London, 1975)

Coward, Noël. *The Noël Coward Diaries* (ed. Graham Payn and Sheridan Morley (Weidenfeld & Nicolson, London, 1982)

Culver, Roland. *Not Quite A Gentleman* (William Kimber, London, 1979)

Day, Doris. *Her Own Story* with A. E. Hotchner (William Morrow and Co. Inc., New York, 1976)

Dukore, Bernard F. *The Collected Screenplays of Bernard Shaw* (George Prior Publishers, London, 1980)

Edwards, Anne. *Vivien Leigh* (Simon and Schuster, New York, 1977; W. H. Allen, London, 1977)

Eyles, Allen. *Rex Harrison* (W. H. Allen, London, 1985)

Farrer, William and J. Brownbill B. A. *The Victoria History of the County of Lancaster* Vol. 3 (Archibald Constable and Co Ltd, London, 1907)

Forbes, Bryan. *Ned's Girl: The Life of Edith Evans* (Little, Brown and Co., Boston, 1977; Elm Tree Books, London, 1977)

French, Harold. *I Thought I Never Could* (Secker and Warburg, London, 1973)

Geist, Kenneth L. *Pictures Will Talk: The Life and Times of Joseph L. Mankiewicz* (Scribner, New York, 1978)

Goldie, Grace Wyndham. *The Liverpool Repertory Theatre* (University Press of Liverpool, 1935)

Graham, Sheila. *My Hollywood* (Michael Joseph, London, 1984)

Gussow, Mel. *Darryl F. Zanuck; Don't Say Yes Until I Finish Talking* (Doubleday and Co., New York, 1971; W. H. Allen, London, 1971)

Harrison, Elizabeth. *Love, Honour and Dismay* (Weidenfeld and Nicolson, London, 1976)

Harrison, Rex. *Rex: An Autobiography* (Macmillan, London, 1974)

If Love Be Love: Poems & Prose Chosen by Rex Harrison (W. H. Allen, London, 1979)

Harwood, Ronald. *Sir Donald Wolfit* (Secker and Warburg, London, 1971)

Heston, Charlton. *The Actor's Life: Journals 1956–1976* (E. P. Dutton and Co., New York, 1978)

Higham, Charles. *Audrey: The Life of Audrey Hepburn* (Macmillan Publishing Co. New York, 1984; New English Library, London, 1985)

Hodson, Gillian and Michael Darlow. *Terence Rattigan: The Man and His Work* (Quartet Books, London, 1979)

Holloway, Stanley. *Wiv A Little Bit O' Luck: The Life Story of Stanley Holloway* (As told to Dick Richards) (Leslie Frewin, London, 1967)

Lambert, Gavin. *On Cukor* (W. H. Allen, London, 1973)

Lamparski, Richard. *Whatever Became of . . . ?* Vol. 4 (Crown Publishers, Inc. New York, 1973)

Laye, Evelyn. *Boo To My Friends* (Hurst and Blackett, London, 1958)

Lerner, Alan Jay. *The Street Where I Live* (Hodder and Stoughton, London, 1978)

Marshall, Norman. *The Other Theatre* (John Lehmann Ltd, London, 1947)

Mills, Sir John. *Up in The Clouds Gentlemen Please* (Weidenfeld and Nicolson, London, 1980)

Minnelli, Vincente. *I Remember It Well* with Hector Arce (Doubleday and Co., New York, 1974)

Minney, R. J. *The Films of Anthony Asquith* (A. S. Barnes and Co., New York, 1976)

Morley, Sheridan. *The Other Side of the Moon: The Life of David Niven* (Weidenfeld and Nicolson, London, 1985)

Neagle, Anna. *There's Always Tomorrow* (W. H. Allen, London, 1974)

Niven, David. *The Moon's A Balloon* (Hamish Hamilton, London, 1971)

Olivier, Laurence. *Confessions of an Actor* (Weidenfeld and Nicolson, London, 1982)

Palmer, Lilli. *Dicke Lilli – gutes Kind* (Droemer Knaur, Germany, 1974)
  Change Lobsters – and Dance (Macmillan Publishing Co., New York, 1975)
  The Red Raven (W. H. Allen, London, 1976)

Parish, James Robert and Don E. Stanke. *The Debonairs* (Arlington House, New York, 1975)
  The Swashbucklers (Rainbow Books, New York, 1977)

Pascal, Valerie. *The Disciple and His Devil* (Michael Joseph, London, 1971)

Roberts, Rachel. *No Bells On Sunday: The Journals of Rachel Roberts* Edited with a documentary biography by Alexander Walker (Michael Joseph/Pavilion, London, 1984)

Saroyan, Aram. *Trio* (Linden Press, Simon and Schuster, New York, 1985)

Selznick, Irene Mayer. *A Private View* (Alfred A. Knopf, New York, 1983; Weidenfeld and Nicholson, London, 1983)

Sharaff, Irene. *Broadway and Hollywood: Costumes Designed by Irene Sharaff* (Van Nostrand Reinhold Co., London, 1976)

Simmons, Dawn Langley. *Margaret Rutherford: A Blithe Spirit* (McGraw Hill Book Co., New York, 1983; Barker, London, 1984)

Tierney, Gene. *Self Portrait* with Mickey Herskowitz (Wyden Books, New York, 1979)

Vickers, Hugo. *Cecil Beaton* (Weidenfeld and Nicolson, London, 1985)

Wanger, Walter and Joe Hyams. *My Life With Cleopatra* (Corgi, London, 1963)

Wilcox, Herbert. *Twenty-Five Thousand Sunsets. The Autobiography of Herbert Wilcox* (Bodley Head, London, 1967)

Windeler, Robert. *Julie Andrews* (W. H. Allen, London, 1982)

Rex Harrison has always been most generous to the press, and shown great co-operation towards the people for whom he has worked, in allowing himself to be interviewed at important times during his long and distinguished career. To all the fine journalists who have had the privilege of interviewing Mr Harrison, and to all the publications: newspapers, periodicals and magazines who have published their work, we express our thanks.

THEATRE APPEARANCES

LIVERPOOL REPERTORY THEATRE COMPANY
1925:   *Thirty Minutes in a Street*
1926:   *Old English*
        Doctor Knock
        Gold
        A Kiss For Cinderella
1927:   *Milestones*
        Abraham Lincoln
        Charley's Aunt (Tour)
1928:   *Potiphar's Wife* (Tour)
1929:   *Alibi* (Tour)
        The Chinese Bungalow (Tour)
1930:   *A Cup of Kindness* (Tour)
        Richard III New Theatre, London. *d.* Caspar Middleton,
            John Counsell, Barbara Curtis, with Baliol Holloway.
        Getting George Married Everyman Theatre, Hampstead,
            London. *d.* Malcolm Morley, with Louise Hampton,
            Bruce Belfrage.
1931:   *The Ninth Man* Prince of Wales Theatre, London. *d.*
            Campbell Gullan with John Longden, Nora Swin-
            burne, Edward Ashley-Cooper.

CARDIFF REPERTORY THEATRE
1931:   *Square Crooks*
        The Berg
        The Joan Danvers
        Meet The Wife
        Other Men's Wives
        After All (Tour)
1932:   *For The Love of Mike* (Tour)

1933: *Another Language* Lyric Theatre, London with Herbert Marshall.

Road House (Tour)

Mother of Pearl (Tour)

1934: *No Way Back* Whitehall Theatre, London, *d.* A. R. Whatmore with Mary Clare, Esmé Church, Sophie Stewart.

Death at Court Lady Shilling Theatre, Fulham, London, with Nigel Patrick.

Division Shilling Theatre, Fulham, London, *d.* Jack Minster with Donald Wolfit.

Our Mutual Father Piccadilly Theatre, London, *d.* Reginald Tate with Basil Radford, Joan White, Joyce Barbour, Fabia Drake, Eric Portman.

Anthony and Anna Shilling Theatre, Fulham, London, *d.* Jack Minster with Carol Goodner, Herbert Lomas, Bruce Belfrage.

1935: *Man of Yesterday* St Martin's Theatre, London, *d.* Campbell Gullan with Leslie Banks, Ann Todd.

The Wicked Flee (Tour)

Short Story Queen's Theatre, London, *d.* Tyrone Guthrie with Marie Tempest, Sybil Thorndike, Margaret Rutherford, A. E. Matthews, Ursula Jeans.

1936: *Charity Begins* Aldwych Theatre, London, *d.* Henry Kendall with Cathleen Cordell, Katie Johnson, Nigel Patrick, Iris Hoey.

Sweet Aloes Booth Theatre, New York, *d.* Tyrone Guthrie with Evelyn Laye, Nicholas Joy, John Litel, Joyce Carey, John Emery.

Heroes Don't Care St Martin's Theatre, London, *d.* Claud Gurney with Carol Goodner, Coral Browne, Felix Aylmer.

French Without Tears Criterion Theatre, London, *d.* Harold French with Kay Hammond, Jessica Tandy, Robert Flemyng, Trevor Howard, Roland Culver.

1939: *Design for Living* Theatre Royal, Haymarket, London, *d.* Harold French with Diana Wynyard, Anton Walbrook, Cathleen Cordell.

1941: *No Time For Comedy* Theatre Royal, Haymarket, London, *d.* Harold French with Diana Wynyard, Lilli Palmer, Elisabeth Welch.

1945: *French Without Tears* (Tour) *d.* Daphne Rye with Anna Neagle, Roland Culver.

1948: *Anne of the Thousand Days* Shubert Theatre, New York, *d.* H. C. Potter with Joyce Redman, John Williams.

1950: *Anta Album* Ziegfeld Theatre, New York, *d.* Sir Cedric Hardwicke with Lilli Palmer, Peggy Wood, Francis L. Sullivan.

The Cocktail Party New Theatre, London, *d.* E. Martin Browne with Margaret Leighton, Ian Hunter, Alison Leggatt.

Bell, Book and Candle Ethel Barrymore Theatre, New York, *d.* John Van Druten with Lilli Palmer, Jean Adair, Scott McKay, Larry Gates.

1952: *Venus Observed* Century Theatre, New York, *d.* Laurence Olivier with Lilli Palmer, Eileen Peel, John Williams.

1953: *The Love of Four Colonels* Shubert Theatre, New York *d.* Rex Harrison with Lilli Palmer, Leueen McGrath, Robert Coote, Larry Gates.

1954: *Bell, Book and Candle* Phoenix Theatre, London *d.* Rex Harrison with Lilli Palmer, Athene Seyler.

1955: *Nina* Theatre Royal, Haymarket, London, Rex Harrison as director only with Coral Browne, Michael Hordern, James Hayter.

1956: *My Fair Lady* Mark Hellinger Theatre, New York, *d.* Moss Hart with Julie Andrews, Stanley Holloway, Robert Coote, Cathleen Nesbitt.

1958: *My Fair Lady* Theatre Royal, Drury Lane, London, *d.* Moss Hart with Julie Andrews, Stanley Holloway, Robert Coote, Zena Dare.

The Bright One Winter Garden Theatre, London, Rex Harrison as director only with Kay Kendall, Gladys Cooper.

1959: *The Fighting Cock* ANTA Theatre, New York, *d.* Peter Brook with Natasha Parry, Arthur Treacher, Roddy McDowall, Michael Gough.

1960: *Platonov* Royal Court Theatre, London, *d.* George Devine, John Blatchley with Rachel Roberts, Rosalind Knight, Frank Finlay.

1961: *August for the People* Edinburgh Festival and Royal Court Theatre, London, *d.* George Devine with Rachel Roberts, Hugh Latimer, Donald Sutherland.

1969: *The Lionel Touch* Lyric Theatre, Shaftesbury Avenue, London, *d.* John Gorrie with Joyce Redman, Christopher Cazenove.

1973: *The Emperor Henry IV* Ethel Barrymore Theatre, New York, *d.* Clifford Williams with Eileen Herlie.

1974: *Henry IV* Her Majesty's Theatre, Haymarket, London, *d.* Clifford Williams with Yvonne Mitchell.
In Praise of Love Morosco Theatre, New York, *d.* Fred Coe with Julie Harris, Martin Gabel.

1976: *Monsieur Perrichon's Travels* Chichester Festival Theatre, Sussex, *d.* Patrick Garland with Keith Michell, Clive Francis.

1977: *Caesar and Cleopatra* Palace Theatre, New York *d.* Ellis Rabb with Elizabeth Ashley.
Our Theatres in the Nineties Edinburgh Festival *d.* Patrick Garland.
The Devil's Disciple Ahmanson Theatre, Los Angeles, *d.* Frank Dunlop.

1978: *The Kingfisher* Biltmore Theatre, New York, *d.* Lindsay Anderson with Claudette Colbert, George Rose.

1980: *My Fair Lady* (Tour) *d.* Patrick Garland with Cheryl Kennedy, Milo O'Shea, Cathleen Nesbitt.

1981: *My Fair Lady* Uris Theatre, New York, with Nancy Ringham as Eliza.

1983: *Heartbreak House* Theatre Royal, Haymarket, London, *d.* John Dexter with Rosemary Harris, Diana Rigg, Mel Martin.
Heartbreak House Circle in the Square Theatre, New York, *d.* Anthony Page with Amy Irving, Dana Ivey, Stephen McHattie.

1984: *Aren't We All?* Theatre Royal, Haymarket, London, *d.* Clifford Williams with Claudette Colbert, Francis Matthews, Nicola Pagett, Madge Ryan, Michael Gough.

1985: *Aren't We All?* Brooks Atkinson Theatre, New York, *d.* Clifford Williams with Claudette Colbert, Jeremy Brett, Lynn Redgrave, George Rose.

FILM APPEARANCES

1930: *The Great Game* Gaumont-British, *d*. Jack Raymond.
The School for Scandal Paramount–British, *d*. Maurice Elvey with Madeleine Carroll.

1934: *Get Your Man* Paramount–British, *d*. George King with Sebastian Shaw, Kay Walsh.
Leave It To Blanche Warner Brothers–First National, *d*. Harold M. Young with Henry Kendall, Griffith Jones.

1935: *All At Sea* Fox–British *d*. Anthony Kimmins with Googie Withers.

1936: *Men Are Not Gods* London Films, *d*. Walter Reisch with Miriam Hopkins, Gertrude Lawrence, A. E. Matthews.

1937: *Storm in a Teacup* London Films, *d*. Victor Saville, Ian Dalrymple with Vivien Leigh, Cecil Parker, Ursula Jeans.
School for Husbands A Wainright Production, *d*. Andrew Marton with Diana Churchill, June Clyde, Henry Kendall, Romney Brent.

1938: *St Martin's Lane* US Title: *Sidewalks of London*, Mayflower Pictures, *d*. Tim Whelan with Charles Laughton, Vivien Leigh, Larry Adler, Tyrone Guthrie.
The Citadel Metro-Goldwyn-Mayer, *d*. King Vidor with Robert Donat, Rosalind Russell, Ralph Richardson, Emlyn Williams, Nora Swinburne, Athene Seyler.

1939: *The Silent Battle* Paramount, *d*. Herbert Mason with Valerie Hobson, John Loder.
Over The Moon London Films, *d*. Thornton Freeland with Merle Obcron, Ursula Jeans, Robert Douglas.

1940: *Ten Days in Paris* Irving Asher Productions, *d*. Tim Whelan with Kaaren Verne, Leo Genn.
Night Train to Munich (US Title: *Night Train*) Twentieth Century Productions, *d*. Carol Reed with Margaret

Lockwood, Paul von Hernreid (Paul Henreid), Basil Radford, Naunton Wayne, Roland Culver.

1941: *Major Barbara* Pascal Film Productions, *d.* Gabriel Pascal with Wendy Hiller, Robert Newton, Sybil Thorndike, Deborah Kerr.

1945: *Blithe Spirit* Two Cities/Cineguild, *d.* David Lean with Constance Cummings, Kay Hammond, Margaret Rutherford.

I Live in Grosvenor Square (US Title: *A Yank in London*) ABP, *d.* Herbert Wilcox) with Anna Neagle, Dean Jagger, Nancy Price, Irene Vanbrugh.

The Rake's Progress Individual, *d.* Sidney Gilliat with Lilli Palmer, Godfrey Tearle, Griffith Jones, Guy Middleton, Jean Kent.

1946: *Anna and the King of Siam* Twentieth Century-Fox, *d.* John Cromwell with Irene Dunne, Linda Darnell.

1947: *The Ghost and Mrs Muir* Twentieth Century-Fox, *d.* Joseph L. Mankiewicz with Gene Tierney, George Sanders, Edna Best, Anna Lee, Robert Coote, Vanessa Brown, Natalie Wood.

The Foxes of Harrow Twentieth Century-Fox, *d.* John M. Stahl with Maureen O'Hara, Richard Haydn, Victor McLaglen, Vanessa Brown, Patricia Medina.

1948: *Escape* Twentieth Century Productions, *d.* Joseph L. Mankiewicz with Peggy Cummins, Norman Wooland, Jill Esmond.

Unfaithfully Yours Twentieth Century-Fox, *d.* Preston Sturges with Linda Darnell, Rudy Vallee, Barbara Lawrence, Kurt Kreuger.

1951: *The Long Dark Hall* Five Oceans. A Cusick International Presentation *d.* Anthony Bushell, Reginald Beck with Lilli Palmer, Denis O'Dea, Raymond Huntley.

1952: *The Four-Poster* Stanley Kramer Company, *d.* Irving Reis with Lilli Palmer.

1953: *Main Street to Broadway* Lester Cowan, *d.* Tay Garnett, guest appearance with Lilli Palmer.

1954: *King Richard and the Crusaders* Warner Brothers, *d.* David Butler with Virginia Mayo, George Sanders, Laurence Harvey, Robert Douglas.

1955: *The Constant Husband* Individual/London Films *d.* Sidney Gilliat with Margaret Leighton, Kay Kendall, Robert Coote, Cecil Parker.

1958: *The Reluctant Debutante* Avon/Metro-Goldwyn-Mayer, d. Vincente Minnelli with Kay Kendall, John Saxon, Sandra Dee, Angela Lansbury.

1960: *Midnight Lace* Ross Hunter, d. David Miller with Doris Day, John Gavin, Myrna Loy, Natasha Parry, Herbert Marshall, Roddy McDowall, Hermione Baddeley.

1961: *The Happy Thieves* Hillworth, d. George Marshall with Rita Hayworth, Alida Valli.

1963: *Cleopatra* Twentieth Century-Fox, d. Joseph L. Mankiewicz with Elizabeth Taylor, Richard Burton, Roddy McDowall.

1964: *My Fair Lady* Warner Brothers, d. George Cukor with Audrey Hepburn, Stanley Holloway, Wilfrid Hyde-White, Gladys Cooper, Jeremy Brett.

The Yellow Rolls-Royce Metro-Goldwyn-Mayer, d. Anthony Asquith with Jeanne Moreau, Moira Lister.

1965: *The Agony and the Ecstasy* Twentieth Century-Fox, d. Carol Reed with Charlton Heston, Diane Cilento, Harry Andrews.

1967: *The Honey Pot* Famous Artists, d. Joseph L. Mankiewicz with Susan Hayward, Cliff Robertson, Maggie Smith.

Doctor Dolittle Apjac, d. Richard Fleischer with Samantha Eggar, Anthony Newley, Richard Attenborough.

1968: *A Flea in Her Ear* Twentieth Century-Fox, d. Jacques Charon with Rosemary Harris, Louis Jourdan, Rachel Roberts.

1969: *Staircase* Stanley Donen Films, d. Stanley Donen with Richard Burton.

1977: *The Prince and the Pauper* (US Title: *Crossed Swords*) Film Trust, d. Richard Fleischer with Raquel Welch, Charlton Heston, Mark Lester.

1978: *Shalimar* Laxmi/Judson, d. Krishna Shah with Sylvia Miles, John Saxon.

1979: *Ashanti* Beverly/GAV, d. Richard Fleischer with Michael Caine, Omar Sharif, Peter Ustinov.

The Fifth Musketeer Sascha/Wien Films, d. Ken Annakin with Beau Bridges, Sylvia Kristel, Ursula Andress, Cornel Wilde, Olivia de Havilland.

1983: *A Time To Die* Carnation International Pictures, d. Matt Cimber with Rod Taylor, Edward Albert Jr.

Mr Harrison has appeared many times on television in guest appearances in all manner of presentations in the United States, Great Britain and many parts of the world. Listed below are the major plays which Mr Harrison has brought to the television screen:

The Walking Stick (1950) NBC, with Dennis Hoey, Una O'Connor (US)

The Man in Possession (1953) ABC, with Lilli Palmer, Robert Coote (US)

Dear Arthur (1960) NBC, with Hermione Baddeley (US)

The Datchet Diamonds (1960) NBC, with Tammy Grimes, Robert Flemyng (US)

The Adventures of Don Quixote (1973) BBC/Universal, with Frank Finlay (Great Britain)

Platonov (1971) BBC, with Sian Phillips (Great Britain)

The Kingfisher (1982) Anglia Television, with Wendy Hiller, Cyril Cusack (Great Britain)

Heartbreak House (1985) Cable TV with Amy Irving, Rosemary Harris, Stephen McHattie (US)

INDEX

In the sub-headings throughout this index the abbreviation 'RH' is used for Rex Harrison, and his wives are referred to by Christian name only.

To avoid overloading an already long index, the places of Rex Harrison's numerous stage appearances have not been included: these may be ascertained from the chronological listing on pages 326–9 or by looking up the references to the relevant play or plays. For the same reason, it has not been possible to include entries for all his frequent comings and goings between London, Hollywood and New York in later years.

MORE BIOGRAPHIES FROM
HODDER AND STOUGHTON PAPERBACKS

PATRICK AGAN
☐ 41731 X   Hoffman Vs Hoffman   £2.50

PETER & LENI GILLMAN
☐ 41346 2   Alias David Bowie   £4.95

PAUL FERRIS
☐ 05534 5   Richard Burton   £2.25

MARGARET CROSSLAND
☐ 41370 0   Piaf   £2.95

NANCY SINATRA
☐ 39748 9   Frank Sinatra, My Father   £3.50

All these books are available at your local bookshop or newsagent, or can be ordered direct from the publisher. Just tick the titles you want and fill in the form below.

Prices and availability subject to change without notice.

Hodder and Stoughton Paperbacks, P.O. Box 11, Falmouth, Cornwall.

Please send cheque or postal order, and allow the following for postage and packing:

U.K. – 55p for one book, plus 22p for the second book, and 14p for each additional book ordered up to a £1.75 maximum.

B.F.P.O. and EIRE – 55p for the first book, plus 22p for the second book, and 14p per copy for the next 7 books, 8p per book thereafter.

OTHER OVERSEAS CUSTOMERS – £1.00 for the first book, plus 25p per copy for each additional book.

Name ....

Address ....

....